Bombers versus Battleships

BOMBERS VERSUS BATTLESHIPS

The struggle between ships and aircraft for the control of the surface of the sea

David Hamer

Naval Institute Press
Annapolis, Maryland

First published in 1998 by
Allen & Unwin, 9 Atchison Street, St Leonards, NSW,
2065, Australia.

Published and distributed in the United States of America
and Canada by the Naval Institute Press, 118 Maryland
Avenue, Annapolis, MD 20402-5035.

Library of Congress Catalog Number is available on request.

ISBN 1-55750-043-6

Printed in Singapore

Contents

Acknowledgements

Many people have helped me, but I should like to give formal thanks to Mr David Brown, Head of the Naval Historical Branch in Whitehall, Dr Evelyn Cherpak of the US Naval War College in Newport, Rhode Island, Mr Teruaki Kawano, of the National Institute for Defence Studies, Tokyo, Commander James Goldrick, RAN, Commodore Bruce Loxton, RAN (Rtd) and Commander Sadeo Seno, IJN (Rtd).

I would also like to thank Ian Bowring, Emma Cotter and Ann Crabb of Allen & Unwin and Chris Coulthard-Clark for their support and assistance.

Maps and illustrations

ILLUSTRATIONS

Weights and measures

One of most difficult problems to be tackled in a work such as this is the question of weights and measures. After all, there are no less than three 'tons': the imperial ton of 2240 pounds, the American ton of 2000 pounds, and the metric tonne of 1000 kilograms. Further, a British battleship at the end of the Second World War could have 14-*inch* and 5.25-*inch* medium-calibre guns, as well as 2-*pounder*, 40*mm* and 20*mm* close-range guns.

What has been done in this work is to use the weights and measures which were commonly understood in the English-speaking countries involved at the time of the various actions. Ship displacements are given in imperial tons, at 'standard' displacement unless otherwise indicated. The standard displacement is a peculiarity of the 1922 Washington Treaty, which was introduced during the period between the wars when there were attempts to limit by treaty the sizes of warships and the total naval strength of the various powers. Its definition excluded the weight of fuel and reserve feed water, and was therefore substantially less than the 'full-load' displacement. For instance, the battleship *Rodney* was 33 900 imperial tons standard, but more than 38 000 tons full load.

The calibres of heavy- and medium-calibre guns are given in inches, and close-range weapons usually in millimetres. Aircraft are a mixed bag. Speeds are given in knots, and ranges in nautical miles. On the other hand, heights are given in feet. Bomb weights are usually given in pounds, though if a bomb was usually known by its kilogram size that is used. With missiles one is moving into more recent times, when the metric system is more generally accepted, and this is reflected in the way in which the capabilities of missiles are described.

Times are shown as a.m. and p.m. While all navies used the 24-hour clock, it is felt that the twelve-hour clock is clearer to

those who are interested in naval warfare without being direct
participants.

DISTANCE

Nautical miles	km	Land miles	Yards	Feet
0.1	0.19	0.11	203	608
0.2	0.37	0.22	405	1216
0.5	0.93	0.56	1013	3039
1	1.9	1.1	2026	3079
2	3.7	2.2	4052	12157
3	5.6	3.3	6079	18236
4	7.4	4.5	8105	24315
5	9.3	5.6	10131	30394
10	18.5	11.2	20262	60787
20	37.1	22.3		
30	55.6	33.5		
40	74.1	44.6		
50	92.6	55.8		
60	111.2	67.0		
70	129.7	78.1		
80	148.2	89.3		
90	166.8	100.5		
100	185	112		
200	371	223		
300	556	335		
400	741	446		
500	926	558		
1000	1853	1116		
2000	3706	2232		
5000	9264	5581		

SPEED

Knots	km/h	M/H
1	1.9	1.1
2	3.7	2.2
5	9.3	5.6
10	18.5	11.2
15	27.8	16.7
20	37.1	22.3
25	46.3	27.9
30	55.6	33.5
35	64.8	39.1
40	74.1	44.6
50	92.6	55.8
100	185	112
150	278	167
200	371	223
250	463	279
300	556	335

Knots	km/h	M/H
350	648	391
400	741	446
500	926	558

ALTITUDE

Feet	Metres
10	3
20	6
50	15
100	30
200	61
300	91
400	122
500	152
1000	305
2000	610
5000	1524
10 000	3048
20 000	6096
30 000	9144

WEAPON CALIBRE

Inches	mm
0.30	7.6
0.35	9.0
0.50	12.7
1.0	25.4
1.6	40.0
2.0	50.8
3.0	76.2
4.0	101.6
4.7	119.4
5.0	127.0
6.0	152.4
8.0	203.2
10.0	254.0
12.0	304.8
15.0	381.0
16.0	406.4
18.0	457.2

Introduction

This story endeavours to trace the history of the struggle between aircraft and ships for mastery of the surface of the sea. It begins in 1903, when the first powered heavier-than-air machine flew. In the early days the tale is of the battle of individuals for recognition of the capabilities of these new machines. Between the two world wars, there was bitter and sustained controversy over 'bombers versus battleships'. Eventually, in the Second World War, the influence of aircraft became almost all-pervading; so much so that, in order to keep this history down to manageable proportions, it has been necessary to limit it to the description of selected battles which seem to have interesting tactical or material features. All these battles have been extensively written about, so only brief descriptions are given, designed to highlight developments in the fundamental struggle between ships and aircraft. There is a short introductory narrative to each battle to outline important new technical advances up to that time, and a concluding section which outlines the lessons learnt (or which should have been learnt) and the changes in equipment and tactics which resulted from the battle.

Some light is also thrown on the reactions of a conservative profession to the introduction of a new form of warfare. The indignant reactions of conservatives must, however, be considered in the perspective of their time. When governments are preparing for imminent war, it is often the path of wisdom to refuse visionary solutions which may not mature for some time, if ever. The most outspoken prophets are not always the wisest counsellors. Soon after the First World War, Brigadier-General William Mitchell, of the US Army, said that if aircraft were 'allowed to develop essential air weapons', they could 'carry war to such an extent . . . as almost to make navies useless on the surface of the water'. This would have been very dangerous advice to follow in the early 1920s. Countries must not only prepare for a future war, they must be ready for the present, and weapons which cannot be effective for several years may fritter away the resources which should have been used to keep the present forces properly equipped. The balance is most difficult to strike; and conservative decisions will certainly be bitterly assailed by the advocates of advanced weapons.

Prophets have an almost irresistible tendency to exaggerate; and they usually fail to distinguish between the qualitative and the quantitative. Put in its simplest terms, the vehement advocates of air power tended to reason thus: a bomber can sink a battleship, therefore in war all battleships will be sunk by bombers; and the even more vulnerable aircraft carriers would have no chance of survival in the face of shore-based bombers. Yet remarkably few battleships were sunk by shore-based air attack in the Second World War, and even fewer aircraft carriers. Of more than 200 aircraft carriers operated by both sides in the six years of the Second World War, only *one* was sunk by shore-based bombing attack.

An even more striking case of the tendency to exaggerate the capabilities of a new weapon was given in 1942, when Lord Cherwell (formerly Professor Frederick Lindemann), Churchill's scientific adviser, calculated the likely results of Royal Air Force bombing of German cities. As a result of these calculations, the decision was made to launch the disastrously ill-directed campaign—the so-called strategic bombing offensive—against the built-up areas of German cities. Post-war analysis has shown that Cherwell exaggerated the effects of such bombing at least *tenfold*.

All this, though, is being wise after the event. If, as General Wolfe said, 'war is an option of difficulties', preparing for war at an indeterminate future date against an unspecified enemy is an option of imponderables. It is only to be hoped that our generation does no worse than its predecessor.

1

The beginnings of air power

At the start of the twentieth century the Royal Navy ruled supreme across the world's oceans and waterways—so much so that British naval power, represented most visibly by its battleships, was an article of faith to most English people. The growth of the German fleet was not yet a subject of general concern, and the two weapons with which Germany was to bring the British Empire almost to its knees were not yet developed as there were only a few small, unreliable submarines and not many people took them seriously. Regarded even less seriously were attempts to produce a powered, heavier-than-air flying machine.

The first flight by such a machine in 1903 produced virtually no publicity, and the Wright brothers continued their experiments almost in secrecy. No-one, except for a few ardent disciples, believed they could actually fly, and the US government would not touch their invention. The Wrights then offered it to Britain, but it was three times refused—twice by the War Office and once by the Admiralty. At length the Wrights realised that they had to come to Europe to convince governments that they could really fly.

The development of military flying dates from the demonstrations Wilbur Wright gave in France in 1908. Although many were experimenting at this time, no-one in Europe had been able to hop more than a short distance off the ground. Therefore the effect of Wright's flight of more than one-and-a-half hours was electrifying. The impact was increased when, in the following year, Louis Blériot flew an aircraft across the English Channel. By this time France, Germany, Britain and Russia had all purchased

1

aircraft for their armed services, though none were very clear about what to do with them.

Meanwhile, dramatic developments in naval aviation were happening in the United States. In 1910 the US Navy obtained the services of Eugene Ely to fly an aircraft from the cruiser *Birmingham*, following an announcement by the Germans that one of their Hamburg-America steamships was to launch an aircraft to speed the mails. How could America, the originator of flying, accept such a thing? On 14 November Ely took off in his machine (a 50 horse-power biplane built by Glenn Curtiss, one of America's aviation pioneers) from a 60-foot long sloping platform built over the cruiser's forecastle.

Two months later, on 18 January 1911, Ely made the first deck landing on the US cruiser *Pennsylvania* using a similar but slightly heavier aircraft. A 120-foot platform had been fitted over the ship's quarter-deck and after turret, and primitive arresting gear installed comprising sandbag-weighted ropes stretched at intervals across the deck. Canvas screens were fixed over the sides and at the far end of the landing deck, to stop the aircraft in case the

Ely landing on board USS *Pennsylvania*, 18 January 1911. (*NH 82737, US Naval Historical Center*)

arresting arrangements failed. After a successful downwind landing, Ely turned his aircraft round and took off again. He was keen to join the navy, but there was no place for him at the time, so he continued with his demonstrations and races, which at that stage were still very dangerous. Within a year he was killed in a crash.

Ely's performance was duly noted, though not always with acclaim. Technically, the flights had not achieved very much, since the ships had been at anchor on both occasions. All that was really proved was that aircraft could land on and take-off from very small spaces. Many people considered that the deck landing was pointless exhibitionism, with one British magazine commenting:

> this partakes too much of the nature of trick flying to be of much practical value. A naval aeroplane would be of more use if it 'landed' on the water and could then be hauled on board. A slight error in steering when trying to alight on deck would wreck the whole machine.[1]

This same publication declared in January 1912 that:

> it must be obvious to anyone who understands aviation that . . . the only possible naval aeroplane for use at sea is one which is launched from the ship by auxiliary power, and on return alights on the water as near the ship as may be.[2]

Another method of surviving a landing on the sea, other than airbags, was by now becoming available. Why should an aircraft not be fitted with floats rather than wheels? In March 1910 the French aviator Henri Fabre had managed to take-off and land in a machine fitted with four pontoons, but this arrangement was not really practical.

The first successful seaplane was produced by the American, Glenn Curtiss, early in 1912. On 17 February he took off in San Diego Bay and landed alongside the *Pennsylvania*—the same ship on which Ely had made the first deck landing. The aircraft was hoisted aboard the cruiser, then hoisted out again for a take-off from the sea and a successful return to its base. Other countries were producing seaplanes at about the same time. France had one flying in April, and Britain soon afterwards. The original name for these aircraft was 'hydroaeroplane'—the name 'seaplane' being coined in 1913 by Winston Churchill, then First Lord of the Admiralty.

Following this approach, a number of aircraft were flown off British battleships during 1911 and 1912—that of Commander C.R. Samson from *Hibernia* in May 1912 being the first launch from a moving ship. The tactical idea behind these experiments was that an aircraft should be launched, perform its mission and then land alongside; airbags would cause it to float and it could then be hoisted in, and with luck re-used. In order to launch these aircraft from a ship what was called a 'scenic railway' was temporarily erected above the forecastle and forward turret. These launching ramps were much criticised because they would interfere with the firing of the guns, and the structures were so flimsy that they would certainly be knocked down by heavy seas.

The increasing success of aeroplanes led to the formation in 1912 of the Royal Flying Corps (RFC) in Britain. Military flying was given the rather quaint name of 'aerial navigation', and pilots were described as 'drivers'. The corps had naval and military 'wings', and it was the original intention that each was to be available to support the other in the event of a war in which the other service was not involved. In fact, the naval wing devoted itself almost exclusively to naval problems right from the start, and its separation was finally given official recognition just before the First World War when it was renamed the Royal Naval Air Service (RNAS).[3]

The availability of seaplanes led all the important navies to develop them to the exclusion of the aeroplane. The causes of this attitude are not difficult to see. In the early days naval aircraft were envisaged purely as scouts. For this, seaplanes seemed to have obvious advantages over aeroplanes. They could be carried in existing ships with a minimum of modification; they needed only a crane to hoist them in and out, and somewhere to stow them; and as aircraft engines were singularly unreliable it seemed a real advantage if, in an emergency, the scout could land on the sea and await rescue.

When, in 1913 and 1914, investigations began into using naval aircraft for offensive roles, carrying bombs or torpedoes, it was found that the weight-lifting capability of seaplanes was greater than that of contemporary aeroplanes. A torpedo fitted more easily between the floats of a seaplane than underneath an aeroplane, whose undercarriage was rarely long enough to keep a torpedo clear of the ground when the aeroplane was in the tail-down position.

The first seaplane carrier was produced in 1912 by the French, by converting a repair ship, *La Foudre*. The old British cruiser *Hermes* was converted to carry seaplanes in 1913, and operated two during that year's manoeuvres. She was fitted with a scenic railway of the type fitted earlier to the battleships, and wheeled trolleys were put under the seaplanes' floats. However, the runway was too short and the ship's speed too low to allow take-offs from

4

the runway unless there was a fairly strong natural wind. The alternative method was to hoist the seaplane into the water, but most of the current types were too flimsy for this to be successful except in calm seas. One of *Hermes'* Short seaplanes was fitted with folding wings, a space-saving device which was to be widely adopted in future carrier aircraft; it was another of Winston Churchill's suggestions.

The United States was making similar experiments, and the seaplane carrier *Mississippi*, carrying three aircraft, was present at the occupation of Vera Cruz in Mexico in 1914. One of her scouting seaplanes was damaged by rifle fire from the ground, and has the distinction of being the first carrier-based aircraft to be in action.

The policy of all the major navies was that aircraft were to be used for scouting to increase the vision of surface ships, and even in this role aircraft were frequently considered to be inferior to airships. Some officers soon realised their attack possibilities, however, and as early as 1911 an Italian, Captain Guidoni, got airborne with a 350-pound torpedo in a Farman biplane. The Air Department of the British Admiralty had already been struck with this possibility, which offered a way of inflicting more serious damage on a warship than was possible with the small bombs then available. Early in 1913 a French Borel seaplane was bought by the Admiralty and dropped a small practice torpedo. Further trials were then ordered with a 14-inch torpedo, the smallest operational type available, but even so weighing 810 pounds. Such a torpedo was actually successfully dropped from a Short seaplane towards the end of the year. At this time, seaplanes were the only type which could lift such a weight; the first aeroplane designed to carry a torpedo was not produced until several years later.

The other possible offensive weapon against ships was the bomb, but opinion sharply differed whether this would be successful or not. In 1911, when it was suggested that aircraft might be used to attack battleships, the magazine *Aeroplane* commented that such a machine would be 'expensive and useless'. Other authorities were nevertheless investigating the possibilities. Wrote an Italian:

> The height must not be too great, but the aeroplane must take advantage of its manoeuvring powers to descend fairly close above the ship, throw its bombs, and then rapidly depart, so as to avoid the wave of explosion created. There must be two persons in the aeroplane, one as a pilot, the other as an observer, armed with chart,

Short Seaplane dropping a 14-inch torpedo. (*Imperial War Museum, Q60866*)

note-book, camera etc. Having rapidly made the necessary calculations, he should be able to throw the bombs with some accuracy.[4]

In America Glenn Curtiss had already dropped dummy bombs on imaginary warships, and from a very low height had obtained a high proportion of hits.

The arguments raged round two points: whether an aircraft would be able to hit a ship *at sea*; and whether it could carry a big enough bomb to do any significant damage. There were still no definite answers to these questions when the British naval wing commenced bombing experiments in 1912. The whole subject was new. No-one knew exactly how the stability of an aircraft would be affected by the release of a heavy bomb. No-one could be sure that a bomb explosion would not damage the aircraft which dropped it. Commander C.R. Samson dropped a dummy 100-pound bomb in 1912, and to everyone's surprise the flight of the aircraft was scarcely affected.

Later, experiments were carried out to find out the lowest height at which bombs could be dropped without endangering the aircraft. The risks were again less than the pessimists had predicted; nevertheless there was no unanimity about the prospects of bombing warships. One authority wrote in *Flight* magazine that:

bomb dropping is not likely to be effectual. Any aeroplane should be kept at least 3,000 feet by massed and controlled rifle fire . . . There is no future for bomb dropping on warships.[5]

He went on to suggest that the proper roles for naval aircraft were scouting and possibly observing the fire of the ship's guns.

All these theories were soon to be put to the test. At the outbreak of the First World War in 1914 the old *Hermes* was the only seaplane carrier the Royal Navy possessed. The RNAS then had 39 aeroplanes and 52 seaplanes (of which not more than half were in flying condition), and six airships; its personnel strength was 128 officers and 700 ratings. By 1918 there were eleven carriers, as well as nearly 3000 land and seaplanes and more than 50 non-rigid airships; the personnel strength was 55 000 officers and men.[6]

The maritime air power of the other navies also increased during the war, though not so spectacularly. The German service was heavily reliant on its Zeppelins for reconnaissance. These were hydrogen-filled airships of rigid construction, and of considerable size. The early naval types were 518 feet long and capable of 40 knots, but by the end of the war some were as large as 743 feet long with a speed of 70 knots. The German Navy was in fact rather slow to adopt Zeppelins, and had only one available when the war began.[7] The construction program was immediately sped up, and before the end of the war 61 Zeppelins had been received as well as twelve airships of other designs; only seven of the whole number were to survive the war. Their size, their unhandiness and the use of highly-inflammable hydrogen made them vulnerable both to gunfire and to accidents. No less than 26 of them were lost from causes that had nothing to do with combat.

Despite the attention given to Zeppelins, the German Navy did not totally ignore seaplanes and aeroplanes. At the beginning of the war the total aircraft strength was nine seaplanes, but by the conflict's end the front-line strength was 673 seaplanes and 191 landplanes. The Germans took little interest in the development of aircraft carriers. They did convert four merchant ships into seaplane carriers, but these ships had no launching arrangements and were too slow to accompany the High Seas Fleet.

The Russians and French both used seaplane carriers, but they were employed defensively and there was little development of their attack potential, though Russian seaplane carriers (called 'hydro-cruisers' by them) made several attacks on shore targets in the Black Sea during 1916. At this time the US Navy did not develop aircraft carriers at all. When the US entered the war in April 1917

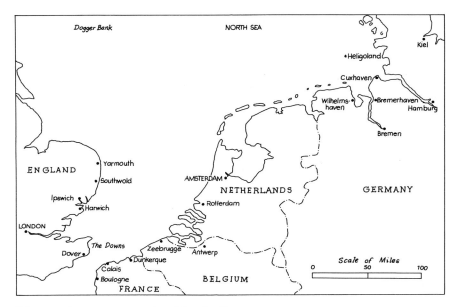

The main ports on the North Sea

their naval air service was tiny, with only 43 officers and 209 enlisted men. Eighteen months later it had expanded to more than 3000 officers and 47 000 enlisted men, with 1865 flying-boats and seaplanes.

None of the navies devoted much effort to aerial attacks on ships. The first such clash occurred on Christmas Day 1914[8] and was a singularly ineffectual affair against a force of British ships withdrawing after an unsuccessful attack on the Zeppelin sheds at Cuxhaven, near the main German naval base of Wilhelmshaven. There were no hits from the bombs dropped by German seaplanes and Zeppelins, and though anti-aircraft fire from the ships was enough to scare off a few of the attackers it was equally ineffective in scoring hits. The main result of the brush was to relieve the Royal Navy of a great part of its fear of air attack, the force commander later reporting he was quite convinced that 'given ordinary sea room, our ships have nothing to fear from seaplanes and Zeppelins'.

The next milestone occurred in the Dardanelles eight months later, when pilots from the seaplane carrier *Ben-my-Chree* scored several successes in Short seaplanes each fitted to carry a 14-inch torpedo. On 12 August 1915 Flight Commander Charles Edmonds sighted a 5000-ton cargo ship in the Sea of Marmara, glided to within fourteen feet of the water and launched his torpedo from 300 yards. The torpedo ran truly, and the last Edmonds saw was a large explosion and the target settling in the water.[9] It did not really matter that the ship was subsequently discovered to have been already beached when hit, a result of being torpedoed and shelled by a submarine. Edmonds had shown that the air-launched torpedo was an effective attacking weapon, and nothing can take from him the credit of being the first man to carry out such an attack in action.

Five days later Edmonds carried out another attack, this time against a steamer which was underway. The ship was hit and seriously damaged but eventually got to Constantinople. On the same day a second British seaplane tried to carry out a similar attack, but unfortunately suffered engine trouble and had to land in the Sea of Marmara. Not daunted by this, the pilot taxied his seaplane towards a large steam tug and fired his torpedo. The tug was sunk. The seaplane, without the weight of the torpedo, was just able to take off after a run of two miles.

The *Ben-my-Chree* pilots had proved one thing beyond dispute—that it was possible to hit ships at sea with torpedoes dropped from seaplanes. Two other things were equally clear to the pilots themselves. They needed a torpedo with a much bigger warhead than the old 14-inch model, so that when a ship was hit it would sink; the 14-inch torpedo had been designed for use by picket-boats against enemy ships in harbour, and was obsolete. Even more importantly they needed a better torpedo-carrying aircraft. When loaded with a torpedo the Short seaplane could take-off only when there was a combination of a calm sea, a slight breeze and a perfectly-running engine, and was so heavy that the amount of petrol which could be carried limited the duration of flight to 45 minutes.

There were no more successes for the torpedo-carrying seaplanes during this campaign, though there were some minor results from bombing attacks. More than 70 bombing attacks were made during 1915, and two large steamers and a tug were damaged, and one lighter and six dhows wrecked. Although these may seem meagre results, it must be remembered that the bombs were small, and bomb-sights non-existent.

A better torpedo-bomber, the Sopwith Cuckoo, was tried out succesfully in July 1917, and the new Commander-in-Chief of the Grand Fleet, Sir David Beatty, proposed a torpedo-bomber strike against the German Fleet in Wilhelmshaven. This was to be launched from flying-off decks on eight converted merchant ships which would also be fitted with 'flying-on' decks. Beatty wanted the Cuckoos to attack in three waves, each of 40 aircraft, supported by bomb-carrying flying-boats operating from bases in England. The attack was to be launched from the carriers at a distance of not more than 'one hour's fly' (about 100 miles) from Wilhelmshaven. After dropping their torpedoes, the Cuckoos were to remain in the area, supporting the succeeding waves with their machine-guns, before heading back to land on their carriers in shoal water under the lee of the Dutch coast.

Beatty wanted the attack to be made in the Spring of 1918, as soon as the ships and aircraft could be ready,[10] but the Admiralty had been disappointed by the results achieved by naval aircraft based in the Dunkirk area (though there were no torpedo-bombers involved there) and did not consider the proposed operation worthwhile. On 25 September Beatty was sent a statement of Admiralty policy on aircraft to be carried in ships,[11] which dismissed his proposal rather curtly, but did announce that an order had been placed for '100 torpedo-carrying aeroplanes of the Sopwith type',[12] with deliveries commencing in April 1918.

There is no doubt that Beatty's proposal was pushing the limits of capability, considering difficulties with the availability of suitable ships and aircraft, and unsolved problems with deck-landing techniques. These problems might have been successfully tackled by a regime such as that of Winston Churchill and Jackie Fisher, but their successors were much less dynamic. It was to be 1940, at Taranto, before a torpedo-bombing attack on the lines proposed by Beatty was to be successfully launched.

The Germans were slow to adopt torpedo bombers, but early in 1916 an order was placed for a twin-engined Gotha floatplane as a torpedo-carrier and deliveries started in July 1917. In the meantime a torpedo-seaplane flight was formed from existing aircraft, and on 1 May 1917 a machine from this unit attacked, hit and sank the small steamer *Gena*. Before the vessel went under, she fired two rounds from her gun—one of which shot down the seaplane.

During the next six weeks the Germans made several ineffective attacks, in one of which two seaplanes were shot down by the armed yacht *Diana*. The pilot of one of these expressed sentiments which would strike a chord with many future pilots. 'Once you are given a two-seater', he said, 'the authorities start loading you up with cameras, machine guns, bombs and wireless, and now to crown all, they actually hang a torpedo on your machine.'

The next successful attack was made in the middle of June, when a ship off Harwich was sunk by a torpedo claimed to have been dropped from a range of 3000 yards. Early in July five seaplanes attacked a convoy without success; that evening two other seaplanes attacked some ships east of Southwold. One of the attacking seaplanes was shot down, and seeing this, the pilot of another German seaplane gallantly, but rather foolishly, landed to rescue the crew. With the increased weight the rescue seaplane was unable to take off again, and eventually the crew had to surrender ignominiously to an armed trawler.

After this incident there was a lull in the attacks for two months, until in September seven seaplanes attacked a small steamer. Hit by two torpedoes and several bombs, the 264-ton ship sank in two minutes. Despite this success, the Germans had had enough. They did not feel that the results were worth the effort. But before they gave up these attacks, they did carry out an interesting investigation which bore fruit more than a quarter of a century later. They realised that large, slow, hydrogen-filled Zeppelins were much too vulnerable to come close enough to a ship to drop a torpedo. To overcome this problem, they designed a glider which could carry a torpedo. This glider was to be released by a Zeppelin but would remain connected by an electric wire, by which the parent ship could control the glider and drop the torpedo. The Zeppelin *L17* experimented with such a glider during 1917, but the concept was far in advance of the techniques of the time and never worked satisfactorily.

The war did not end without a trial of strength between an enemy capital ship and the RNAS. In 1914 the German battlecruiser *Goeben* and cruiser *Breslau* had taken refuge in Constantinople from the pursuing Allied fleets. They were 'sold' to the Turks (the *Goeben* being renamed *Yavuz*), and they were an important factor in the Turkish decision to fight on the side of Germany. In January 1918 these two ships emerged from the Dardanelles with the object of attacking two British monitors off Imbros Island, and of bombarding Mudros on the island of Lemnos—both islands being occupied by the British.

The monitors were quickly sunk, but each of the German ships had been damaged by mines before Imbros was reached. Initially *Goeben* tried to take her companion in tow—despite the ineffectual attention being paid to the pair by British aircraft from Imbros—but eventually abandoned the hazardous attempt and left *Breslau* to her fate, the latter sinking after hitting another mine. The German admiral, von Rebeur-Paschwitz, realised that *Goeben*, too, was seriously damaged as a result of striking a second mine, and that the only sensible thing to do was to retire to Constantinople. On the way back *Goeben* struck yet a third mine, but although listing to port she could still make a fair speed.

The battlecruiser escaped back into the Dardanelles having spent only five hours out in the Mediterranean, but owing to a navigational error she ran aground south of Nagara while attempting to pass through the anti-submarine nets. Before she ran aground an attack was delivered by two seaplanes escorted by Camel fighters, but the *Goeben*'s escort of ten seaplanes rendered the attack ineffective. An attack by four aircraft on the beached ship on 20 January also failed, but four separate attacks the following day resulted in one hit being made with a 112-pound bomb. Over the

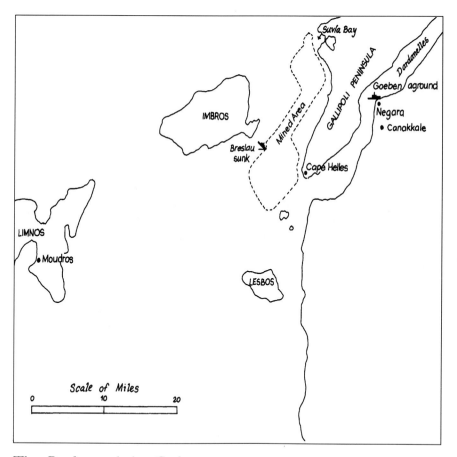

The *Breslau* and the *Goeben*

next two days and nights the air attacks were kept up, but no further hits were achieved. The bombers were escorted by fighters, but there was no opposition other than heavy gunfire, by which one attacking aircraft was shot down.

Desperate attempts were made to fit a 14-inch torpedo to one of the Short seaplanes in *Ark Royal* at Mudros, but the old aircraft could not lift the load. On 24 January the carrier *Empress* arrived, followed (much more importantly) on the next day by the carrier *Manxman* bringing with her two seaplanes each capable of lifting an 18-inch torpedo. There was a most unfortunate delay in using these seaplanes, in part caused by unsuitable weather. By the time they were ready for use the *Goeben* was gone. In poor visibility on 26 January she was towed off by a Turkish battleship and reached Constantinople the same day. Thus ended a bitterly disappointing episode for the RNAS. During the six days the *Goeben* was aground fifteen tons of bombs (but no torpedoes) had been dropped, but only two of the bombs had hit and the damage was insignificant.

It cannot be denied that air attacks on ships achieved little during the First World War. No warships were sunk or even seriously damaged, and only a handful of merchant ships was destroyed. Air attack on ships had not yet been proved to be effective. In this role the aircraft was still a weapon of promise, not yet of performance.

Aircraft were much more successful in the other roles to which they were assigned—reconnaissance and anti-submarine patrols were the ones to which most effort was devoted. The RNAS had some massive additional tasks. From 1914 to 1916 it was responsible for home air defence against attacks by Zeppelins and bomber aircraft. There were also naval squadrons based in France, initially to watch the Belgian coast and to attack the Zeppelin bases, but the role broadened into strategic bombing of German factories, and in 1917 a strategic bombing unit was set up in central France with the aim of attacking German defence industry. The carriers also made several attacks on the Zeppelin bases, for the Zeppelins were regarded as a serious threat.

The first Zeppelins were designed purely for reconnaissance, and had no arrangements for dropping bombs. (They did not have much defensive power, either; the Zeppelin *L3*, the only one available at the outbreak of the war, had a total armament of two machine-guns, mounted on a platform near the nose.) Zeppelins did occasionally attempt to bomb ships, but they did not achieve anything. Level-bombing of manoeuvring ships from any height is very rarely effective, and the Zeppelins were far too vulnerable to attempt low-level bombing or torpedo attacks. Attention was soon diverted to strategic bombing.

By the middle of 1915 the German Navy had ten airships, and it was decided to use some of them to cooperate with army airships in attacks on England and Scotland. As their numbers increased the naval Zeppelins made 177 bombing flights over England and Scotland, losing eleven of their number in the process. Little actual damage was caused though the disruption was extraordinary. The raids reached a peak in 1916, but the vulnerability of the Zeppelins became obvious as the British fighter-defence improved. By 1918 raids by airships had almost ceased, the task being taken on by bombing aircraft.[13]

There were a number of developments during the First World War which, while they had no immediate effect on the effectiveness of air attacks on ships, were to have a significant impact later. The first was the problem of recovering aeroplanes which had been launched from ships. If land was not within range, the aeroplanes had to crash-land near a destroyer—relying on flotation bags to keep them afloat until they could be rescued and the aircraft possibly salvaged. The problem seemed intractable until in 1917 when, for the first time, a fast modern vessel was made available for conversion to a carrier.

Furious was one of a class of three giant cruisers ordered by Admiral Lord Fisher, the First Sea Lord. These ships were heavily gunned, very fast and lightly armoured, and the concept became unpopular after three ill-protected British battlecruisers had blown up at Jutland. The Admiralty therefore ordered the building of a hangar on *Furious* in place of the forward 18-inch turret. On top of the hangar there was room for a flying-off deck more than 200 feet long and 50 feet wide and this space, coupled with *Furious'* speed of more than 30 knots, made take-offs easy for both aeroplanes and seaplanes.

The problem of recovering the aircraft remained unsolved. Could an aeroplane land on the large flying-off deck on *Furious*? This had not been designed for landings, and a direct approach was prevented by the funnel and masts. Nevertheless on 2 August 1917—over six years after Ely made the first deck landing on a ship in harbour—Squadron Commander Ernest Dunning made the first landing on a ship under way. There were no arresting arrangements as there had been when Ely landed, just a party of officers waiting on deck to seize ropes hanging from the wing tips, fuselage and tail skid while the slow-moving aircraft was still in the air. Five days later Dunning was drowned after he attempted to abort his third such landing, stalled, and fell over the side.

The first deck landing on a ship under way. (*Imperial War Museum, Q20637*)

Although these trials ended in disaster, they showed that landings on a ship were practicable, but that the existing arrangements were much too dangerous. *Furious* was therefore again rebuilt, and when she reappeared in March 1918 the after turret and mainmast had been removed, and a landing deck nearly 300 feet long and 70 feet wide had been built between the stern and the funnel. The arresting system consisted of ropes similar to those used by Ely stretched at right angles across the path of the aircraft, and a hook fitted to the fuselage of the aircraft which could be lowered by the pilot.[14] To ensure that the aircraft was kept straight after landing—Dunning's swerve over the side was ever in their minds—fore-and-aft wires were fitted a few inches apart and supported about six inches off the deck. The aeroplane was fitted with skids instead of wheels, the idea being that horns on the skids should catch under the fore-and-aft wires, keeping the aircraft running straight up the landing deck, and in addition assist in stopping. It did not work. Out of twelve landings made, nine resulted in crashes, and many pilots abandoned their approaches because of the extreme turbulence caused by the ship's superstructure. Use of the landing deck was suspended.

A skid-fitted Sopwith Pup landing on the deck of
HMS *Furious*. (*Imperial War Museum, Q20634*)

Further deck-landing trials were pending in *Argus*, which was
nearing the completion of her conversion from the ex-Italian liner
Conte Rosso. The original concept of *Argus* was that her flight deck
should be clear, with no obstructions in the way of approaching
aircraft or causing turbulence for them, but in fact the flight deck
ended up cluttered with upperworks as a result of modifications
made by non-fliers. After the trials in *Furious* these obstructions
were removed, but *Argus* was so delayed that she was not completed
until September 1918, too late to take any operational part in the
First World War, although successful deck-landing trials were
carried out with Sopwith 1½-Strutters.

Two new methods of launching aircraft were being developed
at about the same time. During 1917 the German Zeppelins became
a thorough nuisance to the Grand Fleet and to Rear-Admiral
Tyrwhitt's Harwich force. Whenever ships put to sea they were
liable to be shadowed by one of these airships, which seemingly
watched and reported everything[15] out of range of retaliation—
unless a seaplane carrier was present and the weather was suitable
for operating aircraft. As an urgent measure fighter aeroplanes were
fitted in as many ships as practicable, typically being launched

16

A Sopwith 1½-Strutter being launched from a turret of
HMAS *Australia*. (*Imperial War Museum, Q18729*)

from a small platform above the conning tower, allowing a 20-foot
run for the aeroplane. By the autumn of 1918, 22 light cruisers
were carrying Sopwith Pup fighters.

Fighters were not initially carried in battleships, because they
were usually the slowest ships in the fleet and the admiral did not
want to have to slow down so one could catch up after turning
into the wind to launch an aeroplane. To use the top of one of
the big-gun turrets was the obvious solution, although opinion was
sharply divided whether this would give a long enough run. Despite
these doubts a successful flight was made by a fighter from a
turret on the battlecruiser *Repulse* in October 1917.

Soon, all battleships and battlecruisers were carrying two
aeroplanes—a fighter and a scout—and by the end of the war the
Grand Fleet could launch over 100 aeroplanes, not counting any
support provided by the seaplane carriers. There was a problem,
though, in the use of these aircraft. Because they were usually
wrecked on landing, and recovery of the crew sometimes presented
problems, ships were reluctant to launch these aircraft until they
were certain that there would not be a better opportunity later,

A fighter on a towed lighter (*Imperial War Museum, Q65606*)

and consequently the fighters were often launched too late or not launched at all.

The US Navy also experimented with the use of turret platforms to launch fighters. When the battleship *Texas* was in England in November 1918 launching ramps were built over two of her 14-inch turrets, and she was assigned two Sopwith Camels and a Sopwith 1½-Strutter. Seven other battleships were similarly fitted, and many successful launches were made, but the US Navy dropped this activity as a dead-end in August 1920.

An alternative method of getting a fighter into the air at sea was from a towed float. The floats were 60 feet long and sixteen feet wide, and 40 were built during 1917 and 1918. Destroyers could tow them in calm weather at speeds of up to 32 knots, and Sopwith Camel fighters could take off from them.

Each method of launching had a success. A fighter launched from the cruiser *Yarmouth* destroyed the Zeppelin *L23* in August 1917, and in July 1918 a fighter from a towed lighter destroyed the Zeppelin *L53*. Although only two Zeppelins were destroyed by the ship-launched fighters, by the middle of 1918 they had made shadowing by the Zeppelins almost impossible, and if the war had

continued the Zeppelins would have been replaced in the reconnaissance role by Dornier flying-boats.

At the same time the US Navy was developing a better method
of launching aircraft from ships. A compressed-air catapult had
been successfully tried from a barge in 1912, and in 1915 an
aircraft was successfully catapulted from *North Carolina*. In 1916
two cruisers were fitted with catapults, but neither used them
operationally during the war.

The most important wartime development was the formation
on 1 April 1918 of the Royal Air Force, through the merging of
the RNAS and the RFC. There were many factors which led to
this outcome, though the dominant motive was the political need
to be seen to be doing something about German bombing attacks,
particularly those on London. Although the formation of the RAF
was undoubtedly a wise move—it is hard to imagine that the Battle
of Britain would have been won otherwise—many problems were
created for the navy, particularly because most air-minded officers
left to join the new service. The Royal Navy would suffer greatly
from their loss.

2

Between the wars

In 1921 Admiral William Sims, the President of the US Naval War College, carried out a series of simulated exercises to assess the value of aircraft carriers. These exercises seemed to prove conclusively that, given good weather, a force of aircraft carriers would always defeat a force of battleships. Sims told his friends in Congress that a fleet which was superior in aircraft carriers 'will sweep the enemy fleet clean of its airplanes, and proceed to bomb the battleships, and torpedo them with torpedo planes. It is all a question as to whether the airplane carrier, equipped with 80 planes, is not the capital ship of the future'.[1]

Sims' assessment of the offensive importance of aircraft carriers ran counter to the mainstream of naval thought. Attention was at that time concentrated on fixing the deficiencies revealed by the last war. Improved defences against submarines, the development of effective long-range gunnery, the perfection of massed torpedo attacks by destroyers, and the improvement of night-fighting techniques were all being pushed forward as fast as resources would allow. The aircraft carrier was relegated to the role of scouting for the surface forces and providing observation for their guns. As late as 1926 Sims complained that the US Navy had no policy towards air power, but hoped that if they took absolutely no notice of it, it would go away.

The possibility of effective aircraft attacks on ships was bought dramatically before the public by the activities of Brigadier-General William Mitchell of the US Army. When Mitchell returned to America from France early in 1919 he was a man with a mission. Having studied the organisation of the RAF, he was convinced that an independent air force was not only desirable but that air power was the sole requirement for future national defence. While the agitation for an independent air force remained an internal army squabble, the US Navy was content to watch from the sidelines. What brought the navy into the fight was Mitchell's statements to the Military Affairs Committee of the House of Representatives which raised, both publicly and privately, the question of the vulnerability of battleships.

As a result of the violent controversy whipped up by Mitchell's agitation, bombing tests were conducted in 1921 although unfortunately the aims of the navy and the general were different. The navy aimed to determine three things: the ability of aircraft to locate ships at sea; the probability of scoring hits on manoeuvring ships; and the damage such hits would cause. Mitchell had one aim: he wanted to prove that bombers could sink battleships, and this he achieved when six of his bombers sank the ex-German cruiser *Frankfurt* in front of the assembled Atlantic Fleet in 35 minutes. Three days later the ex-German battleship *Ostfriesland*, of 22 800 tons, was similarly attacked and sunk—albeit after Mitchell breached the rules he had previously agreed to with the navy by using some specially prepared 2000-pound bombs. Twenty-two minutes after the first bomb was dropped and scored a hit, *Ostfriesland* went to the bottom.

Mitchell had achieved his aim. It would be quite impossible for anyone in the future to say that bombers could not sink battleships. They could say—as indeed they did, repeatedly—that the tests were unrealistic: that anti-aircraft gunfire would destroy the bombers before they could drop their bombs; that a manoeuvring ship would never be hit; that the target ships were obsolete; and that damage-control parties would minimise the effect of any damage. But the sight of these ships sinking beneath the Atlantic waves produced pictures more convincing than any amount of abstract argument.

Mitchell's methods inevitably produced antagonism and his outspokenness earned him many enemies. In 1925 he accused the War and Navy Departments of 'incompetency, criminal negligence and almost treasonable administration of the National Defence'.[2] For this he was court-martialled and suspended from rank and duty for five years. He died in 1936, but was posthumously honoured in 1945 when the Senate voted him the Congressional Medal of Honor and promoted him to major-general. His activities had one effect he would not have foreseen. The vehement attacks made the navy realise that its internal arguments were trivial compared to the necessity of saving naval aviation from extinction, and that the best answer to General Mitchell was to show that the navy could use air power effectively.

The arguments stirred up by Mitchell set the pattern for the 'bombers versus battleships' debate which lasted 20 years. His ideas were certainly not immediately accepted, for the report of a Special Board of the US Navy in 1925 concluded that 'the battleship is the element of ultimate force in the fleet, and all other elements are contributory to the fulfilment of its function as the final arbiter in sea warfare' and that 'airplanes cannot . . . exercise control of the sea'.[3] The issue could not be settled until the Second World War, because there were so few facts to go upon. The attacks on *Goeben* in 1918 were endlessly refought, and each of the incidents between ships and aircraft in the inter-war years was appropriated by the advocates of either side to prove their points.

A similar debate was taking place in Britain, where the situation was further confused by the understandable desire of the newly-formed RAF to claim an important role for itself—a role which would inevitably be at the expense of the other services. In 1919 a 'Post War Questions' Committee was set up in the Admiralty to investigate, among other matters, the likely role of aircraft in attack and defence, and in the following year a cabinet committee investigated the need for new battleships to match the 1916 program of the US Navy. Nothing decisive emerged from either inquiry, for there were so many unresolved issues. Could aircraft reliably find ships at sea? Could an effective strike be organised? And could aircraft weapons inflict serious damage on battleships?

The dominant Admiralty view was expressed in 1926 by Admiral Chatfield, then Third Sea Lord and controller of the navy, who wrote that 'any Admiralty representations . . . should be guarded in *admitting* any effectiveness in bomb-dropping on ships at sea . . .'.[4] After rehearsing the usual claims in favour of battleships, he also said that he thought that anti-aircraft fire would cope with torpedo-bombers on their necessarily slow, steady approach and drive bombers to heights from which they could achieve few hits. Chatfield was, in fact, an advocate of aircraft carriers, for in 1921 (when he was Assistant Chief of the Naval Staff) he had written that 'the number of aircraft carriers present in a fleet action will decide who is to command the air, and command of the air is likely to be vital in the next naval battle'. But he saw carriers as ancillaries to the decisive force, the battlefleet. This role for aircraft and their carriers—locating, harassing and delaying the enemy fleet—was the dominant view in the Royal Navy in the inter-war years.

DEVELOPMENT OF AIRCRAFT CARRIERS

Aircraft carriers had developed rapidly during the war years, but with the onset of peace the pace slackened. During war there is an impulse of urgency, risks are taken and departmental obstructions are overcome. In peace more prudent counsels prevail. Plans must be proposed, estimates prepared and solutions debated. All this, although no doubt admirable, means delay. Added to it was the general feeling that the war-to-end-all-wars had been fought and won, so what was the point of preparing weapons for a hypothetical and improbable future conflict? And then there were airships, which for a decade diverted quite a lot of attention in both the British and American navies, until their severe limitations were revealed in a string of accidents.

America

Ten years after Ely's first deck landing, the US Navy resumed experiments with aircraft carriers. The first carrier, *Langley*, was a converted collier of 11 500 tons which joined the fleet in 1922.[5] Experiments with deck landing were conducted using fore-and-aft wires of the British type, the US Navy having paid for the rights to use this gear, and resulted in refinements to this system involving athwartship wires.[6] Progress was slow but by 1923 *Langley* could land three aircraft in seven minutes; she was also fitted with two catapults similar to those fitted in cruisers during the First World War.

It was then decided to go ahead with the conversion of two partly-completed battlecruisers, *Lexington* and *Saratoga*, both of which commissioned in 1927. These were ships of 33 000 tons,[7] with flight decks nearly 900 feet long and 100 feet wide. Both were fitted with a lowerable crash barrier, a decisive step in the development of carriers which enabled them to quadruple the rate of landing aircraft. For twenty years it remained the key to the rapid operation of aircraft from a carrier, and like many inventions it was simple, even obvious, in concept—although the Royal Navy was extraordinarily slow to recognise it.

Before the introduction of crash barriers it was dangerous to allow an aircraft to land while another was still on the flight deck, because of the risk of a crash if the second aircraft failed to catch an arrester-wire. After landing, an aircraft usually had to go down to the hangar in the lift (and the lift come up to flight-deck level again) before the next aircraft could land, meaning there was a minimum interval of about two minutes between landings. The introduction of the lowerable crash barrier enabled carriers to carry

The three US carriers, *c.*1930. From the front: *Langley, Saratoga* and *Lexington.* (*US Naval Historical Center, NH 95037*)

many more aircraft because of the great increase in the rate of landing and also because the ships were able to carry a permanent deck park—extra aircraft for which there was no room in the hangar.

The use of the crash barrier enabled American carriers to operate two or three times the number of aircraft which could be operated by contemporary British carriers. Whereas it took two hours to land 50 aircraft on the British carrier *Courageous, Saratoga* could land 70 in a little over half-an-hour. In the American carriers the hangars were largely used for maintenance and for the storage of non-operational aircraft, while in the British carriers they were designed as the storage for the entire aircraft complement.[8]

Deck landing on the American carriers was aided by a landing signal officer, who guided aircraft onto the deck with outstretched bats. This technique was adopted by the Royal Navy some years later, but unfortunately with the signals having the opposite meaning, which caused considerable confusion during the Second World War when pilots from one navy endeavoured to land on a carrier of the other.[9] The Japanese never used landing signal officers, but did use a light beam to help guide aircraft coming in to land, a system which was to be adopted, in a much more

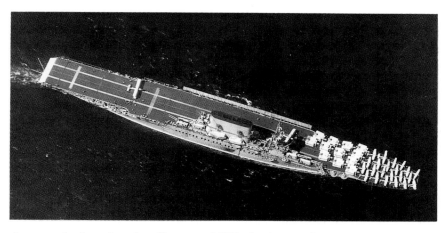

A torpedo-bomber landing on USS *Lexington* in 1929. Note the size of the deck park. (*Naval Historical Foundation, Washington, NH 75713*)

sophisticated form, by the Americans and British after the Second World War.

Further development of American aircraft carriers was complicated by treaty restrictions. The Washington Treaty of 1922 established a 5:5:3 ratio between the navies of Britain, the United States and Japan. As far as aircraft carriers were concerned, this meant that the United States and Britain were each allowed to build aircraft carriers to a total of 135 000 tons, and Japan 81 000 tons. France and Italy were allowed 60 000 tons each, but Germany was not allowed anything (being already controlled by the Treaty of Versailles).

After *Lexington* and *Saratoga* were completed, the US Navy had 69 000 tons of its allowance remaining. There was lengthy argument whether five carriers of 13 000 tons or three of 20 000 tons should be built. Arguments for the smaller type won the day, and in 1934 the 13 800-ton *Ranger* was completed. This was a remarkable design, carrying 72 aircraft on that small displacement (and able to stow the aircraft in the single hangar), and with a greatly-improved catapult which could launch a 9000-pound aircraft at 55 knots. On the other hand, *Ranger* had serious drawbacks and has been described by an American admiral who served in her as an 'atavistic anomaly'. Her speed was only 27 knots, and her construction was very light.[10]

Even before *Ranger* was completed, it was decided that the remaining two carriers to be built under the 1934 program should be of 20 000 tons. These two, *Yorktown* and *Enterprise*, were commissioned in 1937 and 1938 respectively. By this time all restrictions on aircraft-carrier tonnage had been lifted under the spur of general rearmament, and a new carrier was ordered in 1938. It was felt that insufficient experience had been gained with the *Yorktown* design, so the new carrier, *Wasp*, was built to the same basic design as *Ranger*, but was fitted with an interesting new development: a deck-edge lift. The conventional lifts in the middle of the ship were unpopular because they weakened the flight deck, and because the dimensions of every aircraft with its wings folded had to be limited to the physical size of the lift. The deck-edge lift became standard in all subsequent American carriers, and was eventually adopted by the Royal Navy nearly twenty years later.

By this time all the US carriers were fitted with catapults on the flight deck. These catapults were important because the large number of aircraft carried by US carriers in permanent deck parks restricted the space on the flight deck available for take-offs. Although the normal way of launching aircraft was by free take-offs, it was a great advantage to deck-handling if enough aircraft could be catapulted to provide sufficient space for free take-offs. If there were more than sixteen aircraft on the flight deck of *Wasp*, for instance, a catapult was the only way of getting the first aircraft into the air. The US Navy was now far in advance of the other navies in the development of catapults, and by 1939 each of their carriers was fitted with at least two catapults, each capable of launching two aircraft a minute.

American carrier aircraft were in the front rank, far in advance of the comparable British aircraft. The three basic aircraft—the F4F Wildcat fighter, the SBD Dauntless dive-bomber and the TBD Devastator torpedo-bomber—were all useful aircraft, although to the surprise of the Americans two of the three were to be outperformed by their Japanese equivalents, the dive-bomber being the exception. In the early days with *Langley* it became obvious that carrier aircraft could not possibly carry the bombload of shore-based aircraft, so accuracy had to be the key. After Marine pilots had experimented with dive-bombing in 1919 it was taken up by the US Navy and by 1926 had become part of the fleet exercises. In 1934 dive-bombing was accepted into standard US carrier practice, and by the time war came to the Pacific most carriers had at least eighteen Dauntless aircraft.

The Americans did have a serious problem with the torpedo to be used by their torpedo-bombers. The Mark 13 weapon available before Pearl Harbor had a 400-pound warhead, but its performance was marred by numerous defects affecting accuracy, depth-keeping and reliability of the exploder. Worse (from the point of view of the pilots) was a requirement that it had to be dropped from no higher than 60 feet and at a speed of not more than 115 knots. These problems were gradually overcome, but it was to be 1944 before the Mark 13 torpedo became a satisfactory weapon.

In an important development, not matched by other navies, American naval officers were properly trained in aviation matters. A course in aeronautics was started at the Naval Academy in 1925 and by the following year half the graduates had received flying instruction. Senior officers were encouraged to learn to fly so they could acquire what became an essential requirement for command of an aircraft carrier, for in 1926 legislation was passed which laid down that aircraft carriers, seaplane tenders and naval air stations could be commanded only by naval aviators.[11] It must not be assumed, though, that the aviators dominated US naval policy. There was a struggle for supremacy between the aviators (nick-named 'brown shoes') and the battlefleet advocates ('black shoes'); before Pearl Harbor the 'black shoes' were definitely in the ascendancy.

A great deal of the credit for the rapid development of US naval aviation must be given to the drive and sense of publicity of Rear-Admiral William A. Moffett, chief of the navy's Bureau of Aeronautics for ten years after its formation in 1923. By 1931 *Lexington* and *Saratoga* were easily the most effective aircraft carriers anywhere, and the US Navy had achieved the astonishing number—by the standards of other navies—of 1000 aircraft, including those based ashore. Yet Moffett went seriously wrong in two areas.

He was a strong advocate of the small aircraft carrier, though he did have the grace to acknowledge the design problems of *Ranger* and to direct attention to larger 20 000 ton carriers. He was an even more passionate advocate of the merits of helium-filled rigid airships as a solution to the problems of naval reconnaissance in the vast distances of the Pacific. The outcome was a series of disasters, one of them—the loss of *Akron* in April 1933—costing Moffett his life. *Akron* and her sister *Macon* were 785 feet long, and each carried five fighters inside the hull which were launched and recovered while the airship was in flight by a device like a trapeze. When *Macon* also crashed two years later it effectively ended this program. The reconnaissance role conceived for rigid airships was taken over by long-range flying boats.

Great Britain

In 1918 the Royal Navy was unquestionably the leader in naval aviation, but over the next two decades Britain fell far behind both America and Japan in this field as a result of the absorption of the RNAS into the RAF. By 1919 all the RAF was able (or prepared) to make available to the Royal Navy was one spotter-reconnaissance squadron, a fighter squadron and half a torpedo-bomber squadron. The relatively poor performance of the Royal Navy in aviation matters in the inter-war years can be explained only by the decisions being made by officers with no feel for the possibilities of aviation, though financial constraints undoubtedly played a part.

Successive Boards of Admiralty pressed for the return of the Fleet Air Arm. Some concessions were gradually wrung as to the use of naval officers as pilots and observers in carrier aircraft, and in 1923 it was agreed that the Admiralty should pay for the Fleet Air Arm and be provided with the equipment it wanted (and could afford) by the Air Ministry. All the observers and 70 per cent of the pilots were to be naval officers (the pilots being attached to the air force but wearing naval uniform). When an aircraft carrier was in harbour the aircraft were usually disembarked to an RAF station, the pilots remaining with the RAF while the rest of the aircrews remained with the ship. When these arrangements were announced by Prime Minister Stanley Baldwin it was specifically stated that they were experimental. 'It is impossible', he said, 'without experience to pronounce a final judgement on these arrangements'.[12]

There were, of course, further disputes as to how the arrangements should be implemented, and in 1926 the Admiralty was specifically told not to attempt to control shore-based Fleet Air Arm establishments or the Coastal Area Command. One particular area of dispute was over the navy's desire, because of the shortage of officer volunteers, to have rating pilots and observers. It was not until 1936 that rating observers were introduced and the rating pilots two years later, and only in 1939 was full control of the Fleet Air Arm returned to the Admiralty. Even then, Admiralty control extended only to carrier-based aircraft; the land-based Coastal Command continued to be part of the RAF, and the naval commanders were not given operational control of these aircraft until April 1941. It took still longer before aviators had an appropriate place in the navy's policy-making structure. In contrast to the American approach, the Royal Navy has never required commanding officers of aircraft carriers to have some flying qualifications.[13]

Deck-landing trials had been resumed soon after the end of the 1914–18 war, but it was to be many years before the problems were solved; they would have been solved much sooner if the American developments had been studied. It was 1928 before fore-and-aft wires were removed, and for the next seven years the carrier aircraft landed without any arresting device at all other than their wheel-brakes, if they had them. The early aircraft did not have wheel-brakes, and for them there was usually a rope barrier at the end of the flight deck to stop them going over the bows if the pilot misjudged the landing. This could not last, for in order to make such landings possible the carrier had to steam at high speed into the wind—which frequently meant that the carrier could make no effective progress at all if the wind happened to be from the wrong direction. Besides, the increasing weight and landing-speed of carrier aircraft were making it more and more difficult to land them without some sort of arresting device.

Friction-type athwartship arrester-wires were tried in *Courageous* in early 1931, but they did not work satisfactorily. The Admiralty accordingly authorised experiments being carried out during 1933 in *Courageous* with an American-style system controlled by hydraulic cylinders. Arrester wires were generally introduced in 1935, but it was not until 1938 that crash barriers were first installed, and several more years elapsed before all carriers were fitted with them. In any case the first carrier to have a crash barrier, the new *Ark Royal*, did not initially use the barrier for its proper purpose—to permit the use of a deck park so as to avoid the delay of taking an aircraft down on a lift before the next aircraft landed.

The launching of aircraft from British carriers suffered from comparable problems. Nearly all the Royal Navy's capital ships and cruisers were fitted with catapults so that they could launch their reconnaissance flying-boats or seaplanes. The Admiralty had not forgotten the success of the ship-borne fighters in 1917 and 1918, and had therefore laid down that all types of Fleet Air Arm fighters must be capable of being launched from the catapults of battleships and cruisers. This apparently reasonable order had most unfortunate results.

In order to avoid an excessive weight penalty in the aircraft the same system of catapulting had to be used in the carriers as in battleships and cruisers. Thus it came about that in order to catapult an aircraft from a British carrier, the tail of the aircraft had to be jacked up onto a trolley and four heavy steel spools sticking out of the aircraft fitted into claws. The whole procedure

A Fairey Swordfish being launched in the 'tail-up' position.
(*FAA Museum, SWFH/644*)

took two minutes—four times as long as on the US carriers.[14] Different trolleys had to be used for different aircraft, which introduced more delays, and the spools sticking out of an aircraft so that it could be attached to the trolley caused aerodynamic damage. Moreover the trolleys had to be removed before aircraft could do free take-offs, and this caused further delays. It was only well into the Second World War, and as a consequence of the use of American aircraft, that a more efficient system of catapulting was adopted.[15]

In 1919 the Royal Navy possessed one aircraft carrier (*Argus*) and had two others (*Eagle* and *Hermes*) under construction which were not completed until 1924.[16] In addition nine seaplane carriers were still in commission, but all except three—*Furious, Ark Royal* and *Pegasus*—were soon disposed of, and the last two were used mostly for aircraft transport. The flush-deck design of *Argus* caused problems both for navigation and for control of flight-deck operations, so experiments were carried out with dummy superstructures on *Furious*. It was found that an island structure could be erected on the flight deck over to one side of the ship without causing turbulence for the aircraft, and *Hermes* and *Eagle* and all subsequent aircraft carriers (of all nations) had such a structure on their

30

starboard side, except for the Japanese ships *Akagi* and *Hiryu*, which had their islands on the port side—the only carriers ever to do so.

In 1928 and 1930 *Courageous* and *Glorious*, sister ships to *Furious*, completed their conversion into aircraft carriers. They were able to stow 52 aircraft, but there were very real doubts about their ability to operate this number with current operating practices. In 1932 *Courageous* operated her 52 aircraft but reported that it took nearly an hour for them to take-off and over two hours for them to land. Those involved with *Furious* considered that the maximum number of aircraft that could be operated from any carrier was 32, of which not more than eighteen should be in the air at any time. (This was at a time when American carriers were comfortably operating twice that number of aircraft.)

Despite the warnings, when a new 22 000-ton carrier named *Ark Royal* was ordered in 1935, she had two hangars and was designed to carry 72 aircraft (48 torpedo-spotter-reconnaissance and 24 dive-bombers). Of course she could have no chance of operating that number of aircraft with current Royal Navy techniques, so she became the first British carrier to experiment with the crash barrier, and she had two rather bulky and primitive catapults (called 'accelerators'). *Ark Royal* had three lifts, but these were small, and it was not possible for aircraft without folding wings to be taken down to the hangars. The two-level hangar design also created problems in getting aircraft from the lower hangar on to the flight deck. In practice *Ark Royal* could not operate more than 54 aircraft, but she represented a considerable step forward for British aircraft-carrier design.

In the same year that *Ark Royal* was ordered, the London Treaty fixed the maximum tonnage of an aircraft carrier at 23 000 tons. Japan did not sign this treaty and within two years all treaty restrictions were swept aside by the march towards rearmament. Nevertheless the next class of six British carriers was laid down to conform with the London Treaty requirements, although the last three were of considerably modified and enlarged designs. Five of this class (*Illustrious*, *Formidable*, *Victorious*, *Indomitable* and *Indefatigable*) were laid down before the outbreak of the Second World War, and a sixth (*Implacable*) soon afterwards. They were usually referred to as 'armoured-deck' carriers, but 'armoured-hangar' would be a better description, for the two lifts and the flight deck outside the hangar area were not armoured, while the sides of the hangar had heavy armour.

The design of these ships was the product of two very false premises: that the main threat to aircraft carriers would be from the gunfire of surface ships; and that the maximum number of aircraft which could be satisfactorily operated from a carrier was about 35. Only a naval staff with no understanding of the potential of carrier air power could possibly have made such decisions. The perceived need for protection against gunfire meant that 5000 tons of the total displacement was taken up by the weight of armour, although—as the experience of the Second World War would show—it was a rare event indeed for carriers to become involved in a surface action. Many disadvantages flowed from such an approach, not the least being that if a bomb penetrated the flight deck and exploded in the enclosed box-like armoured hangar the damage was much worse than in an open one.[17]

As for the conclusion that aircraft numbers should be limited to 35, the Americans and the Japanese were already operating more than double that number in ships of comparable size. Experience with *Ark Royal* eventually convinced the Naval Staff that the 35-aircraft limit was wrong, and the last three of the *Illustrious* class were substantially larger and could carry more aircraft— though still only about half as many as American or Japanese carriers of comparable size. The increased carrying capacity was achieved by adopting a two-hangar arrangement, with a lower hangar under the after end of the upper hangar, serviced only by the after lift. The cost of this was lowering the height of the upper hangar from sixteen feet (which had been the standard in British carriers since 1924) to fourteen feet (which caused problems later with aircraft stowage). The reason such a reduction was thought to be acceptable was because it was suitable for all existing and projected British naval aircraft, which had rearward-folding wings— the much more efficient upward-folding design had not yet been considered.

There was yet another problem with these armoured-hangar carriers. They were substantially shorter than US carriers of similar displacement, which significantly limited the number of aircraft which could be parked on the flight deck. This became critical later in the war when permanent deck parks became standard. Worse still, the bow and stern ends of the flight decks were sloped downwards to improve the airflow, and the slopes were too steep for aircraft to be parked there.[18] Although the Royal Navy was to suffer severely in the war because of the small number of aircraft it was possible to operate from its carriers, it is nevertheless worth noting that in September 1939 Britain had the greatest number of aircraft carriers of any of the naval powers: seven completed and five under construction—compared with five completed and two being built for the US and six completed and two being built for Japan.

The Royal Navy's position with regard to aircraft was even more unhappy. In 1939 the standard Fleet Air Arm fighter was the Skua, a two-seater designed to combine the duties of dive-bombing with fighter defence and reconnaissance—no doubt as one means of overcoming the small number of aircraft in British carriers. Combining several functions in one aircraft, although attractive on paper and particularly so in periods of peacetime economy, is rarely successful. It usually works only when the basic aircraft is outstanding in one sphere, for such an aircraft often lends itself to other duties. The Skua, however, was obsolete as a fighter even before it entered squadron service in 1939, its low top speed of 195 knots making it 40 knots slower than the German Heinkel 111 bomber and totally outclassed by the Messerschmitt 109 fighter. Perhaps this justified the saying going round the fleet at this time that you should always remember that the Skua was 'a bird that folds its wings and dives into the sea'.

It may be wondered why the Royal Navy did not use single-seat fighters, comparable with the Hurricanes and Spitfires then being built for the RAF. The answer was that the Admiralty did not really consider it desirable to operate an aircraft at sea without an observer (always a naval officer, whereas the pilots were often from the RAF) to do the navigation. It is also because they wanted the fighters to double as reconnaissance aircraft, for which role an observer was thought to be essential. This was despite the fact that both the Americans and Japanese were successfully operating single-seat aircraft from their carriers, and had been doing so for several years.

In any case, in pre-radar days there were serious doubts about whether fighters would be very effective against attacking torpedo or bombing aircraft. These doubts were reinforced by the results of peacetime exercises, a 1935 Admiralty report conluding that 'it is the exception rather than the rule for fighters to succeed in interfering with aircraft in Fleet exercises'.[19] Eventually the Admiralty was forced to modify its views, but very reluctantly and only slightly.

Because of delays with the Skuas, in 1938 the Admiralty took over some obsolescent RAF biplane Gladiator fighters to bolster the fleet defences. These aircraft, called Sea Gladiators, were modified by the fitting of arrester hooks and catapult points, but did not have folding wings, though fortunately they were small enough to be carried down on the lifts into the hangars in most of the carriers. Although the Sea Gladiator was capable of only

214 knots, it was manoeuvrable and was popular in the fleet chiefly because it was a single-seater—another example of the remoteness of the thinking of Admiralty staff from that of personnel in operational units.

The last pre-war fighter to reach the fleet was the Roc, the turret-armed brother of the Skua. The Roc was intended to be used as an escort fighter, but it had no forward-firing guns, its speed was far too low (only 172 knots), and it was a complete failure operationally. Thus, when war finally came in September 1939 the fighter strength in the carriers of the Royal Navy consisted of eighteen Skuas and twelve Sea Gladiators, a totally inadequate force with which to confront the Luftwaffe! Without radar, the first warning of an attack would be visual; by then it would almost certainly be too late for the carrier to launch fighters, and the small number of fighters embarked in the carriers made it impossible for them to maintain effective standing patrols.

As a result of all this the Royal Navy's tactical doctrine in 1939 was that, if an air attack developed on a force containing an aircraft carrier, the carrier was to recall all its aircraft, land them, take them down into the hangar and drain their petrol tanks (to reduce the fire risk). The force was to be defended by gunfire, the likely effectiveness of which was as exaggerated as the fighter defence had been neglected. Leaving air defence to the ships' guns also had the advantage of increasing the proportion of carrier aircraft that were available to attack the enemy. The prevailing attitude was well summed by the Commander-in-Chief of the Home Fleet (Admiral Sir Charles Forbes) during the Munich crisis when he announced his intention, 'in view of the greater value of [torpedo-spotter-reconnaissance] aircraft than fighters in the present emergency, to disembark all fighters from HMS *Furious* and all except two Gladiators from HMS *Courageous*.'[20]

Nor was the offensive position much better. During the inter-war years the Royal Navy had retained confidence in the torpedo as the best weapon for strike aircraft. The Cuckoo of 1917 was followed by a series of similar but slightly improved aircraft, culminating in the Swordfish which joined the fleet in 1936 and of which 140 were operational in the Fleet Air Arm when war came. The Swordfish was a biplane of antique appearance with fixed undercarriage and open cockpits, but despite its very low maximum speed of 122 knots and its cruising speed of 80 knots when carrying a torpedo, over 2000 of these machines were to be built before production ceased in August 1944.

The Royal Navy, like the US Navy, had doubts about the effectiveness of high-level bombing. While the Americans were developing very effective dive-bombers, however, attention in Britain was focused for some years on a proposal for a buoyant bomb. Such a weapon was intended to be dropped ahead of the target ship, sink initially, then rise to hit the vessel's bottom—its most vulnerable area. Only after a great deal of effort had been wasted on this device was it abandoned in favour of dive-bombing. Even then the Admiralty did not go the whole way, merely adding dive-bombing (with a 500-pound bomb) to its design requirements for the new Skua fighter. Not surprisingly the Skua was never a satisfactory dive-bomber. It did not even have a dive-bomb sight, the pilots releasing the bomb when the target ship disappeared below a mark on the engine cowling.

The RAF could do little to supplement the air striking power of the navy against ships at sea. Although some Bomber Command squadrons had taken part in practice attacks on a radio-controlled battleship, few of the crews were really trained for finding and striking a ship at sea. Coastal Command could do even less. Its total offensive strength was two squadrons of Vildebeeste torpedo-bombers, which were even more old-fashioned than the Swordfish.

Germany

At the outbreak of the 1939–45 war the Luftwaffe strength was 3750 aircraft, of which 1270 were twin-engined bombers, mostly Heinkel He.111 and Dornier Do.17, but with a few of the new Junkers Ju.88. There were also 335 Junkers Ju.87 (Stuka) dive-bombers, but these had an operational radius of only 100 miles. The employment of torpedo-aircraft had been part of the German pre-war plans but very little progress had been made. Early in 1939 the Luftwaffe held courses in the technique of attacking ships, but the service as a whole remained virtually untrained in navigation over the sea. The only part of the Luftwaffe trained in sea navigation was the Fleet Air Arm, whose officers and enlisted men had been recruited almost entirely from the navy and merchant service.

The command of the Fleet Air Arm was in the hands of a Luftwaffe general, who was expected to plan his operations in conjunction with the Naval High Command. At the outbreak of war he had 225 aircraft, consisting of obsolescent float biplanes and flying boats. There were also experimental formations of Ju.87 dive-bombers and Messerschmitt Bf.109 fighters intended for the aircraft carrier *Graf Zeppelin*, which was launched in 1938 but destined never to be completed.[21] It is interesting that the German naval and air staffs were planning to equip their first carrier with high-performance single-seat fighters at a time when the British Admiralty would not contemplate such a move. On the other hand, the German Navy clearly did not understand the true potential of the aircraft carrier, for *Graf Zeppelin* was designed with no less than sixteen 5.9-inch guns in double casements to protect itself against surface ships.

In the last months of peace the Luftwaffe became convinced of the need to provide modern bombers to attack shipping. The Fleet Air Arm was useless for this purpose, since it possessed neither the necessary crews nor aircraft. Besides, the navy wanted the Fleet Air Arm to be used solely as the eyes of the fleet. The only alternative for the Luftwaffe was to train its bomber force in navigation over the sea and in attacks on ships. Two squadrons each of 30 twin-engined aircraft were therefore formed—one equipped with He.111s and the other with Ju.88s—and attached to Luftflotte 2.

Because of the very short radius of action of the Ju.87 dive-bombers some of the early Ju.88 twin-engined bombers were specially fitted with dive-brakes, but this attempt to produce a long-range dive-bombing force was not pursued. The overwhelming bulk of Luftwaffe strikes on shipping were normal high-level or low-level attacks, but for such attacks to be successful a great deal of work needed to be done with training and tactical development. Fortunately for Britain very little time remained; the war came too soon.

Japan

Japanese naval aviation was initially organised and equipped by a British mission which was in Japan from 1921 until 1925. It was during this period that the first Japanese carrier, *Hosho*, was completed.[22] Although she was only 7500 tons she had an unobstructed flight deck more than 500 feet long. From the lessons learnt from this ship the Japanese converted two ships under construction, the battlecruiser *Akagi* (1927) and the battleship *Kaga* (1928), into carriers. These were often described as sister ships, but were actually more like cousins. They originally had double-decked hangars, with a flying-off deck at the forward end of each hangar, 53 feet long for the upper hangar, 175 feet for the lower one. The three take-off decks enabled a strike to be launched very rapidly, but the hangar flying-off decks became unworkable as aircraft weights and sizes increased, and the flight deck was lengthened to the bow.

The development of the Japanese Navy was shrouded in a secrecy unmatched by the other major powers. The naval base at

Kure was in a forbidden zone and the available information about the Japanese Navy was meagre and unreliable. At the same time Japan was closely watching developments in other countries, particularly America, and by the early 1930s had introduced arrester-wires and crash barriers into its carriers. This was years in advance of the Royal Navy; *Akagi* and *Kaga* could operate 63 and 72 aircraft respectively, twice as many as comparable British ships. The Japanese carriers were not equipped with catapults, and there was no real interest in fitting them until the latter stages of the Second World War, and by then it was too late.

The lack of catapults meant that Japanese carriers could not have a deck park to take aircraft additional to those that could be stowed in the hangars, and as the Americans progressively increased the size of their deck parks the Japanese carriers fell behind their US equivalents in the number of aircraft carried. The lack of catapults also necessitated a great deal of re-spotting of aircraft on the flight deck so that take-offs and landings were possible, although the fact that the Japanese carrier aircraft were generally smaller and lighter than their US and British equivalents reduced that problem somewhat.

Japan adhered to her Washington Treaty obligations until 1936, when the intention was announced of revoking the agreements. Before Japan did this, carriers had been planned to the limit of the allowance—or rather beyond it, as the Japanese tended to understate the displacements of their ships. After the completion of *Kaga* and *Akagi* only some 27 000 tons remained of Japan's official aircraft-carrier allowance. It was decided to build one carrier of 8000 tons (*Ryujo*) and two of 10 000 tons (*Soryu* and *Hiryu*). *Ryujo*—laid down in 1929 and completed in 1933—was the first Japanese carrier designed as such from the beginning, but she was not a success; any attempt to design an 8000 ton ship capable of operating 48 aircraft was doomed to failure. In 1934 she was considerably modified, but still had poor stability and seaworthiness and was unable to operate most of the later front-line aircraft. The after lift, for instance, was only 35-feet by 24-feet, and by 1940 the only front-line aircraft which could fit on it were the Kates,[23] and they had to be carefully placed at an angle.

After the revocation of the treaties *Soryu* and *Hiryu* were redesigned as 15 900 and 17 300 ton ships, and two new carriers of 25 675 tons (*Zuikaku* and *Shokaku*) were laid down. Two submarine support ships of 11 260 tons were also converted into aircraft carriers capable of 28 knots and carrying 30 aircraft; *Zuiho* commissioned at the end of 1940 and *Shoho* in January 1942. Two 24 000-ton 25-knot passenger liners—*Hiyo* and *Junyo*—and three

37

17 800-ton 21-knot ships—*Taiyo*, *Unyo* and *Chuyo*—were also being converted into aircraft carriers. Only *Taiyo* was commissioned before the Pacific war started, and the three 21-knot carriers were to be used during the war exclusively as aircraft transports and for aircrew training.

Thus, when war came to the Pacific at the end of 1941 the Japanese Navy possessed ten (soon to be eleven) carriers compared to only seven in the US Navy, and not all of the American carriers were in the Pacific. Moreover, the Japanese Navy had made arrangements for the further expansion of its carrier fleet, as two seaplane carriers and two passenger liners had been specially designed and stiffened for eventual use as aircraft carriers.

A unique Japanese carrier development was the building of the island structure on the port side; this was done with *Akagi* when that carrier was modernised in 1936, and *Hiryu*, completed in mid-1939, was built with such an island. The idea was that the carriers with their islands on opposite sides would be able to operate their aircraft when steaming in close company, with the aircraft using opposite traffic patterns. In practice the tactical advantages did not turn out to be very great, and the idea was not pursued in later ships. *Hiryu* was also the first Japanese carrier to have arrester wires at the forward end of the flight deck, for emergency landings—the same idea had been used in USS *Ranger* some years earlier. Like the Americans, the Japanese never used this equipment operationally, primarily because the crash barrier would not be effective if struck from the opposite direction.

One problem which was to become critical in the Japanese carriers was the height of the hangars. The standard was only 13–14 feet, and a mere 10 feet was provided in the lower hangar of *Junyo* class. This caused difficulties both in the design and the stowage of Japanese carrier aircraft.

A serious shock for the Americans and British was the performance of Japanese carrier aircraft. The Zeke (usually called the Zero), a highly-manoeuvrable fighter with a speed of 296 knots, armed with two 20mm guns and two 7.7mm machine-guns, and the Kate, a torpedo-bomber with a very long range, entered service in 1940. Both were superior to their US equivalents, the F4F Wildcat and the TBD Devastator, and of course far outclassed any British naval aircraft, although the lack of armour and self-sealing fuel tanks was later to prove a problem for the Zeke. Only in dive-bombing, which they pioneered, did the Americans have the advantage. Their Douglas TBD Dauntless was undoubtedly the best carrier-based dive-bomber of its era, but even here the Japanese had a very serviceable machine in the Val, a monoplane

A Japanese Mitsubishi A6M5 Zero-Sen. (*National Archives, 80-G-248975*)

with a fixed undercarriage, rather like the German Ju.87. The Japanese had also managed to increase the effective striking power of their large carriers by assigning the reconnaissance duty to the 60 or more long-range scouting seaplanes carried in the heavy cruisers and fast battleships which accompanied the carriers. This was a duty which in the British and American navies was carried out by the carrier-based aircraft if no land-based maritime-patrol aircraft were available.

The training of Japanese aircrew was equally impressive. Only those of high physical standards would be accepted as candidates, and pilots had 300 hours of flying time before joining an operational unit (compared to between 110 and 150 hours for a British Fleet Air Arm pilot in 1941). The Japanese pilots in the Pearl Harbor attack had an average of 800 hours flight time, three times the average of their US equivalents. Their attacking skill was extraordinary, and in pre-war torpedo exercises against fast battleship targets they achieved 80 per cent hits in daylight and 70 per cent at night.[24]

There was a downside to the very high standards for which the Japanese aimed, reflected in the low aircrew numbers produced—under

100 a year. Although adequate in peacetime, such a rate was quite unable to cope with the heavy attrition of even routine wartime operations, let alone battles such as Midway and the Philippine Sea. The Japanese never managed to modify their wartime training system so as to produce sufficient aircrew with adequate skills. At the time of Pearl Harbor the average standard of Japanese naval aircrew was distinctly higher than that of the Americans; by the end of the war it was much lower.

It was the fashion in pre-war years to disparage the efficiency of the Japanese. It was claimed that Japanese designers could merely make inferior copies of the products of other countries, that their pilots suffered from defective vision, and so on. Winston Churchill thought that Naval Intelligence, which equated Japanese capabilities with those of the Italians, was 'very much inclined to exaggerate Japanese strength and efficiency'.[25] It was to take a major war to dispel these illusions.

France and Italy

The other major naval powers, France and Italy, were insignificant in the development of the struggle between bombers and battleships. France did indeed have an aircraft carrier, *Béarn*, converted from a 1914 battleship and completed in 1927. However, she played no significant part in the Second World War, being too slow (twenty knots) to be an efficient aircraft carrier with the aircraft available to her, and having very poor flight-deck design; in fact, although she could carry 40 aircraft, she could not operate more than ten simultaneously. A long-range naval aviation program, produced in 1922, envisaged the contruction of two 30 000-ton cruiser-carriers, but financial stringency prevented any progress on them. Two 18 000-ton carriers, *Painlevé* and *Joffre*, were authorised in 1937, but although one was laid down in late 1938 it was at a very early stage at the time of the French surrender in 1940.

As for the Italians, they had developed the elements of naval aviation during the First World War, but upon the establishment of the Italian Air Force in 1923 the navy had been ordered to discontinue all aviation activity. When Italy entered the war in June 1940 the navy had at its disposal 100 air force reconnaissance aircraft, but nearly all of these were very obsolete single-engined flying boats. These were, moreover, out of production so that there were no replacements for the inevitable attrition. The air force attempted to fill the gap with its medium bombers, but being untrained in maritime reconnaissance they were useless; there was never any night reconnaissance by Italian aircraft. Any maritime air strikes would have to be by the untrained (in maritime operations) Italian Air Force, though there was agreement in September 1940 to the development of a torpedo-carrying capability (which the air force had previously strenuously resisted) and the first effective strike was conducted in the following month. Faced with reality, the Italian government did authorise, in March 1941, the conversion of two transatlantic liners into aircraft carriers, but neither was ready at the time of the Italian surrender in September 1943; nor were their aircraft.

DEVELOPMENT OF ANTI-AIRCRAFT GUNFIRE

It must not be imagined that the majority of naval officers regarded fighters as the main defence of ships against air attack. On the contrary, naval opinion generally had an altogether unwarranted confidence in the ability of gunfire to destroy attacking aircraft, or at least to prevent them bombing accurately. The anti-aircraft guns used in 1939 could be divided into two groups: those of medium calibre, ranging from 3-inch to 5.25-inch, which fired timed-fused shells at the estimated future position of the target aircraft; and close-range (up to about 1500 yards) guns, which were automatic and had a high rate of fire, and whose projectiles were either solid or designed to explode on contact. The large anti-ship guns could also be used to augment the anti-aircraft fire by firing barrages of shells designed to burst at pre-set ranges—usually about 1500 yards.

In 1939 the only navy to have a satisfactory control system for medium-calibre anti-aircraft guns was that of the United States. They had the essential requirements of a stable element from which the movements of a target aircraft could be accurately measured, a good stereoscopic rangefinder, and an automatic computer to calculate the future position of the target. Almost as importantly, the guns followed automatically—thereby eliminating the errors which inevitably occurred if two operators at each gun had to follow pointers to aim their gun. The first modern control system was the Mark 33 director, which entered service in 1934. The only defect of the Mark 33 director was its weight of 20 000 pounds, caused by the fact that the stable element and the computer were both carried in the director, mounted high in the ship so that it would have good visibility. The Mark 37 director, with the computer and stable element below decks, was ordered in 1936, and began to be fitted in 1940. These two systems were so far in advance of those available to other navies that even ten years later they were still unequalled.

41

The 5-inch guns, too, were of a high quality, being capable of elevation to 80 degrees (and thus useful against dive-bombers) and with a rate of fire of fifteen rounds per minute, substantially faster than comparable guns in other navies. The 5-inch 38-calibre single open mounting was first installed in destroyers in 1934, and a single 5-inch turret was produced three years later; a twin 5-inch turret began production in 1940. The layouts varied. Destroyers usually had four or five 5-inch guns, and one director system. Cruisers had eight guns and two directors, as did carriers. The new battleships being built—for by 1939 the Americans were rearming and had two battleships under construction and six more ordered—were to have ten twin-turrets and four director systems. The only weaknesses in the Mark 37 system was the accuracy of the rangefinder—though the stereoscopic rangefinders used by the US and German navies were markedly superior to the coincidence rangefinders used by the other navies—and this weakness could not be overcome until radar was available to provide ranging for gun control; in 1939 this was still some time off.

There was a problem with the arcs of fire of the 5-inch anti-aircraft guns in battleships, aircraft carriers and cruisers. In the battleships and cruisers the 'main armament' turrets—the anti-ship guns—were given the best positions, and the 'secondary armament'—the 5-inch guns—tended to be tucked away with restricted arcs of fire. In the aircraft carriers the positioning of the 5-inch guns was restricted because of the requirement for a clear flight deck. There was pressure for an anti-aircraft cruiser, with the 5-inch guns dominant, and eight such ships were built, the first of them (*Atlanta*) being ready in time for the battle of Midway in June 1942.[26] These cruisers had sixteen 5-inch guns in twin turrets and were very effective anti-aircraft ships, although 5-inch guns were too light to be really effective in the anti-ship role, as the Americans were to find out in the Solomons.

The Japanese Type 91 anti-aircraft control system, which was being fitted in their larger ships from 1931 onwards, was inferior to the US systems in several crucial areas—chiefly in that its mechanical computer was operated manually by no less than ten operators, and the guns did not follow automatically. A much improved system, the Type 94, was introduced in 1937. This had a computer comparable with the US one, but the guns still did not follow automatically. It was not to be until 1943 that the Japanese introduced an automatic stabilising system, and even then it was not completely satisfactory; they never had automatic-following guns. The battleships and cruisers usually had eight 5-inch guns, but these could not fire more than twelve rounds a minute. The destroyers were much worse off. A typical destroyer had five or six 5-inch guns, but could not fire more than five broadsides a minute, because the guns had to be brought down to a low elevation in order to re-load. They were of so little use that Japanese destroyers did not have an anti-aircraft fire-control system. A new twin 4-inch turret for destroyers was being developed, but was not yet ready.

The German Navy's anti-aircraft gunnery was of about the same standard as the Japanese. The earlier cruisers had six or eight 3.5-inch guns, which could fire twelve rounds a minute. The heavy cruisers of the *Prinz Eugen* class had ten and the two *Scharnhorst* class battleships fourteen of a new twin 4.1-inch mounting, of similar design and performance to the earlier 3.5-inch mounting. The Germans, like the Japanese, had not succeeded in providing their destroyers with efficient anti-aircraft guns. Their 5-inch guns could not elevate above 30 degrees and they did not have an anti-aircraft predictor; all they could do was fire a barrage in the general direction of attacking aircraft. Some of the destroyers had a single 4.1-inch anti-aircraft gun which could at least elevate so that it could fire at dive-bombers, but the German destroyers, unlike their Japanese and British counterparts, were fortunate in that they did not have to face a serious dive-bombing threat.

By 1918 all the Royal Navy's battleships and cruisers had been fitted with 3-inch anti-aircraft guns, but as they had no control arrangements the chance of hitting an aircraft, or even a Zeppelin, was remote. A 1919 Admiralty post-war committee recommended the adoption of the 4.7-inch gun as the standard medium-calibre anti-aircraft weapon, with six or eight mounted in all ships of cruiser size and above. This gun was fitted in the 1920s battleships *Nelson* and *Rodney* but in few other ships, primarily because the Admiralty already had a stock of smaller 4-inch guns which could be relatively easily fitted in place of the old 3-inch anti-aircraft guns. Later, more modernised battleships, and the new carriers, were fitted with 4.5-inch or 5.25-inch guns with a rate of fire of about ten rounds a minute.

The Italian crisis of 1935 brought home to the Admiralty the frightening weakness of the anti-aircraft gun defence of the fleet, and eight First World War cruisers had their 6-inch guns removed and replaced with 4-inch so they could act as anti-aircraft ships, defending the fleet against high-level bombing attacks, which were thought to be the main threat. The weakness of these ships was that the 4-inch guns were too light for them to perform the other traditional roles of cruisers: helping to defend the fleet against surface attack and supporting the destroyers when they were attacking the enemy fleet.

To attempt to provide for all these roles a new class of cruisers was redesigned to carry ten 5.25-inch dual purpose guns in five turrets—the first of these ships, *Dido*, was due to come into service in 1940, to be followed by fifteen more.[27] The guns in the destroyers were of yet another type—4.7-inch. These were not the anti-aircraft gun but a First World War anti-shipping weapon, and had the drawback that even in the latest ships they could not elevate above 40 degrees.[28] The heavy losses British destroyers were to suffer at the hands of German dive-bombers needs little other explanation.

There were also some convoy escorts with twin 4-inch guns capable of high elevation, usually in two twin-mountings, sometimes three. Fifteen of these ships were conversions of First World War destroyers, and there were fifteen other anti-aircraft convoy-escort vessels completed and four more under construction. Finally, there were twenty of a new class of small destroyers being produced, designed for anti-aircraft defence and armed with two twin 4-inch mountings (three mountings in later ships), but these *Hunt* class destroyers would not begin to enter service until 1940.

None of the turrets or mountings in any of the ships followed the director automatically, and the manual pointer-following inevitably introduced substantial errors. As a last straw, the muddle of anti-aircraft guns—5.25-inch, two types of 4.7-inch, 4.5-inch and 4-inch—imposed enormous logistic problems on the Royal Navy.

The second major recommendation of the Admiralty 1919 committee was that the medium-calibre anti-aircraft guns should be controlled by a tachometric system on the principles later adopted by all the other major navies. Although various experiments were conducted, the Admiralty was worried about the 'involved nature' of the proposed calculator systems and, as no satisfactory stabilisation system had been produced, the Admiralty fell back on guesswork for the calculation of the amount of aim-off required.

In all of the navies there were many older ships whose guns had no form of anti-aircraft predictor. All that could be done with these guns was to fire a continuous barrage in the general direction of the enemy aircraft while under attack, with the shells set to burst at a fixed range, usually about 1500 yards. The chances of hitting were small, but the barrage had some deterrent effect. The Japanese also used the heavy anti-ship guns in their cruisers and battleships to fire such a barrage, and practised it assiduously.

It can be seen that, except for the Americans, the navies were very ill-prepared to defend themselves with gunfire against air attack. The Royal Navy was clearly the worst prepared. What was extraordinary was the confidence many Royal Naval officers had in their ability to defeat air attack by gunfire despite the crudity of their anti-aircraft systems, of which they should surely have been aware. There were some sceptics about the efficiency of the fleet's anti-aircraft gunnery,[29] but in 1936 Chatfield (by now First Sea Lord) told Winston Churchill that even one anti-aircraft gun in a merchant ship would keep bombing aircraft at such a height that the chance of the ship being hit would be very small! In the same year he wrote that 'we shall, however, so completely equip the Fleet with anti-aircraft guns that I do not believe it will be a profitable thing for aircraft to approach it.'[30]

In addition to the medium-range guns, all warships were fitted with close-range automatic guns, ranging from 0.303-inch machine guns to 40mm, but in 1939 the number of such guns was tiny compared to what all ships would be carrying in a few years time. In 1939, for instance, a typical close-range armament of a major British warship would be two 8-barrelled 2-pounder pom-poms and four twin Lewis guns. In 1939 most of the close-range guns were fired over open sights, the sailor estimating on a fixed-sight on the mounting itself the amount of aim-off to be applied.

With weapons such as the 8-barrelled pom-poms the amount of smoke generated by firing made local aiming difficult, so separate directors were fitted well away from the guns. These directors were simple open sights, transmitting to pointers at the mounting itself, where sailors followed the pointers to aim their gun, but war experience proved them a failure. It was not reasonable to expect men under fire to follow pointers accurately when close air action was developing in their immediate vicinity. Remote directors were not a success until the mountings followed the director automatically. This was done in the US Navy in 1942 and the Royal Navy two years later. In 1936 the Japanese produced a remote director with two or three 25mm mountings following it automatically, but it was not used at sea until 1941 and production delays meant that many ships were never fitted with it.

The most effective automatic weapon in the Royal Navy was the 2-pounder pom-pom, which had been fitted in many destroyers and other small ships during the First World War. Indeed, the development of 8-gun or 4-gun mountings was the only recommendation of the 1919 committee which the Admiralty implemented. Although it had some drawbacks, the pom-pom's rate of fire (120 rounds a minute) made it probably the best naval anti-aircraft weapon of its time—which was, however, running out by 1939. Battleships usually carried two or four 8-barrelled mountings, cruisers two 8-barrelled, and the latest destroyers one 4-barrelled. The other significant automatic gun used by the Royal Navy was the Vickers 0.5-inch machine-gun, usually fitted in quadruple mountings. They fired solid shot and were soon found to have too short a range and have too little hitting-power to be useful in defending a ship against air attack. As for the 0.303-inch Lewis guns fitted in some ships, they were purely for morale purposes.

By the mid-1930s the Admiralty was becoming aware that the close-range armaments of its ships were inadequate but faced the problem that resources and time would not permit the development of new weapons in the United Kingdom. Trials were conducted with various European weapons, the Swiss 20mm Oerlikon and the Swedish 40mm Bofors being clearly the best. A few Oerlikons were ordered just before the outbreak of the 1939 war, to arm merchant ships (or so the Treasury was informed), but they soon became standard weapons in both the Royal Navy and the US Navy. More problems were experienced with the Bofors (undoubtedly by far the best close-range anti-aircraft weapon of the Second World War) because, when inquiries were made as early as 1936, the Admiralty was told that the Bofors firm could take no more orders because production capacity was fully stretched by existing orders, largely from the British army.[31] Bofors guns did not become generally available until massive American production started in 1942.

The US Navy was in an unhappy situation with its automatic weapons in 1939. A new 1.1-inch (28mm) automatic gun on a quadruple mounting was just being introduced, but these proved very unreliable in practice. Even as late as 1941 the only automatic weapons in many US warships were 0.5-inch machine-guns. The weapons which were to arm and defend the US fleets in their campaign across the Pacific—the Swedish Bofors 40mm and the Swiss Oerlikon 20mm—were not ordered until a few months before Pearl Harbor.

The Japanese had begun producing a French 25mm gun of Hotchkiss design in 1935. These guns had a rate of fire of 200 rounds a minute and many twin mountings were fitted. Triple and single versions of the 25mm were developed later in the war, and were eventually fitted in very large numbers. Another Hotchkiss gun, the 13.2mm machine-gun, was also built in Japan and fitted in nearly all their warships.

In 1939 the German automatic guns were in some respects the most advanced of all. They had a 20mm gun of substantially the same performance as the Swiss Oerlikon. A twin 37mm had also been produced, but it was not a success even though nearly 400 were built. The 37mm gun could not fire more than 50 rounds a minute, and the mounting was over-elaborate. Despite its defects this 37mm mounting remained standard in the German Navy throughout the war, even though a greatly improved 37mm gun with a rate of fire of 160 rounds per minute was available. This new gun was fitted in single mountings, but the design effort could not be found to produce a new twin mounting.

What is notable is that in 1939 none of the planning staffs of the various navies realised the scale of close-range armament which was going to be necessary to meet the air threat. In the Royal Navy in 1940 the recently-modernised battleship *Queen Elizabeth* had a close-range armament of four eight-barrelled pom-poms and four quadruple 0.5-inch machine-guns; by the time the war ended in 1945 the machine-guns had been replaced by 52 20mm Oerlikons in twin mountings. Similarly in the US Navy the battleship *West Virginia* had a total close-range armament of ten 0.5-inch machine-guns in 1939, but in 1945 she had ten quadruple 40mm Bofors mountings, each with its own director (with a tachometric sight) remotely controlling the mounting, and 52 20mm Oerlikons. The Japanese battleship *Yamato* had 24 25mm guns when she was commissioned in December 1941, but by the time she was sunk in 1945 she was carrying 40 triple 25mm mountings and 30 singles. And the German *Bismarck* had eight twin 37mm and twelve single 20mm automatic guns when she was commissioned in 1940, but by the time she was sunk in May 1941 the number of 20mm guns had been increased to 36 (and eventually to 70 in her sister ship *Tirpitz*).

DEVELOPMENT OF RADAR

An essential part of effective air defence was warning of the approach of attacking aircraft, both so that guns would be ready and fighter defence (if any) was properly deployed. All ships placed lookouts, but they could rarely see an aircraft more than ten miles away and often failed to see high-level bombers at all. Various expedients were tried during the inter-war years, such as the stationing of destroyers or cruisers at some distance from the fleet in the likely direction of attack, at a cost of placing the ships concerned at some risk and weakening the number available for close screening of the battlefleet. Patrolling aircraft were also tried, but although it was found that they sometimes saw low-flying aircraft they were completely ineffective against those approaching at any height.

It soon became obvious that visual warning was of very limited usefulness, although it would have to be retained as a last resort.

The answer obviously lay in some instrumental method of detection. A great deal of work went on for nearly twenty years with acoustic detectors, but even when mounted under ideal conditions ashore these devices rarely achieved success beyond ten miles. Their range was obviously going to be much less if they were mounted in a ship, where inevitably there would be severe restrictions on the size of aerials.

The solution was found in radar, with successful systems being evolved independently and at nearly the same time in the United States, Britain, France and Germany during the years 1934–40. Development of British radar dates from early in 1935, and led to the Air Ministry beginning construction of radar stations covering the Thames estuary from 1936. By the time of the Munich crisis two years later, these stations were in operation and other stations were under construction to cover the rest of the country.

The Royal Navy was also interested in radar, and long-range air warning sets (the Type 79, later Type 279) were fitted in a battleship and two cruisers in 1938–39. At this stage the RAF's radars operated on a 12–13 metre wavelength, but the 7-metre wavelength was the longest for which a practicable aerial could be mounted on a ship's mast, with each set requiring two aerials—one for transmitting, the other for receiving. These sets, of which 40 were ordered in September 1939, could give warning of approaching high-flying aircraft at a distance of about 100 miles, and some estimate could be made of their height. It was far from being a perfect system, because the information was sometimes indecisive, but it was better than nothing. A more efficient 3.5-metre set (the Type 281) was under development, but it would not be available for shipfitting until October 1940. Other sets on the much shorter 50cm wavelength were also being developed to supplement and possibly replace optical rangefinding in the control of gunfire, but they too could not be at sea for at least a year.

In America it was the navy which originated radar, and the frequencies chosen were naturally ones which would be best for sets to be fitted in ships. The US Navy's first success with radar came in April 1937 when a 1.5-metre set was fitted in a destroyer for trials, and eventually it was able to follow aircraft out to 40 miles. A development of this set, known as the XAF, was fitted in a battleship in December 1938. A further development, known as the CXAM, was fitted in a battleship, the carrier *Yorktown* and four cruisers in 1940; before Pearl Harbor all American carriers and seven battleships were to be fitted. The CXAM had surface-warning as well as air-warning capabilities, and had the great advantage, compared to the Type 79 and Type 281, that only a single aerial was required. The CXAM could detect an aircraft at high altitude at 80 miles and at 35 miles at 3000 feet, but in the early days there were considerable problems with its reliability.[32]

The first radar experiments in the German Navy were carried out in 1934. In 1937 a prototype 80cm radar set—the first to be used operationally by any navy—was installed in the pocket battleship *Graf Spee*, and trialled off the Spanish coast during the Civil War. When war broke out only two German ships—*Graf Spee* and the cruiser *Königsberg*—had been fitted with the 80cm radar, but the battleships *Scharnhorst* and *Gneisenau* were soon fitted and eventually every significant German warship was radar-equipped. In its air-warning role, the German set could detect aircraft out to about 60 miles, but it was also useful for surface warning and in ranging guns against both ships and aircraft; the set was also used ashore by the Luftwaffe. Thus it can be seen that in the early days of the Second World War the German radars were superior to the British in surface warning, but inferior with regard to aircraft. The Germans concentrated on radar for gunfire control, and did not develop the kind of air-warning sets which were common in the US and British navies.

The French Navy had been interested in the possibility of radar, but at the outbreak of war they had no operational sets. There was experimental work going on with a 16cm magnetron, from which the power output was much greater than anyone else had been able to produce at such a frequency. Fortunately a sample was passed to England before everything was destroyed when the Germans marched into France in 1940, and this sample was of considerable use to British scientists when they were developing 10cm radar.

Japan lagged far behind Germany, Britain and America, and in 1939 Japanese radar was still in the exploratory phase. Work began on a 3-metre shore-based air-warning radar in April 1941, but a Japanese military mission which visited Germany the next month was very surprised to learn the extent to which the British were using radar. Research was stimulated by British sets captured in Singapore in January 1942 and American sets captured in the Philippines.[33] Two Japanese ships (*Ise* and *Hyuga*) had primitive sets at the time of the Battle of Midway, but it was not until some months later—after the disastrous defeat at Midway—that ship-fitting commenced, though as late as 1944 many ships had no form of radar. The performance of Japanese radars suffered badly from being underpowered, and the Japanese never managed to develop height-finders or radars for anti-aircraft gunfire control.

The Italian Navy started investigating the possibilities of radar in 1936, but ship-fitting of a workable warning-set did not begin until 1943, although some German sets had been received in the previous year. The Italian EC–3 could detect an aircraft at 50 miles and had useful surface detection performance. Fifty sets were ordered, but only twelve had been delivered by the time Italy surrendered in September 1943. The sets were fitted in the *Littorio* class battleships, four cruisers and five destroyers.

It can be seen that in 1939 the British, American and German navies were all at about the same stage of radar development, with the Japanese and Italians far behind. The great advance, the invention of the resonant cavity magnetron, which was to give the British and Americans the decisive lead in radar development, was still a year away. The magnetron made possible very short-wavelength radar, which in turn made possible a narrow radar beam and roles for radar such as the accurate determination of an aircraft's height or the radar aiming of gunnery systems. When scientific liaison between the United States and Britain started late in 1940, the magnetron was one of the devices given to the USA.[34] It was described by an American as the most valuable cargo ever brought to their shores. The Germans did not believe that high-powered microwave radar sets were practicable until a British bomber carrying such a set was shot down over Germany in February 1943. By then it was too late for them, although they did manage to rush some microwave sets into service before the war ended.

REPLENISHMENT AT SEA

It is one thing to have efficient aircraft carriers, anti-aircraft gunfire and radar equipment, but another to be able to maintain ships with these capabilities on station when and where required. In the Second World War it became crucial to be able to replenish ships at sea and avoid the necessity to return to harbour, which might be many miles away. Fuel was usually the most critical need, and it was generally thought to be undesirable to allow a ship to have less than 50 per cent of her fuel capacity since it could be very awkward to be caught short if a crisis developed. From this it can be seen that unless the ships could be refuelled in or near their operational area their military usefulness was greatly reduced; of course, the further they were operating from their base the greater the reduction.

In the US Navy the first refuelling at sea of a major ship occurred in 1924 with a light cruiser, and over the next three years experiments were also made with battleships. The best method was the abeam method, the ship being refuelled steaming close, usually about 100–150 feet, to the fuelling ship (oiler or major warship), which had to have suitable cranes, oil fuel hoses and pumps. The alternative was the astern method, with the ship being towed by the oiler, but this ultimately proved much less satisfactory than the broadside method. The experiments continued, and by the late 1920s refuelling destroyers at sea by the broadside method became almost a standard part of each fleet exercise.

The same progress was not made with the refuelling of the larger ships, until in 1938 the Chief of Naval Operations directed that tests were to be made with the fuelling at sea of battleships, carriers and cruisers by tankers whilst underway. The carrier *Saratoga*, steaming at seven knots, was successfully fuelled from a tanker in June 1939. By the following year a standard procedure had been adopted, and a directive was issued that all major warships were to be fitted with the necessary fuelling-at-sea installations at their next regular overhaul. At the same time three fast tankers being built for the Standard Oil Company were requisitioned, and formed the basis of the superb Fleet Train which later supported the advance across the Pacific. Although battleships and carriers did refuel by the abeam method, this was done by the tanker coming alongside the warship, and it was not until 1943 that the procedure was reversed so that the warship made the approach to the tanker.

Things were not nearly so advanced in the Royal Navy. Fuelling-at-sea experiments had begun in 1906, but were then given little priority because nearly all ships were coal-powered and there was no prospect of transferring coal at sea. When experiments in refuelling with oil began, the techniques used involved the astern method, a 5-inch bronze hose, and extremely slow speeds. It was not until 1937 that trials began with fuelling abeam, accompanied by great problems caused by the inflexibility of the hoses and steering difficulties created for destroyers by the low speeds required. Although steps were taken to solve these problems, it remained the case that connecting was very complicated and protracted, and there were plenty of things to go wrong. Nevertheless by the time the war started battleships could refuel destroyers, albeit slowly and at slow speed, but if major ships had to be refuelled (and this was rare) it had to be done from oil tankers by the laborious astern method.

Improvements did not really begin until 1941, when two of *Bismarck*'s supply ships were captured intact in the Atlantic and the Royal Navy was able to inspect the rubber hoses used by the

Germans and make trials with such hoses beginning in March 1942. However there were to be problems for the British with rubber supplies, and their refuelling standards improved only slowly. It was really not until 1945 that they were approaching the standards of the other major navies.

The German Navy had given a much higher priority than the Royal Navy to refuelling at sea. This was because of their intention to use long-range surface raiders and their lack of overseas bases. They had developed a system of refuelling ships astern of tankers, using inflatable rubber hoses which could be floated to the ship being refuelled. It worked quite well, although it was rather slow.

The Japanese were substantially better than the Royal Navy at refuelling at sea, largely because they used rubber hoses but also because senior officers regarded the capability as tactically important. However the Japanese did lag substantially behind the Americans, particularly in the pumping rates of their tankers. The Japanese used the abeam method of refuelling for destroyers and light cruisers, though they sometimes were refuelled while being towed by the tanker. The battleships and aircraft carriers reversed the positions, towing the tanker while being refuelled.

During the war the Japanese did not advance as rapidly as the Americans in refuelling capability for another reason—the battle squadrons had top priority, and logistical support was a poor relation. However they did change to abeam refuelling for their battleships and carriers, though it was the tanker which made the approach to the warship rather than the other way round.

Although oil was the most critical requirement, ships needed many other supplies if they were to remain in operational areas as long as the physical state of their crews permitted, or until crucial equipment needed servicing which was beyond the capability of ships' crews. Aircraft carriers needed aviation fuel, and replacement aircraft and crews; all ships needed ammunition, food and spare parts, and hospital arrangements for the wounded and seriously ill. It took time and immense efforts to provide such support, very little of which was available at the start of the Second World War. By 1945, however, ships—particularly US ships—could remain in operational areas for periods which would have seemed inconceivable a decade earlier.

It is always difficult to summarise briefly the relative capabilities of different navies, because not only is their capability a factor but also their direction and morale. Throughout the inter-war years Britain, France and the United States had found it difficult to maintain and update their military forces, because of pressure for disarmament and restrictions on armaments. In Britain this took a

52

particularly pernicious form through the Ten Year Rule which asserted that, in planning defence organisation and equipment, it was to be assumed a major war was unlikely for the next ten years.

First established in 1919, the rule was made self-perpetuating in 1928 at the instance of Winston Churchill, who was Chancellor of the Exchequer at the time. It was eventually abolished at the end of 1933 but by then had done great damage. In 1939 the British clearly lagged far behind both the Japanese and Americans, not only in air defence of their ships by gunfire or fighter aircraft, but in their ability to mount effective air strikes on ships and to replenish their ships at sea. Fortunately, the Royal Navy's early adversaries—the Germans and Italians—were no better and perhaps a little worse in these fields than it was.

3

Norway:

9 April–13 June 1940

From the first hours of the Second World War the Royal Navy became engaged in an unrelenting struggle against submarines and surface raiders of the German Navy, but its first serious clash with the German Luftwaffe did not occur until the Germans invaded Norway in April 1940. As early as September 1939 the First Lord of the Admiralty (Winston Churchill) had proposed mining Norwegian waters to stop the Germans transporting iron ore southwards from Narvik, but it was only after the war between the Finns and the Russians ended on 13 March 1940 that this scheme gained acceptance. It was expected that minelaying would probably provoke a German reaction, and that retaliation would largely be by air strikes, so the British dispositions to deal with this threat are interesting.

Because of the reported presence of four Norwegian warships in the Narvik area, when the minelayers went out on 8 April the battlecruiser *Renown* was sent to protect them. Four cruisers were held at Rosyth with four battalions of troops on board, and there were loaded troop transports in the Clyde ready to occupy key Norwegian cities if the Germans launched an invasion *and* the Norwegians accepted British support. The main body of the Home Fleet—two battleships and a battlecruiser, three cruisers and ten destroyers—was at Scapa Flow.

The air-defence capability of the Home Fleet had changed little in the six months since the outbreak of war. Two battleships now had air-warning radar, as did some of the cruisers, for they had been given priority over the carriers (none of which was yet fitted). The radar-fitted ships were not organised to direct fighters by radio, a system which by now was standard in RAF Fighter

Command; in any case, the Home Fleet had no fighters at sea at the time. As far as gun defence was concerned, its effectiveness, or ineffectiveness, was unchanged. Work was going on with radar sets to supplement rangefinders in the anti-aircraft directors, but none had yet been fitted. A few 20mm Oerlikon guns (diverted from their original destinations to merchant ships) had been installed.

At the outbreak of the Second World War the Royal Navy had a total strength, ashore and afloat, of 232 operational aircraft—85 per cent of which were biplanes with fabric-covered wings, constant-pitch propellers, no flaps, fixed undercarriages and no voice radio. There were six aircraft carriers in commission, but the only one available was *Furious*. She was without catapults or crash barriers, and there were grave doubts as to whether she could operate Skua fighters as well as her two squadrons of Swordfish; although Skuas had been assigned to the ship they had never actually been embarked.

Such a situation was extraordinary for the moment when the Royal Navy had chosen to provoke probable heavy German air strikes on the fleet, but they illuminate the disregard senior British naval officers then had for carriers in this sort of operation, and for air defence generally. Only two months before the Norwegian campaign the Fifth Sea Lord (who was Chief of the Naval Air Service) had argued that:

> the Fleet when at sea with its destroyer screen in place presents quite the most formidable target a formation of aircraft could attack and the presence of fighter aircraft to protect the Fleet is by no means a necessity. They should be looked on as an added precaution if available.[1]

The RAF was not intended to be part of the operation either. 'No air forces', wrote the Chiefs of Staff, 'need accompany the . . . army forces in the first instance . . . A decision on [the later provision of an RAF contingent] can be deferred.'

The strategic importance of Norway was not lost on the Germans, although they did not attach nearly as much importance to the iron-ore traffic as did Churchill. In October 1939 Admiral Erich Raeder, the German Naval Commander-in-Chief, drew Hitler's attention to the desirability of gaining bases in Norway, to forestall a British move. Hitler was not convinced, and only after a series of incidents had persuaded him that Allied intervention in Norway was inevitable did he give approval for the invasion option on 1 March.

The German plan was extraordinarily bold; indeed, as Raeder

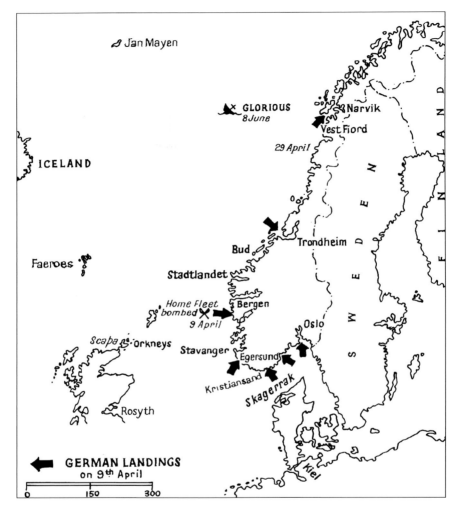

The battle of Norway

pointed out to Hitler, it was 'contrary to all principles in the theory of naval warfare'.[2] In the face of the very superior British Navy it was planned to land forces at six points at once, along with airborne forces at a seventh. In the early stages it was hoped that surprise would compensate for German naval inferiority; later, aircraft operating from captured Norwegian air bases would play their part. The two battleships *Scharnhorst* and *Gneisenau* were to be used to provide a diversion during the early stages. The invasion date was set for 9 April.

Code-breaking, which later gave some Allied commanders the appearance of remarkable prescience, did nothing useful to unmask the German plans in this case. The first information received by Admiral Sir Charles Forbes, the Commander-in-Chief of the Home Fleet, was on 6 April when he was warned of unusual German activity. Late the next day he was told that German heavy ships were at sea, but not their destination. Forbes at once disposed the Home Fleet, not to deal with an invasion of Norway, but on the assumption that the German heavy ships were trying to break out onto the Atlantic trade routes. When the main body of the Home Fleet departed Scapa Flow at high speed, it was therefore in a north-easterly direction, and every hour took them further away from the Skagerrak area of the North Sea.

Meanwhile, the Germans had broken the British naval ciphers and thereby obtained considerable information about the movements and intentions of British ships.[3] The planned German assaults accordingly proceeded smoothly in the early hours of 9 April. As soon as he realised that the Germans were actually invading Norway, Forbes turned south. Early on the morning of the invasion he was joined by more cruisers and destroyers, bringing his force to three capital ships, twelve cruisers and 23 destroyers—but no aircraft carriers. Forbes planned an immediate counter-attack against enemy ships in Bergen, and detached four cruisers and seven destroyers for this purpose. Before the blow could be delivered, it was stopped on orders from London—the first of several unfortunate Admiralty interventions during the campaign.

During the afternoon the expected German air attacks developed on Forbes' forces. Two anti-shipping squadrons, formed at the outbreak of war and equipped with He.111 and Ju.88 aircraft, comprised the nucleus of a newly-raised Fliegerkorps 10. At the outset of the Norwegian campaign this formation had about 500 combat aircraft and 500 transports. The core of the operational force was 290 medium bombers (mainly He.111 and Ju.88) together with 40 Ju.87 Stuka dive-bombers, though the latter were of limited usefulness against ships because their crews were inexperienced in anti-shipping strikes and their radius of action was less than 100 miles. Initially Fliegerkorps 10 operated from airfields in Germany, but as Norwegian airfields were captured or new ones built the force moved to bases closer to the action.

The actual attacks on the British ships on the first day were not very heavy, with only the two original anti-shipping squadrons involved in launching low and medium-level bombing attacks. One destroyer was sunk,[4] the battleship *Rodney* was hit by a 1000-pound bomb which failed to penetrate the armoured deck, and three cruisers were damaged. Although the damage was slight, the limitations of the fleet's anti-aircraft gun defences were clearly exposed, particularly in the appalling sea conditions which prevailed. Some of the larger ships fired nearly half of their stocks of ammunition, but only one German aircraft was shot down.

What was dramatic was the change in attitude of senior British commanders. Forbes himself had stated shortly before the war that the effectiveness of anti-aircraft fire made daylight attack on ships uneconomical. Confidence had been high both in the Admiralty and in the Home Fleet that naval ships at sea would not be seriously menaced by the Luftwaffe, but as Forbes afterwards commented, somewhat ruefully, 'the scale of air attack that would be developed against . . . our naval forces off the Norwegian coast was grievously underestimated when the operations were undertaken'.[5]

What was Forbes to do? Even if he had believed that carrier-based fighters could defend the fleet, *Furious* (who had just joined him) could make no contribution. When *Furious* was given the urgent order to sail by the Admiralty, her fifteen Skua fighters were disembarked at an airfield 100 miles away—'too far off to comply with what was obviously an urgent order'[6]—and the ship sailed without them. So all *Furious* had to offer was two squadrons of outdated Swordfish torpedo-bombers.

Recognising that his fleet could not continue to operate close to the bases being used by the German bombers (which did not yet extend to Norwegian airfields), Forbes abandoned plans for an attack on Bergen the following day by Swordfish from *Furious*. Instead, he proposed to the Admiralty that the Home Fleet should concentrate its efforts on Trondheim and the coast further north, leaving the approaches to Stavanger, Kristiansand and Oslo to submarines, and Bergen to bombers operating from Britain. It is doubtful if there had been such a sudden and decisive change of naval direction since 18 March 1915—the day the British Fleet failed to force the Dardanelles.

Two days later there was another historic event: the first torpedo-bombing attack by carrier-based aircraft. There had been reports of two German cruisers and other ships in Trondheim harbour, and *Furious*' Swordfish were ordered to attack them. The attack was a fiasco. The main German force had already left, leaving only three destroyers in the harbour, and the British torpedoes—set to run at twenty feet—ran aground on sandbanks and did no damage.

Another attack, this time against Bergen, carried out by fifteen

Skuas of the Fleet Air Arm based in the Orkneys, was more successful. Although most of the German ships involved in the landing there had departed on the evening of 9 April, the cruiser *Königsberg* had been rendered unseaworthy by damage from Norwegian shore batteries and remained to supplement the harbour defences. For the Skuas (aircraft of two squadrons left behind by *Ark Royal* when she went to the Mediterranean) this was the first (and almost the only) chance they had to show what they could do as dive-bombers.

To attack Bergen required a return flight of 560 miles—very nearly the limit of the Skua's endurance. Surprise was complete, although it may have been helped by a German standing order which said that all single-engined aircraft sighted must be assumed to be friendly. *Königsberg*, hit by two bombs, burned out and capsized—the first cruiser ever to be sunk by air attack and the first ship to be sunk by dive-bombers. Only one aircraft was lost. There was nothing wrong with the efficiency of Fleet Air Arm crews. What they badly needed was much better aircraft and properly-fitted aircraft carriers.

Naval surface operations off the southern coasts of Norway had been virtually ruled out after the action of 9 April, but two sorties were still made into this area. The first—the bombardment of Stavanger airfield by the heavy cruiser *Suffolk* on 17 April—appeared to confirm Forbes' appreciation of the threat. There was a muddle over the arrangements for RAF fighter protection and *Suffolk* was left without air cover for nearly six hours. Subjected to repeated attacks, she was hit by a 1000-pound bomb from a Ju.88 but managed to struggle back into Scapa Flow with her quarterdeck awash.

The second sortie showed that operations were possible if proper fighter defence was available. Within a week of *Suffolk*'s return to Scapa Flow, three French destroyers made a sweep through the Skaggerak to try to destroy the German anti-submarine patrols. The destroyers left Rosyth during the afternoon of 23 April, attacked the German trawlers during the night and by the following morning were withdrawing at high speed. This time the arrangements for Blenheim fighter support worked well, and although the ships were heavily attacked they escaped without damage.

During the remainder of the naval operations in Norway there were two surface actions in the Narvik fiord in which ten German destroyers were sunk. There was also an ineffective bombing attack on the enemy ships by two squadrons of Swordfish from *Furious*, torpedo attacks being temporarily out of fashion after the failure of the Trondheim strike. Landings of British troops were eventually made near Narvik and north and south of Trondheim, but it was too little too late. The Germans held all the key towns, and all the airfields. The RAF could do little to counter the Luftwaffe. Ineffective raids were made on the German airfields in Norway, but targets in Germany were still off-limits.

Some RAF fighters were ferried across to Norway by the carriers *Glorious* and *Ark Royal* (both belatedly recalled from the Mediterranean) to operate from temporary landing strips hacked and blasted out of the ice and snow in the face of German bombing. The first contingent, a squadron of eighteen Gladiator biplanes flown off from *Glorious* on 23 April to occupy a landing field (actually a frozen lake) near Aandalsnes, achieved little before being destroyed—mostly on the ground—by Luftwaffe bombers.

It was nearly a month before a second attempt was made, this time much further north, near Narvik. By then the Germans had launched their great offensive in the west and the strength of Fliegerkorps 10 was being reduced, but the second detachment of RAF fighters achieved little more than the first. A squadron of Gladiators flew off from *Furious* on 22 May, and a squadron of Hurricanes from *Glorious* on 26 May. For a while they achieved local air superiority, but there were too many things against them: a primitive airfield, no radar for warning or for fighter direction, and ineffective radio communications. It was remarkable they remained in operation at all.

Meanwhile *Ark Royal* and *Glorious* were operating further down the coast. When *Ark Royal* arrived at Scapa Flow for the Norwegian campaign she embarked the survivors of her two squadrons which had, eleven days before, carried out the triumphant sinking of *Königsberg*. These Skuas did not last long after being re-embarked; almost none of them survived the Norwegian campaign, some being shot down, two landing on neutral Swedish soil and being interned, some being abandoned in Norway and others failing to find *Ark Royal* and ditching at sea.

In order to make room for the transport of RAF fighters *Glorious* had disembarked two of its squadrons when it reached Britain, and it arrived off the Norwegian coast with no Swordfish on board and a fighter complement of eighteen Sea Gladiators and eleven Skuas. The broad aim of the two carriers was to protect naval ships and convoys, to give cover to the troops at the landing places and to attack the German air bases in Norway. The trouble was that, both numerically and in quality, the Fleet Air Arm was quite inadequate for the task.

There were no arrangements for re-supply of aircraft while the carriers were at sea, so they had to return to Scapa Flow to replace losses from enemy action and accidents, and replacements were by no means always available. While in Norwegian waters the two carriers had to stay at least 100 miles off the coast to remain outside Ju.87 range, which limited the time their aircraft could spend on task over the coast. The requirement for a continuous combat air patrol over the carriers further limited the number of aircraft available for offensive operations. Despite these limitations, carrier-based pilots did what they could to help the army in the Namsos and Aandalsnes areas.

Fortunately Fliegerkorps 10 was also concentrating its declining strength in support of army operations, and at this stage was not paying much attention to distant ships. By early May increasing German military and air pressure forced the withdrawal of the Allied forces in central Norway. Although the troops were success-fully evacuated the escorting ships suffered at the hands of the Luftwaffe, which by now was able to concentrate on them as army-support requirements had virtually ceased. The admiral com-manding *Ark Royal* and *Glorious* admitted that he could not 'maintain a position from which aircraft could give support to our forces in the Namsos and the Aandalsnes area owing to continuous bombing'.[7]

Carrier support was then shifted to the Narvik area, where things were rather easier because the Luftwaffe had no local bases and had to bomb from airfields at Trondheim, 300 miles away; this ruled out dive-bombing attacks. Narvik was finally captured from the Germans at the end of May, but things were by then going so badly for the Allies—the evacuation from Dunkirk was just beginning—that this force, too, was evacuated after destroying the port facilities. The withdrawal was again harassed by the Luftwaffe.

During the campaign Forbes lost one cruiser, four destroyers and one frigate sunk by enemy aircraft, and a battleship, eight cruisers, six destroyers and two frigates were damaged, at a cost to the Luftwaffe of not more than twenty aircraft. The relatively low cost to the Royal Navy was in part because Fliegerkorps 10 concentrated on army support, partly because it was being weak-ened by the demands of the Western Front, but mainly because the Germans, particularly the Ju.87 dive-bomber crews, were untrained in attacking ships. It is worth pausing to think what a highly-trained dive-bomber force such as that deployed by Admiral Nagumo at Pearl Harbor in 1941 and in the Indian Ocean in 1942 would have done to the almost defenceless British ships.

The campaign ended with two dramatic events. During the evacuation of Narvik, the troop and storeship convoys got away safely between 7 June and 9 June but there were problems with the RAF fighters. *Glorious* was detached to embark them, but neither the Gladiators nor the Hurricanes had arrester hooks. There was no problem about landing the ten Gladiators, but it was feared that the ten Hurricanes would have to be destroyed, for not only had *Glorious* no experience with landing such high-performance aircraft but none of the Hurricane pilots had ever done a deck landing before.

The pilots themselves decided to make the attempt, the intention being to try *Ark Royal* (which had a longer flight deck) if a landing on *Glorious* proved impossible. A stiff breeze helped to create a wind of more than 40 knots down the flight deck of *Glorious*, and the outcome was that all the Hurricanes safely landed during the morning of 9 June. With the recovery of the RAF fighters completed, all the aircraft were stowed in the hanger.[8] The eyes of the navy were opened to the possibility of having such high-performance fighters for themselves, a point emphasised by Admiral Forbes in his report to the Admiralty.

The story has a sad sequel, however. Although the Germans had no knowledge of the evacuation of Narvik, their surface fleet was not inactive. On 4 June the battleships *Scharnhorst* and *Gneisenau* left Kiel, accompanied by a cruiser and four destroyers, aiming to relieve the pressure on their troops in the Narvik area. They kept well out to sea, searching an area that code-breaking had indicated was likely to be used by British ships. They sank a few independently-routed vessels and, shortly after 4 p.m. on 9 June, were lucky enough to fall in with *Glorious*.

After embarking the RAF fighters *Glorious* had been ordered to return to England, accompanied by only two destroyers. This was done because the captain of *Glorious* wished to get back to harbour to conduct a court martial of one of his officers, which was an absurdly trivial reason for such an important tactical decision.[9] In order to make room for the RAF fighters, *Glorious* was carrying only a squadron of Sea Gladiators and six Swordfish, only three of which were fitted to carry torpedoes. Inexcusably, *Glorious* did not use its Swordfish for reconnaissance, or even have them ready for torpedo strikes.

Within half-an-hour *Scharnhorst* and *Gneisenau* had opened fire, despite the smoke-laying efforts of the British destroyers. The German gunnery, aided by radar rangefinding, was excellent and soon scored a hit. This was decisive, for *Glorious* had still not yet armed or launched her Swordfish—an indicator of a very poor level of organisation—and the shell started a fire in the hangar. The fire curtain had to be lowered, which blocked access to the torpedoes for the Swordfish. After this the end was certain. The Germans could make 31 knots, *Glorious* not more than 29. Hit repeatedly, *Glorious* sank within an hour. The escorting destroyers fought gallantly until they were overwhelmed, one of them managing to torpedo the *Scharnhorst*. There were very few survivors, and among those lost were nearly all the RAF pilots who had saved their aircraft that morning.

The last blow of the campaign was, appropriately enough, struck by the Fleet Air Arm. After the clash with *Glorious*, the German ships retired to Trondheim where they were unsuccessfully attacked by RAF bombers on 11 June. Forbes then decided to see what he could do against them with *Ark Royal*'s aircraft. In thick weather the Home Fleet ran south, hoping to reach the flying-off position without being detected. But German reconnaissance aircraft found them during the afternoon, and shadowed until dusk. Despite the loss of surprise, Forbes decided to launch an attack the next day with fifteen Skua dive-bombers, each carrying a 500-pound bomb; a daylight attack by the Swordfish torpedo-bombers was rejected as suicidal.

The Skuas had to fly 30 miles at 11 500 feet up Trondheim fiord to reach the German ships, and by the time they arrived the defences were thoroughly alert. It had been arranged for the RAF to bomb the neighbouring airfield and also provide fighter support for the fleet, for with the Skuas used for dive-bombing Forbes had no fighter defence at all and no fighter escorts for his dive-bombers. The airfield bombing by the RAF achieved nothing, however, and the Blenheim fighters failed to appear. The skies were buzzing with German fighters, and eight Skuas—over half the attacking force— were lost to them and to gunfire; most of those who survived escaped by low-flying tactics. After recovering the survivors Forbes withdrew unmolested; the demands of the campaign in France, which was reaching a crescendo, had drained much of the bomber strength from Fliegerkorps 10.

At the time it was believed that *Scharnhorst* was hit. This was true but the bomb had failed to explode—a gallant failure which was symbolic of the whole campaign. A week later *Scharnhorst* was reported to be at sea and heading for home. The Fleet Air Arm aircraft based at Hatston, near Scapa Flow, were ordered to attack with whatever they had. The only available aircraft were six Swordfish which had been employed mainly on anti-submarine patrols, but despite their lack of training and the range of the target (240 miles) they managed to find and attack *Scharnhorst*, the first torpedo-bombing attack on a battleship at sea. Unfortunately the inexperience of the Swordfish crews now showed up, for they went straight into the attack without coordination or manoeuvring for a favourable position, and no hits were scored. Two Swordfish were lost to the heavy anti-aircraft fire.

What lessons could be learned from this campaign? It could only be regarded as a decisive win for air power, for the Home Fleet had effectively abandoned the whole eastern half of the North Sea to the Luftwaffe. The pre-war belief of the Royal Navy that surface ships would have little to fear from daylight bombing evaporated in the first test. The air-defence deficiencies of the navy—the very inaccurate medium-range gunfire, the inability of destroyers to fire their 4.7-inch guns at attacking dive-bombers, the inadequate numbers of effective close-range guns, the poor performance of the carrier-based fighters and the lack of any efficient fighter-direction arrangements in the carriers—were all starkly revealed.[10] The First Sea Lord, Sir Dudley Pound, wrote to Admiral Cunningham in the Mediterranean that the 'one lesson we have learnt here is that it is essential to have fighter protection over the fleet whenever they are within range of enemy bombers'.[11]

What to do about these problems was more difficult. The navy was stuck with its very sub-standard medium-calibre gun systems for there were no alternatives immediately available. However it was hoped that the introduction of radar-ranging would result in some improvement and the first sets, ordered in May 1940, began to be installed from September. Many of the destroyers armed with 4.7-inch guns had one set of torpedo tubes removed and a 4-inch gun put in its place. The 4-inch guns could elevate to 80 degrees and although there were no fire-control arrangements they could at least fire barrages at attacking dive-bombers. The Swiss 20mm Oerlikons were coming into service, but the fall of France cut off supplies from Switzerland after only about 150 weapons had been delivered. It would not be until the end of 1940 before deliveries from British manufacturers could be expected; orders were also placed with American firms but deliveries could not be expected until 1941. In the meantime the British ships would have to survive if they could with what they had, although as with the medium-calibre guns there was hope of radar-ranging in the future—200 sets for pom-pom directors had been ordered in April.

The shortcomings of the carrier aircraft were obvious. 'Our Fleet Air Arm aircraft are hopelessly outclassed by everything that flies in the air and the sooner we get some different aircraft the better', wrote Forbes after the campaign.[12] But even if the Admiralty had been prepared to fight to have Hurricanes and Spitfires modified for immediate carrier operations, there was no chance of such aircraft being released by the RAF with the Battle of Britain looming. A new fighter, the Fairey Fulmar, had just entered service but, in accordance with earlier Admiralty policy, it had a crew of two. Moreover its performance was nowhere near that of modern single-seat fighters, and its top speed was below that of most German bombers.

The first delivery from America of Grumman F4F–3 fighters (called Martlets by the Royal Navy) was expected by August. These aircraft (81 in all) had been ordered by France, but were diverted to Britain after the French surrender. The Royal Navy had also ordered 100 Martlets—like the French ones, with fixed wings—but when the Admiralty heard that a folding-wing version was being designed it was decided to change the British order to that type, accepting the inevitable delay.

It was clear that it would be a long time before British ships could expect efficient fighter defence from their carriers, a problem which was compounded by the continuation of the policy of giving priority to battleships and anti-aircraft cruisers in the fitting of long-range aircraft-warning radars. The new *Illustrious* did have a radar set, but the remaining carriers had to wait.

As for the direction of fighters by a ship using radar information (assuming that there were any useful fighters to direct) there had been some experiments in the Mediterranean in January 1940, but the first ship to do it operationally was the carrier *Ark Royal* during the Norwegian campaign. As *Ark Royal* did not have a radar set she received reports from radar-fitted cruisers when they were in company. The reports were normally transmitted (rather slowly) by flag hoist, but they were permitted to use morse radio when the force had been obviously located by the Germans. An officer in *Ark Royal* received the reports, and initially merely passed on the position of the enemy aircraft to the defending fighters, leaving it to them to work out what to do. Soon, though, he found that by plotting the positions of both the enemy aircraft and the defending fighters he could give courses, speeds and heights to the fighters in order for them to intercept, and thus naval fighter direction was born.

It was not an easy birth, for the rotation of the cruiser's air-warning radar had to be stopped in order to take a bearing of a target, and this delay coupled with the time taken to get the reports to *Ark Royal* meant that the information the fighter director was using was several minutes out of date.[13] The orders to the fighters were sent by morse radio, which was read by the observers in the back seats of the Skuas. (Voice radio was little used by the Royal Navy. It had to be used with single-seat fighters such as the Hurricanes and Sea Gladiators, and a few voice-radio sets had been borrowed from the RAF, but they were found to be unreliable.)

However, the Luftwaffe was not without its problems as well, though it does not seem that the German Air Staff really appreciated them. Attacking warships at sea requires special techniques and training, which the ordinary Luftwaffe squadrons, particularly the Ju.87 dive-bombers, did not have. If the whole of Fliegerkorps 10 had been trained in anti-shipping operations much more would have been achieved against the ill-defended British ships.

4

Taranto:

11–12 November 1940

The collapse of France and Italy's entry into the war on 10 June 1940 left the British fleet in the Mediterranean highly exposed, a position only slightly eased once French warships outside metropolitan France were destroyed or neutralised. When it had become clear that Italian involvement was imminent, the British Fleet in the Eastern Mediterranean had been heavily reinforced during May by four battleships, the carrier *Eagle*, and a number of cruisers and destroyers. Despite these additions, British naval forces in the Mediterranean were still thought to be inferior to the Italian Navy in nearly every category of warship.

In fact, the weight of the Italian Fleet at this time was four battleships of the *Cavour* class; old ships which had been recently modernised, although two of these were still not ready. Two new 35 000 ton battleships of the *Littorio* class would not be available until August. The other obvious material weakness of the Italian Navy was in aircraft carriers, although this lack was to some extent thought to be compensated by a powerful (but, as it turned out, incompetent) shore-based air force.

Early in July, when the Eastern Mediterranean Fleet under Admiral Sir Andrew Cunningham was covering two convoys from Malta to Alexandria, the first action between the fleets developed. The opposing forces were on paper roughly equal, but the Italians beat a precipitate retreat and used their superior speed to avoid Cunningham who pursued them to within 25 miles of the Calabrian coast. Thereafter the Italian battlefleet rarely ventured to sea, and did not seriously contest British control of the central Mediterranean. Even so, as a 'fleet in being' it could never be entirely ignored.

At the end of August Cunningham received welcome reinforcements in the shape of the modernised battleship *Valiant*, the new aircraft carrier *Illustrious*, and two anti-aircraft cruisers. Thus augmented, the balance of forces was now adjudged as favourable for making a carrier attack upon the main Italian fleet base at Taranto. The possibility of launching such an operation had been studied before the war—not least by Rear-Admiral Lumley Lyster, now commanding Cunningham's two carriers, who had worked out such a plan at the time of the Munich crisis in 1938.[1] Now, two years later, he was given the chance to implement it.

The plan Lyster evolved was for a night torpedo-attack on the ships in Taranto. A daylight attack by the slow, lumbering Swordfish would have been suicidal, for they could make no more than 80 knots when carrying a torpedo. For a night attack to be successful three requirements had to be met: it was essential to have photographic reconnaissance of the harbour so that the pilots could be briefed on the exact positions of their targets; there had to be moonlight for the attack and for the deck landing on return; and the range of the Swordfish somehow had to be increased so that the carriers would not have to make an obvious move towards Taranto in daylight.

It was not until September, when the RAF transferred three American-built Maryland bombers to Malta, that the necessary reconnaissance became possible. The Fleet Air Arm crews also needed special training in night flying, and could not be ready before mid-October. The attack was first planned for 21 October—the anniversary of Trafalgar—but a serious fire in *Illustrious*'s hangar destroyed a number of aircraft and forced a postponement. Then it became apparent that *Eagle* would not be fit to take part. She had received several near-misses in air attacks off Calabria in July, and as a result had developed defects in the petrol-refuelling system for her aircraft.

Illustrious had only nineteen Swordfish, but five more aircraft and eight crews were transferred from *Eagle* before *Illustrious* left Alexandria. The number of Swordfish available for the attack was eventually reduced to 21 because of crashes and forced landings during the transit from Alexandria, caused by contaminated fuel. The original plan had been for two strikes, each of fifteen aircraft, but the losses forced a change in the plan to successive flights of twelve and nine Swordfish. The problem of the inadequate range of the Swordfish was met by giving each aircraft an extra 60-gallon fuel tank, which occupied half of the rear seat of the torpedo-carrying Swordfish but was strapped on externally in the other aircraft.

A Swordfish dropping a torpedo. (*Imperial War Museum, MH167*)

The attack on Taranto

Lyster had arranged for these tanks to be brought out from England in *Illustrious*.

Taranto did not look like an easy harbour to attack. The Italians had no radar, either for warning or to assist their guns, but as well as the ships' armament they did have more than 200 guns and eight searchlights in position. Balloons and anti-torpedo nets were placed to protect the ships in the outer harbour, the Mar Grande, but only a third of the planned length of anti-torpedo nets was in position by November and there was room inside the nets for the torpedoes to be dropped. To make things worse for the Italians, bad weather (and the incompetence of the crews) destroyed two-thirds of their barrage balloons early in November, and at the time of the attack they had only 25 in place. They had no plans to cover the harbour with a smokescreen although this would have frustrated an attack such as Lyster was planning.

It was important that the attack be a surprise, for *Illustrious* would have to launch her Swordfish from not more than 180 miles from Taranto. Therefore it was planned that she would approach her launching position in darkness and before moonrise. *Illustrious* had a fighter complement of fifteen Fulmars, but replacements were so difficult to obtain that two Sea Gladiators had to be embarked from *Eagle* to bring the actual number of fighters up to fourteen. And if the Italian reconnaissance and air strikes were even moderately efficient *Illustrious* might have a difficult time.

In order to confuse the Italians as to the intentions of *Illustrious*, the attack on Taranto was part of a complicated pattern of operations. Convoys were to be passed to and from Malta, reinforcements were to be sent through from the Western Mediterranean, and other convoys were to be sent to Greece and Crete. A force of three cruisers and two destroyers was sent to raid Italian shipping off the Albanian coast. Cunningham's main battlefleet, with *Illustrious* in company, cruised in the central Mediterranean 250 miles south-east of Taranto to cover all these movements. In fact, though this could not have been assumed in the planning, they were unopposed by the Italian Air Force.

On 10 November a Fulmar was sent to Malta to pick up the latest photographs taken by the RAF reconnaissance aircraft. These showed that five battleships were in the Mar Grande, and the incomplete torpedo nets and the surviving barrage balloons could be clearly seen. The next day further photographs showed that a sixth battleship had arrived, so that now all the Italian battleships were in Taranto.

Under Lyster's plan the new 35 000-ton battleships *Littorio* and *Vittorio Veneto* were to be the main targets. To distract attention

70

from the torpedo-bombers, and particularly to keep the searchlights pointed upwards so that they would not dazzle the pilots as they came in to drop their torpedoes, bombing attacks were to take place at the same time on the smaller ships in the inner harbour— the Mar Piccolo. Because of the restricted space inside the Italian torpedo nets, it was decided that not more than five or six aircraft in each flight would drop torpedoes. Target identification was obviously going to be a problem, so in addition to planning the raid for a moonlit night two aircraft in each flight were assigned to drop flares.

There were problems with the torpedoes. They were fitted with magnetic pistols, which were designed to detonate under the bottoms of their targets, where an explosion does much more damage than one against a ship's side. In order to attack the bottoms of their targets the British torpedoes were set to run at a depth of 30 feet. The intended dropping area in the Mar Grande was only 80–90 feet deep, and the torpedoes dived after being dropped and took some distance to come to their set depth. To prevent the torpedoes hitting the bottom of the Mar Grande after being dropped, the torpedo-aircraft had to be flying at a height of less than 30 feet. To do this by night, under fire, required resolution and flying skill of the highest order.

At 6 p.m. on 11 November Cunningham detached *Illustrious* and her escort of four cruisers and four destroyers to proceed to her launching position 170 miles south-eastwards of Taranto. At 8.40 p.m. the first flight of Swordfish roared one by one down the flight deck. Six were carrying torpedoes and six were carrying 250-pound bombs; two of the bombers were each carrying sixteen flares as well. It took a few minutes for the aircraft to form up, but just before 9 p.m. they took their departure. The plan was for them to fly up the centre of the Gulf of Taranto, and then to attack Taranto from westward, to avoid flying over land.

The Italians were by no means unprepared, for although they were without radar they had sound-locating apparatus. As early as 8 p.m. they had heard suspicious noises and the defences were manned and alerted. The noise was in fact a Sunderland flying boat patrolling off the entrance to the harbour. Cunningham had been concerned about the possibility of a sortie by the Italian fleet against *Illustrious*, which was only six hours steaming away, and had asked for this patrol to be flown to give him warning of any movement by the Italians. (This was poor planning, since similar flights should have been made on previous nights to lull the Italians.) At 10.50 p.m. the Italian listening posts heard the noise of the approaching Fleet Air Arm aircraft, and the order was given to the guns to fire a barrage in all four quadrants. Such unaimed barrages look impressive, may do some good to the defender's morale and may cause concern to the attackers, but they very rarely destroy any aircraft.

Numerous targets were available for the Swordfish. In the Mar Grande there were six battleships, three heavy cruisers and eight destroyers, all of them vulnerable to torpedo attack. In the smaller Mar Piccolo there were six cruisers, 21 destroyers, five torpedo-boats, sixteen submarines and many smaller vessels. The first wave of torpedo attacks lasted only five minutes and by 11.20 p.m. the torpedo-bombers were making their getaway, leaving the new 35 000 ton battleship *Littorio* heavily damaged and the older battleship *Cavour* sinking.

The diversionary bombing attacks lasted longer. Three of the bombers attacked the cruisers and destroyers in the Mar Piccolo, but although one destroyer was hit the bomb failed to explode. The fourth bomber could not identify its target, so after a fruitless search for a suitable ship to bomb, dropped its bomb on the

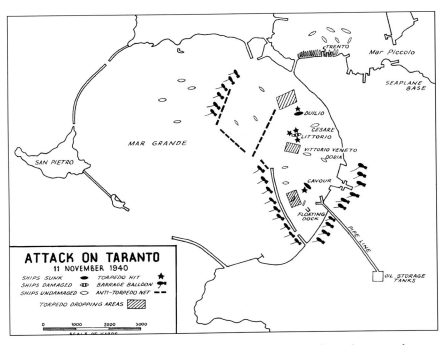

ATTACK ON TARANTO
11 NOVEMBER 1940

SHIPS SUNK ●	TORPEDO HIT ★	
SHIPS DAMAGED ⬤	BARRAGE BALLOON ⥿	
SHIPS UNDAMAGED ◇	ANTI-TORPEDO NET ▬▬	
TORPEDO DROPPING AREAS ▨		

SCALE OF YARDS 0 1000 2000 3000

The disposition of ships in Taranto Harbour after the attack seaplane base, starting a large fire. By 11.35 p.m. they had all withdrawn and the first wave of attacks was over.

All this time the Italian shore guns were putting up a heavy, aimless barrage, supplemented by the machine-guns in the ships when they could see a target and frequently when they could not. The guns did not cease firing when the first wave withdrew, for by then the second wave was approaching, though not yet within range. This second flight was reduced to a mere seven aircraft, because one had been forced to turn back with a defective petrol tank and another was damaged in a collision on the flight deck when taxying into position to take off. The crew of the latter were so determined to take part in the attack that they begged permission to follow as soon as their aircraft could be repaired, and eventually took off 25 minutes after the rest of the second wave.

At 11.55 p.m. the two flare-droppers of the second wave dropped their flares, and six minutes later the five torpedo aircraft made their attack. Two of their torpedoes hit *Littorio* (making four hits in all on that ship) and another torpedo hit the older battleship *Duilio*, but unfortunately one of the torpedoes which hit *Littorio* did not explode. The two flare-droppers, having completed their illumination job, dropped their bombs on the oil tanks, starting a small fire. Just as the other aircraft were leaving the scene, the lone straggler arrived, carrying six 250-pound bombs. Not deterred by having to make the attack without support, this aircraft bombed the ships in the Mar Piccolo, hitting the cruiser *Trento*, but the bomb failed to explode.

All the surviving aircraft had landed on board *Illustrious* by 2.50 a.m. and the carrier then steamed southwards to rejoin the battlefleet, greeted by the laconic signal from Cunningham 'manoeuvre well executed'. It was some time before the results of the action were known in detail, although photographs taken by the RAF the next day made it clear that a great blow had been struck. *Littorio* had been damaged by three torpedoes, and was badly down by the bows. She was to be out of action for four months. Two of the older battleships of the *Cavour* class were in worse shape, although they had been hit only once each. *Cavour* was beached and abandoned, with her upper deck under water; she was not refloated until the following July, and was never fully repaired. *Duilio* had also been beached, and was under repair for six months.

It had originally been intended to repeat the attack the following night, but the weather deteriorated and Cunningham decided to cancel the second attack. The surviving major Italian ships had in

Taranto Harbour after the attack. (*Imperial War Museum, CM164*)

---

any case left Taranto during 12 November and taken refuge in the safer harbours of Naples and Spezia.

Great results stemmed from this action, which was the most successful Fleet Air Arm action of the war. As Cunningham pointed out, Taranto is probably unsurpassed in naval history as an example of economy of force.[2] All the damage was done by eleven obsolete torpedo-bombers, just two of which were lost. In describing this battle, the behaviour of individual aircraft is significant. Three years later, carrier air groups or even the aircraft of a division of carriers were the significant combatants, but they often did no more damage than the eleven Swordfish from *Illustrious*, though perhaps they were up against tougher opponents.

There were material lessons to be learnt by both sides. For the

Royal Navy something had to be done about the magnetic pistol on the torpedoes, although it took the Admiralty six more months to recognise the problem. Five torpedoes had failed to detonate correctly: one of them hit *Littorio* but did not explode, one hit something (it is not clear what) but did not explode, and three exploded harmlessly between *Vittorio Veneto* and *Andrea Doria*, possibly as a result of grounding in shallow water.

Neither of the 250-pound bombs which had hit a cruiser and a destroyer had gone off, probably because they were dropped from so low a height that the safety device was still active. There should have been concerns, too, about the performance of the 18-inch torpedo; it was effective against the old battleships, but *Littorio* took four hits (three of which detonated) and was out of action for only four months. And, despite the sensational success of the night attack by the Swordfish, the fact that a daylight attack by them could not be contemplated was a stark indication of their limitations.

The Italians had much more to learn, if they were prepared to do so. It was a gross reflection on their reconnaissance and air striking power that an enemy carrier could approach within 200 miles of their main fleet base without being shadowed and harassed. Although they were obviously preparing for a possible attack by torpedo-carrying aircraft, the defensive arrangements were poorly conceived and more poorly executed.

Even more significant were the strategic advantages for the Royal Navy. The Italians abandoned any idea of disputing the control of the central Mediterranean, and Cunningham was able to release two of his older battleships for employment elsewhere. Italian naval morale had suffered another heavy blow, and their failure to take advantage of the disasters the British were to suffer in the following year must in large measure be attributed to this action.

The success of the British attack did not pass unnoticed elsewhere. The force used by the Japanese against Pearl Harbor was very much greater—some 360 aircraft—but of these it was the 40 torpedo-bombers which did most of the damage.

5

Crete:

20 May–1 June 1941

In the months after they entered the war the Italians suffered a series of defeats, both on land and sea, and Hitler transferred German forces to the Mediterranean theatre to support them. On 10 January 1941 the carrier *Illustrious* was heavily hit by German dive-bombers south of Sicily. Incapable of operating her aircraft, she managed to make it to Malta, where she was patched up so she could make the voyage to a repair yard in America. The day after *Illustrious* was hit, two cruisers were surprised by German dive-bombers; neither ship had radar, and the cruiser *Southampton* was hit twice and later had to be sunk. The command of the central Mediterranean had clearly changed hands.

Although Cunningham defeated the Italian Fleet off Cape Matapan in March 1941, the strain on the Mediterranean Fleet was enormous, with convoys to Malta, supplies to the garrison of Tobruk, support for the army in Egypt and Libya, and provision of light naval forces in Malta to harass Italian convoys to North Africa. These commitments were soon dwarfed by the effects of the German invasions of Yugoslavia and Greece, for which the Germans concentrated more than 1000 aircraft. Yugoslavia quickly collapsed, and it soon became clear that the British and Greek armies could not possibly hold the Germans.

By 21 April the British cabinet had given approval for the removal of British forces from the Greek mainland. This evacuation seemed likely to be an even more desperate undertaking than Dunkirk, for here the navy had no air support at all over the embarkation ports and all loading had to be done in darkness. Nonetheless, more than 50 000 men—80 per cent of the original force—were lifted, most of them to Crete, and the naval casualties

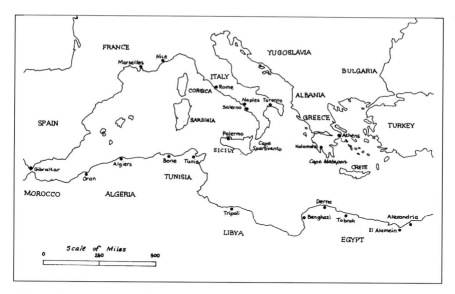

The Mediterranean theatre

were not excessive, only four transports and two destroyers being sunk during the operation.

There was to be no rest for the Mediterranean Fleet, as by this time the German threat to Crete was growing ominous. The whole operation to invade the island was in Luftwaffe hands, an assault being planned by airborne troops (who were part of the Luftwaffe) supported by Fliegerkorps 8 comprising more than 500 serviceable front-line aircraft. In addition 530 Junkers tri-motor transport aircraft and 72 gliders had been assembled in the Athens area. Fliegerkorps 8 concentrated its 150 Ju.87 dive-bombers and the 90 single-engined fighters on the forward airfields of Mulaoi, Milos and Scarpanto. The twin-engined fighters and the bombers were held further back, but the Germans had ten airfields within 250 miles of Crete.

By now British code-breakers had penetrated both the German and Italian naval and air force ciphers, and the British command was well informed of German intentions. But with resources stretched to the limit, the problem was how to respond? At the beginning of May the fighter strength on Crete comprised the remnants of three fighter squadrons from Greece and one from the Fleet Air Arm (mostly survivors from *Illustrious*). These totalled about 24 fighters—mostly Hurricanes, supported by three Fleet Air Arm Gladiators and three Fulmars. Only about half of these aircraft were serviceable, because there were no proper servicing or spare-parts arrangements, particularly for the Fleet Air Arm aircraft. The Germans began concentrated attacks on the three airfields in use on the island, and within five days the only fighters fit for action were four Hurricanes and three Gladiators. This was despite two or three Hurricanes having been flown over from Egypt each day to try to keep the numbers up. There was no hope of further reinforcement, so the remnants were withdrawn to Egypt. The garrison was on its own.

The navy was already making desperate attempts to supply the ill-equipped garrison, but suffered severe damage and casualties because of the lack of fighter protection. The fighter aircraft on Crete were gone, those in North Africa were out of range, while the sole aircraft carrier—*Formidable*, which had replaced the damaged *Illustrious*—had only four serviceable fighters left after recent operations, and had to wait until 25 May for replacements to arrive. Some additional guns for the Crete garrison had been scraped together in Egypt, but the Luftwaffe was very active and nearly half of them were lost at sea on the way to Crete. Of 27 000 tons of supplies despatched from Egypt after 1 May, only 10 per cent got through. It was clear that the survival of the island garrison would depend largely on the ability of the navy to continue to operate without fighter support.

The War Cabinet ordered that Crete was to be held at all costs, though it is unlikely that they understood what the expression really meant. General Bernard Freyburg, the commander of the British forces on Crete, thought that the island could be successfully defended against a purely airborne assault. 'With help of Royal Navy', he signalled, 'I trust that Crete will be held'.[1] But Cunningham had formidable problems in giving that help. Because of the persistent air attacks and the lack of effective fighter support, his ships could not refuel or replenish their ammunition at Suda Bay, on the north coast of Crete. Instead they had to work from Alexandria, more than 400 miles away.

Starting on 14 May, Cunningham's plan was to use three forces, each made up of cruisers and destroyers, to sweep the area north of Crete each night and to retire south of the island by day, outside the 100-mile radius of the Ju.87s based in Greece, Milos and Scarpanto. To support these forces a covering force of two battleships and five destroyers cruised to the west of the island, for the possibility of intervention by the Italian battlefleet could never be totally ignored. In reserve in Alexandria Cunningham had two battleships, the carrier *Formidable* (waiting for the arrival of replacement aircraft), four cruisers and sixteen destroyers.

The German attack started on the morning of 20 May. It was entirely by airborne forces: first there were heavy bombing-attacks, then landings by gliders. As soon as he heard the invasion had started Cunningham gave orders for the establishment that night of anti-shipping patrols north of the island, in the Aegean Sea. He also ordered three destroyers to bombard the Italian airfield on Scarpanto, where many fighters and dive-bombers were based. The destroyers had no observation for their fire, and did little damage; blind gunfire at an airfield is unlikely to be more than an irritant. Nor did the cruiser patrol have any success that night, for the Aegean Sea north of Crete was clear, the Germans not having yet launched the seaborne part of their operation.

By dawn on 21 May all the British ships had left the Aegean Sea. Cunningham had two strong groups of ships—the covering force of battleships and destroyers under Rear-Admiral Bernard Rawlings and another group of cruisers and destroyers under Rear-Admiral Irvine Glennie—off the western end of Crete, and a smaller group of cruisers and destroyers under Rear-Admiral E.L.S. King patrolling off the eastern end of the island. So far he could reckon that things had gone well. His ships were well placed to prevent an invasion of Crete by sea, and the Luftwaffe had not troubled them much. But this comparative calm was soon to be rudely shattered.

During the afternoon of 21 May there were reports of groups of small craft moving towards Crete, escorted by Italian destroyers. Cunningham ordered King and Glennie to take their forces into the Aegean that night, searching northwards after dawn on 22 May. Shortly before midnight the western force fell in with the first-wave German troop convoy bound for Maleme, sinking ten craft and scattering the remainder. At 3.30 a.m. Glennie decided to withdraw, to avoid the heavy air attacks that he knew must be expected if he stayed in the Aegean after daylight.

Meanwhile at the other end of the island King had spent the night patrolling uneventfully. In accordance with his orders he turned northwards at dawn, and soon afterwards came under air attack which continued without respite. By 10 a.m., when King was 75 miles north of Crete, he encountered another large troop convoy escorted by two Italian destroyers. But King's ships were running out of ammunition, the convoy was withdrawing under a protective smokescreen, and the relentless dive-bombing attacks continued. For all these reasons King decided that he could not risk a pursuit, so he ordered his destroyers to abandon the chase and withdrew to the westward through the Antikithera Channel.

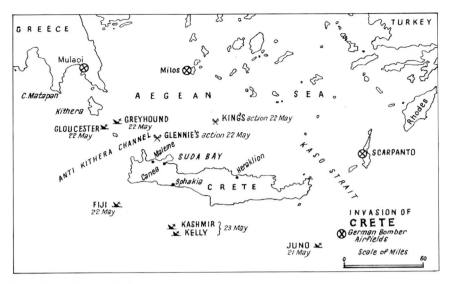

The invasion of Crete

When he learned that King was withdrawing, Rawlings decided to meet him in the Antikithera Channel. As the day wore on, however, it became apparent that King was in serious trouble. King's flagship, the cruiser *Naiad*, had two turrets put out of action and her speed reduced to less than twenty knots, and it seemed only a matter of time before more ships were disabled. So although Rawlings' ships were short of ammunition too, he determined to enter the Aegean. At the least his ships would provide additional targets and take some of the weight of air attack off King.

It was with tremendous relief that Rawlings' two battleships were sighted at 1.20 p.m., steaming at over twenty knots to King's assistance. Ten minutes later Rawlings' flagship, *Warspite*, was attacked by three Messerschmitt 109 fighter-bombers, which suddenly swooped out of some low clouds. One bomb hit and half of the battleship's anti-aircraft guns were put out of action and her speed reduced to less than eighteen knots. The air attacks continued until dusk, by which time the destroyer *Greyhound* and the cruisers *Gloucester* and *Fiji* had been sunk, and the battleship *Valiant* was also hit though not seriously damaged.

By now reinforcements were on the way, with six destroyers coming from Alexandria and five from Malta. The latter group, under the command of Captain Lord Louis Mountbatten, joined King at 4 p.m. but were soon detached again under orders to patrol inside Kissimo Bay and Canea Bay, on the north-western side of Crete. One of these ships, *Kipling*, developed steering problems on the way to the patrol area and was sent back, but for the rest of the night Mountbatten with two of his destroyers patrolled in Canea Bay, intercepting two caiques and bombarding Maleme. His other two destroyers searched Kissimo Bay, ten miles to the west, but finding it empty they sailed independently for Alexandria.

At the other end of the island another force of four destroyers patrolled off Heraklion, but sighting nothing during the night they too returned to Alexandria. On the way they were bombed for five hours, and two of the destroyers were damaged by near-misses. King's forces, including Rawling's battleships, had remained south of Crete, but during the night Cunningham, acting under the mistaken impression that the two battleships were very short of ammunition, told him to return to Alexandria.

Since dawn on 23 May, Mountbatten in *Kelly* with *Kashmir* in company had been heading south at full speed. They had been late leaving Canea Bay, and now had to bear the consequences. By 8 a.m. they had survived two air attacks, and had passed Gavdo Island, twenty miles to the south of Crete. Mountbatten had some reason to think that he was out of the worst of the danger, but then he was hit with an attack by 24 Ju.87 dive-bombers, in which both ships were sunk. Fortunately *Kipling*, returning after repairs to her faulty steering, came into sight at this time and picked up nearly 300 survivors. *Kipling* remained in the area until 11 a.m. and although over a period of five hours she was attacked by more than 40 bombers, she escaped undamaged. She was so short of fuel, though, that she had to be towed the last 50 miles into Alexandria.

Meanwhile attempts were still being made to run reinforcements and supplies to the army in Crete. On 24 May Cunningham informed the Admiralty that the scale of air attack made it no longer practicable to operate in the Aegean in daylight without suffering heavy loss, and therefore he could not guarantee to prevent a seaborne invasion. The Chiefs of Staff replied that if enemy convoys were reported north of Crete the fleet might have to operate in that area by day, regardless of the losses.[2] In the event, Cunningham did not have to take any action on the Chiefs of Staff directive, since the Germans did not again attempt to run their convoys to Crete until the battle was won. However, he did not know this, and stuck to his policy of sending ships to sweep through the Aegean after dark.

By 25 May *Formidable* had at last managed to build her fighter strength up to twelve Fulmars, although some of them were rather decrepit. In addition she had 21 Albacores. Cunningham decided to use the carrier offensively against the German bomber-base at Scarpanto. She sailed in company with the battleships *Queen Elizabeth* and *Barham* at noon on 25 May, and at dawn the following morning her striking force of four Albacores and five Fulmars attacked the airfield. The Germans were completely surprised, but the carrier force was far too small to be more than a nuisance, and only two German aircraft were destroyed on the ground. By 7 a.m. the aircraft had landed back on *Formidable*, and the force retired southwards, attacked by German aircraft as they went.

Formidable by then had only four serviceable Fulmars and, although she was capable of radar-controlled fighter-direction, the number and performance of her fighters were simply inadequate. In an attack by twenty Ju.87 dive-bombers at 1.20 p.m. the destroyer *Nubian* had her stern blown off and *Formidable* was hit twice by 1100-pound bombs. The carrier was hit on the forward end of the flight deck and the bomb passed through and detonated below the hangar deck. A hole 52-feet by 14-feet was blown in the ship's side, and there was serious damage internally. The second bomb hit aft, passed through the ship's structure and burst underwater, damaging the starboard propeller. The carrier's maximum speed was reduced to twenty knots and the forward aircraft lift was out of action. As she could no longer operate aircraft she had to be sent back to Alexandria that evening, escorted by four destroyers. Her involvement in the campaign had lasted just over one day.

The remainder of the force stayed to the south-west of Kaso Strait, to cover the withdrawal of ships sent to land reinforcements and supplies in Suda Bay during the night. Shortly before 9 a.m. on 27 May it was attacked by fifteen Ju.88 and He.111 bombers; the battleship *Barham* was hit on one of her 15-inch turrets (putting it out of action), two of her anti-torpedo bulges were flooded by near-misses and a fire was started which took two hours to extinguish. Cunningham ordered the force to return to Alexandria. It could achieve nothing useful by staying where it was, a mere target for air attack, and it was urgent that the ships should be replenished and the crews rested.

By this stage the military situation in Crete had collapsed. After enduring a bitter fight for six days, and in the face of overwhelming air superiority, the British troops in the Suda area were forced to retreat towards Sphakia, on the south coast. Heraklion could obviously no longer be held with the Suda area in German hands. Evacuation, or surrender, was now inevitable, although Churchill still exhorted Wavell with a message to 'Keep hurling in all you can'. Wavell replied on 27 May that he feared it must be recognised that Crete was no longer tenable, and that as far as possible the troops must be withdrawn.

Nearly half the ships in the Mediterranean Fleet had already been sunk or damaged, and the crews were nearly worn out after weeks of almost-continuous operations. Now they were faced with the evacuation of the army in the face of complete enemy air superiority. 'I have never been prouder', wrote Cunningham afterwards, 'of the Mediterranean Fleet than at the close of these particular operations, except perhaps, at the fashion in which it faced up to the even greater strain which was soon to be imposed on it'.[3]

Early on 28 May two groups of ships sailed to start the evacuation. One group, the destroyers *Kelvin* and *Kandahar* and the Australian destroyers *Napier* and *Nizam*, was destined for Sphakia. They picked up 700 soldiers, and got back to Alexandria suffering only one attack in which *Nizam* was slightly damaged. They had some fighter support as they headed for Alexandria, for the RAF had managed to fit a few twin-engined Blenheims with extemporised long-range fuel tanks. But the converted Blenheims were not really very useful fighters and the ships had no effective radar with which to direct them. The support could at best be only meagre and spasmodic.

The ships in the other group, three cruisers and six destroyers commanded by Rawlings, had a much worse time. For nearly five hours from 5 p.m. on 28 May the force was under almost constant air attack, but although there were some near-misses no ship was hit. By 3 a.m. the following morning, Rawlings' ships had embarked the whole of the Heraklion garrison of 4000 men, and were heading for the open sea at 29 knots when mischance occurred. The destroyer *Imperial*, which had been near-missed the previous evening, suddenly ran amok with jammed steering gear. Rawlings could not afford to wait, so he sent back the destroyer *Hotspur* to take off *Imperial*'s crew and then sink her.

Rawlings was not a man willingly to abandon a ship to her fate, and soon after *Hotspur* had been detached he reduced the speed of the rest of his ships so that she could overtake him. *Hotspur*, and the 700 men on board, were thus saved, but the delay was fatal to Rawlings' hope of getting through the Kaso Strait undetected. He had fallen more than an hour behind his schedule, and it was broad daylight by the time his ships reached the strait. By then German aircraft were patrolling the narrow gap, and attacks began almost at once. The destroyer *Hereward* became the first casualty, and Rawlings was forced to take the distasteful decision of leaving the ship to her fate.

At 6.45 a.m. *Decoy* was damaged by a near-miss, and Rawlings had to slow down to 25 knots. Three-quarters of an hour later the speed had to be further reduced because of similar damage to the flagship *Orion*. The situation was beginning to look ominous. Fighter cover had been promised from daylight, but it had still not arrived. This was partly due to the fact that Rawlings was behind schedule, but mostly to the inexperience of the pilots in navigating over the sea. It was not until noon that the first fighters arrived—two Fleet Air Arm Fulmars from Alexandria—and by then Rawlings' ships had suffered severely. Both the cruisers had been hit, and with hundreds of soldiers below decks the casualties were cruel. Of the 1100 troops on board *Orion*, more than 500 became casualties.

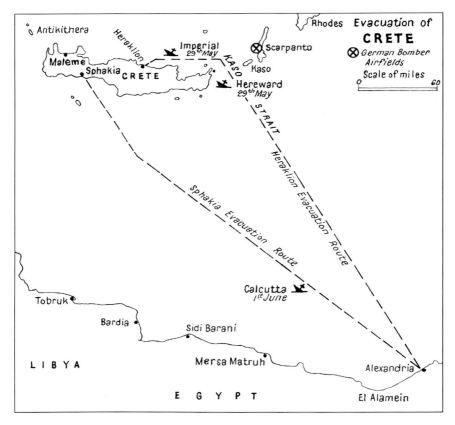

The evacuation of Crete

By the time the fighters eventually arrived, the worst was over. Rawlings was more than 100 miles from Scarpanto and outside the range of the Ju.87s, so all they had to put up with were high-level bombing attacks, which finally ceased by 3 p.m. The ships had survived, but they had fired practically all their ammunition, and Cunningham's feelings can be imagined as he saw them finally steam into Alexandria, 'the guns of their fore-turrets awry, one or two broken off and pointing skyward, their upper decks crowded with troops, and the marks of their ordeal only too plainly visible'.[4]

It looked as if the evacuation might become a major catastrophe. Nearly a quarter of the troops so far rescued from Crete had become casualties while on the passage back to Egypt, and the fleet could not possibly go on accepting such losses of ships if control of the Eastern Mediterranean was not to be jeopardised. But Cunningham was never lacking in resolution, and after consulting the Admiralty and General Wavell he decided that the evacuation must go on.

It was a sound decision. As so often happens on such occasions, the worst was already over. While the army was retreating towards Sphakia on the south coast of Crete, it was no longer necessary for Cunningham's ships to make the dangerous passage through the Kaso Strait to Heraklion. On the night of 29 May the transport *Glengyle* with three cruisers and three destroyers rescued 6000 men from Sphakia. For most of the daylight hours of the return journey the ships were covered by RAF fighters, and the only damage was a bomb hit on the Australian cruiser *Perth*.

The following night four destroyers tried to repeat the success, but there were problems. Soon after leaving Alexandria *Kandahar* developed engine trouble, and had to turn back. At 3.30 p.m. the three remaining ships were surprised by Ju.88s which dived on them from astern. One bomb fell close to *Kelvin*, and the damage caused her speed to fall to twenty knots. So she, too, had to be sent back to Alexandria, reducing the evacuation force to the Australian destroyers *Napier* and *Nizam*. They arrived at Sphakia without further incident, and by 3 a.m. the next morning they had embarked all the 1400 troops originally intended for the four destroyers. With their upper decks crowded with men, they turned for Alexandria at full speed. Soon after daylight they were attacked by twelve Ju.88s. One bomber was shot down, but both destroyers were damaged by near-misses and *Napier*'s speed was reduced to 23 knots. Fortunately there were no more attacks, and the troops were landed at Alexandria that evening.

King was already on his way with another force, consisting of a cruiser, the fast-minelayer *Abdiel* and three destroyers. Cunningham had decided that this was to be the last night of the evacuation, and King was told to fill his ships to capacity. On the way to Sphakia he was attacked three times, without loss to either side, RAF fighters helping to break up the attacks. By 5 p.m. on 1 June King's ships disembarked more than 4000 troops in Alexandria after a pleasant, uneventful passage. They were the last of more than 16 000 soldiers (half of the original army strength) to be rescued by the navy. Meanwhile two anti-aircraft cruisers which left Alexandria early on 1 June to reinforce King on his passage back from Sphakia were surprised by Ju.88s when only 100 miles from the Egyptian coast. One of the ships was hit twice by bombs and sank within minutes.

The battle of Crete was over. Nothing can disguise the fact that it was a heavy British defeat. For the six decisive days of the battle the navy had succeeded in preventing German troops or supplies reaching Crete by sea, but this had not saved the island. The Mediterranean Fleet had given all it had in the way of courage and a determination to play its part to the limit of its ability. Cunningham divined this feeling, saying in a signal to his ships: 'Stick it out. Navy must not let the Army down. No enemy forces must reach Crete by sea'. To his staff he is said to have remarked that 'it will take us three years to build new ships. It would take us three hundred to build a new tradition'.[5]

New ships would indeed be needed. Three out of four battleships and the only aircraft carrier had been damaged. Cunningham had lost three cruisers (sunk) and six were damaged (leaving only one unscathed), and of his 33 destroyers six had been sunk and seven damaged. If these ships had been casualties of a major fleet action, at least comparable damage would probably have been inflicted on the enemy. But in this campaign the only compensation for such losses to the fleet was a small number of enemy aircraft (certainly not more than twenty) shot down, and the knowledge that they had not failed the army. With the equipment they had, no other navy could have done more.

What lessons could the Royal Navy learn from this defeat? It was already clear that existing British naval anti-aircraft gunfire was quite unable to handle attacking dive-bombers, who would be decisive unless there was effective fighter support to prevent the dive-bombers making coordinated attacks. The moves going on to fit all ships with radar-ranging sets on the directors controlling their medium-calibre anti-aircraft guns would make some slight improvement, but would do nothing to eliminate the guesswork used in establishing the necessary aim-off for the guns.

Similarly the bigger ships were to be fitted with radar-ranging sets on the directors for their multiple pom-poms, but the same limitations applied here too. Nothing could be done about the limited elevation of the 4.7-inch guns in the existing destroyers, and the 4-inch guns fitted in place of one set of torpedo tubes in most destroyers were more for show than for effect. Cunningham's statement that he could not operate in the Aegean by day without suffering heavy loss was a clear admission of the victory of the bombers, unharassed by fighters, over the contemporary British anti-aircraft fire.

But where were the Fleet Air Arm fighters? The new carrier *Formidable* played a negligible role in the campaign. Like *Illustrious* she had a very small complement of aircraft, but in this campaign it was not her aircraft carrying-capacity that limited her involvement. Rather it was the delays in providing replacement aircraft from England along the lengthy, tortuous supply routes, and the diversion of Fleet Air Arm aircraft to other places such as the airfields of Crete. *Formidable* was fitted with air-warning radar and was capable of directing her fighters, though these were the low-performance Fulmars. In her sole action in the campaign her four surviving Fulmars were unable to defend her effectively, and the damaged carrier made a rapid exit, having made an insignificant contribution. But better fighters were on the way. The first carrier-type Martlets (the Royal Naval version of the Grumman F4F Wildcat, with folding wings) were about to go to sea.[6]

Even better, with increasing aircraft production and the end of the battle of Britain, the Admiralty had been able to prise some Hurricane production from the Air Ministry, as well as some fairly well-worn models which had fought in the Battle of Britain. They had originally been intended to be catapulted from merchant ships to deal with long-range German reconnaissance-bombers in the Atlantic (in which role they were of some limited use) but some were fitted with arrester hooks, and were just about to go to sea in *Furious* in July 1941. But the Sea Hurricanes were verging on obsolescence, and did not have folding wings, so that they took up a lot of space on the flight deck and could not be struck down to the hangar for stowage and maintenance.

It was to be some time before the far-superior Spitfires were to be modified for carrier service, where they were known as Seafires. Part of the delay was because of Air Ministry reluctance to give up the aircraft, and part because there were naval doubts whether the Spitfire, with its short endurance and narrow, rather flimsy, undercarriage was really suitable for carrier operations. Sea trials were conducted in December 1941 and the Seafires first saw operational service during the invasion of North Africa in November 1942. The early Seafire versions, like the Sea Hurricanes, did not have folding wings, but the Seafire III, with manually-folded wings, was doing sea trials before the end of 1942.[7]

Of equal importance, fighter direction at last began to be taken seriously. A three-week course for fighter directors was started at the Naval Air Station at Yeovilton, although there were initial problems. There was a shortage of aircraft for training, so the trainees spent some time on mobile ice-cream tricycles, each of which acted as a fighter or a bomber. The tricycles were fitted with voice radio and a compass, and were screened to limit visibility to a couple of yards. It was crude but it worked. By the end of the year reasonably-trained fighter directors began to be available in all the carriers.

Another lesson which should have been learnt was the urgent necessity of improving the arrangements for refuelling and re-ammunitioning the combat ships. The battleships did fuel a few destroyers at sea, but it was very slow because of low pump-capacity in the battleships.[8] The result of these replenishment deficiencies was that the force Cunningham could deploy in the combat area was sharply cut, possibly by as much as a third. The Admiralty did not seem to grasp the problem, which was occurring at the same time in the hunt for the German battleship *Bismarck*. They were apparently regarding it as one of the facts of maritime warfare, and unaware that the Royal Navy was lagging far behind both the American and Japanese navies in this field. There were some improvements in refuelling at sea over the next couple of years, but it was not until the British ships were preparing to join the Americans in the Pacific in 1945 that the problem was tackled seriously.

In the light of this campaign, and the earlier attacks on *Illustrious*, one issue which should have been questioned was the value of the heavy armour on the sides and flight decks of the new British carriers. Quite apart from halving the number of aircraft which could be carried, compared to contemporary American and Japanese carriers of similar size, what did it achieve defensively? The purpose of armour is twofold: to permit a ship to continue to fight effectively after being hit, and to make its destruction more difficult. *Illustrious* was hit by six 1000-pound bombs off Malta, and *Formidable* by two off Crete, although in the latter case neither of them hit the armoured hangar. The anti-shellfire side-armour was irrelevant in both cases, and neither carrier was able to continue to operate aircraft after the first bombs hit.[9] Moreover, the massive construction of the flight decks made temporary repairs almost impossible. Even after ten days being patched up in Malta dockyard *Illustrious* could still not use her flight deck, and the time which elapsed from the date of the bomb hits to the carrier being ready again for operational service was eleven months for *Illustrious* and seven months for *Formidable*.

The value of the armour was possibly higher when considering the survival of the aircraft carriers. It is true that none of the six *Illustrious* class carriers was sunk by bombing during the war, but then neither were any of the American equivalent, the seventeen carriers of the *Essex* class. Carriers proved to be much more vulnerable to torpedoes, particularly from submarines, than they did to bombing. It was perhaps fortunate that only one of the British armoured carriers was torpedoed during the war, for it seems that they were very vulnerable to such damage. *Indomitable* was surprised by a solitary torpedo-carrying Ju.88 off Italy in July 1943, was hit amidships and very nearly sank.[10] The aircraft escaped without a shot being fired at it. *Indomitable* was put out of action for nearly a year, whereas the comparable American carriers showed a remarkable ability to absorb several torpedo hits, and to be rapidly repaired and returned to service.

The American carriers did have an armoured deck but it was under, not above, the hangar. This allowed a much larger and more open hangar and a deck-edge lift, so that not only could many more aircraft be carried but they could be operated and maintained more efficiently. From the point of view of the carrier's survival the armoured-deck below the hangar seems to have been at least as good as the armoured flight deck.[11]

The Germans had lessons to learn too. The High Command, and Hitler in particular, were appalled at the losses suffered by the airborne troops during the invasion—4500 parachute and glider-borne troops killed or missing, as well as 170 Junkers 52 transport aircraft lost—and they were never again employed on such a mission.[12] There should have been concern, too, about the low strike-rate of the German bombers, most of whom had little or no experience in attacking ships. In view of the total lack of fighter cover in the Aegean and the weakness of the anti-aircraft fire, experienced anti-shipping bombers would have been able to inflict much more damage on the Mediterranean Fleet.

Other deficiencies of the Luftwaffe were their total lack of ability to launch anti-shipping strikes by night, and their poor reconnaissance south of Crete. None of the reconnaissance aircraft were drawn from the experienced squadrons in Sicily or Africa, and they were not fitted with anti-shipping radar, which Coastal Command of the RAF had in place for some time and which was just being fitted in Fleet Air Arm Swordfish.[13] Despite their deficiencies, the Luftwaffe had nevertheless won a stunning victory.

6

The hunt for *Bismarck*:

21–27 May 1941

While the Mediterranean Fleet was fighting desperately to save Crete there was another crisis for the Royal Navy. This time it was in the Atlantic, where the trade routes, long under submarine threat, were now threatened by a surface force. In the first eighteen months of the war the German Navy had made several forays, using at one time or another the pocket battleships *Scheer*, *Deutschland* (later renamed *Lützow*) and *Graf Spee*, the cruiser *Hipper* and the battleships *Scharnhorst* and *Gneisenau*. Although they sank only some 58 ships between them, their influence on British naval strategy was immense.

A successful Atlantic raid by *Scharnhorst* and *Gneisenau* encouraged Raeder to plan an even bigger operation by the new 41 700-ton battleship *Bismarck* and the 10 000-ton cruiser *Prinz Eugen*. The commander of the German squadron was Vice-Admiral Günther Lütjens, who had successfully commanded the earlier sortie by *Scharnhorst* and *Gneisenau*. His first problem was to penetrate the British defences of the northern exits. All shipping was cleared from the Baltic before the two German ships sailed, but they were unlucky enough to encounter the Swedish cruiser *Gotland* and a report that the German ships were moving reached the Admiralty the next day, 21 May.

The Commander-in-Chief of the Home Fleet was now Admiral Sir John Tovey. He had at his disposal the new battleships *King George V* and *Prince of Wales*, the battlecruiser *Hood*, ten cruisers and twelve destroyers—but no aircraft carrier. Of the major ships only *King George V* could be considered a fair match for the *Bismarck*. *Hood* was twenty years old and was known to be

91

Bismarck in a Norwegian fiord, photographed from the *Prinz Eugen*. (*Imperial War Museum, HU375*)

ill-protected, while *Prince of Wales* was very new and her main armament of 14-inch guns was not yet working properly.

When the news was received that *Bismarck* had sailed, the Admiralty placed the aircraft carrier *Victorious* and the battlecruiser *Repulse* at Tovey's disposal, withdrawing them from a troop convoy sailing from the Clyde the following day bound for the Middle East. *Repulse* was an old ship, armed with six 15-inch guns, but so lightly protected that it would be suicidal for her to oppose *Bismarck* in a gun action. *Victorious*—the third of the *Illustrious* class to be completed—had been in commission for two months, but she did not finally leave dockyard hands until 16 May (four days before the sailing of *Bismarck*) and had then been sent to Scapa Flow to commence training her crew and aircraft.

Victorious was carrying 48 crated Hurricanes to be delivered to Gibraltar for onward transit to Malta, and had only two squadrons of operational aircraft for her convoy-escort duty—825 Squadron of nine Swordfish and 800 Squadron of six Fulmars. The Swordfish squadron had three aircraft equipped with radar[1] and had done some training with it, but the squadron was intended to operate from airfields and had not done any deck-landing training. Indeed, most of the pilots had never landed on an aircraft carrier. The Fulmars were not a squadron in the true sense, as the pilots and observers were a scratch lot who had been gathered together for the convoy-escort trip. Deck-landing training started on 21 May, but only two or three pilots had done practice landings before the ship had to return to Scapa Flow for the night.

Tovey was very doubtful whether he was justified in employing such an untrained ship as *Victorious* in operations against *Bismarck*, so he sent for the captain and his senior Fleet Air Arm officers. Although the aircrews were obviously very inexperienced, Tovey was impressed by the commander of the Swordfish squadron, on whom the principal responsibility would lie. Lieutenant-Commander Eugene Esmonde was a very experienced pilot (who less than a year later was to win a posthumous Victoria Cross for leading a forlorn hope against *Scharnhorst* and *Gneisenau* as they escaped up the English Channel) and Tovey thought that under his leadership even an untried squadron might strike a vital blow.

Meanwhile, Coastal Command aircraft were searching the North Sea for the German ships. During the afternoon of 21 May *Bismarck* and *Prinz Eugen* were located near Bergen, but then the curtain of mist and rain descended over the North Sea. Nothing more was known of the movements of the German ships until late on 22 May when, despite appalling weather conditions, a Fleet Air Arm aircraft managed to make a visual search of the fiord where the German ships had been seen. At 8 p.m. the vital message reached Tovey that they had left the fiord.

Tovey decided that it was time to act. *Hood* and *Prince of Wales*, screened by six destroyers, were ordered to join cruisers already watching the Denmark Strait (between Iceland and Greenland). Tovey in *King George V*, accompanied by *Repulse*, *Victorious*, four cruisers and seven destroyers, steamed westwards into the Atlantic to cover the Iceland-Faroes passage. At 7.22 p.m. on 23 May the German ships were sighted near the edge of the ice in the Denmark Strait, and subsequently shadowed by British cruisers. When *Hood* and *Prince of Wales* arrived at dawn the next day the result was a completely unexpected disaster. After an action lasting 23 minutes, *Hood*—the largest ship in the Royal Navy—blew up and sank, and *Prince of Wales* was hit seven times and forced to break off the action.

Prince of Wales had managed to hit *Bismarck* twice, and one of these hits had a decisive effect on subsequent events. It caused *Bismarck* to lose so much oil by leakage and contamination that Lütjens decided that the battleship would have to make for St Nazaire, 110 miles south-east of Brest and the only port on the French Atlantic coast with a dry dock which could take a ship of that size. *Prinz Eugen*, he decided, could continue with the trade offensive on her own, and at about 6.30 p.m. he managed to

The search for the *Bismarck*

detach the cruiser without her departure being noticed by the shadowing British ships. At the same time Lütjens ordered *Bismarck* to steer more to the westwards, a decision which made it more difficult for *Victorious* to get within range.

When *Hood* blew up, Tovey was about 330 miles to the south-eastwards and he was badly placed to intercept *Bismarck* unless her speed could be reduced. Therefore at 2.40 that afternoon Tovey ordered *Victorious* to close and attack the German battleship from a distance of 100 miles. The weather was worsening, and there were grave doubts whether any of the untrained pilots would be able to land safely after the attack, although it was hoped that they would at least be able to save themselves—even if they had to crash their aircraft in the sea. Moreover, with so small a torpedo squadron it was clear that all the Swordfish must attack and that none could be spared for shadowing or reconnaissance.

The strike force—nine Swordfish followed by three Fulmars—took off soon after 10 p.m. There were heavy rain squalls and low cloud, but the visibility near the surface was good except in the squalls. Soon after midnight *Bismarck* was found and attacked by the Swordfish. Considering the inexperience of the pilots it was a remarkably well-conducted attack; one hit was registered, but it struck the heavy 13-inch armour-belt of the battleship and did no damage. Even so, *Bismarck*'s violent manoeuvring to avoid the torpedoes caused increased flooding from the earlier damage, and a boiler room had to be abandoned. Tovey was delighted to hear of the success of the torpedo-bombers, although it soon became clear that the hit had no noticeable effect on the German ship's speed.

There were high hopes of bringing *Bismarck* to a surface action the following morning, but during the night Tovey suffered a heavy blow when the cruisers who had been shadowing her so tenaciously lost contact. He believed that Lütjens was still heading for St Nazaire (as indeed he was), but could not be certain. The captains of the shadowing cruisers thought the German had headed westwards, which Tovey had to recognise was the most dangerous course for him, for if *Bismarck* could be refuelled from one of the German oilers Lütjens could continue the attacks on British shipping. So Tovey ordered *Victorious*, which had been preparing to search to the south-east, to search instead to the north-west. Nothing was seen by this search, for *Bismarck* was heading in the opposite direction, and *Victorious* was left so far behind the German battleship that she was out of the hunt for good.

Although Lütjens had eluded his pursuers he did not realise his good fortune for some time. He thought he was still being shadowed by the cruisers and that radio silence was therefore pointless, so he continued to send radio messages. Although code-breaking could give no timely intelligence from these transmissions, stations in the British radio direction-finding system duly obtained Lütjens' bearings and passed these to Tovey. Unfortunately for Tovey, the bearings were incorrectly plotted in his flagship and he formed the impression that *Bismarck* had reversed course and was breaking back to the north-eastwards, which in many ways was the obvious thing to do. Accordingly, for several hours most of his ships headed to cut the German off from the Iceland-Faroes passage, while *Bismarck* steamed steadily towards France. By the time Tovey realised his mistake he was more than 100 miles behind *Bismarck*.

But now, however, there were many other ships in the chase. Several battleships and cruisers which had been escorting Atlantic convoys were ordered to join in the hunt, the best-placed being the battleship *Rodney*, 350 miles to the south-east of *Bismarck*. *Rodney* had correctly plotted the bearings of *Bismarck*'s radio transmissions and had assessed that the German battleship was heading for Brest. *Rodney*'s captain acted on this assumption, ignoring Tovey's instructions to move to the north-east. At the same time Vice-Admiral Sir James Somerville, with Force H from the Western Mediterranean—*Ark Royal*, the battlecruiser *Renown*, and the cruiser *Sheffield*—was 1300 miles to the southward.

Coastal Command, too, was doing everything in its power and it was a Coastal Command Catalina which found *Bismarck* at 10.30 a.m. on 26 May, after she had been lost for 31 hours. All

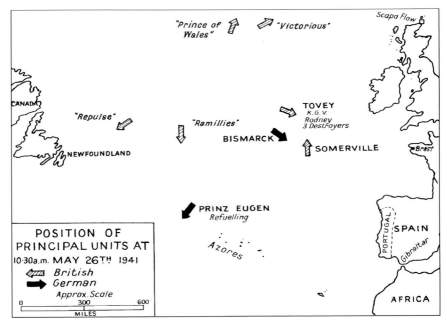

The position of the principal units at 10.30 a.m., 26 May 1941

Tovey's ships except the battleship *King George V* had returned to harbour to refuel, and he continued on alone until he was joined by *Rodney* and three destroyers during the afternoon. But the two battleships were more than 130 miles to the north of *Bismarck*, and as *Rodney* could not make more than 22 knots they had no chance of catching the German unless her speed could be radically reduced.

Time was pressing, and the situation seemed nearly hopeless, for *Bismarck* was within 700 miles of Brest and could easily reach that harbour by the evening of 27 May. Worse still, the remaining British ships were short of fuel and had no oilers available, and there was a serious threat from the Luftwaffe if the pursuit was continued too close to the French coast. The only hope seemed to be Force H (particularly *Ark Royal*) which all the previous night Somerville had been driving northward in the teeth of a rising gale. When *Bismarck* was found Somerville was only 55 miles away, directly barring the way to Brest.

The crucial question was whether *Ark Royal*'s Swordfish could stop *Bismarck*. Somerville was keen to attack as soon as possible, but *Ark Royal* had only 23 serviceable Swordfish and before launching a strike it was essential to get back aircraft which had been sent out on reconnaissance, refuel them and arm them with torpedoes. This was easier said than done, for the weather had been worsening all day, and the stern of *Ark Royal*'s flight deck was now rising and falling through more than 50 feet. It was also essential that *Bismarck* should be kept under continuous observation, so relays of shadowers were organised throughout the day, all the strain falling on the Swordfish because the weather was much too bad for the Fulmar fighters to operate.

Somerville's problem was to take up a convenient position from which *Ark Royal*'s aircraft could attack, without running the risk of becoming embroiled in a surface action with *Bismarck*. The wind was blowing at gale force from the northwest, and *Bismarck* was steaming almost directly downwind, straight towards *Ark Royal*. With the sea conditions as they were it was possible that *Ark Royal* might have to spend protracted periods heading into the wind while her Swordfish were landing or taking off. It was essential therefore for Force H to get clear of *Bismarck*'s path, which Somerville achieved by moving to a position 50 miles to the north-eastwards of her track.

At 2.50 p.m. fifteen torpedo-armed Swordfish began to leave *Ark Royal*'s heaving deck, the crews having been briefed that they would find *Bismarck* on her own, 40 miles away. But *Bismarck* was not on her own, for at 1.40 p.m. Somerville had sent the cruiser *Sheffield* to shadow the battleship. The visibility was poor,

Ark Royal's officers were busy and did not notice the departure of *Sheffield*, and it was not until the strike had been gone for an hour that a message from Somerville to the Admiralty, copied to *Ark Royal* 'for information', was deciphered and it was realised that *Sheffield* was in the target area. An immediate message was sent in the clear to the strike leader to 'look out for *Sheffield*', but it was already too late.

At 3.50 p.m. the strike leader, flying the only Swordfish fitted with radar, had made a detection in roughly the expected position of *Bismarck*, and attacked through the clouds. As they dived to the attack some of the pilots recognised the target as *Sheffield* and withheld their fire, but eleven torpedoes were dropped. *Sheffield*'s crew, knowing that a strike from *Ark Royal* was on the way, had expected to sight a formation of Swordfish, but were horrified when it was realised that the aircraft were attacking them.

Luck was with *Sheffield*. The torpedoes were armed with the magnetic pistols which had been used with apparent success at Taranto, but these pistols were liable to fire prematurely if there was a heavy swell, which there certainly was. Some thus exploded on hitting the water and *Sheffield*, manoeuvring desperately at full speed, managed to avoid the remainder. Great hopes had been pinned on this Fleet Air Arm attack, and this fiasco was a sad anticlimax. Somerville told Tovey that the attack had scored no hits, but understandably did not give the reason.

Somerville also advised Tovey that a further attack force would leave *Ark Royal* at about 6.30 p.m., but they could have little hope that it would be any more successful than the first. By 7 p.m. the second strike of fifteen aircraft—every available Swordfish—was refuelled, rearmed (this time with contact pistols on the torpedoes) and ready. This time they found *Bismarck*, but in the low cloud the strike became disorganised—the attacks being spread over more than half-an-hour, from 8.47 to 9.25 p.m. Two hits were scored. One was on the armour belt and had no apparent effect, the other was right aft and wrecked the battleship's steering gear and damaged her propellers. This hit was decisive.[2]

Tovey knew nothing of this success. The strike leader had only three aircraft with him when he attacked, and afterwards reported that they had scored no hits. It was assumed by all that this referred to the whole strike, and hope was virtually abandoned. Somerville had warned Tovey that after one more small torpedo-bomber attack, planned for later that night, all torpedoes would be expended. Then it was realised that *Bismarck* was behaving in a very peculiar manner. First *Sheffield*, then a shadowing aircraft, reported that she had altered course to the northwards—back towards Tovey's battleships. As soon as it became clear that this was not merely an evasive manoeuvre, hopes soared again.

Bismarck could no longer steer, and nothing the crew could do could prevent her from heading into the wind, which was blowing at gale force from the north-westwards. At 9.40 p.m. Lütjens sent a farewell message to Hitler that the ship was unmanoeuvrable, but the crew would 'fight to the last shell'. An hour later five British destroyers arrived, and they safely delivered *Bismarck* into Tovey's hands the following morning. The only really interesting point about the surface battle which followed is the incredible amount of punishment absorbed by *Bismarck*. When she finally sank at 10.36 a.m., she had been pounded at short-range by the 16-inch guns of *Rodney* and the 14-inch guns of *King George V* for over an hour, but still required three torpedo hits and the assistance of some scuttling charges detonated by the Germans before she would go down.

Force H was still over the horizon during this engagement. By 8.55 a.m., when Force H was within twenty miles of *Bismarck* and the sound of gunfire could be heard, Somerville decided to attempt another torpedo attack. The weather was still very bad, with the wind gusting over *Ark Royal*'s flight deck at 60 knots, but twelve Swordfish were safely dispatched by 9.26 a.m. They had no difficulty in finding *Bismarck*, but soon realised that an attack would be most unwise, for four ships were firing at the German ship and some of the shots were falling very wide. Somerville was just planning another attack by his Swordfish when he received the signal that *Bismarck* had sunk.

Its task completed, Force H returned to Gibraltar. Somerville's two major ships had never sighted either *Bismarck* or Tovey's battleships. The chase of *Bismarck* was the only occasion when the classical pre-war concept of surface action—the carriers finding and fixing, the battleships catching up and destroying—came off. Twenty more capital ships were to be lost during the war; five of them were to be sunk by ships, and twelve by air attack, but none by the two in combination.

There were many lessons which could have been learnt from this campaign, but by no means were all of them learnt. The shortcomings of the British refuelling-at-sea capability were starkly revealed—as they were at the same time in Crete—but the Admiralty reaction was slight. It seemed to be blithely accepted that the Germans could expect to refuel in the Atlantic, an ocean supposedly dominated by the Royal Navy, whereas the British ships could not. The Admiralty, at Churchill's instigation, actually ordered that *Bismarck* must be sunk even if it meant that *King George V* would

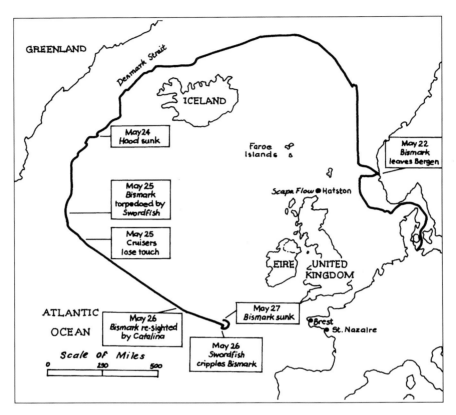

Overview of the search for the *Bismarck*

run out of fuel and would have to be towed home after the action, a signal fairly described by Tovey as 'the stupidest and most ill-considered signal ever made'.[3] To be fair to Churchill, he had long been a critic of the Royal Navy's inefficiency in refuelling at sea, and in his usual forthright way repeatedly pointed it out to the Admiralty.[4] It was nevertheless to be three more years before the Royal Navy really tackled this problem.

Then there was the reconnaissance capability. Radar was in its infancy, and visual identification of targets located by radar was not easy in the prevailing weather conditions. The failure of air reconnaissance to detect *Prinz Eugen* after she had been detached by Lütjens, and the fact that two German oilers could be waiting, undetected, to refuel the German ships is a fair indication of its limitations at this time. (In fact the foray of *Prinz Eugen* turned out to be abortive. After successfully refuelling she developed

100

engine defects and returned to Brest without intercepting any British merchant ships.)

The staff work on the British side was twice seriously defective. The inaccurate plotting of the bearings obtained on Lütjens rash (and unnecessary) radio transmissions was inexcusable, causing Tovey to go charging off in the wrong direction and almost putting him out of the hunt. Somerville's detachment of the cruiser *Sheffield* to shadow *Bismarck* was potentially even more damaging, and to do it without asking or even directly telling *Ark Royal* was clearly wrong.

The confusion in the briefing of *Ark Royal*'s first strike, as well as the earlier problems over the efficient use of fighters to defend *Illustrious* off Malta, bring up the question of the most suitable ship for the admiral in tactical command of the force. Off Malta, and again in Force H against *Bismarck*, the admiral was in a capital ship although the carriers and their aircraft were the key weapons. Perhaps the admiral was more comfortable in a battleship or battlecruiser, but he would have been in much better tactical control of his force if he had flown his flag in an aircraft carrier.

On the armament side, the shortcomings of the magnetic pistols in the 18-inch torpedoes were starkly revealed, and they were immediately taken out of service. Less could be done about the warheads on the torpedoes, which were too small—*Bismarck* accepted the first two hits without being significantly damaged. However, it was not until the Royal Navy adopted the American Grumman Avenger TBF torpedo-bomber in 1943 that its strike aircraft could carry a larger 22-inch torpedo with a 400-pound warhead.

The operation did dramatically demonstrate the mobility of carrier-based air power. On 21 May *Ark Royal* was in the Western Mediterranean flying off two dozen Hurricanes to Malta. Six days later her Swordfish were successfully attacking *Bismarck* 450 miles west of Brest.

7

Pearl Harbor:

7 December 1941

In April and May 1940 (six months before the British naval air attack on Taranto) the Japanese used war games to test the possibility of a carrier-based torpedo-aircraft raid against a fleet in harbour. Following the British success at Taranto, Admiral Isoroku Yamamoto (the Commander-in-Chief of the Combined Fleet) asked for full information about the raid from the Japanese naval attachés in Berlin and Rome—particularly in regard to the use of torpedoes in shallow water. After reading the reports obtained, Yamamoto directed the Chief of Staff of the 11th Naval Air Force to consider the practicability of an attack on the US Pacific Fleet base at Pearl Harbor in Hawaii, using specially modified shallow-running torpedoes. The report resulting from this study, which became available to Yamamoto in February 1941, concluded that a carrier attack on Pearl Harbor was practicable, provided that all the Japanese Navy's large carriers were used and that complete secrecy could be maintained.

At this time the Japanese Naval War Plan envisaged a southward thrust to capture the oilfields of the Dutch East Indies. If, and when, the US Fleet at Pearl Harbor endeavoured to intervene, it could expect to have to fight its way across the central Pacific, where the Japanese aimed to exact a heavy toll by submarine and air attacks from their bases in the Marshall and Caroline island groups. The surviving American ships would be destroyed in the Philippine Sea by the overwhelming power of the Combined Fleet.

This was not an unreasonable scenario, for in December 1941 the Japanese had ten battleships to the US Pacific Fleet's nine, 36 cruisers to 21, and 113 destroyers to 67. In aircraft carriers the Japanese strength was overwhelming—ten (six large and four light) to three—although Japanese intelligence incorrectly assessed the US strength as five. The US Navy had diverted two carriers into the Atlantic, but even if all the American carriers were concentrated in the Pacific these would still be outnumbered ten to seven.

Yamamoto did not adopt the plan of attack on Pearl Harbor without further thorough investigation. From September 1941 he conducted a series of war games and practical trials which tested every aspect of the plan, and at the same time continued the training of the Combined Fleet with the utmost vigour. Manoeuvres, air exercises and gunnery practices succeeded each other almost without pause, with particular emphasis on night torpedo-attacks (at which the Japanese were already unsurpassed), and the air groups from the six large carriers started training specifically against Pearl Harbor. Meanwhile production began of torpedoes with wooden fins, which were especially designed to run in Pearl Harbor's shallow waters.

To this point Yamamoto had not yet been able to convince the Naval General Staff or the government that such an attack was desirable, even though relations between the US and Japan had been deteriorating for some time. Events seemed to be clearly heading towards war, especially following the decision of the US Congress in July 1940 to place an embargo on the export of certain strategic materials to Japan, and the subsequent freezing of Japanese assets in America. That war would be the eventual outcome was widely accepted, and on the American side Secretary of War Henry Stimson later admitted that the problem had been how to manoeuvre the Japanese into firing the first shot without allowing too much danger to themselves.[1]

The Naval General Staff did not easily agree to the alteration to their original war plan, since the war game conducted in September 1941 seemed to indicate that the Japanese would suffer heavy losses in such an attack. Yamamoto, however, was 'firm and unbending'[2] and, unable to withstand his prestige and personality, and the threat of resignation[3], the Naval Staff at last yielded. However, not until 3 November did Admiral Osami Nagano, the Chief of the Naval Staff, finally agree to the change. The Pearl Harbor operation was to be an addition, rather than an alteration, to the original scheme, and the southern attacks against the Philippines, Siam, Malaya and ultimately the Dutch East Indies were to go ahead as planned.

The Japanese government had already decided that war would be commenced if a diplomatic agreement had not been reached with the Americans by the end of the month. Therefore, on 26 November the striking force set sail secretly for a waiting position 2000 miles to the north-west of Pearl Harbor. This force, commanded by Vice-Admiral Chuichi Nagumo, was the most powerful carrier fleet yet assembled in war. The large carriers *Akagi*, *Kaga*, *Hiryu*, *Soryu*, *Shokaku* and *Zuikaku* were to achieve almost legendary fame in the next few months. They carried a complement of 393 aircraft—114 Zeke fighters, 135 Val dive-bombers and 144 Kate level-bombers or torpedo-bombers—and were accompanied by two fast battleships and a screen of three cruisers and nine destroyers, as well as eight oilers and supply ships. One of the carriers, *Zuikaku*, was so new that she had completed her shake-down cruise only on 25 September, and her sister ship, *Shokaku*, was only one month older.

A major problem for Yamamoto was the selection of a safe approach route for his carriers. The dominant requirement was to avoid detection by the Americans, but he had to consider also the refuelling of the destroyers, which had insufficient endurance for the round trip. It was ultimately decided to steam at economical speed (fourteen knots) through the stormy and deserted waters south of the Aleutians, accepting that if the weather was too bad to refuel the destroyers they would have to be left behind.

The crew cheers 'Banzai' as a Kate torpedo-bomber takes off. (*US Naval Historical Center, NH50603*)

Only the carriers *Kaga*, *Shokaku* and *Zuikaku* and the two battleships had the normal endurance to carry out the operation without refuelling. To eliminate the necessity for refuelling at sea, the other carriers and the heavy cruisers carried additional oil (in drums, trimming tanks and other watertight compartments). The light cruiser *Abukuma* and the destroyers, which could not carry additional fuel, assiduously practised refuelling from tankers both by the broadside and astern methods. Efficiency rose steadily, as well as the speed at which the refuelling could be done. The greatest problem was the low pumping rate of the tankers (about 60 tons an hour) which inevitably caused delays. The availability of fuel was a crucial factor in the planning of the operation.

Nagumo was not himself an aviator, having specialised in surface torpedo-warfare and later enjoyed a distinguished career in battleships, cruisers and destroyers. He was fortunate to have on his staff the brilliant Commander Minoru Genda, who had done a great deal to develop coordinated operations by large numbers of carriers, and the quality of the staff concealed many of the defects of the admiral. Nagumo had initially been dubious of the wisdom of the Pearl Harbor attack—so much so, in fact, that Yamamoto at one stage considered assuming command of the striking force himself.

On 1 December the Japanese government finally made the decision to go to war, and the next day the date for the attack on Pearl Harbor was set as 8 December.[4] This was a Sunday, a day that the Japanese knew the US Fleet normally spent in harbour. The approach to the launching position was made smoothly in accordance with the plan, concealment being helped by fog and heavy seas. Nagumo preserved rigid radio silence; the story that false signal traffic was used to give the impression that the Japanese carriers were still in the Inland Sea seems to be incorrect—the Americans reached that conclusion without any help. Yamamoto had given Nagumo written orders beforehand to abandon the operation if he was discovered on or before 5 December, and the discretion whether to continue the attack if he was discovered on 6 December.[5] The problem did not arise, for there was never a sign of any other ship, submarine or aircraft in the area.

By 11.30 a.m. on 6 December Nagumo had reached a position to the north of Hawaii and turned southwards, detaching the oilers to a rendezvous on the homeward route. By 9 p.m. that night he was less than 500 miles north of Pearl Harbor, and speed was increased to 26 knots. Soon after midnight a message was received from Tokyo that although all seven battleships were in harbour, there were no carriers there. This was a great disappointment, for

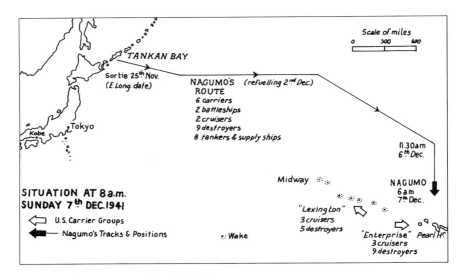

Nagumo's route to Pearl Harbor

the carriers were the priority target and Yamamoto had hoped that four would be in Pearl Harbor. Nagumo decided to continue with the attack as planned, for there was, after all, some chance that the carriers might return to harbour before morning.

At 5 a.m. four reconnaissance floatplanes were launched by cruisers to see whether the conditions were still favourable for the raid. By 6 a.m. the striking force was within 275 miles of Pearl Harbor, and without waiting for the report from the floatplanes the first wave of 183 aircraft—by far the largest attack force ever launched from carriers—took off. Commander Mitsuo Fuchida led in a Kate bomber, followed by 49 more of the same type under his direct command, each carrying a 1600-pound bomb converted from a 16-inch armour-piercing shell. To starboard were 40 more Kates, each armed with a torpedo. To port were 51 Val dive-bombers, each armed with a 550-pound bomb, while above the formation 43 of the incomparable Zeke fighters patrolled watchfully.

The four floatplanes from the cruisers had gone ahead to confirm that the American ships were still in harbour, and it was one of these aircraft which was detected by American radar at 6.45 a.m. The US Army had six mobile radar sets for early warning of an air attack, but the vital set, covering the northern approaches, was operated only from 4 a.m. till 7 a.m., though training continued until 11 a.m. (except on Sundays). On this morning the operators tracked a suspicious aircraft for a quarter of an hour from 6.45 a.m., and soon afterwards picked up a large group of aircraft 132 miles to the north, and closing. The two privates (instructor and trainee) were unable to interest the duty officer in what they had found. He was expecting a group of B–17 Flying Fortresses to approach from that direction, and saw nothing suspicious in the detections. Besides, it was Sunday, and the set was due to be switched off. The main body of Fuchida's aircraft flew above the cloud layer, at 9000 feet, but as they crossed the north coast of the island of Oahu the clouds cleared, and soon Pearl Harbor itself could be seen. 'Pearl Harbour was still asleep in the morning mist' wrote one of the Japanese pilots.

> It was calm and serene inside the harbour, not even a trace of smoke from the ships at Oahu. The orderly groups of barracks, the wriggling white line of the automobile roads climbing up to the mountain; fine objectives of attack in all directions. In line with these inside the harbour were important ships of the Pacific Fleet, strung out and anchored two ships side by side in an orderly manner.[6]

Yet the Americans should have had ample warning. Not only had the Japanese reconnaissance-seaplane been detected by radar before 7 a.m., but at 3.42 a.m.—more than four hours before the air attack—a minesweeper had sighted the periscope of a submarine in the approaches to the harbour. The Japanese intended to supplement the air attack with five midget submarines, while sixteen large submarines were deployed off the approaches to Pearl Harbor to torpedo any ships which might manage to survive the air and midget-submarine attacks and fight their way to sea. The midget submarines had each been carried on one of the larger submarines, and launched about ten miles from Pearl Harbor. They were intended to slip undetected into Pearl Harbor and not to commence their attack until Nagumo's aircraft had struck. If necessary, they were to wait till the next night to launch their attacks, afterwards rendezvousing with their mother submarines seven miles off the coast.

The midget-submarines might have—and in the event should have—compromised the surprise of the air attack, and they were destined to accomplish nothing. Fortunately for the Japanese there had been more than ten unconfirmed reports of Japanese submarines in the Pearl Harbor approaches in the past six months, three of them in the past five weeks, and new reports were inevitably regarded sceptically by US staff officers. The periscope sighting was reported to the destroyer *Ward*, which investigated the area but, when nothing was found, decided not to pass the report on to headquarters. It was three more hours before the alarm finally reached headquarters, after the *Ward* and a flying boat sank a midget submarine in the approaches to the harbour. The *Ward* sighted the conning tower of the midget submarine, fired at it and then dropped depth charges at the submerging vessel. The incident was reported at 6.51 a.m. and the Pacific Fleet commander (Admiral Husband Kimmel) was himself informed of this at 7.41 a.m., but still the general alarm was not given.

The reason for the strategic surprise at Pearl Harbor has been a fertile field for conspiracy theorists, but some points are quite clear. Both the Americans and the British were intercepting and decrypting some Japanese radio messages, notably their diplomatic traffic (codenamed 'Purple'). At this time, it is claimed, the American code-breakers could not read the content of any important Japanese Navy or Army encrypted messages,[7] though they had a good idea from intercepted call signs where most of the Japanese ships were. This source was far from perfect, because ships in harbour used frequencies which could not be intercepted, and those at sea who were preserving radio silence could not be tracked. Moreover, after a change of call signs—which occurred on 1 November 1941 and again a month later—it took some time to re-establish the system.

Kimmel certainly did not receive in timely fashion all the code-breaking information he should have been given; in particular he was not given the transcripts of the Japanese diplomatic traffic.[8] He was nevertheless kept well informed. As a result of Purple intercepts, 'war warning' signals were sent to both Kimmel and General Douglas MacArthur in the Philippines on 27 November, to alert them that negotiations with the Japanese were at breaking point. The Philippines, Thailand, northern Malaya and possibly Borneo were listed as being in danger of imminent attack.

The message to Kimmel specifically stated that it was to be regarded as a warning of an aggressive Japanese move 'within the next few days'. A dispatch to Major-General Walter Short, the Army Commander of the Hawaiian Department, said that future Japanese action was 'unpredictable' but that hostilities were 'possible at any moment'. An even clearer warning was given on 3 December, when American Pacific commanders were told (again as a result of the decryption of an intercepted diplomatic message) that all Japanese embassies except the one in Washington had been ordered to destroy their cipher machines. Thus the question was not whether the Japanese would strike, but where.

There is no doubt that all the American authorities believed that the Japanese would strike only southwards, as had in fact been their strategy until Yamamoto managed to impose his radical modification. Although Secretary of the Navy Frank Knox had sent a memorandum to Secretary of War Henry Stimson after the Taranto attack saying that 'the success of the British aerial torpedo attack against ships at anchor suggests that precautionary measures must be taken immediately to protect Pearl Harbor against a surprise attack in the event of war between the United States and Japan', such a possibility does not seem to have been taken seriously in Washington. Even Knox, when told that Pearl Harbor was under attack, could only express his astonishment, saying: 'This can't be true, this must mean the Philippines'.[9]

Admiral Kimmel also did not believe that the Japanese would attack Pearl Harbor, a view shared by his senior staff. Only a week before the Pacific war began Kimmel asked his war plans officer what the chances were of a surprise attack on Pearl Harbor, and the reply was 'none'. There had been no recent trace of the Japanese carriers, but they were thought to be waiting in the Inland Sea of Japan, poised to counter any moves by the US Pacific Fleet against their southward advance. Kimmel consequently considered his principal task to be the training of the vast numbers of men needed to crew the new ships now coming forward. He did, however, take the precaution of avoiding too predictable a pattern in the movements of his ships, though he was limited by the fact that he had only four tankers fitted for fuelling at sea because priority had been given to the Atlantic Fleet.

The Pacific Fleet was divided into three principal task forces, with all the aircraft carriers in one and the battleships split between the other two. Only rarely were two task forces in Pearl Harbor at the same time, though unfortunately this was the case on 7 December. Kimmel had few long-range reconnaissance aircraft, and these carried out only meagre searches to the west and south; the Japanese, knowing the areas which being searched, approached from the north. (As was shown by the new reconnaissance patrols ordered immediately after the Japanese attack, these searches could have been greatly extended if there had been sufficient sense of danger.[10])

The defensive measures adopted in harbour were no more thorough. Although the British action at Taranto over a year earlier had shown that torpedo attacks on ships in harbour were practicable, anti-torpedo baffles were not fitted in Pearl Harbor, because they would restrict boat traffic. Nor did the ships have anti-torpedo nets, Kimmel stating that 'until a light, efficient net that can be laid temporarily and quickly' was available, he did not want them.[11]

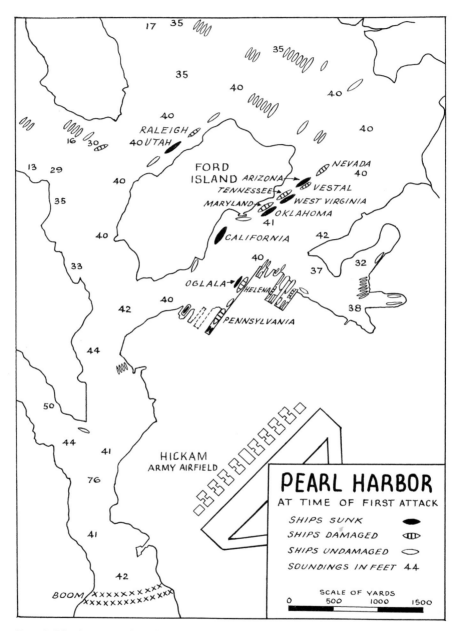

Pearl Harbor at the time of the first attack

The Kate bomber, maximum speed 193 knots, 565 miles range with 1765-pound torpedo. (*National Archives, 80-G-427153*)

Kimmel did not take any additional measures as a result of the warning of 27 November. In his view the fleet was already at an adequate level of readiness, with a quarter of the anti-aircraft guns on 'alert status', although the only anti-aircraft guns actually manned all the time were a pair of 0.50-inch machine guns in the foretop of each battleship. He did not order additional aircraft searches, and did not inform several key officers (including the rear-admiral in command of the patrol aircraft) of the warning messages.[12]

Nor was the army any better prepared, and with it lay the responsibility for the air defence of the fleet in harbour. For this purpose eleven reconnaissance aircraft, 35 bombers (six B–17s[13] and 29 of older types) and 94 fighters (64 P–40s and 30 of older types) were available. There were a further 88 undergoing repair, overhaul or inspection, and many of the aircraft on hand were unarmed. The available fighters were on four-hour flight notice, and were clustered together for easy guarding on the ground, for General Short considered sabotage by Japanese civilians living in Hawaii to be the main threat.

The Japanese attack plan provided for the possibility that the Americans might be on the alert, and Fuchida was to signal the type of attack to be launched by firing a signal pistol, one shot if surprise had been gained, two if it had not. If the Americans were on the alert, the Val dive-bombers would attack the battleships first to draw their fire, and then, in the ensuing confusion, Fuchida's

Kates would drop their torpedoes, while the Kate level-bombers would have the task of neutralising the anti-aircraft guns. But there was no need for the alternative plan, for there was no sign of any reaction by the Americans. It was 7.49 a.m. when Fuchida gave the order to attack, firing his signal pistol once into the clear sky. Four minutes later, when there was still no sign of American fighters or anti-aircraft fire, he sent to Nagumo the code-word 'Tiger', meaning that surprise had been gained.

The task of the dive-bombers now was to gain local air supremacy, and they therefore attacked the three airfields at which the Americans were believed to have fighters—Wheeler, Hickam and the naval station at Ford Island.[14] As the American aircraft were close together, almost wingtip-to-wingtip, they were easy targets for the dive-bombers. The Zeke fighters, finding no opposition in the air, assisted by machine-gunning the parked aircraft, and in a few minutes over 150 machines—more than half the serviceable aircraft on the island—were destroyed or seriously damaged. The surprise was so complete and the damage so heavy

View of Battleship Row during the attack. One battleship (USS *West Virginia*) is listing to port as a result of a torpedo hit and other torpedo tracks can be seen. (*US Naval Historical Center, NH50931*)

that not more than a handful of the Army's 94 serviceable fighters took to the air,[15] and these could do little against the overwhelming Japanese strength. No navy or Marine Corps fighters were able to take part.

While the dive-bombers and fighters were gaining air superiority, the 90 Kates were attacking the ships, their chief targets being the seven battleships moored singly or in pairs alongside Ford Island. The 40 torpedo-bombers had a very restricted area in the narrow channel between Ford Island and the Dockyard in which to drop their torpedoes, and they also had to drop them from a very low altitude, since the depth of the harbour was no more than 40 feet. Genda and Fuchida had made lengthy experiments to ensure that the torpedoes would not hit the bottom, and eventually wooden stabilisers were fitted to the fins of the torpedoes to flatten the angle of entry into the water, and this simple device worked well. The level-bombers attacked at the same time as the

Battleship Row after the attack. From the left: USS *West Virginia*, severely damaged; USS *Tennessee*, damaged; and USS *Arizona*, sunk. (*Imperial War Museum, OEM3604*)

torpedo-bombers, just before 8 a.m. The actual attacks were spread over half-an-hour, the torpedo-bombers approaching their targets individually and the level-bombers dropping their bombs in groups of ten aircraft. Some made two or three approaches in order to gain perfect dropping positions.

When the first wave of Japanese aircraft attacked, the American ships were preparing for the ceremonial hoisting of colours at 8 a.m. Only a quarter of the 780 anti-aircraft guns were manned, and numerous watertight doors were open. Many key officers were ashore, including five of the eight battleship captains. There were a few moments of stunned incredulity, some imagined that it was a practice attack by the marines or army, and some who saw bombs fall thought that live bombs must have been used by mistake. But this state did not last long, and within two minutes some guns were firing, and as time passed the volume of anti-aircraft fire strongly increased. The second wave of Japanese bombers was to have a far more difficult time than the first.

By 8.45 a.m. the first wave of Japanese aircraft was withdrawing. Nine minutes later the leader of the second wave, Lieutenant-Commander Shimazaki, gave the order to attack. His group had left the carriers at 7.15 a.m., 75 minutes after Fuchida's group, and comprised 54 Kates and 80 Val dive-bombers escorted by 36 Zekes. By the time Shimazaki's aircraft had finished, all but 43 of the 390 army, navy and marine aircraft on the island had been damaged or destroyed.

By 10 a.m. the battle was over. The results had been devastating. All the battleships of the US Pacific Fleet had been sunk or damaged[16] at a cost to the Japanese of 28 aircraft (eight fighters, fifteen dive-bombers and five torpedo-bombers). But the American carriers had escaped, and the dockyard installations, which were essential for the rapid repair of the damaged ships, were virtually untouched, as was the fuel depot.

Nagumo decided not to attempt anything more against Hawaii, or to try to find the American carriers. An extensive search for the latter to the south of Pearl Harbor was in any case impossible, because the Japanese ships were short of fuel and the oilers had been given a rendezvous far back along the northerly withdrawal route. At 1.30 p.m. Nagumo ordered a retirement, and his ships headed north-westwards still unsighted by any American ships or aircraft. By this time the US carriers were looking for Nagumo's fleet, but fortunately for them they did not find it, for they would almost certainly have been annihilated by Nagumo's six carriers.

At the time of the attack the carrier *Enterprise*, flying the flag of Vice-Admiral William Halsey, was on her way back to Pearl

Harbor after delivering a marine fighter squadron to Wake Island, and at dawn was more than 200 miles to the westward. Halsey had then launched fifteen SBD Dauntless dive-bombers to carry out a routine 150 mile search ahead of the carrier, with instructions to the aircraft to proceed to Pearl Harbor when they had finished. They were unlucky to arrive at the same time as the Japanese strike, and five were either shot down or made crash landings. Of the other carriers, *Saratoga* was in San Francisco and *Lexington* was heading for Midway Island with a cargo of marine dive-bombers. Kimmel at once ordered the latter ship to abandon that mission and to rendezvous with Halsey south of Pearl Harbor.

A period of total confusion followed, for no-one knew where the Japanese had come from. Kimmel correctly guessed they had come from the north, but the problem was to find them. Few reconnaissance aircraft had survived the attack, and the areas to be searched were vast. The army radar station which had detected the Japanese aircraft as they approached later tracked them northwards as they retired towards their carriers, but this vital information was not passed on to Kimmel. A false sighting report placed two Japanese carriers ten miles south of Pearl Harbor, and an American cruiser which was in this exact position tried to clarify the situation by reporting 'no carriers in sight'. The message was, however, transmitted as 'two carriers in sight', and considerable misunderstanding ensued.

Soon afterwards a directional interception of radio transmissions from a Japanese carrier was received, but the direction finder could not distinguish between reciprocal bearings, so the transmitting ship might be either to the north or to the south. A special set which could have solved the problem could not be contacted because the army had, without warning, taken over the telephone circuit. Confronted with all this confusing evidence Kimmel changed his mind, and ordered searches to the south and west of Hawaii. By the time a correct appreciation had been made, Nagumo's carriers were well beyond his reach.

The Japanese attack on Pearl Harbor was much greater, both in size and efficiency, than anything previously attempted in war from aircraft carriers. The tactical execution of such a difficult operation demonstrated that intelligence assessments had greatly underestimated Japanese naval capabilities. The approach from the north successfully evaded American reconnaissance, and attacking in daylight—relying on surprise and the Zeke fighters to protect the bombers—achieved maximum bombing accuracy. Attacking on a Sunday morning, when most American ships would not only be in harbour but they would not be very alert, certainly paid off.

The ability to replenish at sea in rough weather (which the Royal Navy could not have done at this time) was essential to the success of the operation.

On the other hand the Japanese made some serious errors. It was a mistake for Nagumo to send his oilers so far back along his withdrawal route that they were not available to refuel his fleet if he had decided to hunt for the American carriers after the successful Pearl Harbor attack—and the carriers were, after all, the prime target. More extensive searches at the time of the attack—Nagumo knew the American carriers were somewhere at sea—would almost certainly have found *Enterprise,* which was within 200 miles of Hawaii, and once found her destruction would have been assured. It was also a mistake to use midget submarines to attack Pearl Harbor before the air strike, for they might have given away the element of surprise, and in any event they achieved nothing.

The Japanese were lucky too. Yamamoto apparently did not know about the American radar, which should have given nearly an hour's warning to the US Fleet and the defending fighters, instead of the complete surprise the attackers achieved. The false enemy report from one of Kimmel's cruisers, and the erroneous plotting of the bearing of an intercepted radio signal from a Japanese carrier during the withdrawal, both of which misled Kimmel, were further strokes of luck. (It may be remembered that a similar error in plotting the bearing of a radio transmission misled Tovey during the hunt for *Bismarck.*)

The Americans made many more mistakes, some of which can be explained by the fact that they were not yet on a full war alert, and an attack like Nagumo's would startle anyone in peacetime. Yet, although the Pearl Harbor attack itself was a surprise, the Americans knew that war with Japan was imminent. Kimmel totally failed to penetrate the mind of his Japanese opposite number, though Yamamoto was well known to the Americans, having been Naval Attaché in Washington, and had been assessed as 'aggressive and dangerous'. In the circumstances Kimmel's assumption that Yamamoto's mind would work the same way his did, and as a consequence his failure to provide proper anti-torpedo and anti-dive-bomber defences in Pearl Harbor, is inexcusable. Kimmel was also at fault in not giving the general alarm when the midget submarine attacks were detected.

Kimmel was dismissed for his failure, but it was really the responsibility of his army colleague, General Short, to defend Kimmel's fleet from air attack while it was in harbour. Yet at the time of the attack only four of the army's 31 anti-aircraft batteries were in position, and their ready ammunition had been returned to depots because it was 'apt to disintegrate and get dusty'.[17] The failure to use the air-warning radar effectively, and the lack of communication between the two services, are extraordinary. Even more extraordinary was the lack of any means of using the radar information (if it had been passed on) for direction of the army fighters, remembering that this was more than a year after the battle of Britain.

The whole battle was a tactical embarrassment for the Americans and a stunning blow to American pride, but the disaster was not as overwhelming as it appeared at first sight. Few ships other than the battleships had been damaged. The carriers, cruisers and destroyers—the ships which later bore the brunt of the Pacific war—were almost untouched.

Despite the attack's tactical success, it was not really a victory for the Japanese. In fact, it proved to be close to strategic madness. As Yamamoto himself had predicted, Japan had no hope of total victory in a war with the United States. Japan's only hope of victory lay in the rapid occupation of key strategic areas, followed by the building up of such a formidable defensive system that the Americans would agree to a negotiated peace rather than suffer the losses involved in attempting total victory. Yamamoto's miscalculation lay in his belief that it was essential to cripple the US Fleet before attacking southwards, for the reality was that the US Fleet, heavily outnumbered in carriers and with inadequate and obsolescent anti-aircraft armaments in many of its ships, could not have prevented the Japanese occupation of the Philippines, Malaya and the Dutch East Indies. One of Kimmel's staff officers later said that 'we could not have materially affected their control of the waters they wanted to control, whether or not the battleships were sunk at Pearl Harbor . . . I thought it would be suicide for us to attempt with an inferior fleet, to move into the Western Pacific'.[18]

Yamamoto's successful attack on Pearl Harbor—'the day that will live in infamy', as President Roosevelt described it—had, by making America ridiculous in the eyes of the world, ensured that the US government would never accept a negotiated peace with Japan. 'Remember Pearl Harbor' became a national watchword, and the ultimate defeat of Japan became a certainty. Yamamoto had temporarily eliminated the US Pacific battlefleet, but he had lost the war.

8

The sinking of *Prince of Wales* and *Repulse*:

10 December 1941

The British government had been well aware of the increasing likelihood of a Japanese attack on Malaya and the Dutch East Indies, particularly after the German invasion of the USSR in June 1941 removed the Russian threat to the Japanese position in Manchuria. In August Winston Churchill made proposals to the Admiralty for the creation of a powerful fleet in the Indian Ocean, in the hope of deterring Japan from entering the war. He had in mind sending the recently-completed battleship *Duke of York*, with a battle cruiser (either *Repulse* or *Renown*) and a fast aircraft carrier.

The First Sea Lord, Admiral Sir Dudley Pound, replied that the Admiralty planned to form a fleet of six battleships, one fast aircraft carrier, ten cruisers and 24 destroyers, but that this force could not be assembled before March 1942. Pound went on to say that, if war with Japan had not broken out by the time they were available, it might be desirable to send a deterrent force of the battleships *Nelson* and *Rodney*, the battlecruiser *Renown* and a carrier to Singapore, but 'if war eventuated they would have to retire to Trincomalee' in Ceylon.[1]

Churchill had a different concept. He was much struck by the effect that the presence of the German battleship *Tirpitz* had on all British naval plans, and wished to base a force on Singapore to exert a similar influence on the Japanese. At a meeting of the Defence Committee on 17 October (confirmed on 20 October) it was decided 'to send as quickly as possible one modern capital ship, together with an aircraft carrier, to join up with *Repulse* in Singapore'.[2]

Prince of Wales left for Capetown almost immediately, arriving on 16 November, but there were problems with *Indomitable*, the chosen aircraft carrier. She had commissioned only on 7 September and was training her crew and aircraft squadrons in the West Indies, where she ran aground on 3 November and had to be repaired in Norfolk, Virginia. Churchill and others have given the impression that, under the original plan, *Indomitable* would have arrived in Singapore with *Prince of Wales* and *Repulse*, thereby forming an impressive and balanced force.[3] Even if *Indomitable* had not run aground it is most unlikely that this would have happened, for she was not due to finish her work-up until 22 November and was scheduled to arrive in Gibraltar a week later.

In view of Churchill's urgent desire to get *Prince of Wales* to Singapore as a deterrent to Japan's intervention in the war, it seems inconceivable that she would have been permitted to hang around in South African waters for a month waiting for *Indomitable* to catch up. As it was, the news of the carrier's grounding enabled Churchill to gain agreement for *Prince of Wales* to head for Colombo immediately, where she would join up with *Repulse* and the two of them would make a well-publicised arrival in Singapore; *Indomitable* would follow when she could. In fact, *Indomitable*'s repairs were completed very expeditiously, in only twelve days, but she did not reach Capetown until 6 January 1942.

Acting Vice-Admiral Sir Tom Phillips was selected to command this new Eastern Fleet, and promoted to Acting Admiral for the role. Aged 52, he was an officer with a brilliant staff record and an exceptional capacity for dealing with a large volume of paperwork. Since June 1939 he had been at the Admiralty as, in Churchill's words, 'our trusted Vice Chief of the Naval Staff'.[4] Phillips had his critics, however. He was a terrible centraliser,[5] and his wartime sea experience was extremely limited and had occurred a quarter of a century before. He had never served in an aircraft carrier, and in the opinion of Sir Arthur Harris, later the Commander-in-Chief of Bomber Command, had no real appreciation of the air threat to ships at sea. According to Vice-Admiral Willis, who had a long talk with Phillips in Freetown when he was on his way to Singapore, 'he was inclined to scoff at the air menace, and advocated facing it with anti-aircraft fire alone'.[6]

The new fleet, to be known as Force Z and consisting of *Prince of Wales*, *Repulse* and four destroyers, arrived in Singapore on 2 December. Unlike most wartime arrivals they were greeted with a blaze of publicity, including an announcement by Churchill in London. All this propaganda was in vain, for the Japanese Government had already made the decision for war and only a few more days of peace remained. Indeed, it is hard to see a rational purpose for the publicity, for it might have been safely assumed that Japanese intelligence was aware of the ships' arrival without this help. The result was to prevent the ships from becoming a 'fleet in being' on the *Tirpitz* model, as Churchill apparently had in mind. After all the hype, if the Japanese attacked Phillips had to take action or otherwise morale would be dealt a devastating blow.

Phillips' most urgent task was to try to coordinate the scattered anti-Japanese naval forces in the area. The Dutch had some cruisers, destroyers and submarines in the East Indies, and there were a few ships in Australian and New Zealand waters. The Americans had a small force in the Philippines, but their main strength was far away in Pearl Harbor and Phillips had no time to concert arrangements with Kimmel. The principal British concern was that the Japanese might not attack the Americans at all, but would bypass the Philippines and attack Thailand, northern Malaya and the oil-rich Dutch East Indies, and they were desperate for an assurance of American support if this happened.

At last, on 3 December, Roosevelt promised Churchill 'armed support' if such a Japanese attack occurred. This did not mean that the United States would necessarily declare war (only Congress could make that decision), but Churchill was satisfied; for some months the United States had been giving Britain very substantial 'armed support' in the Atlantic against Germany while remaining technically neutral. Fortified by this promise Phillips flew to Manila on 4 December to see Admiral Thomas Hart, the Commander-in-Chief of the US Asiatic Fleet based in the Philippines, and General MacArthur, the army commander there.

Discussions with Hart were described by Phillips as very friendly, and the American admiral promised to lend eight destroyers to supplement Phillips' anti-submarine screening forces. While Hart was sensible, MacArthur was, in retrospect, totally divorced from reality. He was confident that his handful of B–17 Flying Fortress bombers and his Filipino militia would be able to 'hurl back' a Japanese invasion.[7]

By now, war was evidently imminent. There had been signs of transport movements in a southerly direction, and British, Dutch and American air reconnaissance patrols over the South China Sea started on 29 November. The Admiralty was acutely aware of the exposed position of Force Z, and while Phillips was in Colombo Vice-Admiral Moore (Phillips' successor as Vice-Chief of the Naval Staff), tried to persuade Pound to tell Phillips that his ships should disappear into the Pacific. Pound rejected this advice, claiming that Phillips was sufficiently in the picture to make his own decisions.[8]

Although Pound was not prepared to give direct orders to

Phillips, in the first week of December he made two suggestions for the moving of the Eastern Fleet to less dangerous areas, with the additional thought that its disappearance might mystify the Japanese. *Prince of Wales* could not be moved because seven days in dockyard hands were needed to repair defects in its evaporators. But *Repulse* and two destroyers were despatched on 5 December for a short visit to Darwin only to be hurriedly recalled the next day, when news was received of Japanese convoys entering the Gulf of Thailand.

The guidance given by the first two Admiralty messages was undermined by a third, received by Phillips on the evening of 7 December (Singapore time), asking him to report what action it might be possible to take with naval or air forces in the event a Japanese expedition was located in the South China Sea 'in such a position that its course indicates that it is proceeding towards Thailand, Malaya, Borneo or Netherlands East Indies'. Phillips immediately replied that:

> if relative strength of enemy force permits, endeavour will be made to attack expedition by night or by day. If we are inferior in strength a raid will be attempted and the air forces will attack with bombers and torpedoes in conjunction with our naval forces.[9]

This was a far cry indeed from withdrawing to 'a safe harbour', or, as the First Sea Lord had suggested in his proposal to Churchill the previous August, retreating to Ceylon. There was no direct reply from the Admiralty to Phillips' message.

During the night there was a meeting in the war room at the Singapore naval base, where Phillips discussed his strategy with a group including the Governor and the Commander-in-Chief Far East (Air Chief Marshal Sir Robert Brooke-Popham), who was responsible for air and land operations but had no authority over Phillips. After the meeting Phillips sent a message to the Admiralty proposing that Force Z sail that night to attack the enemy force off Kota Bharu at daylight on 10 December. If Phillips hoped for a veto from the Admiralty he was to be disappointed. In fact, from Phillips' later behaviour with his subordinates it would seem that he was neither expecting nor seeking a veto.

The Japanese were certainly moving somewhere, but perhaps it was only to Thailand. During 6 December large Japanese convoys were sighted by RAAF aircraft off south-east Indo-China,[10] steering into the Gulf of Thailand, though little more was heard of these convoys the next day. The weather conditions for air reconnaissance were bad, and in fact the only Japanese ships sighted were one transport and a cruiser, which fired at the British reconnaissance aircraft. These were the first shots of the Pacific War. It was 6.35 p.m. on 7 December.[11]

Any doubts as to Japanese intentions were quickly dispelled when, soon after midnight on 8 December, Japanese troops landed in northern Malaya and southern Thailand. The troops for all these landings were carried in 28 transports, escorted by a cruiser, ten destroyers and some smaller craft, while four cruisers and four destroyers were cruising off the southern tip of Indo-China as a covering force. Further to the eastward was the Commander-in-Chief, Vice-Admiral Kondo, with two old battleships, two cruisers and ten destroyers. Twelve submarines were also deployed in the Gulf of Thailand.

Even more importantly, there were substantial naval air forces in southern Indo-China, with 39 Zeke fighters and six reconnaissance aircraft at Soktran and nearly 100 bombers and twelve Claude fighters of the 22nd Air Flotilla in the Saigon area. These bombers belonged to three experienced air groups—the Genzan and Mihoro groups, each with 36 Nell bombers, and the Kanoya group with 26 of the new Betty bombers. These three groups comprised more than a third of the Japanese Navy's total strength in twin-engined bombers, at that time 240 Nells and Bettys. The Kanoya group was newly transferred from Formosa, Yamamoto having ordered it to Saigon when he heard of the arrival of Phillips' capital ships. The tasks of the squadrons in Indo-China were to gain control of the air over Malaya, and to frustrate any attempt by the Eastern Fleet to interfere with the landings. Both these tasks were performed with exemplary efficiency.

Phillips had only a sketchy idea of the Japanese ship strength, and very little information about Japanese air strength in Indo-China. The capability of the latter was seriously underestimated, for the Japanese were assessed as being less effective than either the British or the Germans and on about the same level as the Italians. It was not thought at all likely that the Japanese naval aircraft in Indo-China could launch torpedo-bombing attacks on ships 400 miles away on the coast of Malaya, for both the Germans and British had trouble reaching half that distance. Besides, Phillips thought that the aircraft that might attack him would be Japanese Army aircraft operating from southern Indo-China in support of the landing operations, and they would certainly not be carrying anti-ship bombs or torpedoes.

Phillips called a meeting of his senior officers a few hours after the Japanese landings, some time after he had sent his signal to the Admiralty. His officers agreed unanimously that Force Z could not possibly remain idle, or tamely retreat, while amphibious landings were being made on British territory and the army and air force were being driven back. After the publicity that had attended the arrival of *Prince of Wales*, inaction would have a disastrous effect on the morale of the other services and the civilian population.

In London on the evening of 9 December, 36 hours after Phillips had sailed from Singapore and was in the Gulf of Siam heading for Kuantan, Churchill held a meeting at which 'possible naval dispositions and other measures to redress the balance of naval power in the Pacific' were discussed. The meeting (actually a staff conference with the First Lord of the Admiralty and the Chiefs of Staff)[12] dealt with a number of matters, not all of them naval, but there was no suggestion that Phillips' current mission should be aborted. According to Churchill there was general agreement that the ships of Force Z 'must go to sea and vanish among the innumerable islands'. Churchill himself thought that 'they should go across the Pacific to join what was left of the American Fleet', but 'as the hour was late we decided to sleep on it'.[13]

Phillips thought that his two fast capital ships had a good chance of destroying the Japanese invasion fleets off Kota Bharu (in the north-east corner of Malaya) and Singora (in Thailand, 100 miles to the north), provided he could maintain surprise and the air force could give fighter cover. The two landings were more than 300 miles from the Japanese air bases in Indo-China, and the experience of the Royal Navy against the Germans and Italians led Phillips to believe that his ships would be safe from serious air attack at that distance. He thought that torpedo attacks in particular would be most unlikely, and he knew that such attacks were the only ones which could inflict crippling damage on a heavily-armoured battleship.

Planning to attack the Japanese invasion fleet at dawn on 10 December, Phillips sailed with Force Z from Singapore on the evening of 8 December. He left behind his Chief of Staff, Rear-Admiral Palliser, to be his representative in the war room in Singapore. Phillips was flying his flag in *Prince of Wales*, the only modern ship in his fleet. She had sixteen 5.25-inch anti-aircraft guns, but although the four gun-directors had been fitted with radar ranging the other weaknesses of British medium-range anti-aircraft gunnery remained: guessing the target aircraft's speed, inaccurate measurement of direction of flight, and low rate-of-fire and lack of automatic following by the guns.

Repulse was even weaker, for she was an old ship and had only four single 4-inch anti-aircraft guns. (She also had three triple

Prince of Wales leaving Singapore. (*Imperial War Museum, A29068*)

4-inch mountings, but these were intended for use against surface ships and were of almost no anti-aircraft value.) None of the destroyers was capable of predicted anti-aircraft fire, although they could put up a barrage at low elevation for their own protection, which might possibly help the capital ships they were screening.

The picture was a little brighter with close-range automatic weapons, for *Prince of Wales* had six 8-barrelled pom-poms and *Repulse* three, each with its own director and, in the case of *Prince of Wales*, with radar ranging fitted (though in fact only one of the six radars was operational at the time of the action). *Prince of Wales* also originally had eighteen 20mm Oerlikons, and she picked up four more at Greenock before she sailed for the Far East. In Colombo the battleship embarked a hand-aimed 40mm Bofors gun borrowed from the army, and this was mounted on her quarterdeck in Singapore before the final sortie. *Repulse* was much worse off, being armed with only six 20mm Oerlikons and four 0.5-inch four-barrelled Vickers machine-guns. The difficulty was the short effective range of all these visually-aimed guns.

To make matters worse, *Prince of Wales* was far from being an efficient ship. Soon after commissioning she had been hustled out to fight the *Bismarck* and had suffered severe damage. After being repaired she had been used to carry Churchill and his staff to the Atlantic Charter meeting with President Roosevelt, and after taking part in a Malta convoy in September 1941 she had commenced her long voyage round South Africa to Singapore. There were no suitable targets for practice firings on the way, and it was a sadly inefficient ship which arrived in Singapore. It was thus most unlikely that the gunfire of the Eastern Fleet would be capable of beating off a well-conducted air attack.

As he was about to sail Phillips was informed that the fighter cover he had asked for off Singora was doubtful, and soon after he left harbour a message came from the RAF commander that he regretted that 'fighter protection impossible'. Phillips' only outward reaction was the comment: 'Well, we must get on without it'. At 1.25 a.m. the following morning—9 December—a signal from his Chief of Staff confirmed that the fighters could not be provided and that Kota Bharu airfield in northern Malaya had been captured by the Japanese. Palliser added that the Japanese were now believed to have large bomber forces in Indo-China and possibly in Thailand, and that there might be two Japanese carriers off Saigon—a false report, as it turned out.

The air force in Malaya had never been brought up to the level local commanders thought necessary. In October 1940 a proposal was made to increase the establishment to 556 aircraft, but with heavy commitments elsewhere there was no chance of this being achieved. Thus when war broke out in December 1941 there were only 241 serviceable aircraft (153 with squadrons and 88 in reserve) in Singapore and Malaya, and none were front-rank. For reconnaissance there were three Catalinas, for bombing (and some assistance with reconnaissance) there were four squadrons of Blenheims manned by the RAF, and two squadrons of Hudsons of the RAAF, supplemented by two squadrons of very obsolete Vildebeeste torpedo-bombers. There were four squadrons of fighters— one RAF, two Australian and one New Zealand—all equipped with Brewster Buffaloes. The Buffalo was an American carrier type which remained outclassed in every respect except armour by the Japanese Zeke fighters. To add to the problems the fighter pilots were, almost without exception, very inexperienced.

Phillips' plan had been based on air cover and surprise, and now the first of his requirements was gone. He had already decided to continue with the operation as long as he had some chance of achieving surprise, hoping to be able to dash into Singora at high speed with his capital ships alone. He correctly discounted the significance of the two aircraft carriers (even if they were off Saigon they were too far away to be relevant), and thought that the Japanese bombers (which he believed would be army) were unlikely to be carrying torpedoes or armour-piercing bombs, and that he would have to face only hastily-organised attacks during his withdrawal. All this, of course, depended on his ships avoiding detection during the approach.

At 6.20 a.m. on 9 December a lookout in the destroyer *Vampire* sighted an aircraft for a few seconds before it disappeared into cloud. As the weather was bad, with rain squalls and low cloud, Phillips hoped that he had not been sighted and held on to the northward. Later in the day the weather cleared, and three Japanese seaplanes were sighted. All chance of surprise now appeared to be lost. In assuming the worst, Phillips was right—but for the wrong reasons. It later transpired that no report from these seaplanes (which were from the cruisers in the covering force) ever reached the Japanese bombers in Indo-China. Force Z had, however, been sighted by the submarine *I–65* soon after 1.30 p.m. and the report reached the Japanese bomber bases some two-and-a-half hours later.

The bombers were being loaded with bombs for an attack on Singapore, and although frantic efforts were made to exchange the bombs for torpedoes it was not until after 6 p.m. that the aircraft were ready. By this time the sun had set and it was getting dark, but so seriously did the Japanese regard the threat to their invasion shipping that it was decided to attack by night. The result was a fiasco because the aircraft failed to find the British ships and nearly attacked one of the cruisers in the Japanese covering force (actually the flagship of Rear-Admiral Ozawa). After this incident the bombers were recalled, and all returned safely to their bases by midnight.

Unaware of the failed Japanese strike, Phillips continued towards Singora and it was not until 8.15 p.m. that he abandoned his plan and set course for Singapore, without breaking radio silence to inform Singapore of his intentions. This was an extraordinary decision, for he was making a radical change of plan because he believed the Japanese knew where he was, yet he would not break radio silence (which might give away his position) so that he could inform his colleagues of what he was doing.[14]

During the evening Phillips received a stream of disturbing reports from Singapore about the progress of the fighting in northern Malaya, and at 11.35 p.m. he received the message: 'Enemy reported landing Kuantan'. If the Japanese were allowed to establish themselves only 150 miles from Singapore they might be able to cut the army's communications with northern Malaya. Phillips thought he had a good chance of smashing a landing at Kuantan, for it was not far off his return route to Singapore and was more than 400 miles from the nearest Japanese air base. So shortly before 1 a.m. he altered course and increased speed to 25 knots.

Again, Phillips did not inform Singapore of his decision. Being anxious not to break radio silence, he apparently expected that Palliser would realise that he would have abandoned his intention to go to Kota Bharu and would instead be going to Kuantan. Palliser in fact naturally assumed that Phillips was following his original plan, for Phillips had not told him of the sightings by Japanese reconnaissance aircraft, and the only message Palliser received was at 8 a.m. on 10 December from the destroyer *Tenedos*. This message, which Phillips had given to *Tenedos* the previous day before the Japanese seaplanes were sighted, asked for all available destroyers to meet Phillips on his way back to Singapore, the timing of the rendezvous being compatible with a prior attack on the shipping off Kota Bharu. Soon after noon Palliser found out where Phillips really was,[15] as messages came into the war room in Singapore in rapid succession which painted a tragic and almost incredible picture.

Phillips had not, as he had hoped, been successful in concealing his whereabouts during the night, for his ships were sighted and unsuccessfully attacked by submarine *I-58* shortly after 2 a.m. Kondo realised, when he reviewed Phillips' position as given by the submarine and its report that the British were on a southerly course, that Phillips' fleet was out of reach of his surface ships. But the 22nd Air Flotilla could get there, even though by dawn the British ships would be more than 400 miles from the nearest Japanese naval airfields.[16] The weapons available to the Japanese squadrons were 250kg and 500kg bombs, and two types of 18-inch torpedoes—the Type 91 Model 1 with a 170kg warhead, and the Model 2 with a 204kg warhead, the latter roughly the same size as the warhead on the British 18-inch torpedo. The bombs were not armour-piercing, for all the available bombs of that type had been directed to the Pearl Harbor attack.

Soon after 5 a.m. the reconnaissance aircraft—nine Nells from the Genzan group—took off to search a forty-degree arc to a distance of 600 miles. The centre of the search arc was pointed towards Phillips' expected position on the assumption that he was heading for Singapore. The reconnaissance aircraft were followed a little more than an hour later by the leading elements of a strike force of 34 bombers and 51 torpedo-bombers from the three air groups—a total of 85 aircraft. Meanwhile Phillips was approaching Kuantan. All seemed peaceful. The destroyer *Express* was sent to search the harbour, but found nothing untoward. Phillips then decided to have a closer look at a tug towing some barges, which had been sighted earlier, but before this could be accomplished the Japanese aircraft struck.

127

Nakajima G3M2 'Nell' bombers. (*National Archives, 80-G-179013*)

Because of the poor visibility and Phillips' change of plan the Japanese reconnaissance aircraft had experienced difficulty in finding the Eastern Fleet. It was not until 10.20 a.m. that it was sighted, the location being helped by the Japanese aircraft following a Walrus amphibian which had been launched by *Repulse* to fly an anti-submarine patrol, and was returning to Force Z to report (by flashing light, the use of radio being forbidden) the sighting of a small steamer.

The Japanese striking force had by that time searched as far south as the Anamba islands (190 miles north-east of Singapore), and was turning north. The bombing squadron of the Genzan group attacked by mistake the destroyer *Tenedos*, which was south of the Anamba islands on her way back to Singapore to refuel; the attacks did no damage. The picture was confused for the Japanese because, while the reconnaissance aircraft off Kuantan was accurately describing the British force, the report from the squadron which had attacked *Tenedos* 150 miles to the southward claimed that they 'had finished bombing of the enemy's main force', and it was not until 11.40 a.m. that the strike force was informed that the Kuantan report was the correct one.

The Japanese strike squadrons had been sent out in a 'search and attack' formation, with each squadron required to search an arc in the direction of the targets, but they were heading too far to the southward because of the assumption that Phillips was heading for Singapore. By the time the Kuantan sighting report was received the strike aircraft were loosely strung out over a considerable distance in squadrons of eight or nine aircraft. They headed to the northward to investigate the contact. Their fuel situation was critical, and they could not have searched for much longer.

The Japanese reconnaissance aircraft which sighted Force Z was also seen by that force, and the British ships were fully alerted by the attack on *Tenedos*. From 10.30 a.m. onwards the British radar[17] detected large numbers of aircraft approaching from the south, and at 11.15 a.m. the ships opened a heavy fire on the first squadron of eight Japanese high-level formation-bombers of the Mihoro Group. (Phillips had still not told Singapore where he was, that he was under attack, that Kuantan was not being invaded, or asked for fighter cover.) Despite the heavy anti-aircraft fire, and considerable splinter damage to the attacking aircraft, the Japanese level-bombers flew on apparently quite unperturbed and dropped a very accurate pattern of bombs on *Repulse*. One 500-pound bomb hit *Repulse* and temporarily reduced her speed, but she was not very seriously damaged.

Twenty minutes later the two torpedo-bomber squadrons of the Genzan Group arrived, attacking in succession from just ahead of the port beam of the British ships, and surprising them by dropping their torpedoes from up to 300 or 400 feet instead of the 30 feet which was the practice with British torpedo-bombers. *Repulse* was in a loose station about half-a-mile on the starboard quarter of *Prince of Wales*, and she turned away from the attack and evaded the torpedoes. *Prince of Wales* was late in reacting, and instead of turning away she turned towards the attacking aircraft, probably because of concern about *Repulse* hovering on her starboard quarter. Whatever the cause, *Prince of Wales* failed to comb the torpedo tracks and was hit by two torpedoes, one on the port side opposite the after 14-inch turret, in her armoured belt, and the other near the port-side propellers. The effects were disastrous.

The A-bracket supporting the propeller shaft was broken, and the bent shaft thrashed around for some time before the engine could be stopped. Several of the machinery spaces were flooded, both port-side propeller shafts were stopped and her speed dropped to fifteen knots. Within a few minutes *Prince of Wales* was listing heavily and all but one of the 5.25-inch turrets was out of action, which was remarkable damage considering the small size of the

Japanese torpedo-warheads. One Japanese torpedo-bomber had been shot down.

Only a few minutes later, at 11.56 a.m., another squadron of nine torpedo-bombers of the Mihoro Group attacked *Repulse*. This time *Repulse* turned towards the attacking aircraft and again was successful in combing the torpedo tracks. The pilot of a Hudson reconnaissance aircraft, which had arrived in the area and had stayed to watch the attacks with increasing dismay, said later that it 'seemed a sheer miracle watching *Repulse* comb 19 torpedoes aimed at her by four waves of attackers'.[18] While *Repulse* was turning to avoid the torpedoes a level-bomber squadron of the Mihoro Group attacked with 250kg bombs, but this time the attack—although again accurate—was unsuccessful.

The situation confronting Captain Tennant, of *Repulse*, was that his ship was still operational, but the flagship seemed completely disabled. He did not know what messages, if any, Phillips had sent, or indeed if he was still able to transmit at all. At 11.58 a.m. Tennant therefore signalled to Singapore 'enemy aircraft bombing'. This was the first indication that the Singapore war room or the air force had had that Force Z was being attacked. The thirteen Buffaloes of No.453 Squadron, RAAF, at Sembawang airfield on Singapore island had been ordered to be ready to give fighter protection to Force Z as it approached Singapore, and although they responded to the call with admirable promptness it was already too late.

After sending the signal to Singapore, Tennant closed in on *Prince of Wales* to see if any assistance could be given. The flagship was a sorry sight, with a heavy list to port and her quarterdeck awash. Another attack by torpedo-bombers was developing from the starboard side of the two capital ships. The Japanese attack, this time by Betty bombers of the Kanoya Group carrying Model 2 torpedoes, was beautifully executed. When about 6000 yards away—beyond effective gunfire range—the squadron split in half, four aircraft apparently making for *Repulse* and the other four for *Prince of Wales*. *Repulse* turned towards the four aircraft which were threatening her, but when she was committed to the turn the four aircraft which had been heading for *Prince of Wales* suddenly turned and attacked *Repulse* from the port side. Tennant could do nothing, and the battlecruiser was hit squarely amidships. Meanwhile the four aircraft which had made the diversion flew on and attacked the wallowing *Prince of Wales*, scoring three or four hits. Her speed dropped to eight knots, and she was evidently in dire straits.

Repulse bore her hit well, and was still able to manoeuvre at 25 knots, but her luck was running out. At 12.26 p.m. another torpedo-squadron attacked, the three flights coming in from different directions. A hit by one torpedo jammed *Repulse*'s steering gear, and although she could still steam at more than twenty knots she had no chance of avoiding the blows that were raining on her. Three more torpedoes hit her in rapid succession, and she was clearly sinking. Tennant ordered all men up from below, and gave instructions for the release of the life-floats. The ship hung for several minutes with a list of about 60 or 70 degrees to port and then rolled over at 12.33.[19] The destroyers rescued nearly two-thirds of her ship's company. It had been less than two hours since the first Japanese attack.

Meanwhile *Prince of Wales* was steaming north at eight knots. Ten minutes after *Repulse* capsized a formation of nine level-bombers attacked the flagship, hitting her with one bomb which failed to penetrate the armoured deck. Nevertheless *Prince of Wales* was doomed, for the battleship was settling rapidly, though desperate signals were sent to Singapore for tugs. The destroyer *Express* went alongside her starboard quarter to rescue the wounded and the men not required to fight the ship. At 1.10 p.m. the order was given to abandon ship, and ten minutes later the battleship suddenly capsized and sank, the destroyers rescuing 1285 of her total complement of 1612, though Phillips was not among the survivors.

Five Buffalo fighters from 453 Fighter Squadron at Sembawang arrived on the scene as *Prince of Wales* sank. They had responded promptly, arriving a little more than an hour after the first alarm from *Repulse*, but it was too late. The two capital ships had gone, and the Japanese aircraft were no longer attacking, making no attempt to molest the destroyers in their rescue work. One of the Buffalo pilots was very impressed with the high morale of the survivors in the water, reporting that most of them waved at him as he flew over; he did not realise that they were shaking their fists at him, blaming the air force for the errors of their admiral.

On their way back to Singapore with the survivors the British destroyers met four of the US destroyers which Admiral Hart had promised. They were a day too late to help *Prince of Wales* and *Repulse*. Churchill has recalled that in all the war he never received a more direct shock than when he was told of the loss of the two capital ships, but he must take much of the blame. The purpose for which the ships had been sent to Singapore—to deter the Japanese from entering the war—had failed, but two days later, with an invasion of Malaya in progress, Churchill and his advisers were debating where the ships should retreat to, without giving Phillips any indication of their thoughts.

Survivors of *Prince of Wales* being rescued by the destroyer *Express*. (*Imperial War Museum, HU2675*)

In the first week of the Pacific war the Japanese, by sinking two capital ships in the open sea by air attack, had been able to achieve what until then no-one else had ever seriously attempted.[20] Moreover, the Japanese had made the attack more than 400 miles from their bases, a distance at which ships until then had felt safe from heavy air attack. The Japanese achieved their results by accuracy rather than by swamping the defence, for their squadrons—usually of eight or nine aircraft—attacked successively without any attempt at coordination, and at fairly long intervals. The four torpedo squadrons (50 aircraft) scored at least ten hits, an exceptionally high proportion.

Could fighters have saved *Prince of Wales* and *Repulse*? During the Second World War daylight-bombing attacks without fighter escort were almost never successful—or anyway incurred heavy casualties—if the target was defended by high-performance fighters, efficient radar and effective direction of the fighter defence by radio. The Japanese strike force had no fighter escort and its method of attack would have provided perfect targets for efficient fighters. At the very least fighter attacks would have broken up the Japanese formations and made the avoidance of torpedoes much

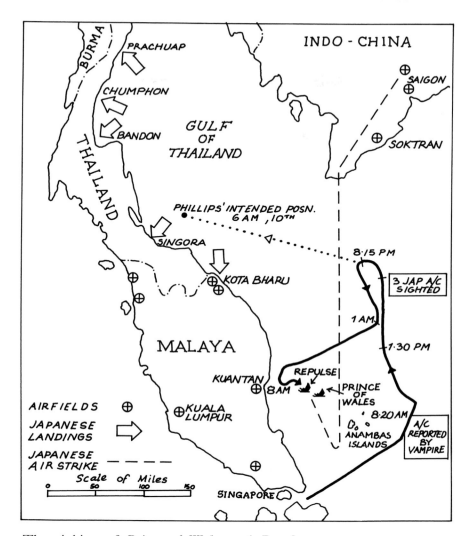

The sinking of *Prince of Wales* and *Repulse*

easier. A Japanese authority says that 'it was completely incredible that the two ships should be left naked to attack from the skies. Interception of our level and torpedo bombers by British fighters might have seriously disrupted our attack'.[21]

Where could fighters have come from? If *Indomitable* had been able to join Phillips' fleet, she would have had 21 fighters (twelve Fulmars and nine Sea Hurricanes). With no requirement to provide escorts for the carrier's bombers, all these fighters would have been available for defence, and *Indomitable* was fitted with the necessary air-warning radar and voice radio to direct them. The Sea Hurricanes had the performance to catch the Nell and Betty bombers (though the Fulmars would have been stretched), so the fighters should certainly have been able to prevent the Japanese from using the tactics they did. Nevertheless it would not have been easy.

It must be realised that if the Japanese had known that an aircraft carrier was part of Force Z they almost certainly would have provided escorting Zeke fighters, of which there were 25 available. The Zekes had the range to escort the bombers to Kuantan, and they would have made short work of the Fulmars and Sea Hurricanes. The most likely result, had *Indomitable* been present, was that she too would have been sunk, for the Japanese torpedo-bombers would have accorded a high priority to an aircraft carrier, and *Indomitable* was very vulnerable to torpedo hits, as was shown when she nearly sank after being hit by a single aircraft-launched torpedo in the Mediterranean in 1943.

Even without *Indomitable*, Phillips could have had fighter cover from daylight on 10 December had he not been so determined to preserve radio silence. There were thirteen Buffaloes at Sembawang standing by to support him, and although these were not great fighters they should have been able to break up the Japanese attacks. Even when he knew he had been sighted—at 10.20 a.m.—Phillips still did not ask for air cover. If he had asked for fighters then, they would almost certainly have arrived before the first Japanese torpedo-bombers attacked. *Prince of Wales* had no qualified or experienced fighter-direction officers and the poor performance and armament of the Buffaloes (four 0.303-inch machine-guns) would have further limited their effectiveness, but they would surely have achieved something. They might not have been able to save the two ships, but they should have been able to make the Japanese pay for their success.

A great deal of the blame for the disaster must rest with Phillips, who on several key occasions behaved with remarkable incompetence. Few of his seniors or contemporaries considered him to be an able seagoing admiral,[22] except possibly Pound. He had seriously underestimated the threat of air attack on ships, though in fairness it must be pointed out that at this stage of the war no capital ship at sea had been sunk by air attack. It was apparently his view that the many smaller ships which had been sunk or seriously damaged by air attack had been unlucky to be caught alone, or else had not been well handled or had shown insufficient resolution. Sir Hastings Ismay, the Chief of Staff in the office of the Minister of Defence who had many dealings with Phillips, recorded that he 'refused to admit that properly armed and well-fought ships had anything to fear from air power'.[23]

Yet some of the criticism of Phillips is undeserved. Faced with the position of the Eastern Fleet, it is certain that any other British admiral would have reacted in the same way that Phillips did. Only the Admiralty (or Churchill) could have stopped him, but although the Admiralty was informed of Phillips' intentions, no such action was taken. As we have seen, they were 'sleeping on it'. Some admirals might have thought twice when they were told that fighter cover would not be available, but it is worth noting that one of Phillips' severest critics, Sir James Somerville, was to take much greater risks off Ceylon four months later. Somerville was lucky, while Phillips was not. As for the diversion to Kuantan, it is inconceivable that any British admiral, hearing of a landing there, would not have made the minor alteration of course to investigate the report.

These were not the faults for which Phillips stood to be criticised, but there were others for which he should be. One of the most important requirements of a successful admiral is the ability to judge what his enemy is capable of, and Phillips grossly underestimated the Japanese—even if, curiously, he grossly overestimated their ability to fix his position if he transmitted on his radio. It is true that intelligence reports gave Phillips a misleading picture, but after the extraordinary Japanese success at Pearl Harbor he should have been wary of such assessments. It is surprising, after his long career in staff appointments, that he was not more aware of the limitations of intelligence assessments. As it was, he conducted the operation like an old-fashioned simulated war game, where the briefest high-frequency radio transmissions inevitably gave away one's position and it was unthinkable that the weapons of the opposition would exceed their laid-down performance. The real world is not like that, but even when Phillips was told that Japanese torpedo-bombers were about to attack his ships, he refused to accept it, claiming that 'there are no torpedo aircraft about'.[24]

Then there was his mania for radio silence, whatever the tactical cost to himself (there is no evidence that any of the British radio transmissions were detected and plotted by the Japanese). His failures to inform the Singapore war room of his change of objective, to ask for the fighter cover which he knew (or should have known) could probably be provided off Kuantan, and to tell Singapore (even after he knew he had been located) that there was no Japanese landing at Kuantan, were bizarre.[25] He seems to have ignored the possibility that his movements would be reported by Japanese submarines, though he was worried about being attacked by them, which was reasonable considering his exiguous destroyer screen. Yet he seems to have assessed the possibility of achieving surprise at Kota Bharu solely on whether he was located by aircraft, though he knew there were quite a number of Japanese submarines operating in the Gulf of Thailand. All in all, it was a very poor performance.[26]

Why did he not ask for fighter support? After all, he had made a big issue of it in his original plan to attack the Singora and Kota Bharu landings. It has been suggested that he thought Rear-Admiral Palliser, in Singapore, would divine that the report of the Kuantan landing would cause him to change his objective, and that Palliser would organise air cover over Kuantan from the early hours of 10 December; and from this that the absence of air cover when they arrived at Kuantan meant that no fighters were available, so that it was pointless to ask for them. Alternatively it has been argued that he misunderstood the message that no fighters would be available (for his Singora/Kota Bharu operation) to mean that no fighters were available anywhere, so again it was pointless to ask for them. Then it has been claimed that Phillips believed that there would be a delay of several hours between a reconnaissance aircraft sighting his fleet and the delivery (after staff contemplation, assessment, arming of aircraft, and transit time) of an effective strike, so there was no urgency about fighter cover. Finally it has been suggested that he might have thought that, as he was beyond the range—so he believed—of Japanese torpedo-carrying aircraft, his ships could survive by means of their armour and anti-aircraft gunfire. It is not possible to determine which of these possibilities dominated Phillips' behaviour, but none of them reflects credit on his tactical sense.

On the equipment side, the performance of the Japanese torpedoes was remarkable, bearing in mind that the warhead of the Model 1 torpedoes was smaller than that of the British 18-inch torpedoes. In the first torpedo attack *Prince of Wales* was hit almost certainly twice (though early reports suggested only one hit), and was mortally wounded.

Despite the installation of radar rangefinders on the directors in *Prince of Wales*, and the widespread fitting of 20mm Oerlikon guns, the British anti-aircraft gunfire was very poor. The Japanese had been prepared to lose a third of their strength in the attack on *Prince of Wales* and *Repulse*. They lost three aircraft.

9

The Channel dash by *Scharnhorst* and *Gneisenau*:

11–12 February 1942

Following a foray into the Atlantic in early 1941 to attack British shipping, the German battleships *Scharnhorst* and *Gneisenau* took refuge in Brest, from where they posed a constant threat to British sea communications across the Atlantic, which were already under almost intolerable strain from U-boats. After definitely locating them on 28 March, the RAF set to work to keep them there. Over the next four months attacks involving more than 1850 British aircraft were made, and although the full results were not known at the time (and hence considerable anxiety remained) in fact the German ships were almost continuously immobilised.

Although the threat to British shipping posed by the two battleships never materialised, it nonetheless sufficed to tie up a large number of British ships and aircraft. By the end of 1941, however, Hitler had persuaded himself that a British invasion of Norway was imminent and that the Brest squadron must return to Germany. Admiral Raeder, with his usual strategic insight, opposed the move, but Hitler was adamant. If such a move was held to be impossible, he decided, then the ships must be paid off and the guns and crews sent to Norway.

At a conference on 12 January 1942 Hitler approved a plan put forward by Vice-Admiral Ciliax, the Commanding Admiral of Battleships, proposing that the ships break through the Dover Straits. Ciliax insisted that there should be a minimum of naval movements before the attempt, so as not to compromise surprise. He also planned to leave Brest after dark, again so as to maintain surprise for as long as possible, even though this would mean passing the straits—the narrowest part of the English Channel—in daylight.[1] Because of this, very strong fighter support would be required from dawn to dusk. Hitler was in full agreement with all these proposals and directed the Luftwaffe to do everything in its power to ensure the safety of the ships.

The arrangements for the fighter defence of the ships was in the hands of Adolf Galland, who in two years had risen from First Lieutenant to General of the Fighter Arm of the Luftwaffe, and was still aged only 30. He had 250 day fighters under his direct orders, along with 30 night fighters for the dawn and dusk periods. He made most elaborate arrangements for their control, and for switching them between airfields if the ships were unable to maintain their schedule. Under the measures he instituted, there was to be a minimum of sixteen and a maximum of 32 fighters over the ships at any time. In order to maintain surprise for as long as possible the fighters were also to remain at low altitude and keep radio silence.

General Martini, the radar expert of the Luftwaffe, arranged to jam the British radar stations, but this was not to start until 9 a.m. on the day of the breakthrough so as to avoid arousing the suspicions of the British. Hitler had said that he considered the air threat to have been exaggerated by Ciliax, and that he did not believe the British were capable of making and carrying out the 'lightning decisions' necessary if they were to attack the ships successfully in the Dover Straits. The results certainly supported this shrewd opinion.

The period between 7 and 15 February was fixed for the operation, because the tidal conditions would then be most favourable. The major ships were fitted with additional close-range anti-aircraft guns for the trip—sixteen more 20mm guns (in quadruple mountings) in the battleships, giving them a total of 34 guns of this size, while the cruiser *Prinz Eugen* had as many as 64 20mm guns. The crews were augmented by naval coastal gunners, who brought the quadruple 20mm mountings with them. All was ready by the planned date. Now they had to wait for a weather forecast which promised poor visibility over British airfields and the channel.

By the end of January 1942 decoded messages had alerted British intelligence that the German ships in Brest were about to make some sort of move, probably back to Germany. Both the Admiralty and the Air Ministry came to the conclusion that the Germans were most likely to attempt to break through the Straits of Dover, for the low state of training of the German ships and the strength of the Home Fleet made it extremely unlikely that they would attempt to pass around the north of Scotland. An Admiralty appreciation concluded that 'we might well therefore find the two battleships and the eight-inch cruiser . . . with twenty fighters constantly overhead . . . proceeding up channel'.[2]

The key to the defence was obviously the Straits of Dover, where the naval commander was Vice-Admiral Sir Bertram Ramsay (of Dunkirk fame). All he had at his disposal were a few motor torpedo-boats and gunboats, although the Admiralty did arrange for six destroyers to be held at Harwich ready to reinforce him at short notice. Ramsay also managed to obtain a further reinforcement of six Swordfish torpedo-bombers of 825 Squadron. Even then these forces were meagre, but they were all that could be spared because until it was certain that the German ships were coming out the convoys could not be deprived of their escorts.

The Home Fleet could not give any assistance to Ramsay, for at this time it was at a very low ebb itself. The battleship *Tirpitz* was in Norwegian waters and the Home Fleet had both to protect the convoys to Russia and also to guard against the possibility of *Tirpitz* breaking out into the Atlantic. Nor was this all. A large troop convoy was about to sail for the Middle East, and the Home Fleet had to provide cover for it as it passed Brest in case *Scharnhorst* and *Gneisenau* should, after all, be intending to make a foray into the Atlantic. The Home Fleet could do nothing to prevent the Germans breaking eastwards up the channel.

Ramsay came to the conclusion that the Germans were most likely to use darkness to cover their approach, passing through the straits at daybreak or shortly afterwards. If the Germans followed the best route, Ramsay could not rely on the shore radar stations detecting them much more than an hour before they reached the straits. He therefore planned to mount a combined attack by his torpedo-boats and Swordfish as the Germans passed Dover, followed some time later by his six destroyers from Harwich. Level-bombing attacks were to be made at the same time by Bomber Command, and additional strikes by Coastal Command torpedo-bombers. The whole plan was known as 'Operation Fuller'.

On 7 February the long-range weather forecast was at last reasonably favourable for the Germans, and the order was given for the ships to sail on 11 February. Ciliax's plan for *Scharnhorst*, *Gneisenau* and *Prinz Eugen*, escorted by six destroyers, to get under way at 7.30 p.m. was, however, almost derailed by a routine Bomber Command raid on the harbour by sixteen Wellington bombers. As soon as the raid started Ciliax cancelled the order to sail. After the 'all clear' was sounded at 9 p.m. he decided to sail at once, despite being 90 minutes behind schedule. He cleared the harbour at 10.45 p.m. and shortly after midnight altered course up the Channel, increasing speed to 27 knots.

The night was pitch-dark, the sea was smooth, and the ships—having caught up the lost time—were off Cherbourg by dawn, when the first escort of fighters arrived on station. These fighters were controlled from radar stations in France, not from the ships, for although each of the three heavy ships had an air-warning radar set and a Luftwaffe liaison officer, they were not organised to direct the fighters. Anyway, the skies were clear of British aircraft for the present. After sunrise two more squadrons of torpedo-boats and a squadron of coastal craft joined the German armada of 30 ships sweeping up the Channel.

How had Ciliax escaped detection after more than ten hours at sea? Hudsons from Coastal Command were flying a series of patrols which certainly should have detected the German ships if the ASV Mark 2 radar sets in the aircraft had worked. These patrols should have been adequate, but on the night of 11 February and the early hours of the following morning a succession of mischances occurred in which the radar sets in two out of three patrols malfunctioned. Replacement aircraft were sent out either too late or not at all (in the latter case without Ramsay being told), while the third patrol was recalled prematurely because ground fog had been predicted in southern England. The outcome was that Ciliax was able to penetrate all three patrol lines without detection.

Although some signs of unusual activity were noted, there was still nothing to indicate clearly to the authorities in England that the German battleships were moving. At 9.20 a.m. jamming of British radar stations began rather ineffectively, but this sort of apparently random interference had been going on for some time and no particular significance was attached to it at first. Numerous German aircraft—Ciliax's fighter escort—were detected north of Le Havre between 8.25 a.m. and 10 a.m., but such detections were also quite common and caused no great concern. Thus it came about that the first report of Ciliax to be received by Ramsay came from the radar station at Hastings, which at 10.45 a.m. detected a group of ships off Cape Griz Nez, 27 miles away.[3] Although the targets located could not be positively identified, it was clear from the range of detection that they must be large ships. Ramsay therefore sent an alerting order to his Swordfish and warned the RAF.

Fortunately the RAF was already looking into what was going on off the French coast. Suspicion had been aroused by the German jamming,[4] and a reconnaissance mission was sent out at 10.20 a.m. to search between Boulogne and Fécamp. A Spitfire soon sighted and reported what the pilot thought was a convoy of

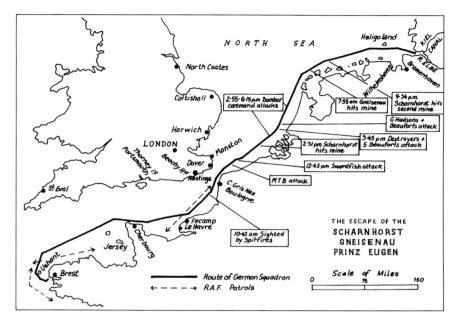

The escape of *Scharnhorst, Gneisenau* and *Prinz Eugen*

25–30 small vessels, but there was no mention of *Scharnhorst, Gneisenau* or *Prinz Eugen*. The report reached Ramsay at 11.05 a.m. but did nothing to clarify the situation. It was not until after the pilot had landed and was being debriefed that he said that one of the ships seemed to have a tripod mast and high superstructure, but by that time the Germans had been identified from another source.

At 10.10 a.m. Group Captain Beamish, commanding the RAF station at Kenley, and another pilot had taken off in their Spitfires to enliven an otherwise dull day by making a sweep across the channel in the hope of 'picking up a stray Hun'. The two British pilots were in hot pursuit of two German fighters when they stumbled across Ciliax's fleet. The time was 10.42 a.m. Although he had no idea that a move by the German battleships was expected, Beamish immediately realised the importance of what he had seen. However, Fighter Command orders laid down that aircraft were not to break radio silence so it was not until he had landed at 11.09 a.m.—having survived heavy anti-aircraft fire and shaking off the attacks of German fighters—that he made his report.

This delay was a most peculiar decision by Beamish. The relevant Fighter Command orders, dated 5 October 1941 and actually signed by Beamish as Senior Air Staff Officer, decreed that 'R/T . . . silence is to be maintained on the outward journey, except in emergency, until such time as the enemy is engaged'. The purpose of the order was to avoid the risk that enemy forces would realise that they had been sighted, but one would have thought that in the circumstances an officer of group captain seniority could have used the 'emergency' escape clause and given the alarm.[5]

Once Beamish's report was received the long-prepared plan for dealing with the German battleships was set in motion, but time was fatally short. The first attack on the German ships was made by five motor torpedo-boats from Dover. The German defences—fighter aircraft, destroyers and E-boats—were much too strong, and the British craft were unable to get near the battleships. They fired their torpedoes from very long range, and the Germans had no difficulty in avoiding them.

At 12.45 p.m., just as the last of the torpedo-boats was attacking, the six Swordfish from Manston appeared. The squadron commander, Lieutenant-Commander Esmonde, had been warned two hours before that there might be a suitable target for him. The attack, of course, would have to be in daylight, when the lumbering Swordfish would be easy targets, but the need was obvious and Esmonde had no hesitation in volunteering to attack. He immediately brought his squadron to readiness, and ordered the torpedoes to be set to run deep—for battleships.

By 11.25 a.m. Ramsay had received Beamish's definite identification of the German battleships and ordered Esmonde to attack, for it was urgent that torpedo hits should be obtained to slow them down. Ramsay considered a suggestion that the Swordfish should be delayed for 90 minutes so they could make a coordinated attack with the Coastal Command's torpedo-carrying Beauforts, but the Germans were already in the Dover Straits and increasing their distance from Manston with every passing minute. Ramsay realised, of course, that an unsupported daylight attack by six Swordfish was a forlorn undertaking, and he asked No.11 Group of Fighter Command to provide the maximum fighter escort. He was promised five squadrons, three to escort the Swordfish and two to attack the German ships in an attempt to divert their anti-aircraft gunfire while the Swordfish dropped their torpedoes.

Esmonde's squadron was not sufficiently trained to be able to carry out a synchronised attack, making full use of cloud cover and using radar to find the German ships. He decided therefore that his best chance of hitting the Germans was to bring his six aircraft in loose column, flying as low as possible to delay radar detection by the ships. The promised fighters were due at 12.25 p.m. and when the first squadron of ten aircraft arrived three minutes later Esmonde, who had been warned that some of the fighters might be delayed, decided he could wait no longer.[6]

After twenty minutes flying Esmonde sighted the German fleet. The heavy ships were in column, with *Prinz Eugen* leading followed by *Scharnhorst* and *Gneisenau,* and a strong screen of destroyers and E-boats protecting each flank. Esmonde led his squadron straight towards the enemy but the odds were overwhelming. The few escorting Spitfires could not hold off the Germans, and his slow biplanes were easy targets for the German fighters and anti-aircraft guns. All six Swordfish were lost, and although three at least were known to have dropped their torpedo before crashing there were no hits scored on the German ships.

The only other available torpedo-bombers were three squadrons of twin-engined Beauforts belonging to Coastal Command. One of these squadrons (No.86) and part of another (No.217) were in Cornwall and the German ships were already beyond their range. The third squadron—No.42—had until two days before been held in Scotland at Admiralty insistence, in order to provide a striking force if *Tirpitz* made a move. Ordered south on 10 February the squadron's move was delayed by snow-covered airfields, and when the first alarm was given at 11.30 a.m. on 12 February the squadron was just coming in to land at an airfield in Norfolk. Thus, the only Beauforts immediately available were seven from No.217 Squadron which had not been sent to Cornwall and remained based at Thorney Island, near Portsmouth.

The attack was a muddle from the start. Two of the Beauforts were already loaded with bombs, and could not be made ready in time, and a third was unserviceable, reducing the attacking force to a puny four aircraft. The crews were briefed by a staff officer who showed more concern for secrecy than commonsense, for he told them they were to attack 'three big enemy merchantmen' whose speed was given as eight to ten knots. Various delays made them late for their rendezvous with the fighter escort, and an attempt was made to recover the lost time by ordering both the Beauforts and the fighters not to go to the rendezvous but to head straight for the position of the German ships. Owing to a communications muddle this order was not received by the Beauforts,[7] so they naturally carried on to the rendezvous where they waited for their fighter escort.

Two of the Beauforts eventually tired of waiting and set off towards the target area. They had no idea that they were to attack German battleships, and as in any case they looked in the wrong area—they assumed, of course, that their targets were doing not more than ten knots, whereas Ciliax was making 27. They found nothing. The other two Beauforts landed at the nearby airfield of Manston, and there they found out for the first time the nature and position of their targets. At 3.40 p.m., about the same time as Ramsay's six destroyers from Harwich were attacking, they dropped their torpedoes at a large warship (probably *Prinz Eugen*) but like the destroyers they achieved nothing.

As it turned out, they were not the first Beauforts to attack. The three stragglers left behind at Thorney Island had been made ready, and set off an hour after the first four. They had not been promised a fighter escort, so they headed straight for the German ships. By this time *Scharnhorst* had been damaged by hitting a mine and had dropped astern. The three Beauforts found *Gneisenau* and *Prinz Eugen*, but although they attacked with determination they failed to score a hit. One of the Beauforts was lost and both the others damaged.

By this time Bomber Command aircraft were entering the fray, but it is convenient to follow first the attempts by Coastal Command to launch successful torpedo attacks, for by these alone could the Germans have been stopped. The fourteen Beauforts of No.42 Squadron had landed in Norfolk at 11.30 a.m., but the airfield (Coltishall) was a fighter base, and naturally did not hold torpedoes for the Beauforts. However at North Coates, little more than 100 miles away, not only were there torpedoes but the Mobile Torpedo Servicing Unit, and orders were at once sent for this unit to move to Coltishall. The unit, which had not in fact moved for several years, proved to be anything but mobile, and did not arrive until the German ships were safe in their home waters.

Fortunately, nine of the Beauforts had brought their torpedoes with them from Scotland, and these nine took off at 2.25 p.m. They had been ordered to go first to Manston, where they would meet their fighter escort and some Hudson level-bombers. The Hudsons were to provide diversionary bombing while the Beauforts dropped their torpedoes, and the Beauforts had been ordered to follow the Hudsons to the German ships. Sure enough, when the Beauforts arrived over Manston at 2.50 p.m. they found the Hudsons circling over the airfield, but what followed had elements of pure farce.

The Beauforts tried to form up behind the Hudsons, but at each attempt the Hudsons moved to get behind the Beauforts. The whole formation continued to orbit Manston for over half-an-hour, each element waiting for the other to take the lead. Finally the Beaufort commander decided to set a course, based on information

144

of the enemy's position given to him before he had left Coltishall, and as he turned out to sea with his squadron, six of the Hudsons followed him.[8] The remainder kept circling over Manston until 4 p.m., when they retired to their airfield in Norfolk.

By now the visibility was worsening, with heavy rain and the cloud base below 1000 feet in places. The Beauforts and Hudsons soon lost touch with each other, but both groups managed to find the German ships. The radar-fitted Hudsons located them without difficulty and bombed them from low level, losing two bombers in the process without damaging the Germans. Shortly afterwards eight of the nine Beauforts (who had no radar) found the Germans as a result of skilful navigation, but their attack was fruitless. The ninth Beaufort had by mistake nearly attacked the destroyer *Worcester*, who was reeling out of action heavily damaged after making a torpedo attack on the German ships. The pilot of the Beaufort recognised *Worcester* in time, but he had lost touch with the rest of his squadron and was unable to find the German ships.

By this time the German ships were in some disorder. The flagship *Scharnhorst* had struck a mine and come to a complete standstill. It was at first thought that the battleship would have to be towed to a Dutch port, and Ciliax and his staff were transferred to the destroyer *Z.29*. The other ships by this time were out of sight, and the destroyer set off after them at full speed, but soon after 5 p.m. she developed engine trouble and Ciliax had to transfer his flag again. The transfer was by boat to another destroyer, in a rough sea and with air attacks in progress, and while Ciliax was making his slow passage between destroyers *Scharnhorst* steamed by at full speed, completely ignoring the admiral. Ciliax's irritation at his predicament was tempered by relief that *Scharnhorst*'s damage was so slight.

Evening was now drawing in, and it was becoming evident in England that the Germans were getting away. The two Beaufort squadrons which had been in Cornwall had been ordered to Thorney Island, where they arrived at 2.30 p.m. They were ordered to attack as soon as they had refuelled, linking up with a fighter escort of Beaufighters over Coltishall, but again the arrangements with the fighters went awry. When the Beauforts arrived at the rendezvous at 5 p.m. they could find no sign of their fighters. The Beauforts could not afford to wait, since it would be dark in little more than an hour, so they set off unescorted. Although they searched until it was completely dark, without radar they could find no sign of the German ships.

There remained only Bomber Command. When the warning that a German sortie was imminent had been received on 2 February, all other operations by Bomber Command were stopped and the entire force held at two hours notice. But as the days passed and still the German ships did not move, Bomber Command became impatient, for surely they could not be expected to remain at this level of readiness indefinitely. On 10 February the Commander-in-Chief, Air Marshal Pierse, ordered that 100 bombers were to be maintained at four hours notice and the remainder released for other tasks. (Neither the Admiralty nor Ramsay were informed of this decision.) When the first news of the German sortie was received at 11.30 a.m. on 12 February, the result was that there were no bombers at less than four hours notice.

Even with the aircraft held on notice there were problems, as these had been fitted with armour-piercing bombs which had to be dropped from at least 7000 feet to be effective. The chances of being able to bomb visually from that height were negligible, since there was a thick cloud layer descending to less than 1000 feet. On the other hand, if the bombers did not use armour-piercing bombs it meant abandoning any hope of inflicting mortal damage on the German battleships. Pierse was reluctantly forced to admit that all Bomber Command could do in the circumstances was to try to inflict superficial damage, and to distract attention from the Coastal Command torpedo attacks. He therefore ordered a change of bomb armament, if this could be done without delaying the bombers' departure.

The total strength of Bomber Command at this time was about 300 aircraft. Fifty of these were Whitleys, which were too slow and poorly-armed to be used in daylight, and some of the remainder were snowbound, so the final number available was less than 250. Of these 100 were already preparing to attack the German ships, and although some of the remainder had operated the previous night they could be made ready within four hours and so they too were ordered into the attack. By 2.20 p.m.—less than three hours after the alarm had been given—73 bombers were ready.

In the thick cloud and intermittent rain squalls the squadrons soon became split up, and the attacks were made individually and without coordination. Most of the aircraft of the first wave reached the target area, but not more than ten of them saw the German ships for long enough to drop their bombs and none scored hits. A second group of 134 aircraft began to take off twenty minutes after the first wave. They reached the target area, either singly or in pairs, between 4 p.m. and 5 p.m. but only twenty managed to attack the German ships, again without scoring any hits. A third wave, of 35 aircraft, took off at 4.15 p.m. but only a third of them even saw the German ships.

During the afternoon Bomber Command had launched 242 aircraft against Ciliax's ships—practically every available aircraft except the Whitleys—but only 39 of them managed to drop their bombs and some of these were dropped on British destroyers. Untrained in attacking ships at sea, and hampered by bad visibility, they achieved nothing, and lost fifteen bombers, mostly from the ships' gunfire or from flying into the sea.

In fact, the only damage the Germans suffered was from mines, which had been laid by RAF Bomber Command with some guidance from the code-breakers who had been decrypting some German messages about a newly-swept channel. *Scharnhorst* had been struck at 2.30 p.m., but the damage was not serious and she was soon able to steam at 25 knots. Five hours later *Gneisenau* was mined off Terschilling, but she too was soon able to proceed at high speed. At 9.34 p.m. *Scharnhorst* was mined again, in almost the same position as *Gneisenau*, and this time the damage was serious. She was completely stopped for nearly an hour, and eventually crawled into Wilhelmshaven flooded with more than 1000 tons of sea water. All the German ships had survived.

The escape of the German ships raised a storm of feeling in Britain, with *The Times* declaring in a leading article that 'Vice-Admiral Ciliax has succeeded where the Duke of Medina Sidonia failed . . . Nothing more mortifying to the pride of sea power has happened in Home Waters since the 17th century'.[9] Churchill appointed a Board of Inquiry 'to allay complaints'. There was nothing surprising in this body's findings, especially in view of its purpose. The chief reason for failure was held to be the delay in detecting the German battleships; the main error made by the commanders was the assumption that the Germans would try to pass Dover in darkness; and Bomber Command was not adequately trained for effective attack on fast-moving warships at sea. Although the inquiry did not know of it, Hitler's assessment that the British would not be able to react to events with sufficient speed was very perceptive, much more so than Admiral Raeder's view that if the British 'were even reasonably alert and prepared, [he] could not see how the dash could succeed'.[10]

The comparison with the sinking of *Prince of Wales* and *Repulse*, frequently made at the time, was misleading. The Germans were greatly aided by poor visibility and the ability of their strong fighter escort to prevent coordinated attacks on the few occasions when a considerable group of British aircraft gained contact with the German ships. Even so, it is true that the German anti-aircraft fire was markedly more effective than that of *Prince of Wales* and *Repulse.*

Nevertheless, the performance of the RAF as an anti-shipping strike force at times verged on the farcical. There was a litany of failures: the incompetence of the three anti-shipping patrols; the delays and bungling in getting together the strikes of torpedo-carrying aircraft; the poor performance of Bomber Command in attacking the German ships—although this was not a major factor, for high-level bombing was never effective against ships at sea during the Second World War (despite the exaggerated pre-war expectations); and the poor coordination of strike forces and their escort fighters, who could not even talk to each other on radio, for Fighter Command was still very separate and the fighters were untrained in the role of bomber-escorts. One cannot help thinking that the Japanese Navy's 22nd Air Flotilla would have been a much more formidable foe for the Germans.

Yet the RAF did learn from this and other unsuccessful attacks on German shipping. In June 1942 approval was given to convert some Beaufighters for torpedo-bombing, and they proved much more useful than the Beauforts and Hampdens. By early 1943 Coastal Command was able to launch coordinated attacks by torpedo-carrying Beaufighters (called 'Torbeaus'), sending these to concentrate on a targetted convoy while other Beaufighters carrying bombs, machine-guns and cannon dealt with the escorts. They began to be extremely effective, particularly from June 1943 when the Beaufighters began to be fitted with rockets. A typical attack force of this period would be twelve Torbeaus, covered by sixteen rocket-firing and eight cannon-firing Beaufighters. But in February 1942 this was all some way away in the future.

Although the performance of the Royal Navy and RAF in the action against the German battleships was mediocre, except in the gallantry of individuals, it must be put in the perspective of the other problems facing the British command. The Atlantic battle against the German submarines was desperate, and any British dispositions had to take into account the possibility that the situation might be made catastrophic by *Scharnhorst* and *Gneisenau* making another foray. The new battleship *Tirpitz*, lurking in Norway, had to be watched lest she attacked Russian convoys or broke out into the Atlantic, and Bomber Command was conducting a strategic offensive against Germany to which much weight was attached.

The Admiralty never really seemed to believe that the Germans could be prevented from breaking through the Dover Straits if they could achieve surprise. From the strategic point of view there is no doubt that the Admiralty would rather have had *Scharnhorst* and *Gneisenau* in Germany instead of Brest, where they were a constant nagging threat to British control of the vital trans-Atlantic convoy routes. The result of the German dash up the channel was well summed up by Admiral Raeder. 'Tactically,' he recorded, 'the dash up the Channel was a great success. Strategically, it was an outright defeat.'[11]

10

Ceylon:

3–9 April 1942

For the Allies the first quarter of 1942 was a period of almost unrelenting disaster in the Far East. Everywhere the Japanese were advancing, seemingly irresistible; everywhere the Allies were retreating, their defensive plans in ruins. There was no British or American fleet capable of challenging Nagumo's six aircraft carriers. What the Allied navies needed was time to reorganise, build new ships and repair damaged ones, and to train. Yamamoto realised the importance of striking further blows at the survivors of the American and British fleets before they were reinforced, but he thought it necessary first to establish a defensive perimeter in the south. During February and March Nagumo's carriers were therefore employed for support of the invasion of New Britain, the destruction of Darwin and preventing the evacuation of Java.

In all these operations the carriers performed with devastating efficiency, but the targets were of comparatively minor importance, and time was slipping by. At last, towards the end of March, Yamamoto decided to strike a blow at the renascent British Eastern Fleet, which was believed to be gathering its strength in the peaceful waters of Ceylon. For this operation Yamamoto allocated Nagumo only five carriers, for the *Kaga* had to return to Japan for repairs. To support the carriers Nagumo had four fast battleships, three cruisers and eleven destroyers.

Japanese intelligence had reported that the British fleet in Ceylon waters consisted of two carriers and two battleships, with supporting cruisers and destroyers. Actually, when the new Commander-in-Chief of the Eastern Fleet, Sir James Somerville, arrived in Colombo on 26 March, he had a fleet consisting of the large new carriers *Indomitable* and *Formidable*, the small carrier *Hermes*, five battleships (*Warspite* and four of the *Royal Sovereign* class), seven cruisers and sixteen destroyers.

Although Somerville's fleet was much larger than his previous command (Force H in the Western Mediterranean) he had no illusions regarding its strength. The ships had been hastily assembled, were unpractised in working together, and many were in a low state of operational efficiency. Moreover, the *Royal Sovereign* class ships could not sustain more than sixteen knots in company, and their anti-aircraft armament and deck armour were woefully inadequate. Churchill stigmatised them as 'coffin ships', declaring that 'if they are of no use and only an encumbrance, why don't they get out of the way . . . and give the aircraft carriers their chance?'[1] (This suggestion was not passed on to Somerville.)

The limitations of his battleships were not Somerville's only worries. His carriers had between them only 58 strike aircraft and 33 fighters,[2] which meant he did not have nearly enough fighters both to defend his own ships and to escort his slow biplane strike aircraft. His force also lacked the ability to refuel quickly at sea, and his bases at Colombo and Trincomalee were exposed and vulnerable. His only other possible base was the secret fuelling-anchorage at Addu Atoll in the Maldive Islands, 600 miles south-west of Colombo, but this harbour was quite undefended against air or submarine attack and could only be used as long as its existence was not suspected by the Japanese.

By chance *Indomitable*, *Formidable* and *Illustrious* had been together for a few days the previous November, all of them being repaired in Norfolk Navy Yard in Virginia, and the fighter-direction officers in the three carriers were able to compare notes. Perhaps more importantly, they were also able to obtain efficient voice-radio sets from the Americans. At the same time the Admiralty made the decision that the Type 279 air-warning sets in the large carriers should be replaced by Type 281s, on the grounds that the latter gave better low cover, though at the expense of high-altitude cover.

Another advantage of the Type 281 was that, as a result of having a much narrower horizontal beam width than the Type 279, it could be used with a Plan Position Indicator (PPI). This was a very important aid to fighter direction and had been in use by RAF Fighter Command since late 1940. A PPI consisted of a cathode-ray tube with afterglow characteristics, the trace radiating from the centre and moving in synchrony with the aerial. An operator could thus see continuously on the PPI the plan position of all targets detected by the radar, an immense boon to a fighter director.[3] Supplies of PPIs from the Admiralty were not yet available, but *Illustrious* managed to 'scrounge' one from the RAF in Ceylon. Even though the fighter-direction was improving, there was still no accurate method of determining an attacking aircraft's height[4] so that Nagumo's striking power would surely have overwhelmed the British defences in a daylight carrier battle.

Being an experienced commander of a fleet at sea, Somerville assessed that if the Japanese attacked Ceylon in strength he could do nothing against them and, if he tried, the Eastern Fleet would merely be annihilated. He also decided that, even if the attack was on a smaller scale, it was his duty to keep his force as a fleet-in-being and to avoid having it destroyed 'in penny numbers' by undertaking operations which did not give reasonable prospects of success. Distasteful as these conclusions must have been to so forceful a character as Somerville, they were undoubtedly wise in view of the state of his fleet. His approach, moreover, was supported by the Admiralty.

Meanwhile, the local defences were being reorganised. Admiral Sir Geoffrey Layton, an abrasive man of great determination and force of character, had on 10 March taken over as Commander-in-Chief in Ceylon and set about eliminating inertia and apathy, of which there was plenty. Pending the arrival of Somerville he simultaneously held command of the Eastern Fleet, and used this authority to divert a cargo of Hurricane fighters being transported to Java in the carrier *Indomitable*—to the considerable irritation of the Air Ministry. He also took strong measures inside Ceylon, including the requisitioning of the Colombo golf links and racecourse so that he could build an airfield, demolishing the houses of the Chief Justice and the Army Commander in the process.[5]

Despite all Layton's efforts he had little with which to defend Ceylon. There were two squadrons of Hurricanes at Colombo and another near Trincomalee—a total of about 50 serviceable fighters—and in addition there were a few Fleet Air Arm Fulmars. For scouting there were only seven Catalinas, while for counter-attacking the Japanese fleet there were a mere fourteen Blenheim bombers and a mixed squadron of Albacores and Swordfish. It was little enough to pit against the 300 aircraft in Nagumo's carriers.

The Japanese operations were directed from Singapore by Vice-Admiral Nobutake Kondo, with the aims of destroying the Eastern Fleet and harassing British shipping in the Bay of Bengal. Kondo ordered Nagumo's carriers and battleships to attack Ceylon, while one light carrier, six cruisers and four destroyers under Rear-Admiral Jisaburo Ozawa were to focus on the Bay of Bengal. Kondo's plan was fundamentally unsound. His aim should have been the destruction of the Eastern Fleet, for after that all else followed. Instead of searching directly for the British fleet, Kondo decided to attack the two major naval ports, Colombo and Trincomalee, in the hope of catching the British fleet napping or otherwise to force it into a major fleet action in which he was confident it would be overwhelmed.

Nagumo did maintain a strike force ready to strike the British fleet if it appeared but nonetheless Kondo was taking risks, for if the unlocated British carriers were well handled they might be able to strike at his carriers when they were most vulnerable—when their main air strike was just returning from the attack on Colombo. But Kondo was lucky, for in the attack on Ceylon the British carriers were caught on the wrong foot, out of position; and in any event, although the Japanese did not know this, they had too few aircraft to strike an effective blow.

On 28 March Somerville received news from the code-breakers of a probable carrier attack about 1 April.[6] He decided that the most likely Japanese plan was for simultaneous attacks on Colombo and Trincomalee from carriers operating south-east of Ceylon. There would be a full moon on 1 April, and Somerville decided that the Japanese would probably attack by moonlight and recover the strike aircraft after dawn. He was faced with a very difficult problem. His fleet could neither fight a surface action with the Japanese—since his four *Royal Sovereign* class battleships could not shoot beyond 23 000 yards and were too slow to force a night action—nor could it withstand a daylight air attack launched from Nagumo's carriers, given that the standard of anti-aircraft gunnery was little improved.

Oerlikon automatic guns (as many as six in some destroyers) were beginning to be fitted to replace the totally inadequate 0.5-inch and 0.303-inch machine guns, but many of Somerville's old ships were still almost helpless against air attack. The close-range anti-aircraft defences of a *Royal Sovereign* class battleship, for instance, was two eight-barrelled pom-poms and four twin Lewis 0.303-inch machine guns. Somerville's only chance was to make use of the one advantage he possessed over the Japanese—radar. He therefore decided to keep his fleet outside the area in which the Japanese were likely to operate during daylight, moving in by night to a position from which he could launch air strikes by moonlight. Such a plan was extremely risky and for it to be successful there would have to be very skilful timing and much good fortune.

Somerville divided his fleet in two. Force A, under his own command, consisted of the battleship *Warspite*, the two large carriers *Indomitable* and *Formidable*, three cruisers and six destroyers. These ships could steam 24 knots in company, or nearly 30 if *Warspite* were to be left behind (although that would leave Somerville behind too, for although the carriers were the crucial strike and reconnaissance elements of Force A, Somerville was flying his flag in the battleship). The two carriers had 33 fighters and 45 strike aircraft between them. Force B was made up of the residue of his fleet—the four *Royal Sovereign* ships, the small carrier *Hermes*, three cruisers and eight destroyers. Nearly half of these ships were more than twenty years old, and their slow speed of advance in company was frequently jeopardised by steering breakdowns among the battleships. It is difficult to see any useful role which Force B could have performed.

By 31 March, Force A was in a position south of Ceylon with Force B in support to the westward. Catalina patrols were searching an arc south-east of Ceylon to a depth of 400 miles. As only three Catalinas could be maintained on patrol, this was as much as could be covered, and Somerville was very exposed if Nagumo approached from any other direction. The Eastern Fleet passed the

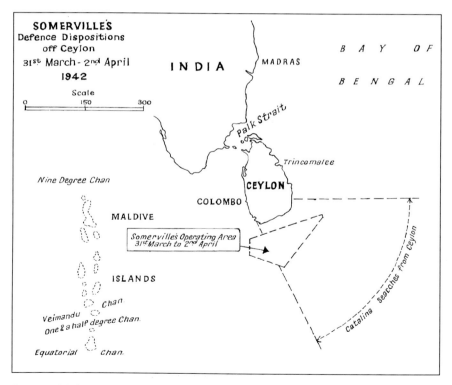

Somerville's defence positions off Ceylon

last day of March and the first two days of April maintaining this patrol pattern, but there was no sign of the enemy.

Somerville could not be certain whether the intelligence he had received was wrong from the start or if the Japanese knew of the movements of his fleet and were merely waiting for him to return to harbour before attacking, but it was certain that he could not stay where he was. His position might well have been reported by submarines, and in any case his fleet was running short of fuel and the *Royal Sovereign* ships were practically out of fresh water.[7] Somerville had the same logistic problems in deploying his forces as bedevilled other British admirals in earlier operations, for his fleet would have to return to harbour to replenish.

Since he could not risk putting into either Colombo or Trincomalee, at 9 p.m. on 2 April Somerville set course for Addu Atoll, where Force A arrived at noon on 3 April and Force B three hours later. Somerville had by this time come to the conclusion that the Japanese attack was not imminent after all, and decided to resume to some extent the ordinary shipping movements in the area which had been suspended for the past six days. Two of his cruisers were ordered to Colombo—*Dorsetshire* to resume an interrupted refit, *Cornwall* to escort a convoy to Australia. The carrier *Hermes*, having been nominated by the Admiralty to take part in the impending invasion of Madagascar, was sent to Trincomalee.

Somerville's fleet had scarcely started fuelling when news came of Nagumo. At 4 p.m. on 3 May a Catalina sighted a large group of Japanese ships 360 miles south-east of Ceylon, steaming towards Colombo. Nothing further was heard from this flying boat, which was correctly assumed to have been shot down. Somerville was caught in the worst possible position, as Force A could not complete fuelling before midnight, and Force B not before 7 a.m. the next day. There was no hope of an attack on the Japanese carriers that night, but there might be a chance to strike them during their withdrawal, and Somerville therefore decided to sail with Force A at midnight, Force B following as soon as it was ready.

Meanwhile Layton had alerted the defences in Ceylon. Since 31 March Colombo had been gradually cleared of shipping, more than 50 ships being sent to other ports or small anchorages. Twenty-five more were sailed on the evening of 4 April with orders to return to harbour the following afternoon. The cruisers *Dorsetshire* and *Cornwall* were sent to rejoin the fleet at Addu Atoll. Yet even after all these ships had left there were still more than 30 ships in harbour. Colombo was as ready as it could be, but the fact that the installations of the radar stations were not yet completed prevented proper direction of the defending fighters. During the night Catalinas continued to shadow Nagumo, but their reports were somewhat confusing as to the exact composition of the Japanese fleet though it was clear that it was substantial.

Launching of the strike at Colombo began at dawn on 5 April. Again led by Fuchida, the attack force consisted of 125 aircraft— 36 Zekes, 36 Vals and 53 Kates. As the formation crossed the south coast of Ceylon, a formation of six Swordfish was sighted flying at a much lower level without any fighter escort. These aircraft were promptly attacked and all quickly shot down.[8] Continuing towards the target, Fuchida's fighters and a few level-bombers attacked the airfields, while the dive-bombers and the rest of the level-bombers attacked the shipping in the harbour. By this time nearly all the British fighters—35 Hurricanes and six Fulmars—were in the air to intercept the Japanese. They were too slow and unmanoeuvrable to compete with the Zekes, however, and 21 were shot down at a cost of only seven Japanese planes. By 9.30 a.m. the attacks were over, and the Japanese were gone. Colombo had been fortunate. Thanks to the timely dispersal of shipping the port

Dorsetshire and *Cornwall* under attack. (*Imperial War Museum, HU2764*)

had suffered surprisingly little, and damage to the airfields was similarly slight.

Nagumo had not overlooked the possibility that the Eastern Fleet might intervene. As was his usual practice he used the float planes from the cruisers and battleships for scouting, reserving his carrier aircraft for offence and defence. At about 11 a.m. one of the scouts reported sighting two enemy destroyers heading south-south-west at 25 knots. The ships were in fact the cruisers *Cornwall* and *Dorsetshire*, on their way to rendezvous with Somerville and Force A about 170 miles away. The two cruisers did not immediately warn Somerville, because they were not absolutely certain that they had been spotted, but when two more shadowing aircraft were sighted at 1 p.m. they did break radio silence. By then it was too late—within 40 minutes they were heavily attacked.

Although *Dorsetshire* was fitted with a primitive type of radar (Type 286) the 80 approaching Japanese dive-bombers were not detected and the actual attack came as a complete surprise. The main radio transmitters were put out of action almost immediately. An attempt was made to transmit a report on *Dorsetshire*'s emergency set, but this message was not picked up by Somerville. The Japanese dive-bombers attacked in groups of three in rapid succession, and apparently nearly all their bombs hit. No cruisers ever built could withstand such punishment, and by 2 p.m. both ships had gone down. The Japanese had no losses.

Somerville was now in a position of acute danger, for Force A was within 200 miles of Nagumo's carriers, although Somerville did not actually know where Nagumo was. All he knew was that shortly before 2 p.m. his radar had detected a large number of enemy aircraft 85 miles to the north-east, roughly where he expected the two cruisers to be. Since they did not report being attacked he hoped that they had escaped and were preserving radio silence, so he continued on a course eastwards (towards Nagumo) so as to reach the prearranged rendezvous with the two cruisers, with Force B trailing more than 100 miles astern. Fortunately for Somerville, Nagumo was satisfied that he had dealt with all British ships in the immediate vicinity and did not send out any more scouts, continuing placidly on his south-easterly course.

One of Somerville's scouting aircraft sighted wreckage in the water at 3.52 p.m. and it soon became obvious what had happened to *Dorsetshire* and *Cornwall*, but any attempt to rescue survivors had to be postponed because reports of Nagumo's fleet at last began to come in. These were most confusing, both as to Nagumo's position and his course, and convinced Somerville that the Japanese were heading directly for Addu Atoll, presumably looking for the

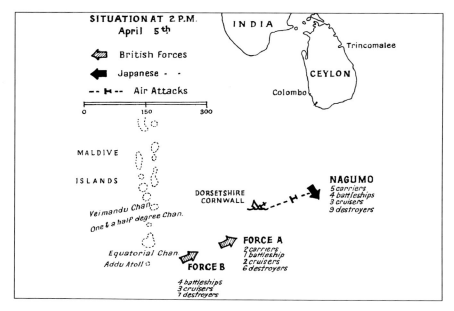

SITUATION AT 2 P.M.
April 5th

British Forces

Japanese

Air Attacks

0   150   300

INDIA

Trincomalee

CEYLON

Colombo

MALDIVE

ISLANDS

DORSETSHIRE
CORNWALL

NAGUMO
5 carriers
4 battleships
3 cruisers
9 destroyers

Veimandu Chan.
One & a half degree Chan.

Equatorial Chan.
Addu Atoll

FORCE A
2 carriers
1 battleship
2 cruisers
6 destroyers

FORCE B
4 battleships
3 cruisers
7 destroyers

The search for Nagumo

Eastern Fleet and scouring the seas ahead with search aircraft. He feared that at any moment he might be discovered and forced into a daylight carrier action. As this was one thing he was determined to avoid at all costs, he ordered all his forces to steer southwards.

At 6.15 p.m. Somerville was given the startling news that the enemy course was north-west, prompting him to switch Force A and Force B to the north-west too and order a dawn rendezvous. He wanted to be in position to launch air attacks on Nagumo that night if he could be found, so during the night radar-fitted aircraft searched over a wide arc to a depth of 200 miles. Nothing was detected, and by dawn the only ships located were those of Force B arriving at the appointed rendezvous.

Where was Nagumo? Somerville had been grossly misled by the reconnaissance reports, for Nagumo had never been within 100 miles of the positions given by the flying boats during the afternoon of 5 April. After recovering the aircraft which had sunk *Dorsetshire* and *Cornwall*, he had retired steadily south-eastwards to put himself beyond range of the Ceylon-based patrols. He had no knowledge of the secret base at Addu Atoll and had never made a move in that direction. He intended to strike his next blow at Trincomalee, and at 6 a.m. he altered course to the eastward. By then he was well beyond the reach of Somerville, who was heading in the opposite direction.

None of this, of course, was known to Somerville, who still thought that Nagumo might be preparing an attack on Addu Atoll and, if this were so, obviously it would be suicidal to retire towards that port. He decided that his best course would be to steer east, so that he would be in position to launch night attacks on Nagumo as he withdrew from Addu Atoll. Admiral Layton had been closely following the progress of the action. He had serious misgivings about the risks Somerville was taking, but realised that to a man of Somerville's temperament it would be difficult not to attempt to destroy an enemy fleet at sea, even if his own fleet was inferior. Layton could not give Somerville direct orders, but he did send an appreciation to the Admiralty pointing out that a strong Japanese fleet was between Addu Atoll and Ceylon and that the Eastern Fleet was facing annihilation. He knew that Somerville would receive this message, and hoped that it would help him in making the difficult decision to refuse action.

Somerville received Layton's appreciation at 2 p.m. and that evening he ordered a retirement to the north-west. He passed through a channel in the Maldive Islands 150 miles to the north of Addu Atoll, and still flying continuous air searches he approached his base from the west. He arrived at 11 a.m. on 8 April and immediately started refuelling his ships.

Meanwhile, the Admiralty had taken a hand in proceedings by telling Somerville that it was realised the *Royal Sovereign* ships might be 'more of a liability than an asset' and giving him discretion to withdraw them.[9] He was also told that his fleet must not use Colombo for the present. The disposal of the four old battleships was a problem for Somerville and his staff, and after studying a pocket atlas of the Indian Ocean it was decided to send Force B to Mombasa, in Kenya, on 9 April.[10] Somerville told the Admiralty that he intended to stay with the remainder of his ships, to prevent the Japanese dominating the Indian Ocean. He would not attempt to operate from Ceylon, and for the present he would base his ships in Bombay.

While these important matters were being decided Nagumo was moving again. On the afternoon of 8 April a flying boat from Ceylon reported three Japanese battleships and an aircraft carrier more than 400 miles east of Ceylon, heading in a north-westerly direction, their obvious targets being Trincomalee or Madras. The tactics which had been so successful at Colombo were repeated at Trincomalee, and the harbour was cleared of shipping that night. Soon after 7 a.m. the next day the radar station at Trincomalee detected a large group of aircraft 90 miles to the east. Thanks to this timely warning all the serviceable fighters (seventeen Hurricanes and six Fulmars) were in the air when the Japanese aircraft—41 Zekes and 91 Kates, again led by Fuchida—arrived.

The attackers did great damage to the dockyard and airfield, and thirteen naval aircraft which were being repaired or assembled were destroyed. Little damage was done in the harbour, partly because most of the ships had left, and partly because the second wave of dive-bombers was diverted elsewhere. Three Japanese aircraft were lost in the attack, at a cost of eight Hurricanes and three Fulmars.

The time had now arrived for the first, and only, British counter-attack against Nagumo's ships. During the attack on Colombo the Blenheim bombers had taken off in search of the Japanese but were directed to the wrong area. Now they had a second chance, and this time they found Nagumo. Nine Blenheims made a high-level attack without being intercepted by fighters (the Japanese having no radar); however, as with almost all high-level bombing attacks on ships at sea, none of the bombs hit.

In a running fight as they withdrew, four Blenheims were shot down by the twenty Zekes of the Combat Air Patrol. The ordeal was not yet over for the five surviving Blenheims because they met *Shokaku*'s Val dive-bombers and *Hiryu*'s Zekes as they were returning from an attack on *Hermes*, and another Blenheim was lost and the four survivors badly shot up. But this attack was the first occasion Nagumo's carriers had ever been threatened in five months of active operations.

While Fuchida's bombers were attacking Trincomalee, the ships which had been hastily cleared from the port during the previous night were about 60 miles to the south, hugging the coast to try to avoid detection. Among them was the carrier *Hermes* who had been hustled to sea at 1 a.m., leaving behind her aircraft (twelve Swordfish). Shortly before 9 a.m. one of Nagumo's scouting float planes sighted the British carrier. This was a great moment for Nagumo, for it was the first time his scouts had ever found an enemy carrier. He at once ordered the second wave of 85 dive-bombers escorted by nine Zekes to attack *Hermes* rather than Trincomalee harbour. The leader was Lieutenant-Commander Egusa, who four days before had distinguished himself by sinking *Dorsetshire* and *Cornwall*.

The naval wireless stations in Ceylon were listening to the Japanese signals, and by 9.30 a.m. it was known that *Hermes* had been sighted. Desperate efforts were made to provide her with fighter cover, but there were delays because of damage to telephone

Hermes sinking. (*Imperial War Museum, HU1839*)

lines (and in one case where the line was intact a message was sent by dispatch rider) and it was more than an hour before the fighters took to the air. The first bomb fell at 10.35 a.m. According to a British eyewitness:

> The attack was carried out perfectly, relentlessly and quite fearlessly, and was exactly like a highly organised deck display. The aircraft peeled off in threes, coming straight down on the ship out of the sun on the starboard side.[11]

Within twenty minutes *Hermes* was gone, and the bombers turned their attention to the escorting Australian destroyer *Vampire*, which lasted a bare ten minutes. Before leaving the area Egusa's dive-bombers sank two merchant ships and a corvette, so that in four days they had sunk seven ships without losing a single aircraft to ships' defences.

At 12.17 p.m., just as the last damaged British ship disappeared, eight Fulmar fighters arrived, too late to save the ships, but able to engage the dive-bombers as they withdrew. Two of the Fulmars were shot down. The Japanese lost four dive-bombers in the two air actions, but it is not clear how many were shot down by the Blenheims and how many by the Fulmars. The Japanese had no losses from anti-aircraft gunfire.

While these heavy blows were being rained on the Eastern Fleet, Ozawa had been causing havoc in the Bay of Bengal among unescorted convoys, sinking 23 ships in five days. Japanese submarines sank a further five ships off the west coast of India, and British shipping was brought to a complete standstill.

By this time Nagumo was withdrawing, and on 12 April he entered the Malacca Strait. In the wake of this highly successful operation he thought it was time to return home, since his ships were in need of maintenance and there were many gaps in the air groups after four months of operations. Two carriers had to be left behind to support impending operations against New Guinea, this role falling to *Shokaku* and *Zuikaku* as the two most modern ships which had been little involved in the operations in February and March. With his remaining ships Nagumo headed for Japan.

Since Pearl Harbor Nagumo could look back on an unbroken run of successes. His carriers had steamed 50 000 miles, rarely sighted and never damaged, while intervening with decisive effect in every Eastern theatre. Yet, though he had accomplished much, he had missed even greater opportunities. He had failed to seek out and destroy the American carriers after Pearl Harbor, and in the attack on Ceylon he missed an opportunity of annihilating the Eastern Fleet. If he had searched in the direction *Dorsetshire* and *Cornwall* had been heading he could scarcely have failed to find Somerville's fleet, and a daylight carrier action between the two fleets could have had only one ending.

Even so, the strategic effect of Nagumo's raid was enormous. The Eastern Fleet had been driven back to the coast of Africa, far away from the US Pacific Fleet—the distance from Mombasa to Pearl Harbor is almost half-way round the world. Coordination between the Eastern Fleet and the Pacific Fleet was markedly lacking, and the Japanese were able to exploit their central position. Worse still, at the very moment that the Americans were desperately gathering all their strength for the crucial battles of the Coral Sea and Midway, the three modern British carriers (*Illustrious* had joined the Eastern Fleet) were committed to a strategically trivial operation—the invasion of the French colony of Madagascar.[12]

Nagumo had shown the possibility of air power, deployed by carriers, dominating shore-based air power through the mobility of the carriers, and also that carrier aircraft could be as good as, if not better than, their shore-based opponents. Neither of these propositions would have been thought reasonable by pre-war theoreticians.

Tactically, Somerville had taken extreme risks off Ceylon, and he could consider himself fortunate to have escaped so lightly. His second-in-command, Vice-Admiral Willis, later wrote that he was puzzled why Somerville took such risks with the fleet on this occasion.[13] It is almost inconceivable that Somerville's attack plan could have worked. The two carriers in Force A had only 45 Albacores between them, and quite a number of these would have been used for searching and shadowing and thus not available for strike purposes. The attackers would have had to carry out an extremely difficult feat—a night torpedo attack on fast, manoeuvring ships at sea—and would have had to disable enough of the Japanese carriers to prevent them destroying Force A the following day. The appearance of the Albacores would have alerted Nagumo to the presence of British carriers in the vicinity, and their direction of flight as they withdrew would have given him a good clue as to where to look. As Force A could not make more than 24 knots, the prospect of its being beyond range by daylight was forlorn.

Because Force B was much slower, it was fortunate to have been further from Nagumo's carriers. It is a pity that Somerville did not get rid of the *Royal Sovereigns*, using their destroyers and cruisers to strengthen Force A—a decision he might have made if Churchill's message had been passed on. Without such support he had a real problem, for he assumed command only on 26 March and three days later had to sail to defend Ceylon. To have banished the four old battleships immediately would have set aside all the Admiralty plans for the building up of the Eastern Fleet.

Somerville was lucky that the alarm signals from *Dorsetshire* were not received, for if they had been he would have faced a distressing dilemma. If he sent fighters he would have revealed his presence to Nagumo, and risked the almost certain destruction of his fleet, while to ignore the cries for help would have been very bad for morale. (Besides, although Somerville could not know this, the fighters would have arrived too late.)

The superiority of the Zeke over the British fighters was most marked, with only the twelve Wildcats in *Formidable* likely to be able to challenge them. The Hurricanes by this time were obsolescent, while the Fulmars were obsolete at the time they came into service. The efficiency of the Japanese dive-bombing was a revelation; nothing like it had been seen from the Germans. Somerville wrote to the Admiralty that 'our Fleet Air Arm, suffering as it does from arrested development for so many years, would not be able to compete on all-round terms with a fleet air arm which has devoted itself to producing aircraft fit for sailors to fly in'.[14] Layton felt similarly, that 'FAA aircraft are proving more of

163

an embarrassment than a help when landed. They cannot operate by day in the presence of Japanese fighters and only tend to congest aerodromes'.[15]

The other problems for the Royal Navy had appeared in earlier battles, and would emerge again. The inability of the fleet to refuel at sea imposed extraordinary tactical problems for an admiral in deploying carrier-based air power. It is clear now that Somerville's decisions on 2 April to disperse some of his ships and to refuel at Addu Atoll were premature, but in light of the intelligence available at the time these decisions were not unreasonable. The standard of anti-aircraft gunnery against dive-bombing was deplorable. Four of Somerville's ships were sunk by the dive-bombers, but not a single aircraft was shot down by them.

From the Japanese point of view the operation was tactically excellent, although it would have been better if the submarines, instead of being sent to the west coast of India, had been deployed outside the ports the carriers were to attack. This would have made the arrangements, used so successfully by Layton at Colombo and Trincomalee, for dispersal of shipping from threatened ports very expensive. The only worry the Japanese should have had was the ability of the Blenheim bombers to attack the carriers without being detected. The lack of radar made them very vulnerable to attackers coming in at high altitude, as they were to find out disastrously at Midway.

11

Coral Sea:

3–8 May 1942

The war plan of the Japanese had been based on the assumption that six months would be needed to capture Malaya and the Philippines, and another six months to repair damaged oilfields; now everything was theirs within four months. Such unexpected ease of conquest caused a sharp divergence of view among Japan's leaders as to what should be the next step. The Naval General Staff was convinced that key areas of Australia should be occupied, to prevent it becoming the base for an eventual American counter-offensive. This proposal was speedily rejected by the army, which argued that it could not possibly provide the ten divisions estimated to be required—quite apart from the difficulty of transporting and keeping up supplies to such a force. Faced with this blunt refusal, the Naval Staff turned to the less ambitious plan of isolating the Australian continent by extending control over New Guinea, the Solomons and the New Caledonia–Fiji area.

At Combined Fleet Headquarters, Yamamoto viewed the problem differently. He knew that Japan had no hope of victory in a long war with the United States. His intention was to destroy the American Fleet by forcing it to fight a decisive action while he still had the initiative, by striking at an objective such as Midway Island in the central Pacific—which the Americans could not afford to abandon since it was 'the sentry of Hawaii'. Yamamoto's view was that:

> in the last analysis, the success or failure of our entire strategy in the Pacific will be determined by whether or not we succeed in destroying the United States Fleet, more particularly its carrier task forces.[1]

A B-25B bomber takes off from USS *Hornet*. (*National Archives, 80-G-41196*)

The Naval Staff reluctantly agreed to Yamamoto's plan, but wanted to delay the attack for three weeks after the proposed date of early June in order to allow more time for preparations. The argument was still continuing when the issue was resolved by an attack on Japan by a handful of American Army medium-bomber aircraft launched from the carrier *Hornet*. This operation, known as the Doolittle raid,[2] did very little actual damage to any of the targeted cities, but afterwards the Japanese Naval Staff no longer felt able to deny the urgency of the threat from the east and withdrew opposition to Yamamoto's scheme.

Meanwhile, the operations planned by the Naval Staff had commenced with the object of isolating Australia. It had been decided as a first step to occupy Port Moresby in New Guinea and Tulagi in the Solomons. Five separate forces were provided for these tasks: two invasion groups, one for Port Moresby and one for Tulagi; a support group, formed around a seaplane carrier, which was to establish a base off the eastern tip of New Guinea; a covering force of four cruisers and the small carrier *Shoho*; and a striking force built round the large carriers *Shokaku* and *Zuikaku*, which had only recently returned from the Indian Ocean. (The remainder of Nagumo's carriers were in Japan preparing for the Midway operation.)

In addition to the sea forces, the Japanese had a supporting land-based air force of 60 fighters, 24 Nell and seventeen Betty twin-engined bombers, twelve flying boats and ten small seaplanes. The majority of the aircraft operated from Rabaul and Lae, with the flying boats being split between Rabaul, Shortland and (after its capture) Tulagi.

The Japanese plan was for Tulagi to be occupied on 3 May, after which the covering force and the striking force were to support the Port Moresby invasion group, which was to sail from Rabaul on 4 May and land the army at Port Moresby three days later. Vice-Admiral Shigeyoshi Inouye, the commander of the Fourth Fleet, was at Rabaul in overall command. The striking force, centred round the two large carriers, was commanded by Vice-Admiral Takeo Takagi flying his flag in a cruiser. A grave weakness of these command arrangements was that neither admiral had any previous action experience of air operations.

From decrypted Japanese messages, signal traffic analysis and submarine sightings Admiral Nimitz realised that something was about to happen in the South Pacific, that at least two aircraft carriers would be involved, and that the most likely place to be attacked was Port Moresby. General MacArthur, the newly-appointed Supreme Commander in the South-West Pacific Area, had only a few cruisers and about 300 land-based aircraft and it was urgent that he be reinforced. On 29 April Nimitz ordered Rear-Admiral Frank Fletcher, then in Noumea, to take his task force centred round the carrier *Yorktown* into the Coral Sea.

Nimitz's urgent problem was to concentrate his carrier forces in the South Pacific, even though that meant leaving the approaches to Hawaii unguarded. He had been told by his intelligence officer that 'nothing appears to be headed for Hawaii yet', but it was still a very bold decision. Halsey's two carriers, *Enterprise* and *Hornet*, had only just returned from the Tokyo raid, and it was most unlikely that they would be able to reach the Coral Sea in time for the battle. His only other carrier was *Lexington*, flying the flag of Rear-Admiral Aubrey Fitch, and he was ordered to join Fletcher by 1 May.

Whereas Fletcher was personally lacking in air experience (he did have an aviator as his chief of staff), Fitch was one of the most experienced carrier admirals in the US Navy. Both task force commanders were told by Nimitz that he believed a Japanese striking force—centred on the carriers *Zuikaku* and *Shokaku*, with cruisers and destroyers—would cover the invasion force heading for Port Moresby, probably through the Jomard Passage at the eastern end of New Guinea. The striking force would probably move into the Coral Sea and cover the invasion force by attacking airfields in north-eastern Australia and at Port Moresby.

The opposing carrier forces were fairly evenly matched after Fitch joined Fletcher. The two large Japanese carriers had 121 aircraft, almost equally divided between fighters, dive-bombers and torpedo-aircraft, while the small carrier *Shoho* had twelve fighters and six torpedo-aircraft. The two American carriers had 134 aircraft between them. In shore-based aircraft the Americans had a numerical advantage, but this was more than offset by the poor standard of training of the US Army Air Force crews for operations over the sea. The US Navy had twelve Catalina flying boats based in Noumea, but they were too far away to search the Solomons. They could have been very valuable in the Coral Sea, but the greater part of this area was in General MacArthur's command and they were not permitted to be used there!

Although the Japanese had fewer shore-based aircraft than the Americans they were much more effective, for they all belonged to the navy and were well trained in maritime operations. The Japanese carrier-based fighter—the Zeke—was definitely superior to the American F4F Wildcat in speed, climb and manoeuvrability, though it was without armour and self-sealing fuel tanks. The Japanese Kate torpedo-bomber was also superior to its American counterpart, the TBD Devastator. Only in dive-bombers—the Japanese Val and the American SBD Dauntless—were the two forces roughly equivalent.

The American carriers had, however, two great advantages over the Japanese: the possession of radar and the ability to use air-warning radar for the direction of defending fighters. As has already been recounted, the US Navy was at roughly the same stage of development of air-warning radar as the Royal Navy. The first operational air-warning set, the CXAM, was installed in late 1940—in the carrier *Yorktown*, an illuminating difference in priorities from the Royal Navy. The CXAM was too large for installation in ships smaller than heavy cruisers, so an air-warning set with a smaller aerial and higher power—the SC—was designed, and went to sea for trials in July 1941.[3] From 1942 onwards the SC became the standard air-warning set in cruisers, destroyers and some battleships, and was also used as a backup set in aircraft carriers.

Specialist fighter-direction officers, nearly all reservists, began to be trained in September 1941, and were available for the Coral

Sea battle. These officers had some formidable problems, principally poor voice-radio communications and the lack of
height-determination capability of radar contacts. They did have
PPIs, for which the rotation of the radar aerial did not have to
be stopped to take a bearing of each target.[4] The radios were
primitive, and the frequency used (HF) meant that transmissions
could be detected at long range, so there was a real possibility of
Japanese monitoring. Finally, the equipment fitted in aircraft so
that radar operators could identify friendly contacts was not widely
available, and the defensive fighters were constantly being used to
check on radar contacts which ultimately proved to be friendly. It
is not surprising that there were some muddles.

The Japanese, on the other hand, had no radar, so they had
no real fighter direction. Visual reports, either from lookouts or
from aircraft who happened to see approaching American formations, were passed to the defending fighters, who made their own
tactical decisions. Interceptions were made—if they were made at
all—very close to the ships being attacked. The voice radios in the
Zekes were very unreliable (indeed many pilots wanted to remove
them from their aircraft in order to reduce weight) and brief
information was usually sent by morse radio.

In anti-aircraft gunfire capability the two fleets were roughly
equivalent. The Americans had an anti-aircraft radar-ranging set—
the Mark 4—in production, but only a few of Fletcher's ships had
been fitted. The Mark 4 (also known as the FD) was excellent
for ranging, but did not track a target with sufficient smoothness
for blind fire to be effective, and below ten degrees elevation it
could not track a target at all. Although the accurate rangefinding
of the Mark 4 made a sharp improvement in the effectiveness of
the American 5-inch gunfire, even without it the systems were
quite good—particularly as their 5-inch guns were markedly superior to the Japanese equivalent.

Lexington had her four twin 8-inch turrets removed, with the
intention of replacing them with twin 5-inch turrets controlled by
the Mark 37 director system, but the new turrets were not available
and as a temporary measure she was fitted with three quadruple
1.1-inch (28mm) mountings. The Japanese cruisers supplemented
the anti-aircraft defences by firing barrages from their main
armaments, but the destroyers still had no anti-aircraft predictors
and were also limited to firing barrages.

Things were more equal in close-range weapons. The 40mm
Bofors guns, which would soon be widely fitted in all US ships,
had still not reached the fleet; although there were some 20mm
Oerlikons these had to be aimed by eye with a ring sight, and

most of the ships had to put up with having only 0.5-inch machine-guns for air defence; a few ships had quadruple 1.1-inch mountings, but these were very unreliable. The Japanese close-range defences, with many twin 25mm mountings and 13.2mm machine-guns, were rather better.

So the stage was set for the first battle ever fought between aircraft carriers. The Japanese were confident—perhaps over-confident—since their carriers had never been checked in six months of active operations. It was to be a clear fight between aircraft carriers, neither side employing any battleships. The Japanese battleships were preparing for the Midway operation, and the Americans kept theirs well out of the way on the west coast of America.

On the evening of 3 May, while Fletcher was refuelling his ships some 500 miles south of Tulagi, he received a delayed report from General MacArthur's headquarters that aircraft had seen Japanese troops disembarking off Tulagi. At this time Fletcher's two carriers were separated by over 100 miles, and he was not

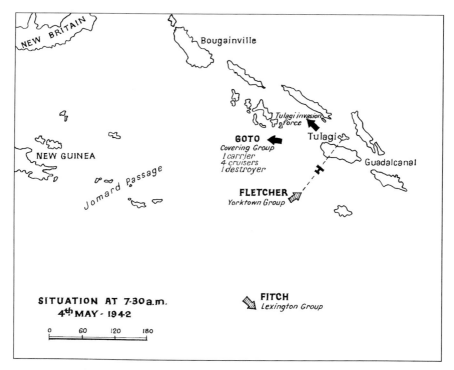

The situation at 7.30 a.m., 4 May 1942

aware that *Lexington* had finished fuelling, so he headed for Tulagi with *Yorktown*'s group alone. It would have been much better if Fletcher had formed all the ships into a single task group, but he did not want to break radio silence and the option of sending a message by aircraft was not used.

At 6.40 a.m. Fletcher commenced strikes against the Japanese ships from a range of 100 miles, and during the day nearly 100 sorties were flown. The results were most disappointing, although the full extent of the failure was masked from Fletcher by the over-optimistic reporting of his aviators. There was little shipping in the harbour (the Japanese invasion and covering forces having withdrawn), and in all of the attacks only one destroyer and three barges were sunk and one minelayer and a destroyer slightly damaged. Nimitz later wryly commented that these poor results showed the necessity for target practice at every opportunity.

During the night Fletcher ran to the south to join up with the *Lexington* group, under the impression that he had struck a heavy blow. He even ordered two cruisers 'to clean up the cripples', but later cancelled the order. It was as well, for the two cruisers would almost certainly have been sunk by the Japanese striking force.

While Fletcher refuelled his force on 5 May, reports began to come in of numerous Japanese ships to the north of him. It was fairly clear that there were three carriers among them, but the forces were scattered and there seemed to be no common direction of movement. What was actually happening was that the invasion group was busy collecting its forces in the north-west part of the Solomon Islands in preparation for the advance on Port Moresby. On the morning of 6 May they were sighted and ineffectively bombed by six B–17 Flying Fortresses from Port Moresby, but the reported course of the Japanese did confirm that the invasion group would pass through the Jomard Passage, with Port Moresby its probable objective.

At this time the Japanese striking force was well to the east, for it had rounded the Solomon Islands during 5 May and turned westwards into the Coral Sea. It had not been sighted by the Americans since 4 May, and Fletcher had no idea of its exact position. So during the morning of 6 May he continued his refuelling, on a south-easterly course because of the weather. This course was taking him further and further away from the Japanese invasion group, so he stopped refuelling and steered to the north and increased speed to be in position for an air strike on the Moresby-bound ships early on 7 May.

During the night Fletcher heard that the Japanese invasion force was nearer the Jomard Passage than he had thought, so he sent

an Australian–American group of three cruisers and three destroyers
ahead to intercept them. This was a peculiar decision. Fletcher
later said that he had detached this group because he expected a
heavy engagement with the Japanese carriers, in which his force
might suffer heavily; by detaching these cruisers and destroyers he
hoped they would avoid damage and therefore be able to drive
back the Japanese invasion force. He does not seem to have
considered the possibility that this small group, without air cover,
might become the target of a major Japanese air strike—which was
indeed what happened. What Fletcher did, without realising it, was
to employ a very useful 'live bait' tactic.[5]

Fletcher still had no information on the whereabouts of the
two large Japanese carriers. At first light on 7 May *Yorktown*
therefore launched ten Dauntless dive-bombers to search an arc of
120 degrees to the north to a depth of 250 miles. At 7.35 a.m.
the searching aircraft sighted two cruisers, but there was still no
sign of the carriers. At last, at 8.15 a.m., the long-awaited report

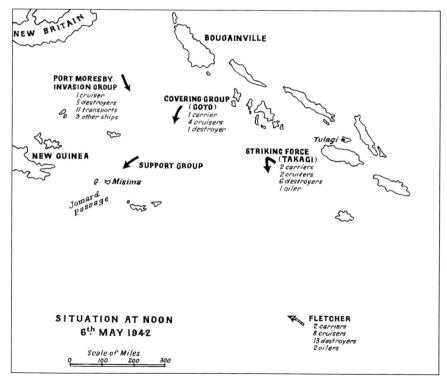

The situation at noon, 6 May 1942

came in. Two carriers had been sighted to the north of Misima Island, steering south-east at eighteen to twenty knots. Fletcher immediately gave orders to launch an all-out strike at them, at a range of 160 miles. At 9.26 a.m. *Lexington* began launching a group of 25 bombers and twelve torpedo-aircraft, escorted by ten fighters. *Yorktown*'s strike, of 25 bombers, ten torpedo-aircraft and eight fighters, was nearly half an hour behind.

At 10.22 a.m. a message was received from General MacArthur that an aircraft carrier (which turned out to be the *Shoho*), sixteen warships and ten transports were a few miles north of Misima Island. A few minutes later *Yorktown*'s scouts began to land, and it was only then discovered that the report of two carriers was false. What the pilot had sighted, and intended to report, was two cruisers and two destroyers. (They were, in fact, two cruisers and some gunboats of the support group.) The air strike was well on its way, so Fletcher decided to let it go on. The leader of *Lexington*'s bombers sighted the carrier, and diverted the strike on to it. He did not know which carrier it was, but at least it was Japanese.

Lexington's aircraft had sighted *Shoho* about 11 a.m. Ten dive-bombers attacked at once and achieved complete surprise. Although *Shoho* launched fighters, these were hopelessly outnumbered and could do nothing to prevent the carrier from being quickly and completely overwhelmed. By the time *Yorktown*'s strike group arrived *Shoho* had been hit by at least seven torpedoes and thirteen bombs, and was clearly sinking. Unfortunately there was no organisation to divert these ten torpedo-bombers onto other targets, so they too attacked the carrier as ordered. She sank three minutes after the attacks were completed; only three US aircraft were lost.

The situation in the American flagship was tense. Fletcher had launched 90 aircraft against *Shoho*, and had nothing left except his defending fighters. There were still two unlocated Japanese carriers in the vicinity, and they might attack him at any moment while he had no means of effective reply. The strike aircraft returned from the *Shoho* mission at 1 p.m., and Fletcher decided not to attack the Port Moresby invasion group or the survivors of *Shoho*'s covering force. He could not risk committing his force on any lesser target while there were the large Japanese carriers somewhere near. A large-scale search would weaken his striking power, so Fletcher decided to rely on shore-based aircraft to locate the Japanese carriers, keeping his own strike aircraft at readiness.

During the day there were numerous indications on the American radar screens of Japanese aircraft searching for them. Fletcher was not to know that he had been located, but that the Japanese carriers, too, were temporarily powerless. Takagi was actually to the south-east of the Americans, so Fletcher's dawn search to the northwards had missed him. Knowing that there were US carriers somewhere, Takagi had launched an intensive air search at almost exactly the same moment that Fletcher had launched his. At 7.22 a.m. one of the scouting Kates from *Shokaku* reported a single carrier, a cruiser and three destroyers 163 miles to the south. Takagi ordered an immediate strike, so that 40 minutes later a total of 78 aircraft—eighteen Zekes, 36 Val dive-bombers and 24 Kate torpedo-aircraft—took off, leaving behind only about twenty Zeke fighters to defend his carriers.

The strike aircraft had barely departed when a reconnaissance aircraft from *Shoho*'s group reported a second US carrier and ten other vessels 260 miles to the north-west of Takagi, but Takagi had committed all his strike aircraft against the first target and could do nothing against the new one until his strike aircraft had returned and been rearmed. *Shoho* was ordered to attack the reported carrier, but she was sunk before she could obey the order.

At 11.05 a.m. Takagi's strike aircraft reached the reported position of the first American carrier, but could find no sign of it. After a fruitless search the strike leader ordered an attack on the only ships in the vicinity—a large tanker, *Neosho* (which the scouting aircraft had mistaken for an aircraft carrier), and an escorting destroyer, *Sims*, which had been detached by Fletcher the previous evening. Like *Shoho* at almost the same time, both American ships were overwhelmed by the weight of the attack.

By the time the strike returned, Takagi knew that *Shoho* had been sunk by a large force of carrier aircraft, and reasoned that he faced at least two American carriers. From the only report he had, they appeared to be at least 300 miles west of his present position. If he launched his strike force as soon as it could be made ready the pilots would have to return to their carriers in darkness, and this in turn would mean that the strike aircraft would have to be without fighter escort, because the Zekes were not capable of night deck-landing.

Despite these problems Takagi decided to attack, but delayed the launch so that the strike aircraft would reach the assumed position of the American carriers at dusk, when their lack of fighter escort would not be so serious. At 4 p.m. twelve Val dive-bombers and fifteen Kate torpedo-aircraft took off—their task being to attack at nightfall, without the assistance of radar, an enemy whose position was only very roughly known and whose strength was only surmised. To add to their difficulties they ran into heavy rain squalls, and after two hours they reluctantly gave up the search, jettisoned their ordnance and turned for home.

Although the Japanese did not know it, their strike force passed within 40 miles of the US carriers, and eleven Wildcat fighters were sent out to intercept them. Lacking a fighter escort, the Japanese were no match for the Wildcats and in a brief battle eight of the fifteen torpedo-aircraft and one dive-bomber were shot down, for the loss of two American aircraft.

By now it was getting dark. The American fighters were recalled so they could land while there was still enough light, but the tribulations of the Japanese strike aircraft were not over yet. Exhausted after flying all day and confused by the battle with the Wildcats, they flew over the American carriers, mistook them for their own, and attempted to exchange recognition signals by flashing lamp. The Americans were equally surprised, and the Japanese managed to escape unscathed, though it was galling for them to have been searching so long for the Americans and to find them accidentally after they had jettisoned their weapons.

The Japanese aircraft eventually did find their own carriers, but not without difficulty, for it was dark and the Americans were accidentally jamming the Japanese voice radio, preventing the aircraft homing on their carrier. In desperation Rear-Admiral Hara (commanding Takagi's two carriers) ordered searchlights to be switched on to guide them home, but nevertheless eleven of the eighteen survivors came down in the sea.

On that same day the cruiser force that Fletcher had sent to cover the Jomard passage was attacked by 33 shore-based Nell and Betty bombers, with an escort of eleven Zeke fighters. This was a force of about half the size of that which had sunk *Prince of Wales* and *Repulse* six months before, and like those two ships the Australian–American force was without fighter cover. This time the result was very different. The Japanese attacked in two waves, the first wave consisting of torpedo-bombers followed closely by for-mation-bombing from about 18 000 feet. Although the Japanese claimed to have sunk one battleship and damaged another, in fact they caused no damage and lost four aircraft in the process.[6] The cruiser force did not even have the satisfaction of a surface action with the invasion group, because Inouye ordered the convoy to turn back until the situation with the American carriers was clearer.

The Americans could reckon they had done well so far. Their two carriers had sunk one of the three opposing carriers, losing only three aircraft in the process, and without being attacked themselves. Although the full details were not known to the Americans at the time, the two surviving Japanese carriers had lost

more than one-sixth of their aircraft, giving the Americans for the
first time a definite numerical advantage in carrier aircraft.

Both Fletcher and Takagi considered a night surface action,
and both rejected it because of uncertainty of the other's position.
After rejecting this option, Fletcher decided to take his carriers
towards where he thought Takagi was, which was a bad move
since it took them out of the zone of poor visibility which had
protected them the previous day and into clear skies to the south.
At the same time Takagi headed north-west to provide air cover
(if required) for the invasion group, which after the sinking of
Shoho was almost defenceless. This confusion of aim, whether to
attack the US carriers or defend the convoy, is typical of several
Japanese actions in this and subsequent battles. In this particular
case it had a fortunate result, for Takagi moved into the area of
rain squalls while Fletcher moved clear of them to the south—the
two forces passing during the night on opposite courses, 200 miles
apart.

It was obvious that everything would depend on the early

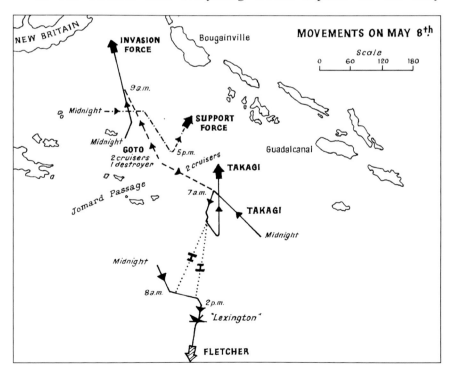

The carriers' movements on 8 May 1942

location of the opposing carriers. Takagi ordered a double search scheme to commence an hour before dawn. With this scheme, aircraft were sent off in darkness and commenced their search at first light some distance from their carrier, while other aircraft were launched at dawn and covered the area the earlier aircraft had missed in the darkness. Such a scheme made extravagant use of aircraft, but Takagi could afford it because his carrier aircraft were supplemented by float planes from the cruisers. Fletcher used a conventional search by carrier aircraft, taking off at first light and, because he had no real idea where Takagi was, searching all round, 200 miles to the north and 150 miles to the south. This search needed 22 aircraft, nearly a fifth of all he had available.

Sightings were made by both sides almost at the same moment. At 8.20 a.m. one of the American scouts which was just turning for home sighted a Japanese carrier almost hidden in rain squalls. The report was confirmed by the adjacent scout, and by 8.28 a.m. Fletcher had an accurate report that the enemy consisted of two carriers, four cruisers and some destroyers. Fletcher ordered an immediate all-out strike, and at 9 a.m. the aircraft began taking off: 46 SBD Dauntless dive-bombers, 21 TBD Devastator torpedo-bombers and seventeen F4F Wildcat escorting fighters.

Just before the first report of the Japanese carriers was received, *Lexington* intercepted a report from a Japanese aircraft giving the position, course and speed of the US carriers. For some reason this report does not seem to have been received by Takagi in his cruiser flagship until 9.25 a.m. Unable to wait any longer Takagi had ten minutes earlier launched a strike of 33 dive-bombers and eighteen torpedo-aircraft, escorted by eighteen fighters. Their orders were to search for the US carriers and attack them when found, but as soon as the scout's report was received they were given the accurate position of the Americans.

Yorktown's aircraft were the first of the Americans to take departure, the dive-bombers going ahead of the torpedo-aircraft. The Japanese were sighted at 10.32 a.m. but there was a lapse of nearly half an hour while the dive-bombers circled, waiting for the slower torpedo-aircraft to catch up. During this interval *Zuikaku* headed for a rain squall, but the other carrier, *Shokaku*, turned into the south-easterly wind and began to launch fighters.

As soon as the American torpedo-aircraft were in position the dive-bombers began their attack. The Japanese were, of course, fully alert, so they were met with fairly heavy anti-aircraft fire and attacked by fighters, both during their dives and after they had pulled out. The Japanese used about sixteen fighters, and the six escorting Wildcats were heavily outnumbered. The dive-bombers scored two hits with 1000-pound bombs on *Shokaku*, but the torpedo-aircraft, who timed their attack well by attacking just as *Shokaku* was turning to avoid the dive-bombers, released their torpedoes from too great a range and the carrier had no difficulty in avoiding them.

Meanwhile, *Lexington*'s aircraft were in serious difficulties. They were ten minutes behind those from *Yorktown*, and could not find the Japanese carriers in the low visibility. The formation became dispersed and, as many of the dive-bombers had been launched without being fully fuelled after returning from their search, half of the strike had to return home without achieving anything. The remaining 21 aircraft re-assembled and commenced a search, and after twenty minutes they came to a patch of clear sky and there, in the distance, were the Japanese ships. They were immediately attacked by Japanese Zekes, but the six remaining Wildcats managed to hold them off, although they lost three of their number in the process.

Again the Americans concentrated on *Shokaku*, *Zuikaku* being obscured in rain squalls. This time the torpedo-aircraft attacked first, followed by the dive-bombers, but the results of this rather disorganised attack were disappointing, only one bomb hit being scored, and seven aircraft were lost in the attack and in subsequent forced landings. They reported that the carrier they had attacked was 'settling fast', but this was not true. *Shokaku* had suffered severe damage and could no longer launch aircraft, but four aircraft did land after the attack, before the fires were extinguished. In the attacks a total of ten US aircraft were shot down by the fighters and anti-aircraft fire, or lost through fuel shortage.

The US carriers were under attack at the same time in this peculiar criss-cross battle. Fletcher had estimated that the Japanese attack would come in at about 11 o'clock, and in order to reduce signalling he had turned over the tactical control of the force to Rear-Admiral Fitch, who commanded the carriers. *Lexington* and *Yorktown* were positioned at the centre of a circular formation, with the cruisers 3000 yards from the carriers and the destroyers 4000. By 11 o'clock all serviceable aircraft were in the air or at immediate readiness on deck—the fighters as a radar-directed combat air patrol, the dive-bombers patrolling at low altitude to intercept Japanese torpedo-aircraft.

The first radar contact was made at 10.53 a.m. as the Japanese approached from the north at a distance of 70 miles. Despite the warning thus received, the force fighter-direction officer in *Lexington* was not successful with his interception. The eight fighters in the air were too low in fuel to be sent far from the carrier, the nine fighters launched after the detection were too late, and as a result only three of seventeen fighters gained contact before the attack began. Nor were the low-level patrols of dive-bombers any more successful. This plan had been based on the Japanese tactics against *Prince of Wales* and *Repulse*, when they approached in squadron formation, but this time the Japanese attacked in small groups from different directions. The American aircraft did not sight the Japanese torpedo-bombers until they were diving to the attack, and could do no more than attempt to hamper them. Because of the failure of their fighter defence the Americans had to rely almost entirely on their ships' guns, and although this fire was heavy, not all of it was very effective. One US cruiser reported that she was more seriously under fire from other American ships than the enemy.

It became clear that the Japanese intended to carry out simultaneous dive-bomber and torpedo attacks on both US carriers. The rigid ring formation of the Americans was soon broken, for the carriers used violent evasive manoeuvres and soon drew apart. The American force, without signal, divided into two—three cruisers and five destroyers accompanying *Yorktown*, two cruisers and three destroyers remaining with *Lexington*. The attacks on *Yorktown* were not very well coordinated. The torpedo-aircraft attacked in three waves from different directions, but there was sufficient time between the waves to enable *Yorktown* to turn towards each new attack and comb the torpedo tracks.

The dive-bombers meanwhile remained overhead, and did not attack until the torpedo-bombers had finished. Eleven Vals then attacked from out of the sun, scoring only one hit which did comparatively little damage. The 250kg bomb made a small hole in the flight deck and penetrated four decks before exploding in a store room. Blast and splinters caused casualties and started fires, for two hours reducing *Yorktown*'s speed to 24 knots, but as soon as the attack was over *Yorktown* was able to turn into the wind and land her aircraft. Another bomb glanced off the side of the flight deck and exploded near the bow, doing some damage to the hull, while a third was a near-miss which did little damage.[7]

Lexington, a much larger and less manoeuvrable ship, had a far worse time. The first attack was by torpedo-aircraft dropping simultaneously from port beam and starboard quarter, which gave little scope for avoiding action and as a result two of the torpedoes hit the carrier's port side. While attention was focussed on the torpedo-bombers, the dive-bombers attacked out of the sun. They were not seen until just before the first bomb was released, and scored three hits and two near-misses which tore holes in the hull.

Within fifteen minutes *Lexington* was on fire in four places, with three stokeholds partially flooded and the ship listing six degrees.

As the Japanese attacks finished and the enemy aircraft departed, the Americans could reckon they had done well. No ships other than the carriers had been damaged, and even in *Lexington* there seemed to be a good chance of getting the fires under control and correcting her list—there was certainly no idea that she was in danger. She was still capable of 25 knots, and although both lifts were jammed—fortunately in the up position— she was able to commence landing her returning strike. However, over an hour after the attacks had finished the ship was abruptly shaken by a heavy internal explosion. Leaking petrol vapour suddenly caused fierce fires to break out again; for a time it was thought that they might be brought under control, but it soon became apparent that the situation was hopeless. Shortly after 5 p.m. *Lexington* was abandoned and she was eventually sunk by five torpedoes fired by American destroyers.

Thirty-six of *Lexington*'s aircraft went down with her and,

USS *Lexington* sinking, after being abandoned. (*US Naval Historical Center, NH51382*)

although nineteen had been transferred to *Yorktown*, Fletcher now had only 28 serviceable aircraft. Still erroneously believing that *Shokaku* had been sunk, he debated whether to launch another attack against the remaining Japanese carrier. Then a returning pilot reported that one of the Japanese carriers was undamaged, and the deduction was drawn that the Japanese striking force had been reinforced by a third carrier. Fletcher felt that the odds were too great and decided to withdraw southwards, a decision reinforced by an order from Nimitz to retire from the Coral Sea.

Takagi had a similar problem in that he had only 39 operational aircraft—a quarter of his original force—including just nine Vals and six Kates. But he also believed that one of the US carriers had definitely sunk while the other, which was left burning, had probably sunk. Feeling that he could do no more with his depleted striking force, Takagi accordingly retired northward. Meanwhile, Inouye recalled the invasion force and postponed the occupation of Port Moresby—not because of the threat from US carriers (which he, too, believed to have been sunk), but because he considered his remaining air strength was inadequate to defend the convoy against American shore-based aircraft. This was practically the only contribution the US Army Air Force made to the battle, but it was a crucial one.

Yamamoto deplored the failure of his admirals to finish off the Americans, but such an opportunity, if it existed, was fleeting. Takagi was ordered to turn back and destroy the remaining American ships, but after an unsuccessful two-day search he gave up and returned to Truk.

The losses of the two sides were very nearly equal. The Japanese lost one light carrier, one destroyer and three small craft sunk, and one large carrier damaged (which would be out of action for nine months), with a total of 77 aircraft lost and 1074 men killed and wounded. The Americans lost one large carrier, an oiler and a destroyer sunk, and a carrier damaged, with a total of 66 aircraft lost and 543 men killed and wounded.

The battle had two dramatic results. The Japanese plans for an amphibious assault on Port Moresby were suspended indefinitely, and the number of aircraft carriers available to each side for the impending battle for Midway moved closer to parity. Neither *Zuikaku* (because of the shortage of replacement aircrews) nor the damaged *Shokaku* were ready in time. *Yorktown* was moved rapidly to Pearl Harbor, repaired with desperate urgency, given aircraft and aircrew replacements for the heavy losses in the Coral Sea battle, and was ready in time to play a decisive part in the next battle.

There were many lessons—strategic, tactical and material—to be learnt from this battle, which was, as Admiral King wrote, 'the first major engagement in naval history in which the opposing ships never came within sight of each other'. By their Tokyo raid the Americans had violated one of the principles of war, the concentration of force. If Halsey's two carriers had been sent to the Coral Sea instead of Tokyo the Americans would have had overwhelming strength and should have been able to win a decisive victory. On the other hand, the Tokyo raid, though designed to fortify American opinion, had an extraordinary effect on the Japanese commanders.

Moreover, as far as the impending Midway battle was concerned, the addition of Halsey's carriers could have achieved no more than Fletcher did, for none of the three Japanese carriers which fought in the Coral Sea was present at Midway; and if Halsey's carriers had fought in the Coral Sea they might have suffered damage or lost key aircrew, and been less effective at Midway as a consequence. The only lesson which can be drawn from all this is that sometimes luck is more important than rigid adherence to strategic principles.

The three tactical areas in which lessons could be learned were in reconnaissance, fighter direction and control of strikes. Both sides had problems with reconnaissance, which at times resulted in near-farcical situations, and both had problems with faulty or delayed messages from their scouting aircraft. Obviously the American reconnaissance effort would have benefited greatly from use in the Coral Sea of the twelve navy Catalina flying-boats based in Noumea, but for the uneasy relations between the US Army and Navy at this time. The Japanese had an advantage in the number of reconnaissance aircraft available in a carrier task force, through the use of the three to five float planes carried by each cruiser, but these were low performance machines and not really suitable for reconnaissance in the vicinity of enemy carriers.

The Coral Sea battle was the first operational trial of the US Navy's new system for controlling defending fighters by specialist fighter-direction officers, using radar information, and the results were mixed. The way the Wildcat fighters dealt with Takagi's unescorted dusk strike on 7 May was exemplary, both in terms of achieving a successful interception and causing heavy losses. To balance this success, the next day was a fiasco. Only three of seventeen defending fighters made contact, largely because of poor tactical direction by the force fighter-direction officer, and they did not succeed in shooting down any Japanese aircraft.

The problems of the fighter-direction officer were compounded by his lack of control over the launching and recovery of the available fighters. At this time these decisions were made by the admiral, and Fitch did not handle them very well. Although the Japanese struck at almost exactly the time Fletcher had predicted, the Americans were caught with their combat air patrol low on fuel, and there was an inordinate delay after the radar detected the Japanese strike before the fighters on deck were launched. It was to be some time in the future before the fighter-direction officers, armed with full information as to the deck condition of each carrier, effectively took over this responsibility during a defensive air battle.

The Japanese also had fighter problems. Although the low visibility hampered the American strikes, it hampered the Zekes too, for they relied totally on visual sightings. In the adverse conditions the Zekes, despite their superior performance, managed to shoot down only a few of the 60 US aircraft which actually attacked Takagi's force.

Looking at the strike performance, both the Americans and the Japanese performed well against weak targets. The Americans against *Shoho* and the Japanese against *Neosho* performed with textbook efficiency, although in the attack on *Shoho* the American command system did not provide for the diversion of the later strike aircraft onto other targets when *Shoho* was clearly sinking.

In the exchange of all-out strikes on 8 May the Japanese performed rather better than the Americans, although they did have the advantage of the visibility which partly concealed their carriers, causing twenty of the American strike aircraft to be unable to find the Japanese task force and making coordinated attacks difficult to organise. The 48 American dive-bombers achieved three hits (all on *Shokaku*) while the 33 Japanese dive-bombers scored four hits (three on *Lexington* and one on *Yorktown*). In the case of the torpedo-bombers, the eighteen Japanese aircraft scored two hits on *Lexington*, but the 21 Americans missed completely.

These statistics were partly the result of the superior Japanese equipment, but here the Japanese had much less to look forward to than the Americans. The Americans had a new fighter—the F6F Hellcat—under development, which would outclass the Zeke in every area except manoeuvrability. The unsatisfactory TBD Devastator torpedo-bomber was in the process of being replaced by the much superior TBF Avenger, which was in the same league as the Japanese Kate. New radars were being fitted in all the American ships, and a flood of new 40mm Bofors guns and 20mm Oerlikons now coming off production lines would soon transform the close-range armaments of American ships. Although those at sea did not yet know anything about it, a remarkable new device called the VT fuse (VT standing for 'variable time', a deceptive codeword for a proximity fuse operated by radar) had also gone into production in America in January 1942. When these came into operational use with US ships the following year they would bring a fourfold increase in the effectiveness of anti-aircraft fire.

The Japanese could not expect anything comparable, for although three ships (none of them in the Coral Sea battle) were trying out primitive radar sets, it would be several months before serious ship-fitting could begin, and the performance of Japanese radars was always far behind the Americans. In any event the benefits of all these equipment changes were inevitably some way off. In the immediate future, in the impending battle for Midway, both sides would have to fight with what they had.

12

Midway:

3–7 June 1942

Early in May 1942 the Americans began to receive indications that the Japanese were about to attack Midway Island, a lonely outpost 1200 miles north-west of Pearl Harbor, leading Admiral King to predict on 15 May that a Japanese invasion force would leave Guam within ten days. The situation seemed desperate for the Americans because the Japanese were estimated—indeed underestimated—to have eleven battleships and at least seven carriers available, against which the Americans had only three carriers, one of which (*Yorktown*) had been damaged in the Coral Sea.[1] It has already been recounted how the Americans tried, and failed, to get the assistance of British Eastern Fleet carriers in the impending battle.

As Commander-in-Chief of the Pacific Fleet, Nimitz accepted the estimate of his intelligence officer that Midway was Yamamoto's objective. Some on his staff thought that the intelligence gathered was all part of an elaborate Japanese deception, and code-breakers in Washington initially believed that the Japanese thrust would be southwards rather than towards Hawaii. Once Nimitz had accepted that Midway was the principal Japanese objective, he acted with vigour. Fletcher's task force, already recalled from the Coral Sea, arrived in Pearl Harbor on 27 May and by extraordinary exertions *Yorktown* was repaired in three days instead of the several months originally estimated.

Task Force 16 (consisting of the carriers *Hornet* and *Enterprise* with escorting cruisers and destroyers), on its way to the Coral Sea after its Tokyo strike, was also recalled to Pearl Harbor. On arrival in Hawaii Halsey had to be taken to hospital, and Nimitz named as his replacement Rear-Admiral Raymond Spruance, who commanded the task force's cruisers. This was a decisive appointment, since it would be difficult to think of more dissimilar personalities than the austere, remote, methodical Spruance and the dashing, colourful, popular Halsey.[2] The latter's great weakness was that he had selected a staff which shared his own rather slapdash attitudes, rather than covering his weaknesses. Spruance was not an aviator—the 55-year-old was a gunnery expert—and he inherited Halsey's experienced but rather overconfident and incompetent staff. Despite this poor support, in the coming battle Spruance showed, by his calm judgement and bold decisions, that he was in the front rank of modern admirals.

By 27 May Nimitz had accepted the intelligence assessment that the Japanese carriers would probably attack Midway from the north-west on the morning of 4 June.[3] He left his carriers divided into two groups, Task Force 16 (*Enterprise* and *Hornet*, commanded by Spruance) and Task Force 17 (*Yorktown*, commanded by Fletcher), and with driving urgency got them well to the west of Pearl Harbor before 3 June. Fletcher, as the senior admiral, commanded the combined force, which Nimitz placed well to the north of Midway where he hoped they would not be detected by Japanese reconnaissance before Nagumo struck but would be well-positioned to deliver a hard flank blow at the Japanese carriers.

One lesson the Americans had learned in the Coral Sea was that more fighters were necessary to provide adequate escorts for strikes while at the same time leaving enough for defence. The fighter strength in the three US carriers had therefore been increased by nearly half, to a total of 81 F4F Wildcat fighters, in addition to 41 TBD Devastator torpedo-aircraft and 106 SBD Dauntless dive-bombers. The F4F Wildcats were the latest model, with armour, self-sealing fuel tanks and folding wings, paid for by a reduction in speed and range.

Nimitz considered using the six battleships which were now based in San Francisco, but concluded that they would be more hindrance than help. He was not prepared to divert from his carrier forces any of the screening vessels which the battleships would have required. This was indeed a far cry from the days when the sinking of the battlefleet in Pearl Harbor had seemed such a disaster.

Admiral King believed that the Japanese plans were designed to trap and destroy a portion of the American fleet, as indeed they were, and for this reason he gave orders to Nimitz that major units were not to be unduly risked. This was an instruction which Nimitz duly passed on to Fletcher and Spruance in writing, telling them that they were to 'be governed by the principle of calculated risk, which you shall interpret to mean the avoidance of exposure of your force without good prospect of inflicting, as a result of such exposure, greater damage to the enemy'.[4]

Nimitz took every precaution that foresight could suggest. Midway itself was heavily reinforced, with the garrison being increased to the point where the Japanese would have had no easy task to take the island by an amphibious assault. Thirty Catalina flying boats were sent there to provide long-range scouting, along with a striking force of seventeen B–17 Flying Fortress heavy bombers and four B–26 Marauders hurriedly converted to carry torpedoes. In addition 68 carrier-type aircraft, mostly manned by Marines, were based on the island. After Nimitz deduced, again correctly, that the Japanese would launch their attack at dawn and that enemy bombers would therefore arrive at Midway soon after 6 a.m., search aircraft were sent out before 5 a.m. each day from 3 May onwards and by 6 a.m. all aircraft were either in the air or ready to take-off.

Yamamoto had issued his orders for the Midway operation while the Coral Sea battle was still being fought. In addition to a

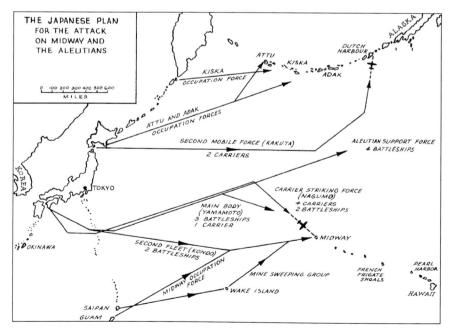

The Japanese plan for the attack on Midway and the Aleutians

direct assault on Midway he decided on a diversion in the Aleutians, to commence the day before the Midway attack. Four battleships, two light carriers and numerous cruisers and destroyers were required for this operation, in which a landing was to be made in the Western Aleutians. The diversion was a complete failure, for Nimitz allocated no more than five cruisers and four destroyers to defending this area and resolutely refused to disperse his meagre carrier strength. It was the Japanese, not the Americans, who were weakened by the diversion.

The Japanese forces attacking Midway were divided into no fewer than four groups. These were:

Advance Force: eleven submarines;

Midway Occupation Force (Vice-Admiral Kondo): two battleships, the light carrier *Zuiho*, ten cruisers and 21 destroyers escorting sixteen transports, two seaplane carriers and various other support ships;

Carrier Striking Force (Vice-Admiral Nagumo): four carriers (*Akagi*, *Kaga*, *Hiryu* and *Soryu*) with a total of 300 aircraft (including 72 Zeke fighters, 72 Val dive-bombers and 81 Kates), two battleships, three cruisers and eleven destroyers;

Main Body (Admiral Yamamoto): three battleships, including the new 64 170 ton *Yamato*, the light carrier *Hosho*, two seaplane carriers, one cruiser and eleven destroyers.

There was also a separate Aleutian Protection Force of four battleships, two cruisers and nine destroyers, which was intended to be detached from the Main Body shortly before the air attack on Midway and to go to a patrol area between Midway and the Aleutians.

Yamamoto's plan was for Nagumo's carriers to make heavy air attacks on Midway, starting the day after the Aleutians diversion, with the aim of forcing the US Pacific Fleet to come out and fight. If challenged by the US Fleet Nagumo was to direct all his effort to its destruction, while the Main Body moved up in support. Meanwhile Midway was to be captured and developed into an air base. It was for this purpose that Nagumo's four carriers had some 40 aircraft on board which were to be based in Midway after the island was secured, including 21 Zekes and two experimental models of the new Judy dive-bomber carried in *Soryu*.

Considering that Yamamoto's aim was to bring about a decisive action with the US carriers his plan was radically unsound, for here he was allowing his own carriers to involve themselves in an attack on Midway without first locating the American ships. Nagumo had made a similar mistake in his attack on Ceylon, but he was not to be so fortunate with the outcome a second time. Yamamoto also dispersed his surface forces widely; much too far apart to give mutual support and liable to defeat in detail. Although in the whole operation, including the Aleutians diversion, the Japanese used eight carriers (this figure could have been ten if Yamamoto had been prepared to wait for *Shokaku* and *Zuikaku*), in the decisive carrier clash the odds were only four to three against the Americans. That is the measure of Yamamoto's failure.

Of course, Yamamoto did not completely discount the possibility of an early sortie by the US carriers, though he certainly had no idea that some of his radio messages were being intercepted and decrypted by the Americans. To give warning of a sortie he arranged for flying boats to be refuelled by submarines off the French Frigate Shoals, and from there to reconnoitre Pearl Harbor on 31 May. A patrol line of submarines was also to be established west of Hawaii. Neither of these measures was successful. When the submarines arrived at the shoals they found the Americans were already using that location as a seaplane base, so the Japanese flying boats could not be refuelled. The muddle delayed some of the submarines intended for the patrol line, others were delayed in sailing because of mechanical troubles, and as a result the submarine cordon was not established until 4 June. By that time the American carriers were far to the westward.

Spruance's task force had actually sailed from Pearl Harbor on 28 May,[5] followed two days later by Fletcher's. While waiting for the completion of repairs, *Yorktown*'s air group was brought up to strength by amalgamation with the survivors from *Lexington*. The two task forces met 350 miles north-east of Midway on 2 June. There they waited. Meanwhile the scouting aircraft from Midway were busy, each day searching to a distance of 700 miles in a semi-circle to the west. Many of the US planes were not yet fitted with radar, and there was an area of fog and rain squalls beyond 300 miles to the north and north-west which could well conceal the Japanese until almost the last moment. Thus passed the last days of May and the first two days of June, as the tension steadily mounted.

At last, on 3 June, the Japanese were sighted. At 9 a.m. that morning a Catalina flying boat reported enemy ships 600 miles west of the island. These vessels were the Midway Occupation Force, and nine B–17s were sent out to attack with 600-pound bombs from 8000 feet. Although the American bombers surprised the Japanese, who were without radar, they scored no hits. (This did not, of course, prevent the airmen from making extravagant claims that they had hit two battleships or cruisers and two transports.) During the night four radar-equipped Catalina flying boats, each with a torpedo secured under a wing by an improvised arrangement, also made an attack on the Japanese force and actually scored a hit on a tanker at the rear of the transport column, although this vessel was not seriously damaged. This daring strike was one of the first successful night air attacks on ships at sea.

Yamamoto was unperturbed by the early location of the Midway Occupation Force and the lack of any reports of the movements of US ships, still confident that the operation was a strategic surprise and it would be some time before the US carriers could intervene. Intent on preserving radio silence so as not to compromise the position of the Main Body, he did not tell Nagumo of the attacks on Kondo's force, nor did his staff pass on intelligence received which indicated that the Americans were on the alert. Thus when Nagumo launched his strike on Midway from a position 210 miles north-west of the island in the early hours of 4 June he had every expectation that surprise would be complete.

Nagumo used 35 Kate level-bombers from *Hiryu* and *Soryu* and 36 Val dive-bombers from *Akagi* and *Kaga,* escorted by 36 Zeke fighters (nine from each carrier). He retained a second strike of equal strength, ready to deal with the US carriers if they appeared. The weakness of Nagumo's plan lay in his arrangements for searching for US ships, which were coloured by his belief that it was unlikely there were any in the vicinity. Only seven search aircraft were used, five of them float planes from the escorting battleships and cruisers. They were to cover an area eastwards to a depth of 300 miles, but were not required to take-off until after dawn. Because of a defective catapult in one of the cruisers its float plane was 30 minutes late, and unfortunately for Nagumo it was in the search-sector assigned to this aircraft that the US carriers were operating. Another aircraft which might have located the Americans was launched by the cruiser *Chikuma,* but developed engine trouble and turned back. In retrospect, Commander Genda thought the search plan was 'slipshod'.

Soon after 7 a.m. Nagumo received a report from Lieutenant Tomonaga, the leader of the Midway strike,[6] that a second attack would be necessary. The aim of the first strike had been to neutralise Midway as a base by destroying US aircraft on the ground, but all the American planes had been in the air when the Japanese strike force arrived. Tomonaga's aircraft found themselves fiercely opposed by 27 Buffalo and Wildcat fighters manned by marines, and although all but ten of these opponents were shot down (for the loss of six Japanese aircraft, mainly to anti-aircraft fire) the goal of putting the airfield out of action was not achieved.

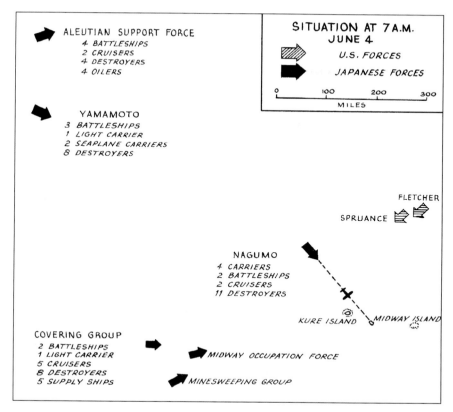

The situation at 7.00 a.m., 4 June 1942

Considerable damage was caused to installations but there was little that could be done to harm the runway. Tomonaga realised that the best hope lay in an immediate second strike catching the surviving American aircraft on the ground being refuelled.

By this time Nagumo had other worries. His carriers had been sighted by a Catalina at 5.52 a.m. and all available strike aircraft on Midway were ordered to attack. They arrived in small groups between 7 a.m. and 8.20 a.m. Every type of attack was made, with torpedoes being dropped, dive-bombing passes carried out in steep and shallow modes, and level-bombing from 20 000 feet. The attacks were gallantly made but very poorly coordinated and uniformly unsuccessful; more than half of the American planes were destroyed by Japanese fighters and anti-aircraft gunfire.

It was while these attacks were in progress that Nagumo had to make up his mind about whether to launch a second strike on

Midway. Clearly the US air strength on Midway had not been eliminated, but were there any US carriers in the vicinity? There was still no report from any of the scouting aircraft, so at 7.15 a.m. Nagumo made his decision. The torpedoes were to be removed from the aircraft held ready to strike the US carriers and replaced with bombs for a second attack on Midway, a change requiring a good hour's hard work.

The two American carrier task forces were by now 200 miles north of Midway, with Spruance about ten miles to the south of Fletcher. Both admirals had received reports of the attacks on the transports during the afternoon of 3 June, but they were after bigger game—the Japanese carriers—which were expected to approach from the north-west. The Catalina's sighting report of the Japanese carriers was intercepted by Fletcher, and at 6.07 a.m. he ordered Spruance to 'proceed south-westerly and attack enemy carriers when definitely located'.[7] He would follow with *Yorktown*.

By 7 a.m. Spruance estimated that he was within 155 miles of Nagumo's carriers—barely within torpedo-bomber range. He could wait no longer, however, and threw every available aircraft into the attack except for essential defensive fighter and anti-submarine patrols. Launching took over an hour, and formations left as soon as they were ready. For his part, Fletcher was reluctant (after his unfortunate experiences in the Coral Sea) to commit all his strike aircraft until he was certain that no other enemy carriers were present. *Yorktown*'s aircraft were accordingly held back until 8.38 a.m. when—no further Japanese carriers having been sighted— Fletcher ordered an attack by half his dive-bombers and all his torpedo-bombers. They were more than an hour behind Spruance's strike.

By this time Nagumo knew that US carriers were in the vicinity. Shortly after 7.30 a.m. a message was received from the cruiser *Tone*, whose float plane had been the one late in taking off, that ten ships 'apparently enemy' had been sighted 200 miles to the eastwards. Immediately he received this message Nagumo ordered the suspension of the changeover from torpedoes to bombs and the preparation of a strike against these ships, though there was no mention of a carrier.[8] But were these ships a serious threat? An urgent message was sent to the scout to identify the types of ships involved, but it was not until 8.20 a.m. that the scout reported that one of the ships 'appeared to be' a carrier.

Nagumo was in a serious dilemma. Nearly all his torpedo-bombers had been rearmed with bombs before he had cancelled his order, and the only strike aircraft immediately ready were the 36 dive-bombers in *Hiryu* and *Soryu*. If he despatched them now they would have to attack without fighter escort, for all his remaining fighters had been used to repel the attacks by the Midway aircraft. Overhead the aircraft returning from Midway were circling, waiting to land, some damaged, many short of fuel. Rear-Admiral Yamaguchi, in *Hiryu*, urged that the dive-bombers should be sent off at once, without fighter escort if necessary, but Nagumo decided that the prudent course was to conserve his strength until he could launch a massive blow by his dive-bombers and torpedo-bombers, with fighter escort. Such a strike could be ready soon after 10.30 a.m., and in the meantime the flight decks could be cleared for the returning Midway strike. By 9.18 a.m. the last Midway aircraft had landed and Nagumo ordered a north-easterly course to close the American ships. Feverish efforts were being made on the flight decks of his carriers to prepare the aircraft for the next strike. Only another hour was needed.

Because of the strength and efficiency of the Japanese fighters the Americans found it difficult to shadow Nagumo continuously, despite the cloud cover. Spruance's aircraft had been given the predicted position of Nagumo's ships, but this was significantly in error. Nagumo had manoeuvred radically while under attack, and had changed course to head for the American carriers after recovering the last of his Midway strike, so that he was actually more than 30 miles north-west of the position predicted by Spruance's staff. Thus, when Spruance's leading formation—35 Dauntless dive-bombers from *Hornet*, escorted by ten Wildcats— arrived in the position they had been given they found nothing but an empty expanse of ocean. Their leader ordered a search to the south, away from the Japanese carriers (although of course he did not know that). The hopeless search continued until the fighters ran out of fuel and crashed; two of the dive-bombers also came down in the sea, but the remainder made it back to their carrier, though thirteen of them had to land at Midway to refuel.

Hornet's torpedo squadron, fifteen Devastators, had become separated from the remainder of the formation, and arrived in the predicted target area after the dive-bombers and fighters had left. Of course they too found nothing, but their leader, Lieutenant-Commander Waldron, ordered a turn northwards (for what reason is not known) and within a few minutes had come across the Japanese carriers. The time was 9.20 a.m. Waldron made a sighting report to *Hornet* and at once attacked, although he was completely unsupported. The Japanese had twenty Zeke fighters in the air, and they made short work of the obsolete Devastators, not one of which survived. The Japanese ships were undamaged.

Nearly an hour passed before the next attacks were made, though at least the Americans now knew where Nagumo was. By chance the torpedo-bombers and dive-bombers from *Enterprise* and *Yorktown*, operating in separate task forces without any real co-ordination, attacked almost simultaneously. The first into action were the fourteen torpedo-bombers from *Enterprise*, which also had been separated from their fighter escort and had to attack unsupported. They sighted Nagumo's carriers at 10 a.m. but because the Japanese carriers manoeuvred radically to keep the torpedo-bombers astern, it was another twenty minutes before they were able to gain a suitable position to commence their torpedo-dropping run. During this long flank movement the Japanese Zekes were steadily reducing the number of torpedo-bombers, only eight surviving long enough to make an attack, and of these half were destroyed. No hits were scored.

Yorktown's torpedo squadron attacked almost simultaneously. Being slower, they had been sent ahead of their dive-bombers and fighters, which had been ordered to link up on the way; this had been achieved, so that *Yorktown*'s aircraft were the only ones to make a properly synchronised attack. But while the dive-bombers were preparing to attack, the torpedo-bombers were being almost wiped out, for their escort of six Wildcats could not hold off the numerous Zekes, and ten of the twelve torpedo-bombers were lost. Again there were no hits.

Of the 41 American torpedo-bombers which had gone in, 35 had been lost, without any compensating success. Nevertheless they played a decisive part in the battle, for the Japanese fighters concentrated on them and neglected the dive-bombers, who were able to attack almost at will. The Japanese had no radar to give warning of impending air attack, and their fighters could intercept the attacking bombers only as and when they could see them and get to them.[9] The American torpedo-aircraft, coming in at low level, had drawn virtually all the Zekes down to them, and the Japanese fighters did not have time to do anything about the dive-bombers even if they saw them.

At 10.20 a.m., though, the situation seemed all in favour of the Japanese. Nagumo had just given the order to launch the strike against the American ships as soon as it was ready, and the attack by the American torpedo-bombers had been beaten off with crippling losses. Then, with perfect timing, came the 32 dive-bombers from *Enterprise*. They were led by Lieutenant-Commander McClusky, who had been given the same target information as *Hornet*'s dive-bombers and had to search for nearly an hour to find the real Japanese position. Now, his attack came just when

A Douglas SBD Dauntless dive-bomber. The SBDs were the decisive force in the Midway battle, causing the loss of all four Japanese carriers. (*National Archives, 80-G-43454*)

the Japanese carriers were supremely vulnerable with all their strike aircraft on deck, fully fuelled and armed.

McClusky's Dauntlesses came down in 70-degree dives, concentrating on the two largest carriers, *Kaga* and *Akagi*. The latter had more than twenty aircraft on deck, and at 10.26 a.m.—two minutes after the last of the torpedoes had been avoided—she was hit twice by bombs. One penetrated to the hangar deck and exploded among the bombs which had carelessly been left there after being removed from the aircraft of the aborted second Midway strike:

> There was a huge hole in the flight deck just behind the amidship elevator. The elevator itself, twisted like molten glass, was drooping into the hangar. Deck plates reeled upwards in grotesque configurations. Planes stood tail up, belching livid flame and jet-black smoke.[10]

Kaga was in no better shape after being struck by four bombs. With her flight deck and hangar deck wrecked, she was soon abandoned. Meanwhile the seventeen dive-bombers from *Yorktown*

(Fletcher had launched only half his available strength) were concentrating on *Soryu*, whose flight deck (like the others) was covered with strike aircraft almost ready to take off. Hit by three 1000-pound bombs she burst into flames and was soon abandoned. In wreaking all this damage, *Enterprise* lost fourteen dive-bombers and *Yorktown* two.

Nagumo was reluctantly compelled to shift his flag to the cruiser *Nagara*, leaving *Akagi* abandoned and burning until eventually sunk by order of Yamamoto at 5 a.m. the following morning.[11] In *Kaga* the fires soon got out of control and, torn by internal explosions, she sank at 7.25 p.m. It was the same story with *Soryu*, who sank ten minutes before *Kaga*. Her captain refused to leave his ship, and as the last survivors left he could be heard on the bridge singing the Japanese national anthem.

The only undamaged Japanese carrier was now *Hiryu*, the flagship of Rear-Admiral Yamaguchi, one of the ablest officers in the Japanese Navy. *Hiryu* had been about ten miles to the north

Yorktown dead in the water and burning after the first Japanese attack. (*National Archives, 80-G-32301*)

of the other three carriers, and had not been troubled by the dive-bombers. Yamaguchi immediately ordered a counter-attack against *Yorktown*, the only one of the American carriers the Japanese had so far discovered. At 10.40 a.m., as soon as the dive-bombing attacks on the other carriers were over, eighteen dive-bombers and six fighters took off from *Hiryu* and headed for the American carrier.

Yorktown had an SC air-warning radar, which gave somewhat better results than the CXAM, but at the height at which the Japanese strike was flying it was detected only at a range of 32 miles. *Yorktown* was well-prepared, with twelve Wildcat fighters in the air, and as soon as the Japanese were detected all aircraft fuelling was suspended and the fuel lines filled with carbon dioxide. The defending fighters intercepted the Japanese fifteen to twenty miles from the carrier, and shot down or drove away all but six of the dive-bombers. These survivors were able to score three hits and within moments most of *Yorktown*'s boilers were out of action and a raging fire was burning. The carrier's construction and damage control stood the test, however, so that by 1.40 p.m. the fires were out, and the ship was able to steam at nineteen knots and operate aircraft, although her radar was temporarily knocked out.

The Japanese had lost three fighters and thirteen dive-bombers in the attack, but despite these losses *Hiryu* was not finished with *Yorktown*. At 1.30 p.m. Yamaguchi sent a second strike of ten torpedo-bombers (one from *Akagi*) escorted by six Zekes (two from *Kaga*). The cruiser *Pensacola*, which had been sent by Spruance to reinforce Fletcher, detected the strike at a range of 45 miles and relayed continuous reports to *Yorktown*. Soon afterwards *Yorktown*, which had managed to get its radar working again, also detected the Japanese. Although the carrier had six fighters in the air when the strike was detected, and managed to launch four more, all interceptions were too late. The fighter-direction officer in *Yorktown* assumed that the Japanese were dive-bombers, and sent his fighters out at too great an altitude, and a belated request for fighter assistance from Spruance's task force was fruitless because the two task forces were by now 40 miles apart.

The Japanese scored hits with two torpedoes, though they lost half their torpedo-bombers to the American gunfire and the visual interceptions by the fighters. Within ten minutes *Yorktown* was listing more than twenty degrees to port, and the order was given to abandon ship. After transferring himself and his staff to a cruiser, Fletcher told Nimitz that Task Force 17 would protect

Kate torpedo-bombers pass near *Yorktown* after launching their torpedoes. *Yorktown* is already listing from a torpedo hit. (*National Archives, 80-G-32242*)

and attempt to salvage *Yorktown* while Spruance engaged the Japanese with Task Force 16. Nimitz raised no objections.

Yorktown did not have to wait long to be avenged. Before she was hit she had sent out ten dive-bombers as scouts, and at 12.45 p.m., just as the Japanese torpedoes were striking home, they sighted *Hiryu*. Spruance received the report and immediately ordered *Enterprise* to launch her remaining 24 dive-bombers (ten of them refugees from *Yorktown*) against *Hiryu*. The American dive-bombers, again led by Lieutenant-Commander McClusky, were not intercepted—mainly because *Hiryu* had committed almost all its Zekes to the task of escorting strikes and had only six left, three of which had just returned from the strike on *Enterprise*.

Attacking from the direction of the sun, the American aircraft scored four hits which turned the Japanese carrier into a mass of flames as bombs and torpedoes in the hangar began to explode, though for a while she could still maintain her speed of 30 knots. The crew fought desperately to save the ship, but the fires and further ammunition explosions ripped her apart. At

Japanese aircraft carrier *Hiryu* burning. (*US Naval Historical Center, NH73065*)

3.15 a.m. the following morning she was abandoned, and two hours later Japanese destroyers were ordered to torpedo her. Admiral Yamaguchi went down with the ship, and with him went the last of more than 300 Japanese aircraft lost in this disastrous battle.

All this time Yamamoto was 400 miles away with the Main Body, informed but impotent. He had heard the successive reports of the damage to Nagumo's carriers, but it was not until 4.15 p.m. that he was informed of the strength of the opposition. Then Yamaguchi reported the claims of returning pilots that they had 'succeeded in damaging two carriers', being under the impression that his second strike had been made on an undamaged American carrier. Within two hours Yamamoto heard that the last of Nagumo's four carriers had been crippled, yet at 7.15 p.m., apparently in order to stiffen morale, he told his Force Commanders that:

the enemy force fleet has retired to the east. Its carrier strength has practically been destroyed . . . The Carrier Striking Force, the

Midway Occupation Force . . . and Advance Force [the submarines] will contact and destroy the enemy as soon as possible.[12]

Nagumo was astounded at this signal, and immediately pointed out that the Americans were believed to have five carriers, four of which were undamaged, and that all his four carriers were out of action. (Nagumo's overestimation of the number of American carriers was caused by a mistake by a reconnaissance seaplane which sighted Spruance's carriers twice within a few minutes, without realising that they were the same force.) Even Yamamoto's faint hope of a night surface action faded when it became clear that Spruance was wisely keeping clear to the east, and at 2.25 a.m. on 5 June Yamamoto accepted the inevitable, ordering the abandonment of the operation and a general retirement.

During the night two cruisers of the Midway Occupation Force collided. As the two ships, *Mikuma* and *Mogami*, limped westwards they were attacked by army B–17s and marine SBD dive-bombers from Midway. The B–17 attacks were ineffective, as indeed they were throughout the battle, but one of the marine dive-bombers crashed on board *Mikuma*, further reducing her speed.

Spruance was in no hurry to begin the pursuit. He had only six torpedo-bombers left, and these were the only aircraft with which he could hope to stop the Japanese battleships if they turned on him. He was also curiously reluctant to use the floatplanes in his cruisers for reconnaissance. So it was not until 9.30 a.m. on 5 June, after the dawn air searches had made certain that the Japanese were not close on top of him, that he set off after them. By this time they were too far ahead and Spruance was able to do no more than harass a couple of stragglers. By nightfall his carriers were approaching the belt of fog and low visibility, where it would be pointless to pursue. Indeed the pursuers might easily become the pursued, and fall victim to the immensely-heavier weight of Japanese gunfire at close quarters.

During the night, therefore, Spruance reduced speed and the following day concentrated his efforts against *Mogami* and *Mikuma*, the other Japanese ships being out of his reach. The two cruisers were still struggling slowly westwards, escorted by two destroyers. Over a period of four hours on 6 June more than 100 aircraft took off from *Enterprise* and *Hornet* to attack them, but although *Mikuma* was sunk, *Mogami*—reduced to a wreck by four bomb hits—was able to limp back to Truk. Spruance could do no more. His ships were short of fuel, his airmen were exhausted. So, at 5.20 p.m. on 6 June, he ordered a retirement to Pearl Harbor.

The only important American casualty had been Fletcher's

flagship, *Yorktown*. She continued to float throughout 5 June and attempts were made to tow her back to Pearl Harbor. Early on 6 June she was boarded by a salvage party, and hopes were high when by noon her list had been corrected. Then at 1.35 p.m. she was hit again, this time by a Japanese submarine which fired four torpedoes at her at short range. Two of the torpedoes struck a destroyer which was alongside providing power, but the other two hit the carrier. The destroyer sank almost at once, but the carrier lasted another fifteen hours until at last, at 5 a.m. on 7 June, she capsized to port and sank in 3000 fathoms. These two ships were the only American ships lost in the battle.

Midway was one of the decisive battles of history. It marked the limit of Japanese expansion. Although the Japanese shipyards were able to build new carriers, the Japanese Navy was never able to replace the experienced aircrews lost in this battle. Thenceforth, the initiative lay with the Americans. The retreat of eleven battle-ships before two American carriers marks the recognition of the end of an era. No longer could the battleships claim to be the decisive surface force. That title had been yielded to the aircraft carrier.

There were three areas in which the Americans had a decisive advantage at Midway: intelligence, radar and damage control. The code-breakers and radio traffic analysts had given Nimitz a clear picture of Yamamoto's intentions, but it is to the credit of Nimitz that he trusted the intelligence assessments and deployed his forces accordingly, despite the fears of some of his staff that he might be falling into a trap. It is not possible to see how Nimitz could have better deployed his available forces; he seems to have thought of everything in his preparations for this battle.

The American advantage in radar, for warning and fighter direction, was critical. The fighter direction was substantially better than in the Coral Sea, but there had been no time to overcome the two serious defects: the lack of height-finding radar and the inferior performance of the F4F. The Japanese had much more serious problems in this area, for the experimental radar sets in the battleships *Ise* and *Hyuga*, employed in the Aleutians Protection Force, made no contribution to the battle, and the Japanese never caught up with the Americans in radar technology.

Nevertheless, it was in damage control that the most dramatic difference was revealed. Each of the four Japanese carriers lost was put out of action by a single dive-bombing attack, set on fire and abandoned. It could be argued that the first three—*Kaga*, *Akagi* and *Soryu*—were unlucky in that they were hit at the most vulnerable moment, with an armed strike ranged on the flight deck.

However, it is obvious that arrangements for stowing the bombs and torpedoes removed from, or waiting to be fitted to, the strike aircraft were grossly defective, as were the safety arrangements for aviation fuel. The fourth carrier—*Hiryu*—went the same way, though she had no strike aircraft on deck.

These results contrasted with the performance of *Yorktown*, which was hit by three bombs from dive-bombers yet two hours later was able to make nineteen knots and operate aircraft again—which none of the Japanese carriers had been able to do. She survived further hits in a torpedo-bombing attack which forced her abandonment, yet still did not sink, so that 36 hours later she still warranted attempts to tow and salvage her—efforts which were apparently successful until she suffered a final crippling submarine attack. Even then she did not sink for another fifteen hours.

The Americans could look forward to a massive aircraft-carrier building program, although they would have to wait.[13] After the shattering defeat at Midway the Japanese Navy completely changed

A formation of Grumman TBF Avengers. (*National Archives, 80-G-238702*)

its building policy. All work on battleships was stopped, and emphasis was switched to constructing new carriers and converting fast merchant ships or uncompleted battleships and cruisers to this role.[14] The building program embarked upon was, however, so ambitious as to be totally unrealistic. With material shortages and extreme overcrowding of shipyards, most of the carriers were never even laid down. The Imperial Navy would have to fight the remainder of the war largely with the carriers which had avoided the Midway debacle.

The disparity in performance of the carrier-based aircraft was also heading to be reversed. The F6F Hellcat, the successor to the Wildcat, first flew just after the battle of Midway. The first operational Hellcats were accepted by the US Navy in January 1943, just six months after the first prototype had flown.[15] Although the TBF Avenger torpedo-bombers made an inauspicious debut at Midway, they were substantially better than the TBD Devastators, which the Avengers were rapidly replacing. They were at least comparable to the Japanese Kate torpedo-bombers.

The shore-based aircraft, particularly the B–17 Flying Fortress high-level bombers, made wild claims about the damage they had done at Midway.[16] In fact they dropped 300 bombs without scoring a single hit, which is not surprising considering that none of them had seen action before and they were untrained in attacking moving ships.

13

Malta convoy:

10–15 August 1942

In the pre-war view of the British Naval Staff, the use of convoys would reduce the air threat to merchant shipping to 'manageable' proportions and surface escorts, suitably armed, would 'prove the answer' to air attacks. This excessive confidence in the effectiveness of anti-aircraft gunnery had now been rudely shattered, and with the whole Atlantic coast from the Spanish border to the North Cape in German hands a formidable air threat to British shipping developed. Vast numbers of guns were obviously needed to give merchant ships some protection, but the guns, and the trained men to crew them, were extremely scarce.

To supplement such weapons as could be scoured from armament depots, many ingenious devices were also tried and installed—such as the Parachute and Cable (PAC), and the Fast Aerial Mine (FAM)—although most were ineffective except against very low-level attacks. Inefficient as they were, and costing more in British productive effort than the worth of the few German aircraft they destroyed, at least these devices gave merchant seamen the feeling that they were not completely defenceless. Possibly they even had some deterrent effect on German pilots.

As the air threat to British merchant ships increased, thoughts naturally turned to the successful use of ship-launched fighters by the Grand Fleet in the First World War. A plan for the carriage of fighters in merchant ships fitted with a catapult was put forward in the autumn of 1940, and although opposed by the Ministry of Transport on the grounds that it would reduce cargo-carrying capacity, the scheme was started as a matter of urgency following the forceful intervention of Churchill. The first ship carrying a Hurricane sailed with a convoy before the end of May 1941, and

A Hawker Hurricane on the launching ramp of a merchant ship. (*FAA Museum, S/HUR#49*)

over the next two years 35 catapult ships completed 170 round voyages with Russian, Atlantic and Mediterranean convoys.

During this period fighters were launched on eight occasions: six German aircraft were shot down, two were damaged and three were driven off. That the results were so poor was due to difficulties with aircraft maintenance and to the primitive radar fitted in the parent ships. By the time these difficulties were being overcome large numbers of small escort carriers were coming off the slipways, and the last catapult-fitted ships were withdrawn in August 1943. The Royal Navy also manned and operated five fighter-catapult ships, launching fighters on ten occasions. Only one German aircraft was destroyed, and by the middle of 1942 all these ships had been withdrawn as not being worth the effort.

The escort carriers which replaced the catapult ships were merchant-ship hulls fitted with a hangar and a flight deck so that their aircraft could both take-off from and land on the carriers. The first of these escort carriers was *Audacity*, which was converted from a captured German merchant ship and entered service in

June 1941. She carried six F4F Wildcat fighters (still called Martlets by the Royal Navy)—the ones ordered by the French, without folding wings—and soon showed her value in convoy defence by shooting down three German aircraft. She was sunk by a submarine in November 1941, but by then many replacements were on the way. Even before *Audacity* was commissioned four more merchant ships were taken in hand for conversion, and the building of six more was ordered in America under the Lend-Lease program. Ultimately 38 US-built escort carriers (CVEs) were provided to the Royal Navy.

The supplying of Malta during the critical months of 1942 was a desperate business for Britain. Not only were the convoys liable to constant air and submarine attack, but they were also threatened by the Italian fleet, which was numerically much stronger than the squadrons Britain could provide in the Mediterranean at this time. Even when ships reached Malta they were often sunk before they could unload. It was obvious that the fighter strength in Malta needed to be increased to enable this situation to be turned around. Strong reinforcements of fighters were flown in from the carriers HMS *Eagle* and USS *Wasp*, and in June another relief attempt was made. This time it was a double operation, with heavily escorted convoys sailing from the west and at the same time from Alexandria. The results were disastrous. The convoy from Egypt was forced to turn back by the combined weight of air attack and the threat of the Italian Fleet, while only two ships of the western convoy got through, the remainder being sunk by air attack.

By August 1942 Malta's situation was becoming desperate, for Rommel had advanced to El Alamein, almost at the gates of Alexandria. Nevertheless the British were determined not to abandon Malta, though little help could be expected from the ships based in Alexandria. That fleet was so reduced in strength that the most it could do was to sail a dummy convoy towards Malta to try to draw some of the Axis surface and air forces away from the real convoy coming from the west.

The support given to the August convoy from Gibraltar (Operation 'Pedestal') was the heaviest yet provided. The fourteen ships in the convoy were escorted by three aircraft carriers—*Victorious*, *Indomitable* and *Eagle*—two battleships, seven cruisers and 24 destroyers. There were also two independent squadrons—two fleet oilers each screened by four corvettes, and the carrier *Furious* escorted by eight destroyers. (*Furious* carried Spitfires which were to be flown to Malta, and she took no part in the main battle.) There were also eight submarines whose task was to

A PAC rocket being inserted into the projector. The wire is in the container. (*Imperial War Museum, MH808*)

attempt to intercept any Italian surface ships which menaced the convoy.

The merchant ships in the convoy were carrying nearly 100 000 tons of supplies, chiefly food and ammunition. Only one tanker, *Ohio*, could be spared, and many of the other ships carried cans of aviation fuel in case the tanker did not get through. The anti-aircraft armaments in all the ships in the convoy had been specially strengthened. Typically a ship would have one medium-calibre gun, usually 4-inch, one 40mm Bofors gun and six 20mm Oerlikons. There were no control arrangements for the medium-calibre guns, so all they could do was to fire barrages over open sights. There were also numerous rockets mounted to fire PACs and FAMs. It was well known by now that these weapons were almost useless, but it was thought they might be good for crew morale.

The whole operation was under the command of Vice-Admiral Neville Syfret, a gunnery specialist who had served all his sea career in cruisers or battleships. He had commanded a cruiser squadron under Somerville during the Malta convoy of July 1941, and later had commanded the escort of a convoy to Russia before taking part in the invasion of the French colony of Madagascar.

Now he was in charge of probably the most difficult convoy operation to be attempted during the whole war.

Rear-Admiral Lumley Lyster commanded the three carriers, flying his flag in *Indomitable*. After his victory at Taranto he had been called to the Admiralty as Fifth Sea Lord and Chief of Naval Air Services, and for more than a year he had worked to get better aircraft for the Fleet Air Arm, in particular modern fighters. After the years of neglect of this arm, the best that could be done was to obtain American aircraft, or to produce modified versions of RAF fighters. Both these measures had been taken, and Lyster had in his three carriers a mixed bag of 72 fighters—46 Sea Hurricanes (without folding wings), ten Martlets and sixteen Fulmars—in addition to 28 Albacores for reconnaissance and strike.

The 72 fighters were few enough, considering the numbers of aircraft available to the Germans and Italians. To make matters worse the convoy had to pass close to the Axis air bases for a long stretch of its voyage, and attacking bombers could thus be given strong fighter escorts. Nor was the only threat in the air, for the convoy had to face the perils of mines, submarines, motor torpedo-boats, and not least the Italian Fleet, which outnumbered the escort by nearly three to one.

Indomitable was an enlarged version of the *Illustrious* class, and had a small lower hangar so that she could stow about a third more aircraft. She also had an enlarged forward lift, so that Sea Hurricanes could be struck down into the hangar. She was the only one of the three carriers who could do this; the other two had to leave their Sea Hurricanes on the flight deck as a permanent deck park, and they took up a lot of room with their fixed wings. As a partial solution to this problem, some of the Sea Hurricanes were placed on outriggers over the side of the flight deck.

During the passage from England the ships in the convoy had been drilled intensively in emergency turns and other likely manoeuvres, for much would depend on their ability to maintain formation under heavy attack. All naval aircraft to be involved in the operation were flown past the convoy in an 'identification parade', in an attempt to cut down the number of aircraft shot down by mistake. Veiled in dense fog the convoy passed through the Straits of Gibraltar early on 10 August 1942. Hopes were high that the convoy had not yet been detected, and that the operation would be at least a partial surprise. But, alas for these hopes, the security arrangements had not been successful, and vague information that a Malta convoy was being planned had reached the Germans and Italians even before the end of July.

Forewarned, the Germans and Italians had acted. There were

already 220 German and 300 Italian aircraft based in Sicily, and a further 130 aircraft in Sardinia. Another 50 bombers from Crete, North Africa and elsewhere were immediately flown in. Eight Italian submarines were disposed in the western Mediterranean, while further east were three German submarines, with the British carriers as their priority targets. In the heavily-mined Sicilian narrows were ten more Italian submarines and the main force of motor torpedo-boats.

The Italians had too little oil to send more than one or possibly two battleships to sea and they were not prepared to risk such valuable (though little used) ships against the heavy convoy escort. They did manage to muster a force of six cruisers and eleven destroyers, which was intended to mop up any members of the convoy who managed to survive the passage through the Sicilian narrows. All Axis shipping movements were gradually suspended, and the German and Italian aircraft, submarines and motor torpedo-boats had a free-fire zone.

Such was the Axis plan. Despite the efforts of the carrier fighters the convoy was continuously shadowed by Italian aircraft from early on 11 August, but it was not from the air that the first blow fell. At 1.15 p.m. on 11 August the carrier *Eagle*, on the starboard side of the convoy, was suddenly hit by four torpedoes

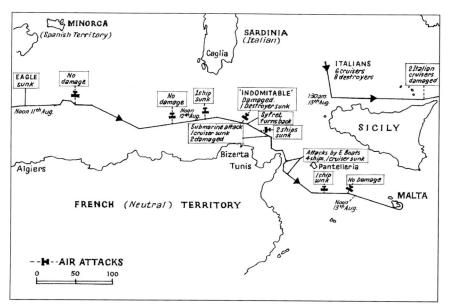

The Malta convoy

fired by the German submarine *U.73* which had penetrated the destroyer screen without being detected. The old carrier sank in eight minutes, but most of her crew were saved, as were four of her Hurricanes which had been on patrol at the time and landed on the other carriers. The loss of *Eagle* was a heavy blow to suffer before the first shock of air attack had been met.

That evening *Furious* flew off her 38 Spitfires to Malta,[1] and turned back to Gibraltar with an escort of destroyers. As she left, the first air attacks developed. The bombers, about 50 strong, appeared as the sun sank below the horizon. The Italians attacked with torpedoes, while the Germans dropped 2000-pound armour-piercing bombs from a height of 8000 feet. The German aircrews made considerable claims, but in fact not a ship was touched—the normal result of high-level bombing, which has been accurately described as the equivalent of trying to drop a billiard ball on a frightened mouse.

The attacks were met with heavy but inaccurate gunfire and the carrier fighters were completely ineffective. These aircraft were not radar-equipped so in the gathering gloom they required to be directed with great precision if they were to find their targets, but none of the directing ships possessed a radar set which could measure the height of an aircraft with any accuracy. Lyster complained that a 'dusk attack must be met with either guns or fighters, both cannot operate together'; here he evidently had in mind the fact that the fighters had come under heavy gunfire as they approached their carriers in order to land, and four had been written-off in deck-landing crashes. 'If fighters are to be used at dusk,' he went on to argue, 'they must be the right type of aircraft properly equipped and directed; Naval Fighters cannot undertake this duty at present.'[2]

The air attacks were resumed next morning, and in the clear light of day the fighter defence was a different story. Both the carriers had fighter-direction officers, although radio silence was permitted to be broken to direct fighters against enemy aircraft only when the latter were certain to sight the convoy! This permission was soon taken up, for not long after 9 a.m. some 30 Ju.88s attempted to approach the convoy from ahead and from out of the sun but were intercepted by fighters when they were 25 miles from the convoy and only a handful of bombers got through, doing no damage.

This was only a precursor of the attacks which were to follow, for the convoy was now within easy range of the Sardinian airfields, and the Italians and Germans mounted a major coordinated attack. The plan was for ten Italian torpedo-bombers each to drop two circling torpedoes, called motobombes, ahead of the convoy, whose formation it was hoped would be disorganised as a consequence. In the confusion, coordinated attacks would be made by 40 German dive-bombers and 20 Italian torpedo-bombers while a further squadron of eight Fiat Cr.42 biplane fighter/bombers, each lightly armed with two 200-pound bombs, tried to confuse the screening destroyers.

The attack was not a success, only one ship in the convoy being damaged. In the first place the motobombes were dropped too far ahead of the convoy, which had no difficulty altering course to avoid them. The Italian torpedo-bombers were late but they finally attacked at 12.45 p.m. They were harassed by fighters on their way in, and met with intense gunfire, including a 16-inch barrage fired by the battleship *Rodney*. The torpedoes were dropped ineffectively at very long range. By this time the belated German dive-bombing attacks[3] were developing, but they too were poorly coordinated and spread over 30 minutes, although they were pressed home with more determination.

As a finale, two Italian Reggiane Re.2001 fighters, each armed with a 100-pound anti-personnel fragmentation bomb, attacked *Victorious* as the Hurricanes were landing. The Italian fighters themselves somewhat resembled Hurricanes, so they were able to approach without being recognised. One bomb burst in the water under the port bow and the other hit the carrier's deck squarely amidships, disintegrated without detonating and fell over the side. There were no casualties and no significant damage. The Italians got away unscathed.[4]

The one damaged merchant ship was unable to keep up with the convoy, and had to be detached with a destroyer as escort. She was sunk the same evening by two torpedo-bombers.

The afternoon slowly wore on, enlivened by numerous submarine scares. The next air attack did not come until late in the afternoon, but it was the most formidable of the day. This time the German and Italian dive-bombers and the Italian torpedo-bombers did manage to attack simultaneously, despite the efforts of the British fighters. The 40 dive-bombers attacked from astern from the direction of the sun, while twenty torpedo-bombers came in from the starboard bow. The Italians again dropped their torpedoes far outside the destroyer screen, but although the convoy, with a well-practised manoeuvre, turned to comb the torpedo tracks, one of the screening destroyers was hit.

Meanwhile the dive-bombers were concentrating on the two carriers. *Indomitable* was hit by two 1100-pound bombs and also had three near-misses, suffering severe damage. Her flight deck was wrecked and she could no longer operate aircraft so her fighter patrol of eleven aircraft (eight Sea Hurricanes and three Martlets) had to attempt to land on board *Victorious*. The small lifts in that carrier meant that the non-folding Sea Hurricanes could not be struck down to the hangar and as the outriggers were already full to capacity the flight deck became very crowded. Landings were delayed, so that two of the fighters had to make forced landings in the sea. *Indomitable* was finished for the rest of the operation. She was eventually sent to Liverpool for repairs, which were to take five months, and she did not become operational again until March 1943.

By 7 p.m. the attacks were over, and it was high time that Syfret's heavy ships withdrew. The convoy was about to enter the mined areas of the Straits of Sicily, and in these narrow waters submarines and motor torpedo-boats were known to be lurking. It would be dark in less than two hours, and such waters were no place for valuable battleships and carriers at night. Besides, Syfret thought that there would not be another heavy air attack before dark. At 7 p.m., twenty minutes earlier than originally planned, he accordingly withdrew to the west, leaving Rear-Admiral Burrough with four cruisers and ten destroyers to take the convoy on.

Indomitable under attack. (*Imperial War Museum, A11298*)

A Fairey Albacore flies over *Victorious*. A Hurricane can be seen on an outrigger just forward of the island. (*FAA Museum, CARS V/41*)

It had been intended to provide a combat air patrol of four Fulmars for the convoy, but the confusion on the deck of *Victorious* prevented the Fulmars landing for refuelling and rearming. The British carriers were not yet organised to operate with a deck park, as the same ships later did successfully in the Pacific. The problem lay with the catapulting arrangements, which still were done with the aircraft jacked-up on to a trolley, and unfortunately differently-adjusted trolleys were needed for the Fulmars and Sea Hurricanes. Moreover, free take-offs could not be done with a trolley in place, so *Victorious* did not use her catapults and there was a tremendous amount of shifting of parked aircraft to clear the forward end of the flight deck for free take-offs, and then the after end for landings. It was all very slow. Despite the failure of the plans for the carriers to provide fighter cover at dusk, the convoy was now within range of RAF Beaufighters based in Malta, and its air defence was up to them until the convoy came within range of the Malta-based Spitfires.

At 8 p.m., while the convoy was changing from four columns into two so that it could be within the area swept for mines by the escorting destroyers, Italian submarines struck devastating blows. First the freighter *Brisbane Star* was torpedoed, then twenty minutes later a single salvo from a second submarine hit two cruisers, *Nigeria* and *Cairo*, and the most important ship in the convoy, the tanker *Ohio*. The tanker was able to stay with the convoy, but *Cairo* sank and *Nigeria* (Burrough's flagship) had to turn back for Gibraltar. Burrough shifted his flag to a destroyer, and was in hot pursuit of the convoy when heavy air attacks began again.

The Germans could not have timed their attack better. Not only was Burrough out of touch with his force, but the two torpedoed cruisers were the only ships capable of directing fighters. Six Beaufighters had been over the convoy, in touch with *Nigeria* and *Cairo*, but these ships were the only ones with VHF radios, and when they were disabled the Beaufighters were unable to make contact with any of the other ships either by high-frequency voice radio or by morse code. Fired on by the convoy when they approached, they had withdrawn to Malta before the dusk air attacks developed.

The convoy was in considerable confusion, for the torpedoed cruisers had been leading the two columns. Thirty German Ju.88s and seven He.111s, each of the latter carrying two 1700-pound torpedoes, came as dusk was drawing in, and found easy targets. Two merchant ships were disabled by bombs, and a third damaged by a torpedo. The convoy disorder was worsened, and during the night Italian submarines and motor torpedo-boats wrought great destruction. Two more cruisers were hit, and one of these— *Manchester*—was eventually scuttled. Six ships of the convoy were also torpedoed, and of these five were lost.

Dawn broke on a tragic scene. The convoy was by now reduced to three ships, escorted by two cruisers and seven destroyers (when Syfret heard of the disasters, he had sent Burrough reinforcements of a cruiser and two destroyers). Behind them straggled the three surviving damaged merchant ships, with destroyers urging them on.

At 8 a.m. the inevitable air attacks began again. Beaufighters and long-range Spitfires[5] from Malta were overhead, but as no ship was capable of directing them they found it difficult to break up the attacking formations. In the first attack one of the ships in the convoy was blown up and sunk. Great efforts were being made to reform the convoy, and by 9 a.m. five of the six survivors—three of them damaged—were in company.

Sporadic dive-bombing and torpedo-bombing attacks continued throughout the morning and in one of them a damaged German dive-bomber crashed on board the tanker *Ohio*. Soon afterwards the convoy was attacked by twenty dive-bombers, and five bombs fell close to *Ohio*, disabling her. In the same attack the already-damaged *Rochester Castle* was set on fire and another ship, *Dorset*, was brought to a standstill.

By noon the air attacks were over. The convoy was within 60 miles of Malta, and inside the cover of the short-range Spitfires. Of much more importance was the fact that the radar in Malta could now be used to direct their operations, and under the protection of the Spitfires the three survivors (including *Rochester Castle*) steamed into the Grand Harbour that afternoon, their crews' exhaustion temporarily forgotten.

It remained to bring in the three damaged stragglers. *Dorset* sank that afternoon, leaving only *Ohio* and *Brisbane Star*. *Ohio* was stopped and almost immovable, but a destroyer and two mine-sweepers managed to tow her the remaining 80 miles to Malta, fighting off several air attacks during the 40-hour trip, and early on 15 August they brought her triumphantly to the island. *Brisbane Star* had arrived independently a few hours earlier, so five sorely-battered survivors of the original fourteen ships finally reached Malta.

The Italians, not without reason, claimed a major naval victory. Indeed, the sinking of nine ships out of an important convoy of fourteen—together with the destruction of one carrier, two cruisers and a destroyer and the damaging of another carrier and two cruisers—might well be considered a great victory, for the Italian Navy lost only two submarines. Yet the odds were all in their favour, and with their air and sea superiority they should never have allowed the convoy to pass at all. Except for their motor torpedo-boats, which were very effective, their surface ships were conspicuous by their absence, though the possibility of their intervention had been one of Syfret's principal worries, and eight submarines had been disposed to intercept them if they ventured east of Pantelleria.

The Italian striking force of six cruisers and eleven destroyers did actually put to sea, with orders to intercept the convoy off Pantelleria at dawn on 13 August, but a furious wrangle broke out at Italian Naval Headquarters. The Commander-in-Chief refused to send his ships beyond Pantelleria unless fighter cover was provided, but as the Italian Air Force claimed they had no suitable fighters, and the Luftwaffe point blank refused to provide any (despite an appeal from Mussolini), the attack was cancelled on the evening of 12 August. To complete a sorry tale, two of the cruisers were torpedoed by a British submarine as they withdrew.

In fact, the British air threat to the Italian striking force was negligible, for the carriers had gone and Malta had too little

The tanker *Ohio* arrives at Malta. (*Imperial War Museum, GM1480*)

strength to mount an effective attack.[6] The RAF in Malta had carried out an elaborate radio bluff to persuade the Italians that attacks on their ships were about to be made by Liberator heavy bombers, but although it is just possible that this may have had some effect the real reason for the failure was the lack of determination on the part of the Italian Naval High Command.

The 15 000 tons of fuel and 32 000 tons of general cargo brought in by the August convoy was enough to keep the island going until the end of the year, and by then the situation had changed dramatically. In early November the Allies had won an overwhelming victory at El Alamein, and a few days later made landings in French North Africa. Malta's long ordeal was nearly over because by the end of the month the Germans had been driven out of Egypt and Cyrenaica, and a convoy of four ships had been safely brought into Malta from Alexandria, covered by fighters operating from the newly-won airfields. In the following month regular sailings to the island were resumed.

Malta was saved, but the margin had been narrow. When the relieving convoy arrived in November there were barely enough supplies to continue siege rations for another four weeks.

216

TACTICAL PHASES

The August Malta convoy fell into three distinct tactical phases. During the first phase—the 770-mile two-and-a-half-day passage from Gibraltar to the western end of the Straits of Sicily—the British lost the carrier *Eagle* (to a submarine) and one merchant ship sank, the carrier *Indomitable* was put out of action and one destroyer was badly damaged by air attack. The British also lost thirteen fighters (not counting the sixteen sunk in *Eagle* and those lost as a result of the damage to *Indomitable*) and the Germans and Italians about 30 aircraft to the fighters and ships' guns.[7] This phase showed, however, that a convoy, with sea room and defended by radar-directed fighters, could survive surprisingly close to enemy bomber-bases. Indeed the early bombing attacks, when the convoy was beyond fighter-escort range, were completely ineffective.

Bombing attacks were much more effective when escorted by fighters, but even so if Malta had been located at the western end of the Straits of Sicily the operation would have been hailed as a great tactical victory for the British, and for sea-based over land-based air power. This was despite the fact that the Germans and Italians could deploy seven times as many aircraft as could the convoy escort, and most of the carrier fighters were obsolescent. Syfret wrote after the action that 'the speed and the height of the Ju.88s made the fighters' task a hopeless one. It will be a happy day when the fleet is equipped with modern fighter aircraft'.[8]

The attack aircraft in the carriers—28 Albacores—were hopeless for the tactically-desirable role of striking at the Axis air bases, and their use for this purpose was not even contemplated.[9] Moreover the lack of any height-finding radar in the British carriers made efficient fighter control very difficult in the half-light of dusk, when most of the British losses occurred.

The second phase—the overnight 140-mile passage through the Sicilian narrows—was a disaster for the British. The only two ships capable of directing fighters were eliminated by an Italian submarine, and German bombers found easy pickings in dusk attacks, as did Italian submarines and motor torpedo boats during the night. Two cruisers were sunk and two damaged, and five merchant ships sunk and four damaged, two of them seriously. This phase was an overwhelming victory for the Germans and Italians, and if the Italian Fleet had attacked at dawn on 13 August as originally planned the British would have been annihilated.

The six surviving merchant ships were extremely vulnerable to air attack during the third phase, but in fact the German and Italian attacks were remarkably ineffective, all but one of the merchant ships surviving the 150-mile remaining passage to Malta. In the early stages this was not because of fighter support from Malta, for the convoy had no ship capable of directing them, but in the final stage—the last 60 miles—when the Spitfires and Beaufighters could be directed from radar stations in Malta the air attacks were easily beaten off.

A tactical change introduced by the British for this operation was the permission given to the aircraft carriers to act independently when operating aircraft, rather than having to wait for the whole force to make a cumbersome turn. The carriers were normally stationed by the Rear-Admiral Aircraft Carriers (Lyster) in a suitable position depending on the direction and strength of the wind, and if a carrier when operating aircraft had to break through the destroyer screen, it merely signalled 'join me' to the two nearest destroyers. A second change was the provision of a separate task group of oilers to refuel the cruisers and destroyers at sea, the first time such support had been available to the Royal Navy in the battles we have considered.[10]

For the Germans and Italians there should have been concern as to why such a large number of sorties—nearly 200 by bombers alone on 12 August—achieved so little. There was also friction between the Axis partners, with the German airmen feeling, not without reason, that they launched a disproportionate number of sorties and pressed them home much harder. The Italians could have replied that the main losses on the convoy were inflicted by Italian submarines and motor torpedo-boats, and that no Germans matched the gallantry of the two Italian fighter-pilots who attacked *Victorious*. The Italians, too, had displayed some tactical ingenuity (without much result, it must be admitted). They had formed two Special Combat Units, and the two Reggiane fighters from one of these units had certainly surprised *Victorious*. The other unit had launched a radio-controlled Sm.79 filled with tons of high-explosive, intending it to crash on one of the British ships. (Its radio-control gear failed, and the aircraft eventually crashed and exploded in Algeria, much to the irritation of the French.)

The Admiralty was developing a greatly increased enthusiasm for aircraft carriers, now that it could no longer be disputed that naval aircraft could sink a battleship at sea, and the progress of the war in the Pacific was demonstrating the crucial role of aircraft carriers. The 1942 naval construction program called for 52 aircraft carriers to be built. Admittedly 32 of these were escort carriers, to be built in America, but the construction program envisaged for Britain was staggering—including completion of *Indefatigable* and *Implacable* (not finally ready until 1944),[11] four more fleet carriers of the *Audacious* class (36 800 tons), ten light fleet carriers of the *Colossus* class (13 190 tons), and six light fleet carriers of the *Majestic* class (14 000 tons).

The 1943 program went even further, authorising three large fleet carriers of the *Gibraltar* class (45 000 tons) and eight improved light fleet carriers of the *Hermes* class (18 300 tons), so that by the end of 1943 the RN had under construction or on order 33 aircraft carriers (not counting escort carriers). The four carriers of the *Audacious* class were designed with armoured decks, but the light fleet carriers had no armour. Interestingly, after prolonged arguments between the designers and the aviators, the *Gibraltar* class were designed to have US-style open hangars with two deck-edge lifts, and without armoured flight decks; there was to be six-inch armour under the hangar. It was all too late. None of the fleet carriers were completed before the end of the war, and although five of the *Colossus* class were commissioned they were not in time for any significant operational service.

The other matter which clearly had to be tackled was the number of aircraft in each carrier. The Admiralty could not help but be aware that US carriers were operating more than twice as many aircraft as British carriers of similar size. This was partly because they had larger hangars than the constricted armoured boxes in the British carriers, but principally because they had a permanent deck park; that is, they carried more aircraft than could be stowed in the hangar. As *Victorious* had found out, for this to work the carrier had to have efficient catapults.

When *Illustrious* was repaired in America after her damage suffered in the Mediterranean in January 1941, her catapults were modified so that they could do tail-down launching—four times as fast as the old trolley style—as well as catapulting on trolleys. After the experience in Operation 'Pedestal' the other armoured-hangar carriers were progressively converted too. There were transitional problems, because existing British aircraft (and US aircraft modified to RN requirements) still had to be catapulted from trolleys, so the carriers had to be ready for both methods. The problems gradually disappeared as new aircraft designed for tail-down launching became available, and by the time the British carriers arrived in the Pacific in 1945 they could cope with substantial deck parks. *Victorious*, for instance, had started with 34 aircraft during Operation Pedestal (including six Sea Hurricanes on outriggers); in the Pacific she comfortably operated 53 aircraft.

Because of their restricted hangar capacity the British carriers were still not operating as many aircraft as their American counterparts, but they were a lot closer. They still had problems, though, for the aviation-fuel capacity of the three carriers of the *Illustrious* class was so restricted that the fuel was exhausted after only two or three days of operations by the enlarged complement of aircraft. This problem was rectified in the later armoured-hangar carriers, and they could operate for roughly twice as long.

The British anti-aircraft gunnery was certainly not very effective, its performance being summed up by Lyster when he wrote:

> that the gunfire is a deterrent to the attacking torpedo aircraft is evident and perhaps it may deter some of the more timid bombers and dive bombers. The fact remains, however, that the dividend paid for a tremendous expenditure of ammunition is remarkably low. I have the strong impression that not only is it inaccurate but also undisciplined.[12]

In the light of the fighter-direction problems that became clear during this operation, the Admiralty issued staff requirements for three new radar sets to provide better coverage: a 3.5 metre warning set to give coverage out to 160 miles, to replace the existing air-warning sets; a 10cm set to give low cover above the horizon out to 150 miles; and a special fighter-direction radar to give gapless cover out to 70 miles and a heightfinding accuracy of 500 feet. All these requirements would ultimately be met, but none of them before the end of the war.

In the meantime a single-mast version of the Type 281 air-warning radar would become available in 1943, and the carriers could then be fitted with both a Type 281 and a Type 79,[13] improving their aircraft-warning and fighter-direction capability. A 10cm height-finding radar, the Type 277, was in production but would not be available until 1944. It then proved a disappointment, for its range was too short for effective fighter-direction, and the only British ship to see action before the end of the war with an effective height-finding radar was the carrier *Indomitable*, which was fitted with an American FM–1 height-finding and fighter-direction set in February 1944.

Perhaps the most crucial development in fighter direction would be the general fitting of PPIs, which were already standard in the US Navy. With a PPI the aerial would not have to be stopped each time the range and bearing of a target was required, so coverage was improved and the fighter director had much clearer and more up-to-date information. Trials of a British naval PPI began in April 1943, and general fitting soon began, at least doubling the efficiency of fighter direction. But that was nearly a year away from now.

14

Santa Cruz:

25–27 October 1942

The Americans wasted no time in exploiting the initiative they had won by their victory at Midway. Admiral King was anxious to halt the Japanese southward advance which was threatening the sea and air routes between the US and Australia. On 4 July 1942 the decision was made that Nimitz's forces should seize Santa Cruz and Tulagi, in the Solomons, and occupy an airfield site on the island of Guadalcanal. When a report was received next day that the Japanese were constructing an airfield on Guadalcanal, that was added to the list of objectives. On 10 July Vice-Admiral Robert Ghormley, the Commander in the South Pacific Area,[1] received the order to proceed; within a month the landings were made. At dawn on 7 August US Marines stormed ashore on Guadalcanal, brushed aside Japanese opposition, and seized the airfield.

Nimitz had given the Guadalcanal operation all the support he could. Escorting the troopships were eight cruisers and a destroyer screen, with a covering force of three carriers—*Saratoga*, *Wasp* and *Enterprise*—the new battleship *North Carolina*, and a number of cruisers and destroyers, all under the command of Vice-Admiral Frank Fletcher. On the evening of 8 August Fletcher felt it necessary to withdraw his carriers because of the torpedo-bomber threat (and also to refuel), a decision resisted by the assault force commander, Rear-Admiral Kelly Turner, whose marines were left ashore short of stores, food and ammunition, and forced to survive on captured provisions. Nevertheless Fletcher went, and the Japanese struck the same night.

A force of seven cruisers and a destroyer surprised the Allied escorting force near Savo Island north of Guadalcanal, sank four cruisers and damaged a number of other ships before escaping practically unscathed. For many months after this action the Japanese controlled the waters round Guadalcanal by night, ferrying-in troops and bombarding the American positions. Ghormley had too few ships to oppose them, but by dawn each day the Japanese ships were gone, for they could not challenge the power of the American carriers.

Meanwhile, the American troops on Guadalcanal set about preparing the captured airfield for use. By 17 August it was ready, and three days later a squadron of fighters and a squadron of dive-bombers were flown in from an escort carrier. Yamamoto was not one to surrender air superiority tamely. Despite the losses at Midway the Japanese Navy's strength was still superior to the US Pacific Fleet, and Yamamoto was prepared to use this factor which he was well aware would not last. By 21 August he had collected three carriers and three battleships with supporting cruisers and destroyers at Truk, under the command of Vice-Admiral Kondo. Another four cruisers and five destroyers were at Rabaul, together with 100 aircraft. Nimitz, too, was reinforcing the South Pacific as quickly as he could. The carrier *Hornet* left Pearl Harbor on 17 August and headed for Noumea, while two modern battleships from the Atlantic Fleet were ordered through the Panama Canal. Both sides knew that a clash was imminent.

It came on 24 August. Fletcher had sent *Wasp* and her escorts to fuel, and as a result had only three carriers to meet the Japanese thrust. The Japanese used their three carriers, as well as two battleships and many other vessels, in an attempt to fight a troop convoy (containing a mere 1500 men) through to Guadalcanal. Yamamoto knew his ships would be attacked by the US carriers, and used the small carrier *Ryujo* as bait, while his other two carriers (*Shokaku* and *Zuikaku*) prepared a counter-stroke.

The bait was duly taken, and *Ryujo* was sunk, but here Yamamoto's plan began to go awry. Although the Japanese bombers did score three hits on *Enterprise* (the flagship of Rear-Admiral Thomas Kinkaid), she was not mortally damaged and within an hour was steaming at 24 knots and operating aircraft. None of the other American ships was touched. Many of the Japanese pilots failed to find their targets, and returned to their carriers after jettisoning their loads.

Fletcher attempted a hasty retaliatory blow, but the 27 aircraft he used, without fighter escort, inadequately briefed, and with only the haziest idea of the position of the Japanese carriers, could not hope to achieve very much. Most of them returned without sighting anything, but a small group found part of the Japanese fleet and, despite being unsupported, gallantly dived to the attack. Two near-misses seriously damaged the seaplane-carrier *Chitose*. Thus ended the battle of the Eastern Solomons. Fletcher withdrew to the southwards to refuel; Kondo, after an unsuccessful attempt to force a night surface action, headed back towards Truk. The Japanese attempt to run a troop convoy into Guadalcanal was frustrated by US Marine bombers based on Guadalcanal and B–17 Flying Fortresses from the New Hebrides.

It was to be two months before the American carriers were again challenged. In the meantime matters continued much as before: a steady slogging battle on the ground to hold the airfield, and frequent attempts by night by the Japanese Navy to reinforce their garrison and bombard the American positions—attempts which were occasionally opposed by the Americans in some of the fiercest night actions of the war. By day the American ships unloaded their cargoes almost unopposed, except for occasional raids by Japanese aircraft from Rabaul. The campaign was becoming a long and bloody struggle of attrition.

Japanese submarines struck some telling blows during August and September. Although control of Guadalcanal airfield by the marines was strengthening, the American carriers still had to operate almost continuously in the restricted waters south of the island to provide them with adequate air support. On 31 August *Saratoga* was torpedoed by a submarine, and although not seriously damaged she was to be absent from the South Pacific for three critical months.[2] On 15 September a second penalty was exacted. A single submarine put two torpedoes into *Wasp* and another into the battleship *North Carolina*. The battleship suffered little damage, but fierce fires broke out in *Wasp* and she had to be abandoned and sunk.[3]

The Americans were now in a desperate position. They had only one fleet carrier in the South Pacific, and Yamamoto could concentrate at least five. Reinforcements of all types were scarce for the Americans, because the Anglo-American invasion of North Africa was about to be launched and was almost unceasing in its demands for more ships. Nimitz decided that it was time for a change of command in the South Pacific. No one could reasonably have done more than Ghormley, but he lacked the spark of showmanship and inspiration necessary in the face of reverses. His successor, Vice-Admiral Halsey, certainly had both these qualities in full measure. He had defects which would be revealed later, but in October 1942 he was undoubtedly the right man in the right place.

The Japanese High Command planned to make a major offensive against Guadalcanal, and by 15 October they were ready.

The army was called upon to capture the airfield within a week, after which the navy would 'apprehend and annihilate any powerful forces in the Solomons area, as well as any reinforcements'.[4] To this end Yamamoto divided his fleet into two task forces. Kondo's advance force consisted of the carriers *Hiyo* and *Junyo*, with two battleships, five cruisers and fourteen destroyers. (*Hiyo* developed engine trouble and returned to Truk, taking no part in the action.) Nagumo's striking force consisted of the carriers *Shokaku*, *Zuikaku* and *Zuiho*, two battleships, five cruisers and fifteen destroyers. Kondo was in overall command and could expect support from the 200 aircraft at Rabaul and from various other surface and submarine forces in the area.

This formidable fleet cruised north of the Solomons for several days, anxiously awaiting the promised capture of Guadalcanal airfield. But the US Marines held firm in a bitter, bloody battle in appalling conditions and the airfield remained in their hands. By 24 October Yamamoto impatiently told the army that his ships would have to withdraw unless the airfield was captured soon. The next day he ordered Kondo to attack American shipping off Guadalcanal, a marked change from his original intention. In accordance with these new orders, Kondo headed south. At the same time, unknown to him, an American fleet was heading towards him. A clash was imminent.

The delay in executing the Japanese plan had given time for Halsey to receive important reinforcements. On 24 October *Enterprise* rejoined the fleet, having received rapid repairs to the damage suffered on 24 August. She was accompanied by the formidable new battleship *South Dakota*. Nevertheless Halsey still had only two carriers to oppose the four Japanese (and with only 171 carrier aircraft compared to the Japanese 222),[5] and was heavily outnumbered in every other class of ship.

The equipment available to the two sides had changed little since Midway. Avenger torpedo-bombers had replaced the Devastators, but otherwise the aircraft operated by the American carriers were the same. Virtually all the US ships now had aircraft-warning radar, but there was still no set available that was capable of determining heights accurately. For close-range anti-aircraft defence, 40mm Bofors fitted in either twin or quadruple mountings had largely replaced the unsatisfactory 1.1-inch guns, with each automatically following a remote director which had a tachometric aiming sight. *South Dakota* had ten of the quadruple mountings, and *Enterprise* had been fitted with four (as well as the number of 20mm Oerlikons being increased to 46) while undergoing repairs after the battle of the Eastern Solomons.

The remote directors used the Mark 14 gun sight, which had originally been ordered by the British Admiralty. This was a design masterpiece which required the gunner merely to aim steadily at the target while the internal mechanism applied the necessary aim-off. The only weakness was that there was no ranging device, so the sights were set to a fixed range through which an attacking aircraft would have to fly. The Mark 14 was originally intended for the single hand-aimed 20mm Oerlikon, which was now being widely fitted. During the war 85 000 of these sights were produced, and Admiral Nimitz thought they filled the war's most pressing need.

The Japanese, on the other hand, had made virtually no improvements to their gun armaments, and although the warning radar set which had been tried by the two battleships during the Midway campaign (the 10cm Type 2 Mk.2) was now fitted in a number of the larger ships, it had a poor performance against aircraft. It had a maximum range of about 50 miles, but its wide beam and poor discrimination between targets at roughly the same range made it useless for fighter direction; the Japanese of course had no PPIs.[6] The best that could be done with the radar sets was to add their information about the direction and range of an incoming attack to reports from lookouts. The voice-radio link with the Zeke fighters was still very unreliable, and much of the information passed to the fighters was done by morse radio. It is to the credit of the Japanese pilots and the manoeuvrability of the Zekes that they made as many interceptions as they did.

Halsey organised his fleet into three task forces: Task Force 16 (Rear-Admiral Kinkaid) built round *Enterprise* and *South Dakota*; Task Force 17 (Rear-Admiral George Murray) comprising the carrier *Hornet* and her escorts; and Task Force 64 (Rear-Admiral Willis Lee) operating independently with the battleship *Washington* and cruisers and destroyers. Halsey, ever keen to assume the offensive, ordered Kinkaid to take the two carrier task forces well north of Santa Cruz and then to sweep in a south-westerly direction to intercept any Japanese forces making for Guadalcanal.

Kinkaid was fairly well informed of the movements of Japanese ships, since Catalinas based near Espiritu Santo in the New Hebrides were searching the area to the north of him. At noon on 25 October one of these aircraft sighted Nagumo's striking force, but was unable to keep touch in the prevailing low visibility. Kinkaid was then 190 miles to the east of the Santa Cruz islands, Nagumo 160 miles to the north-west of them, acting as a shield between Kondo and the expected American retaliation from the south.

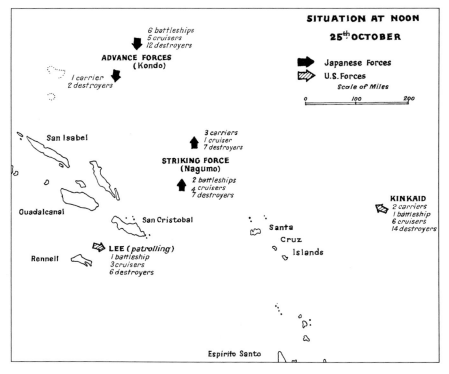

The attack on Guadalcanal

Although Nagumo was almost beyond his reach, Kinkaid decided to attempt a strike, and twelve search aircraft left *Enterprise* at 11.30 a.m., followed 50 minutes later by 29 attack aircraft. In the heavy cloud and thick rain squalls they could find no sign of the Japanese. Worse still, they did not return until after dark; one aircraft crashed on *Enterprise* and six others came down in the sea. It was an inauspicious beginning.

Late that night, believing that Guadalcanal airfield was at last about to be captured, Yamamoto issued fresh orders. He reasoned that the threat to the airfield would force the American carriers to fight, and decided that he would seek to destroy them in the area north-east of the Solomons. The trouble was that his scouting aircraft had still not found any sign of the American carriers, which were much further to the east than he anticipated.

The Americans were obviously in no such doubt regarding the position of his ships, for B–17s bombed Nagumo's battleships during the afternoon (without scoring any hits, of course). After dark five Catalinas took off to try their luck with torpedoes and bombs. One of these managed to drop its bombs so close to Nagumo's flagship, *Shokaku*, that the entire bridge was enveloped in smoke. Nagumo jumped to the conclusion that he was being drawn into a trap, and at 2.50 a.m. ordered a reversal of course to the north at 24 knots; two hours later Kondo ordered his Advance Force to conform with Nagumo's movements. The whole Japanese fleet thus headed northwards, away from the Americans.

Kinkaid at the time was only 200 miles east of Nagumo, having been heading north-westwards at twenty knots. *Hornet* kept her aircraft ready all night, but Kinkaid wanted to reserve his blow for daylight, and he urgently needed a clearer picture of the Japanese dispositions. He had been told the position of Kondo's battleship group soon after midnight, but did not know what had happened to the two carriers that were sighted the previous afternoon. Until they were found he could not risk wasting his strength on anything else.

Dawn began to lighten the eastern sky at 4.30 a.m., but still there was no news of the carriers. At 5 a.m. sixteen SBD Dauntless dive-bombers, each armed with a 500-pound bomb, took off from *Enterprise* with orders to search the north-western quadrant to a distance of 200 miles. Almost simultaneously Nagumo sent sixteen reconnaissance seaplanes and eight Kate bombers to scout to the south-east. Two of the opposing scouts passed, and ignored, each other as they flew outwards on their searches.

The two carrier groups were now less than 200 miles apart, and sightings were inevitable. The first occurred at 6.20 a.m., when an American SBD reconnaissance aircraft found two battleships which Nagumo had stationed 80 miles to the south of his carriers. These ships, under the command of Rear-Admiral Abe, had been intended to act as a buffer, to take the first shock of American air attack, but with the Americans unexpectedly coming from the east they were now badly placed. Kinkaid, however, had no intention of wasting effort upon these battleships until the carriers had been dealt with.

Half an hour later the vital carrier sightings were made, by both sides almost simultaneously. Nagumo was the first to get his attack under way. By 7.10 a.m. 67 aircraft were taking to the air from *Shokaku*, *Zuikaku* and *Zuiho*. But Nagumo was to receive a rude shock from the American reconnaissance aircraft. The Dauntlesses were flying in pairs, and one group, hearing the adjacent pair report the Japanese carriers, decided to attempt an attack. By skill and luck they managed to approach unopposed, and both scored hits on *Zuiho* after a dive-bombing approach. A

50-foot hole was torn in the flight deck, putting the carrier out of action, though (fortunately for Nagumo) not before her first strike was already airborne. All the American reconnaissance aircraft eventually returned safely to *Enterprise*, after a remarkably successful morning's work.

Kinkaid was twenty minutes later than Nagumo in launching his strike, and even then it was a piecemeal effort. First went 29 aircraft from *Hornet* at 7.30 a.m., half an hour later nineteen from *Enterprise*, and finally at 8.15 a.m. a further 25 from *Hornet*. When about 60 miles on its way the leading group of American aircraft passed Nagumo's strike heading in the opposite direction. Each ignored the other—the Americans because they had only 23 fighters with which to protect their bombers and had no wish to risk losing them in unnecessary combat with the Zekes, the Japanese because the fighter leader did not recognise them as enemy. Ten minutes later he had a second chance, when he encountered *Enterprise*'s nineteen aircraft. This time he attacked, and his Zekes shot down three Wildcats and three Avengers, but he lost two Zekes in the process and used up so much fuel and ammunition that most of his fighters had to turn back, leaving the 22 Val dive-bombers and eighteen Kate torpedo-bombers with poor support. They were to pay a heavy price for his impetuosity.

The Japanese bombers were detected by the American radar at 8.40 a.m., but in the confusion surrounding the departure of the American strike the detections were not definitely identified as hostile for nearly twenty minutes, and by this time the Japanese bombers were only 45 miles away. Fighter direction was centralised in *Enterprise*, but the directing officer was inexperienced[7] and too late in sending out his 38 fighters. Additional confusion was caused because command and communication with the fighters was conducted on a single channel, and this quickly became grossly overloaded, particularly as some pilots became orally undisciplined when excited. Fighting started only fifteen miles from Kinkaid's flagship, and most of the Japanese bombers inevitably got through.

Kinkaid had stationed the *Hornet* task force ten miles to the south-east of him, on his disengaged side. Each carrier had its supporting ships in a ring two miles in diameter. At 9 a.m. the *Enterprise* task force was blotted out by a local rain squall, and was not seen by the Japanese, but *Hornet*, ten miles further away, was in clear sunshine. Despite the strong defence—for 25 Japanese aircraft were destroyed—*Hornet* was heavily hit. By 9.20 a.m. the attacks were over. Ten minutes had reduced a fine ship to a shambles. Stopped, without power, and with an eight-degree list,

A Kate torpedo-bomber flies between two US cruisers as it heads for the crippled *Hornet*. (*National Archives, 80-G-32817*)

it was obvious that *Hornet* was out of the fight. It would take the best efforts of the Americans to save her.

While the attacks on *Hornet* were at their height, the first group of American bombers—fifteen Dauntless dive-bombers escorted by four Wildcats—had sighted Nagumo's battleship group. Ignoring them, the Air Group Leader (Commander Felt) led his aircraft towards the carriers 50 miles further north. Some Zekes intercepted them, and although the four escorting Wildcats held them off they lost contact with the dive-bombers, who continued without escort. At 9.30 a.m. Felt's pertinacity was rewarded by the sight of two of Nagumo's carriers, one of them—*Zuiho*—still burning from the bombing two hours earlier; the third carrier, *Zuikaku*, was out of sight to the east.

Shokaku was fitted with radar and had detected the approaching American dive-bombers when they were 60 miles away, and large numbers of Zekes came out to intercept. Two dive-bombers were shot down, and two more forced to turn back, but the survivors fought on, using cloud cover skilfully until finally they were in position to dive at *Shokaku*. Four 1000-pound bombs hit the carrier, wrecking the flight deck and starting fierce fires between decks, so that *Shokaku* could neither launch nor land aircraft. Two of Nagumo's three carriers were now crippled.

This was the only significant success achieved by the Americans. The six Avenger torpedo-bombers in the first wave from *Hornet* lost touch with the dive-bombers, failed to find the carriers and eventually unsuccessfully attacked one of the cruisers in Abe's battleship group. The *Enterprise* group, which had been severely handled in the brush with the Japanese fighters, also ineffectively attacked the battleship group. The second wave from *Hornet* failed to find the carriers, and after searching for some time they too attacked the battleship group. At least they achieved something, for their bombs heavily damaged the cruiser *Chikuma* although she stayed afloat.

Nagumo could reckon that his diversionary battleship group had done well, for only a fifth of Kinkaid's strike of 73 aircraft had reached the Japanese carriers. But *Shokaku*, his flagship, was clearly in no condition to continue the battle and it seemed imperative to get both her and the damaged *Zuiho* out of range of American attacks as quickly as possible. He therefore withdrew all his ships, including the undamaged *Zuikaku*, to the north-west at their best speed. It was not until 12.30 p.m. that Kondo intervened, ordering Nagumo to send back *Zuikaku* to rejoin the battle, and Rear-Admiral Kakuta in *Junyo* to take command of the two undamaged carriers. But *Zuikaku* had lost 70 precious miles, and was almost out of the fight.

While *Shokaku* was being attacked by the US dive-bombers, the second wave of Japanese aircraft was approaching Kinkaid's fleet. Forty-eight aircraft had been dispatched by Nagumo at 8.22 a.m., and a further 30 from Kakuta's flagship, *Junyo*, were not far behind. Kinkaid was ready for them, although *Hornet* was still out of action. *South Dakota* had already detected a group of aircraft 45 miles away which was closing fast. This group was in fact twenty Vals from Nagumo's carriers and their fighter escort. Once again, the American fighter defence failed, and the bombers reached their diving position unopposed—all but one aircraft concentrating on Kinkaid's task force. The lone bomber attacked the damaged *Hornet*, twenty miles to the west, and although it did no damage it interrupted attempts to take the carrier in tow.

Kinkaid had his task force in a very tight circle round *Enterprise*. The powerfully-armed *South Dakota* kept within 1000 yards of the carrier, and two cruisers and six destroyers were similarly placed in other directions. The Japanese dive-bombers were met with withering anti-aircraft fire, but this could not prevent two bomb hits and one near-miss on the carrier. Fortunately there was a ten-minute lull before the torpedo-carrying Kates came in, led by Lieutenant-Commander Murata, the veteran pilot who had dropped the first torpedo at Pearl Harbor. The torpedo attack was a failure because fighters broke up the formation, gunfire destroyed several bombers, Murata was killed and expert manoeuvring by *Enterprise* dodged the nine torpedoes that were dropped. It is a tribute to the seamanship of the American captains that ships in such close formation could cope with radical and unpredictable manoeuvring by the carrier. The only American casualty was the destroyer *Smith*, severely damaged when a crippled Kate crashed in a suicide dive onto its forecastle. By 10.40 a.m. the attacks were over.

There was little respite for *Enterprise*. Fighters from both carriers urgently needed fuel and ammunition, and strike aircraft were beginning to straggle back from their attacks on the Japanese ships. *Enterprise*'s flight deck was rapidly cleared, but the forward lift was out of action and this caused delays in the handling of aircraft. Landings had scarcely started before there was a fresh alarm from *South Dakota* that a suspicious group had been detected approaching from the west. This was the 30 strike aircraft from the *Junyo*, but unfortunately for Kinkaid the American strike aircraft were returning from the same direction. Considerable confusion ensued, and at 11.20 a.m. the fighter director of *Enterprise* informed all ships that there were no enemy aircraft in the vicinity.

Within a minute the carrier was desperately defending itself against *Junyo*'s dive-bombers, which had approached unobserved in low cloud cover. Low clouds were a mixed blessing for the Japanese, making it difficult to select the best targets before the bombers were committed to their dives. For this reason there was less concentration than usual on the carrier, and *Enterprise* escaped with only superficial damage from a near-miss. The two most effective anti-aircraft ships, *South Dakota* and the cruiser *San Juan*, were both hit but neither was seriously damaged. As the last of the Japanese withdrew, *Enterprise* quickly turned into the wind to resume landings, for many of the aircraft were now desperately short of fuel. With the survivors of *Hornet* on board, *Enterprise* was very overcrowded and thirteen dive-bombers had to be sent to the New Hebrides.

Kinkaid was now faced with a hard decision. The *Enterprise* task force had been heading into the south-easterly wind for the past three hours, and it was 100 miles from the *Hornet* task force. Kinkaid knew that *Hornet* was under tow, but was not making more than three knots. His own carrier, *Enterprise*, was no more than 75 per cent effective, and to turn back to support *Hornet*

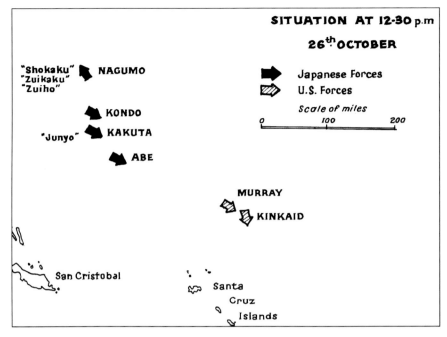

The situation at 12.30 p.m., 26 October 1942

would probably mean that both carriers would be lost. So at 2 p.m. he ordered his task force to retire east, leaving *Hornet* to her fate. There is no doubt that it was the right decision.

When Kinkaid made his decision to retire, Rear-Admiral Murray had by no means abandoned hope of saving *Hornet*. He had transferred his flag to the cruiser *Pensacola*, and all men not required for fire fighting or damage control were also being removed. The cruiser *Northampton* had the carrier in tow, and together they were plodding out of the area while the remainder of the task force circled round them. Unfortunately Murray's most useful anti-aircraft ship, the cruiser *Juneau*, had misunderstood a signal and had left to join Kinkaid.

At 3.15 p.m. Japanese torpedo-bombers were sighted; these were *Junyo*'s second strike of nine Kates escorted by five Zekes. Although the American radar had given plenty of warning of their approach, *Hornet* was a sitting target. She could not operate aircraft, and the fighters from *Enterprise*, now 120 miles to the south-east, arrived too late to do more than harry the Japanese as they retired. Yet so fierce was the American gunfire that seven Kates were shot down and only one torpedo hit the stricken carrier.

Yet this hit—the third—sealed her fate. The list increased to fourteen degrees, and the order was given to prepare to abandon ship.

Hornet's ordeal, however, was not yet over. At 3.40 p.m. the dive-bombers of *Zuikaku's* third strike swooped on the ship, but without doing any damage. Fifteen minutes later six Kates from *Zuikaku* made a level-bombing run, scoring one hit on the flight deck as the crew was leaving. Still *Hornet* did not sink. At 5 p.m. nine dive-bombers from *Junyo* hit her again in the final air attack of the day. By dark all the survivors from *Hornet* had been rescued, and Murray ordered his task force to retire at top speed, leaving two destroyers behind to sink the crippled carrier. They fired nine torpedoes and 500 shells into the carrier's hull, and by 8.40 p.m. the ship was blazing from end to end. With the Japanese battleships just over the horizon, the destroyers could wait no longer and retreated at full speed, leaving the deserted carrier alone in the sea.

All afternoon Kondo's forces had been closing in for the kill. The disabled *Hornet* had no chance of getting away and Kinkaid,

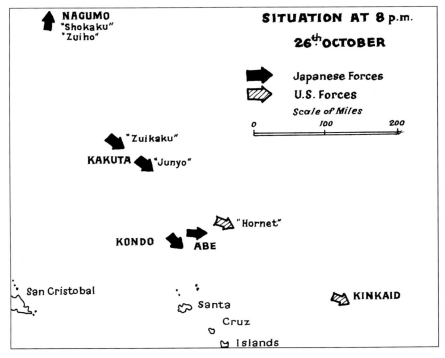

The situation at 8.00 p.m., 26 October 1942

even if he had tried, did not have anything like the strike strength needed to stop the Japanese. Float planes from the battleships and cruisers kept the Japanese admirals fully informed of the *Hornet* group's movements, and both *Zuikaku* and *Junyo* used all their serviceable aircraft to ensure that the carrier did not get away. Yamamoto ordered an all-out pursuit, and if possible the capture of *Hornet*. At 9.20 p.m. Abe's ships sighted the American carrier, but she was obviously too far gone to be taken in tow, and Abe ordered her to be sunk. Four more torpedo hits, making fifteen in all, finally finished her at 1.35 a.m. on 27 October.

The remainder of Murray's task force escaped. Kondo and Abe searched the area thoroughly, but found nothing. American Catalina flying boats dropped torpedoes by night at the scattered Japanese ships, disabling a destroyer and narrowly missing *Zuikaku*. Kondo's ships were by this time seriously short of fuel and his two remaining carriers had only 84 serviceable aircraft between them. When the dawn air searches found no trace of the Americans, the order was given for a general retirement to Truk.

By daylight on 27 October Kinkaid's forces were well out of range of the Japanese scouts, and heading for Noumea. The Americans had been outnumbered two-to-one, and had been defeated, but they were far from disgraced.[8] To offset the loss of *Hornet*, two Japanese carriers had been put out of action for several months; the Japanese aircraft losses were 69 to the American 40. In other ships the Americans lost one destroyer sunk, and a battleship, a cruiser and a destroyer damaged; the Japanese only one cruiser damaged.

Despite the reverse, Halsey was not discouraged and was still determined to attack, sending his surface ships to challenge the Japanese night supremacy around Guadalcanal. The result was two furious battles in November, in which two Japanese battleships were sunk. The Americans also suffered severe losses, but the tide had turned. *Enterprise*, with her forward lift still out of action, gave tremendous support by day, her aircraft administering the *coup de grâce* to one of the Japanese battleships. Yamamoto failed to use his recently won carrier superiority, and the Americans gradually gained the upper hand. They were to receive more unpleasant shocks and unexpected reverses, but by the end of November 1942 their hold on Guadalcanal was secure.

What lessons could be learned from this battle? The fighter direction by the American carriers was poor, caused partly by the inexperience of the fighter-direction officers, partly by the lack of height-finding radars, partly by undisciplined chaos on the voice-radio links, partly because the defending Wildcat fighters were outclassed by the escorting Zekes, and partly by the failure to use IFF effectively to identify hostile aircraft.[9] All these deficiencies could be cured. New radar sets were beginning to pour off the production lines, improved versions of the air-warning radars as well as new 10cm radars to give low cover and height-finding ability. Four-channel VHF radios were fitted in US carrier aircraft, to overcome the problem of jammed circuits during a heavy raid (improved training of pilots helped here too). And there was not much longer to wait for the new F6F Hellcat fighter, which would replace the Wildcats and prove more than a match for the Zeroes.

Kinkaid's decision to leave *Hornet* to her fate was clearly right, but he could still have given her more fighter support as he withdrew. The *Hornet* task force was still capable of directing fighters, but with *Hornet* out of action, it had no fighters to direct. When the Japanese air attacks on *Hornet* developed during the afternoon of 26 October, Kinkaid—at that time 120 miles away and under no air threat himself—would have been much wiser to order *Enterprise* to provide her with a standing patrol of fighters.

There were problems with the American strikes too. It was difficult for relatively low-performance aircraft such as the Dauntlesses or the Catalinas to shadow a Japanese carrier force in daylight in the face of the Zeke fighters, but it was not even attempted. As a result Kinkaid's main strike on 26 October was sent to the estimated position of the Japanese carriers, which was in fact wrong by 60 miles, so most of the American strike failed to find the carriers at all. The strikes took off in very piecemeal fashion, and there were no successfully coordinated attacks between dive-bombers and torpedo-bombers.

The Japanese had much more serious problems. *Shokaku* had radar, and used it effectively to direct fighters onto the US dive-bombers, but the Japanese had much less to look forward to than the Americans as far as new radars were concerned. Even more worrying must have been the declining efficiency of the bomber-pilots, due to the training system's inability to produce sufficient well-trained replacements. In the early months of the Pacific war the performance of the dive-bombers had been awesome, and an effort such as that by *Zuikaku*'s pilots, when they failed to score a single hit on the stricken *Hornet*, would have been inconceivable. At the beginning of the war Japanese carrier pilots had been markedly better trained than their American counterparts; by the time of this battle they were roughly equivalent, and the longer the war went on the more the Japanese fell behind.

The battle of Santa Cruz showed yet again the astonishing resilience of American carriers after being hit. Both *Shokaku* and

Zuiho were unable to operate aircraft again after being hit on the flight deck by bombs. However, *Enterprise* after being hit by a similar number of bombs[10] was operating aircraft again an hour later, remained operational throughout the action, and after the battle she remained in the area for many weeks to give support to Guadalcanal, despite having a damaged forward lift. Added to this was the ability of the Americans to repair their carriers quickly. These two factors were a great advantage for the Americans, and helped to compensate for their numerical inferiority at this time.

15

Bismarck Sea:

1–4 March 1943

Ever since the days of General Billy Mitchell the US Army Air Forces had fervently believed in the superiority of the shore-based bomber over the surface ship. By agreement with the navy (very reluctantly given) the air forces were made responsible for land-based anti-shipping strikes. The introduction of the B–17 Flying Fortress in 1937 and the B–24 Liberator three years later had been largely justified by the requirement to defend the American mainland against attack by sea.

The results of the first months of the Pacific campaign did little to support the sanguine view that heavy bombers would be able to dominate surface fleets. The war opened with a shattering disaster at Pearl Harbor and this fiasco was followed by other failures in the Philippines, the defence of Java, and the Coral Sea.[1] Some of the problems had been overcome by the time the battle of Midway was fought, although aircrews were still inclined towards making extreme claims about their effectiveness. The facts were more prosaic, however, and during fighting around Guadalcanal the Japanese surface ships seemed to ignore high-level attacks by American heavy bombers, sometimes even remaining stationary while an attack was in progress.[2]

Such was the position when Major-General George Kenney, the newly-appointed air commander in the South-West Pacific theatre, arrived in Australia at the end of July 1942. Opinionated, resourceful, and ready to experiment with anything, his rapid rise from lieutenant-colonel in less than two years had marked him out as just the man needed to inject fresh life into the squabbling air command in Australia. His predecessor, Lieutenant-General George Brett, had organised an integrated air staff, an arrangement which resulted in American air units coming under Australian command and caused one irritated senior officer to complain to Washington that 'the present organisation was an affront to national pride and to the dignity of the American Army'.[3]

Kenney reorganised his command so that he had under him the Fifth (US) Air Force and operational units of the RAAF. He gave the Fifth Air Force (which included some Australian squadrons) the responsibility for the vital operations in New Guinea and north-east Australia, and the RAAF the responsibility for the defence of Australia (except the north-east) and for operations against the Netherlands East Indies. By August 1942 the strength of Kenney's American units was about 165 bombers (comprising B–17s, B–26 Marauders, B–25 Mitchells and A–20 Bostons) and 250 fighters. Although much of its strength was still concentrated in Europe and the Middle East, the RAAF had built up to a strength of 31 squadrons, seven of them part of the Fifth Air Force. By early 1943 the RAAF strength in New Guinea consisted of three fighter squadrons (two with P–40s and one with Beaufighters) and four bomber squadrons (two with Beauforts, one with Hudsons and one with Bostons).

Despite its size, this force had some serious weaknesses—chiefly the fact that among the bombers the Marauders were nearly worn out and could be kept going only with great difficulty, while the fighters (mostly P–39 Airacobras and P–40 Kittyhawks) were markedly inferior to the Zekes. Although the Marauders were in the process of being replaced with Mitchells, this changeover was taking place slowly. Kenney was at the end of a very long supply route, and with the war in Europe receiving first priority, replacement aircraft were being doled out with a parsimonious hand.

Kenney's most urgent task was the support of the land campaign in New Guinea, and as a supplement to this he had to devise some means of interrupting the free movement of Japanese ships along the north coast of New Guinea. High-level bombing had been tried, and proved ineffective. He would have to look elsewhere. General Brett had experimented with torpedoes dropped by the B–26 Marauders, but after a brief trial Kenney decided that this task should be left to the RAAF Beauforts which had been designed for that role. Dive-bombing was also discarded, because of the heavy losses suffered by the A–24s (modified versions of the Dauntless) in the early stages of the New Guinea campaign. This left Kenney with only the B–25 Mitchells and A–20 Bostons with which to experiment.

The Boston was a fast light-bomber, but its short range made its use over the New Guinea mountains extremely hazardous, so

two 450-gallon fuel tanks were fitted in the bomb-bay to increase
its range. The armament of four 0.3-inch machine-guns was
increased by four 0.5-inch machine-guns attached to the nose.
Similar gun modifications were made to the Mitchells, the bomb-
aimer's position and the tail gun being removed, and additional
guns were fitted so that each aircraft had eight fixed forward-firing
machine-guns as well as two 0.5-inch machine-guns in an upper
turret.

Intensive bombing experiments were then carried out, using a
wreck in Port Moresby harbour as a target. In the early trials a
skip-bombing technique was used, but this was soon abandoned
in favour of direct bombing from very low altitude. A special
rapidly-armed delay-action fuse was developed so that the bomber
could get clear of the explosion while at the same time ensuring
that the bombs were armed. (One of the continuing problems of
very low-level bombing has been that the bombs may not have
time to become armed.) A few experimental attacks using the new
technique were made on Japanese shipping north of New Guinea,
with fair success. Coordinated rehearsals were then held by the
Mitchells, Bostons and Beaufighters. By February 1943 all was
ready.[4]

In the latter half of 1942 the tide had begun to turn in favour
of the Allies. The Japanese thrust to Port Moresby was beaten
back, and Gona and Buna on the north coast of New Guinea were
recaptured. Further to the east, the Japanese were about to evacuate

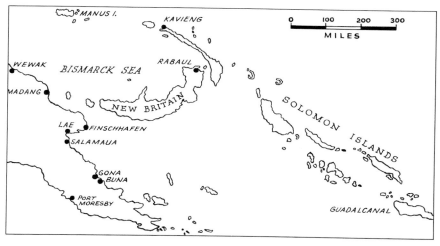

The Bismarck Sea

Guadalcanal. MacArthur was ready to move towards Lae, and with this place in his hands he would be poised to force the island barrier at the eastern end of the Bismarck Sea.

By this time the Allies had established a clear superiority in the skies above New Guinea. The increasing numbers of American aircraft, and particularly the arrival of the twin-engined P–38 Lightning fighter, meant that the Allies outclassed the Japanese in both quantity and quality. The Lightnings, flying high above the ceiling of the Zekes, and with a much higher diving-speed, would swoop down upon the hapless Japanese fighters, destroy several and dive away before any retaliation could occur. The Japanese aircraft were almost swept away, causing one Japanese soldier to remark that the American aircraft 'fly above our position as if they owned the skies'.

The Japanese commanders were determined to reinforce their New Guinea garrisons, and early in 1943 they sent a five-ship convoy to Lae. Kenney's aircraft attacked in force, but the low-level attack technique had not yet been thoroughly practised and only two small transports were sunk. A week later a three-ship convoy reached Wewak without being attacked. On 19 February Allied code-breakers warned that another attempt to run a convoy to Lae was imminent, and on 24 February gave the further detail that the 51st Division was to land at Lae about 5 March. This time Kenney was ready. The training of the anti-shipping squadrons was complete, and he had more than 250 aircraft ready for the job—154 fighters, 34 light bombers, 41 medium bombers and 39 heavy bombers.

The Japanese commanders at Rabaul, Lieutenant-General Imamura and Vice-Admiral Kusaka, decided that 7000 men of the Eighteenth Army should be moved to Lae as soon as possible. Such a large body of men could be moved only by sea, and Kusaka set about collecting transports. Kusaka's principal subordinate was the commander of the Eighth Fleet, Vice-Admiral Mikawa, whose cruisers and destroyers had been operating in the Solomon and New Guinea waters since the previous June. Both Mikawa and Kusaka were very experienced commanders and knew well the dangers to which the convoy would be subjected. Kusaka had been chief of staff to Nagumo at Midway, and Mikawa had commanded the force which had inflicted the dramatic defeat on the Allies near Savo Island.

The convoy consisted of eight transports, ranging in size from less than 1000 to more than 7000 tons, with 6000 troops and some vital stores and aviation fuel on board, and another 1000 men crammed on board eight escorting destroyers. Mikawa placed

Rear-Admiral Kimura, a veteran of the battles of the Eastern Solomons, Santa Cruz and Guadalcanal, in command of the convoy and its escort. After the experiences their ships had recently been having in the waters round Guadalcanal, Mikawa and Kimura expected heavy losses, and were prepared for them. The men and equipment were carefully spread round the ships so that even if as many as half the ships were sunk, the surviving ships would still be able to land a balanced force at Lae. For more than half the ships to be sunk was surely unthinkable!

Yet the Japanese convoy was facing severe odds. The neglect of the merchant marine by the Imperial Navy, both before and during the war, was extraordinary. Despite the fact that Japan's economic survival depended heavily on efficient sea transport, the Navy devoted virtually all its resources to the Combined Fleet.[5] To compound the problem, both the navy and army extensively commandeered merchant ships for military duty and raided them for officers and men. Inadequate training of replacement crews was one resulting problem, but another was that even when ships were commandeered they were not adequately armed. The heaviest armament in any of the ships in the Bismarck convoy was one 4-inch gun, which could not elevate above thirty degrees, and three single hand-worked 25mm guns.

The eight destroyers were better off, but they had not yet received the new armament of 25mm guns which had recently been authorised. It was clear that the principal responsibility for the defence of the convoy would rest with land-based fighters. Forty naval Zekes and sixty army fighters were available, and would give continuous cover during daylight hours. However, the radios in the army and navy aircraft were incompatible so army fighters could not talk either to the navy fighters or to the ships. None of the ships had radar suitable for fighter direction, and if they were to intercept the American bombers the pilots would have to rely on their eyesight, supplemented by warnings (to the Zekes only) from the ships when they sighted something.

Worst of all, the convoy could not make more than seven knots, and would take at least 65 hours to cover the 450 miles separating Lae from Rabaul. It was obvious that the convoy's best chance was to make the trip under cover of bad weather, which would hamper the American reconnaissance aircraft and might permit the convoy to sneak through to Lae undetected.

The convoy sailed from Rabaul punctually at midnight on 28 February. At first all went well. The weather was blowing a gale, and with visibility down to a few hundred yards the convoy ploughed on securely. However, as it crept down the coast of New

Britain the weather improved and patches of blue sky began to appear. Through one gap in the clouds a patrolling B–24 Liberator caught sight of the convoy at 4 p.m. on 1 March. Then the weather closed in again, and eight B–17 Flying Fortresses sent out to attack could not find the convoy, although a shadowing Liberator managed to keep in intermittent touch with the convoy until 9.30 p.m.

Mikawa realised that all hope of surprise was gone, but considered there was still a chance the convoy might get through with only slight losses if the weather continued to be thick. Unfortunately the same conditions which were protecting the convoy were also preventing Kusaka from making the planned attacks on the Allied bomber-bases in New Guinea.

By 8.15 a.m. the following day, in clear weather, the convoy was about to turn into Dampier Strait when a Liberator was sighted. Any faint hope of an unmolested voyage had disappeared, and soon afterwards the convoy was subjected to attacks by 28 B–17s in two waves, the bombers flying in steadily at 5000 feet and dropping their 1000-pound bombs with considerable accuracy. One transport was sunk and two were damaged, a clear example of what heavy bombers could achieve against slow-moving, unarmoured ships if they were allowed to bomb from low altitude. Although both waves of American bombers had failed to link up with their fighter escorts, the two-dozen Japanese fighters could make little impression on the heavily-armed bombers.

Mikawa clearly should have ordered a withdrawal at this point. The Japanese fighters were obviously unable to keep the American heavy bombers away from the convoy, and by dawn on the following day the convoy would be within range of the Allied medium and light bombers as well. Yet Mikawa sent no word, and the convoy plodded steadily on. Two of the destroyers had rescued 950 survivors from the sunken troopship, and were so crowded that Kimura had to send them ahead independently to Lae. They reached their destination safely that night, discharged their troops, and rejoined the convoy the following morning. These were the only troops that were to reach Lae.

All the previous afternoon the convoy had been trailed by a B–17. Kimura was not prepared to risk being attacked in the narrow, rock-infested waters of Dampier Strait, and so he took the convoy round through Vitiaz Strait, even though this meant an additional five hours steaming. There had been only one further attack that day, as dusk was drawing in and the convoy was turning into Vitiaz Strait, when eleven B–17s attacked from a high level; they missed. More than 30 Japanese fighters attacked the formation, but they could make no impression against the massed defensive-gunfire of the B–17s.

By dawn on 3 March the convoy was off Finschhafen. Only 70 miles more and they would be safe, or comparatively safe, in harbour at Lae, but the day was fine and clear and Kimura would have had little doubt that he was going to be heavily attacked. An RAAF Catalina had been shadowing his convoy all night, dropping occasional bombs to keep the gun crews awake. At daylight a B–17 Flying Fortress, which could defend itself against the Japanese fighters, took over the shadowing task.

The Allied air forces were ready to launch their carefully-rehearsed attack, but while the bombers and fighters were forming up over Cape Ward Hunt, a squadron of RAAF Beauforts was sent to make an independent torpedo attack. The Japanese took the conventional evasive measures, the threatened ships turning towards the attacking aircraft as the torpedo-release position was reached. The attack was a failure, but it did have an important (though unforeseen) effect on the success of the next strike.

By 10.30 a.m. the squadrons over Cape Ward Hunt were ready, and headed into the attack. The plan was for thirteen RAAF Beaufighters, each armed with four 20mm cannon and eight machine-guns, to go in first to beat down the anti-aircraft gun defences. Simultaneously thirteen B–17s would bomb from medium altitude, while 28 P–38 Lightnings would keep the Japanese fighters

B-25 Mitchell bombers attack. (*National Air and Space Museum*)

busy. Close on the heels of the Beaufighters would come thirteen B-25 Mitchells bombing from medium altitude, while another twelve, specially trained and equipped, would make a very low-level attack. Finally there were to be level-bombing runs by twelve Bostons and six more Mitchells.

The attack showed the value of careful rehearsal, and was made with great precision. The Japanese reaction was unexpected, for Kimura was much more concerned about the danger from torpedo-attacks than from level-bombing attacks, which his experience in the Solomons had taught him to ignore. The Beaufighters and Mitchells, coming in low above the waves, looked just like the torpedo-attack he had evaded less than an hour earlier. This, then, was assessed as the greatest threat, and his ships duly turned their bows towards the low-flying aircraft. But the Beaufighters flew straight on, sweeping the decks with cannon and machine-gun fire, while the Japanese ships—with very few guns able to bear—were almost helpless. Close behind the Beaufighters came the Mitchells, each with eight 0.5-inch machine-guns blazing. Swooping low over the Japanese ships, which being end-on to the direction of flight presented perfect low-level bombing targets,[6] the Mitchells left devastation in their wake. Seventeen direct hits were claimed.

As the American bombers withdrew, all seven surviving transports in the convoy were sinking. Kimura's flagship, the destroyer *Shirayuki*, was being abandoned, and two other destroyers had been mortally damaged. It was the most decisive single air attack ever launched on a convoy. The cost to the Americans was one B-17 Flying Fortress and three P-38 Lightnings.

The five surviving Japanese destroyers set about the melancholy task of rescuing the survivors. Meanwhile urgent orders went out to the Allied squadrons to mount another attack as soon as practicable. By this stage, however, thick clouds had settled on the high New Guinea mountains and many of the Allied aircraft from the Port Moresby airfields were forced to turn back. In these circumstances a coordinated attack was very difficult, and the one attack which was made achieved comparatively little—some of the already-sinking ships had been hit again, but of Kimura's five undamaged destroyers only one had been hit.

Reconnaissance aircraft scoured the area all afternoon, machine-gunning any survivors they could find.[7] Despite these harassing attacks, the four undamaged destroyers managed to rescue 2734 survivors, with some assistance from submarines. That night Kimura, now flying his flag in the destroyer *Shikinami*, took four destroyers (including one which had joined him from Kavieng) back into the

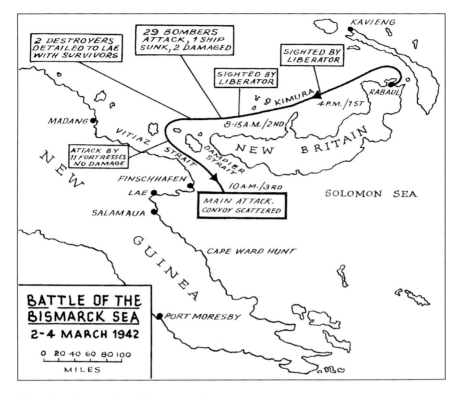

The Battle of the Bismarck Sea

area for a final search. They picked up another 200 survivors, and as dawn was breaking they headed for Kavieng at full speed. Eight US torpedo-boats spent the night searching for crippled ships, finding and sinking a blazing and abandoned troopship.

By sunrise on 4 March nothing remained except two crippled destroyers, and miles of wreckage. The two destroyers were soon despatched, one by a direct hit by a Flying Fortress during the morning, the other by a low-level attack soon after noon. Nothing then floated except wreckage and a few survivors. A few hundred managed to swim ashore or escape in boats. With their departure, the Vitiaz Strait was quiet.

In the first flush of enthusiasm the Allied aircrews made excessive claims, understandable enough after the heat and confusion of action, but subsequent arguments should not be allowed to conceal the fact that they had won a famous victory.[8] There was no precedent for the complete annihilation of a troop convoy by air attack. For the loss of one heavy bomber and three fighters,

245

the Allies had sunk eight merchant ships and four escorting destroyers, as well as shooting down ten Japanese fighters and drowning more than 3000 men. Okumiya writes that 'not during the entire savage fighting at Guadalcanal did we suffer a single comparable blow'.[9]

The battle had a salutary effect on Japanese morale. Yamamoto himself came down to Rabaul to organise a counter-offensive, but it was too late for him to repair the damage that had been done. Japanese Imperial Headquarters was perturbed, and decided to send no more convoys to Lae and Salamaua. The garrisons at those places were thenceforth isolated, nourished only by occasional supplies sneaked in by submarine, barge or other small craft, mostly by night.

To stop this traffic, the Americans were required to develop new techniques, massed air attacks being quite inappropriate. Fighters and the heavily-armed Bostons and Mitchells were effective against the barges by day, but the craft proved difficult to sink. After experimenting with two versions of the Mitchell, each employing a fixed 75mm gun in the nose, rockets began to be fitted in fighters and B–26 bombers towards the end of 1944. These were found to be much more effective, and all thought of fitting a large gun in an aircraft was dropped.[10]

The problem of attacking shipping by night was also tackled with vigour. In August 1943 ten special Liberators, SB–24s, arrived in the South Pacific; these aircraft were fitted with a search radar and a PPI display, a radio altimeter and a bomb-release mechanism which could be operated on radar information. By the end of the month they were operating each night over the Japanese shipping routes, bombing with surprising accuracy from 1200 to 1500 feet. After only a month's experience five of them turned back an eleven-ship Japanese convoy, sinking a destroyer and damaging other ships. In the following month more of these aircraft arrived in the South-West Pacific area, and soon the Japanese could expect no respite by night or day in areas within range of Allied aircraft.

16

The Philippine Sea:

15–20 June 1944

The loss of Guadalcanal marked the end of the Japanese Navy's strategic initiative. Thenceforth Japanese forces were committed to a step-by-step defence of the formidable southern perimeter which had been built up, based on Rabaul. In the central Pacific the difficulties for the Allies seemed even greater, for vast distances were involved and assaults would have to be made far beyond the range of close support from island airfields. Japanese thinking was convinced that shore-based aircraft operating from 'unsinkable aircraft carriers' could dominate the American carrier fleets.

Yamamoto still believed in the policy of striking a decisive blow at the American fleet, but the loss of six carriers in a few months made him cautious. The only carrier reinforcements he could expect during 1943 were two converted merchant ships and two converted seaplane carriers;[1] the 34 000 ton *Taiho* would not be ready before early 1944. Until these new carriers arrived, Yamamoto husbanded his strength.

The position was even less happy with regard to aircraft. The Zeke, which had dominated the skies in the early months of the war, was now outclassed by the new American naval fighters which entered service early in 1943, the F6F Hellcat and the F4U Corsair. Intended replacements for the Zeke had either proved failures or been seriously delayed.[2] Nor was the situation much better with strike aircraft. The obsolete Val dive-bomber had been replaced by the Judy, which had excellent performance but was not suitable for operations from small carriers. The Kate had been replaced by the Jill, a 265-knot torpedo-bomber which could also be used as a light bomber. Early in 1944, 63 carrier-based Zekes were modified to carry 550-pound bombs, in the hope that they would be able to penetrate the American fighter defence, but there were endless problems with this modification.

As far as the performance of the aircraft-warning radars and fighter direction were concerned, the situation had really not improved at all since Santa Cruz. Although radar sets were more widely fitted in Japanese warships by 1944, their performance was much poorer than their American equivalents.[3] Some ships were also fitted with a radar-intercept set (the E–27) which could detect and obtain bearings of transmissions from American air-warning radars and also the surface-search radars used by American aircraft, out to a range of about 200 miles in favourable conditions.

That the United States solved the problems of mounting an offensive across the Pacific is the construction and organisation miracle of the war. By 1943 American shipyards were pouring out vast fleets of amphibious craft, dozens of new aircraft carriers, and tankers and supply ships that could maintain the surge of the US advance. Apart from a rapid improvement in naval aircraft, the new SK air-warning radar was widely fitted in the carriers and other large ships.[4] Even more importantly, fighter directors now had height-finding equipment in the SM radar, which could detect an aircraft approaching at 10 000 feet at a range of 50 miles and determine its height within 500 feet.[5] Added to this was the fitting of reliable multi-channel VHF radio sets, overcoming the communication difficulties which had plagued fighter direction in its early days. Nor was this all.

The fitting of remotely-controlled 40mm Bofors guns and 20mm Oerlikons, each with its own lead-computing sight, had become general. The carrier *Essex*, for instance, completed in late 1942, had forty 40mm guns and fifty-five 20mm guns. Even then some ships' officers complained that their ships were underarmed, with the result that further armaments were added. Perhaps most important of all was the introduction of the deadly radar-triggered proximity fuse, first used in February 1943, which eliminated the necessity, and inevitable errors, of fuse calculation.

In medium-range anti-aircraft gunnery the Japanese had made little progress during the war. A system of automatic stabilisation of the director so that target movements could be more accurately measured began to be installed in 1943, but it was never widely fitted, most ships having to continue to rely on two sailors keeping the director level by sighting on the horizon. Radar ranging was never available, nor did the guns follow the director automatically. Most important of all, the Japanese still had to use pre-set time fuses, as they had not been able to match the American achievement with proximity fuses.

The main batteries of the Japanese battleships and cruisers were used to bolster the anti-aircraft defences, firing barrages of 'sanshiki-dan' (incendiary shrapnel), but as the guns were aimed visually and there was no radar assistance to give the best moment to fire they were more impressive than effective. Things were better in the close-range field, where triple, twin and single 25mm automatic guns were widely fitted; the giant battleship *Musashi*, for instance, had forty triple-25mm mountings and thirty singles.

By the beginning of 1943 Halsey in the South Pacific and MacArthur in the South-West Pacific could slowly inch their way forward, island by island, under the umbrella of shore-based air power, or slog through the New Guinea jungle towards Rabaul. Nimitz still had to build up his carrier and amphibious forces in the Central Pacific before he could attempt an offensive. In April 1943, in order to delay Halsey's advance, Yamamoto collected 350 aircraft—half of them from the Combined Fleet—and based them at Rabaul for a counter-attack. The results were disastrous. Heavy losses were incurred for little result, and the training and experience of the aircrews in the carriers of the Combined Fleet received a further setback.

On 18 April the Japanese suffered an even more serious blow, when Yamamoto was killed. His aircraft was intercepted and shot down while he was visiting Japanese bases in the Solomons. Although Yamamoto's strategy had been marked by a failure to use his overwhelming superiority effectively, and a fatal tactical tendency to disperse his forces, his brother officers were heart-broken at his death. 'There could only be one Yamamoto', said his successor, Admiral Koga, 'and nobody could take his place.'[6]

By October the American advances in New Guinea and the Solomons were becoming more menacing. Koga decided to attempt again the policy which had failed in April, and 173 aircraft were taken from the Combined Fleet carriers and moved to Rabaul. Disastrous losses were again sustained, and less than a third of the Japanese carrier aircraft survived to return to Truk. The training of replacement aircrews became catastrophic.[7]

By this time Nimitz was ready. He had at last built up a powerful fleet in the Central Pacific, where he now had twelve battleships (five of them new), seventeen carriers (ten fast and seven escort), twelve cruisers and 66 destroyers. Spruance had taken command of this force, now called the Fifth Fleet, in August 1943, and immediately started training it intensively. As soon as he felt he was ready he ordered probing strikes against Japanese targets in the Marshalls and Gilberts and on Wake and Marcus Islands, the latter only a little over 1000 miles from Japan.

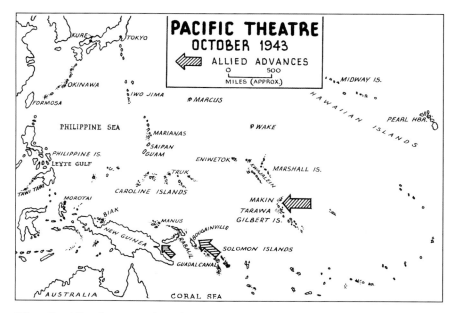

The Pacific theatre, October 1943

By November Spruance was ready for bigger things, and major amphibious assaults were launched which captured Makin and Tarawa islands in the Gilbert group, while the Japanese Combined Fleet, with its aircraft still embroiled in the struggle for the Bismarck barrier, could only watch helplessly. In February 1944 Spruance seized Kwajalein and Eniwetok. He was now within 1000 miles of the Marianas, and was almost ready for the next step, whether it was to be to the Marianas or against the main Japanese naval base of Truk.

The Japanese, of course, did not resignedly accept this step-by-step advance. The 'New Operational Policy' adopted by Imperial Headquarters in September 1943 decreed that the entire strength of the Combined Fleet should be used to destroy the American Fleet 'at one blow'. A new fleet, called the Mobile Fleet, and containing nearly all the effective ships in the Combined Fleet, was formed early in March 1944 under Vice-Admiral Ozawa.

Admiral Toyoda, who had replaced Koga as Commander-in-Chief after the latter's death in an air crash, had formidable problems. The Australian–American forces in the South-West Pacific had broken through the Bismarck barrier, captured Manus and pushed along the New Guinea coast as far as Biak, making the replenishment of the isolated garrisons a serious drain on his

250

ships. At the same time it was obvious that the Americans in the Central Pacific were about to move again, so on 3 May 1944 Toyoda issued orders for Operation 'A-Go', aiming to destroy the US Fleet in the waters between the Philippines and the Carolines. If the Americans struck further north in the Marianas, Toyoda planned to lure their fleet into his chosen battle area where Japanese superiority in shore-based aircraft would, he hoped, be decisive.

While Nimitz was debating what the next step should be—the Marianas or Truk—the Fifth Fleet had an urgent task to perform. Whether or not Truk was to be invaded, the secret and reputedly immensely-strong base there had to be neutralised. Spruance's carriers made a series of devastating raids on 17 and 18 February, and although only a few ships were sunk the Japanese never again used it as a main naval base. It was finally destroyed as an air base by another raid in April.

On 12 March 1944 the Joint Chiefs of Staff decided that the Marianas was to be the next target, with invasions of Saipan, Tinian and Guam starting on 15 June. Nimitz decided to tackle Saipan first. The logistic problems were staggering, for Saipan lay more than 1000 miles from Eniwetok, his nearest advanced base, and 3500 miles from Pearl Harbor. Yet the planned date was kept, and in the early hours of 15 June two marine divisions landed on Saipan. They were given formidable gunfire-support by seven old battleships—most of them survivors from Pearl Harbor—and close air support by Wildcats and Avengers from seven escort carriers.

The only ominous note was a report received from an American submarine 36 hours before the landing that it had sighted four Japanese battleships and accompanying cruisers and destroyers entering the Sulu Sea, near the north-east tip of Borneo. It was not clear whether these ships would head for Saipan, but Spruance made his dispositions on the assumption that they might, and arranged his fuelling schedule so that Task Force 58 would be ready for a Japanese attack by 17 June, the earliest the Japanese force could reach Saipan.

On 14 June Nimitz, having the benefits of the Ultra code-breaking teams, had sent Spruance a very prescient warning of the probable Japanese plan. American intelligence was also helped by an operational plan recovered by Philippine guerillas from a wrecked Japanese aircraft. This document made it clear that, if the Americans attacked in the Marianas, the Japanese would concentrate their forces and 'attack and annihilate' them. Nimitz made sure that his senior officers had translations of this plan as soon as possible.

All seemed to be going well on Saipan, when at 7 p.m. on

15 June—the day of the landing—Spruance received a report from a US submarine that a Japanese carrier fleet was heading towards him from the central Philippines. Nine hours later he received a report from another submarine that a second Japanese fleet was steaming northwards up the east coast of the Philippines. Spruance decided it was time to act. He postponed the landing on Guam planned for 18 June, and ordered forward six radar-fitted Mariner flying boats in the hope that they might be able to operate from a tender in the open seas off Saipan. He also ordered some of the cruisers and destroyers from the bombardment force supporting the landing to join the fast carriers, but left behind all the old battleships and escort carriers. Then, satisfied that the landing was secure, he steamed out in his cruiser flagship to join the carrier fleet.

Ozawa's Mobile Fleet had an unhappy time during the weeks of waiting. Since 16 May the nine carriers and various other ships had been at Tawi Tawi, in the south-west Philippines, where they were close to the Borneo oilfields but were very vulnerable to submarine attack. Prowling US submarines sank four destroyers and three of Ozawa's precious tankers, and so restricted the movements of the carriers that it was impossible to give the inexperienced air groups the training they so desperately needed. The six light carriers were slow and hampered by short flight decks, and it proved difficult, under ordinary conditions, to launch from these carriers the new Judy dive-bombers which had been brought into service after the Battle of Midway. Even the new Jill torpedo-bombers were difficult to use efficiently when aboard the small carriers, because of the lack of catapults.

It was a relief for Toyoda, in his flagship in the Japanese Inland Sea, when news came on 11 June that American carrier aircraft were attacking Saipan. He at once ordered all the ships of the Mobile Fleet to a rendezvous east of the Philippines, and it was these movements which were observed by the two US submarines on 15 and 16 June. On 15 June, after the Americans had started landing on Saipan, Toyoda ordered implementation of the A-Go operation to 'attack the enemy in the Marianas area and annihilate the invasion force'. After fuelling from his six oil-tankers, Ozawa headed east. He was seeking battle against apparently overwhelming odds, for he had only nine carriers against Spruance's fifteen, and was seriously outnumbered in every class of ship except heavy cruisers. But Ozawa had, or thought he had, three important advantages. American aircraft had only two-thirds the range of his own planes, which could search out to more than 500 miles and safely strike at 300, and this advantage might be further increased through the possession of the airfields on Guam and Tinian. Secondly, he expected that under the A-Go plan he would have up to 500 shore-based aircraft from Yap, Palau, Tinian and Guam cooperating with him. Finally, he knew that his side possessed a useful technique for deceiving the radars upon which the Americans' highly-efficient fighter direction system was dependent. The use of metal (usually aluminium) strips called 'window' (also known as 'chaff' by the Americans) created echoes on radar screens which could conceal real attacking aircraft or give the spurious impression of a non-existent strike.[8]

As he steamed towards Saipan, Ozawa's reconnaissance aircraft, both land- and carrier-based, scoured the seas in front of him to a distance of more than 400 miles—75 miles more than Spruance could cover. Soon after 3 p.m. on 18 June one of Ozawa's aircraft, at the very limit of its search, sighted the northernmost of Spruance's carrier task groups, and 30 minutes later another scout reported the southernmost carrier group 40 miles away.

Ozawa had already acted. At 3.30 p.m. he ordered his fleet into battle formation, and ten minutes later, when he calculated he was 360 miles from the US carriers, he altered course to the southwards to avoid closing the range any further. Soon afterwards he issued Operation Order No.16, in which he declared his intention to retreat temporarily and to contact and destroy the American forces the following morning. Ozawa's battle formation was designed to make full use of the float planes in the battleships and cruisers for scouting, while at the same time protecting his fast carriers and hoping that American strikes would destroy themselves by attacking the heavily-armed battleships and cruisers.

In the van Ozawa placed his three light carriers (*Chitose*, *Chiyoda* and *Zuiho*[9]) six miles apart, each with its own circular screen. He supported these escort carriers with four of his five battleships (including *Yamato* and *Musashi*) and five of his nine cruisers, but he could only spare them a mere nine destroyers. Vice-Admiral Kurita was given command of the van, although Rear-Admiral Obayashi, in the carrier *Chitose*, took over tactical command during flying operations. Ozawa held his remaining six carriers 100 miles to the south-west, divided into two groups ten miles apart. One group was protected by two cruisers and nine destroyers, the other by a battleship, a cruiser and ten destroyers, with Ozawa flying his flag in the new carrier *Taiho*. Between the nine Japanese carriers there was a total of 450 aircraft, less than half the American carrier strength.

Ozawa was for a time confused by a report from an army aircraft of another American task force several hundred miles to the north of the earlier contacts, and it was not until nearly 6 p.m. that he was informed by Tokyo that this report was completely false. Meanwhile Obayashi in the van was acting on his own initiative. He had heard the reports from the scouting aircraft, and decided to strike without delay at Spruance's carriers. He started launching at 4.37 p.m., but only a few aircraft were in the air when he received Ozawa's operation order announcing the intention of striking the following morning and he dutifully recalled them.

The American fast carrier fleet was formed into Task Force 58, commanded by Vice-Admiral Marc Mitscher. A pioneer airman, he had commanded the air forces under Halsey in the South-West Pacific and for the past three months had been in charge of the fast carriers in the Pacific Fleet. He had under his command the most powerful fleet ever assembled until then: fifteen aircraft carriers (seven large, eight light) organised into four separate task groups, and a fifth task group under Vice-Admiral Lee comprising seven modern battleships.

Nearly 1100 aircraft were carried in the American carriers—including 483 fighters, nearly all F6F Hellcats. Task Force 58 had a complex fighter direction organisation. Each carrier had its own fighter-direction centre, using the warning and height-finding radars. The activities of the three or four carriers in each group were controlled by a Task Group fighter director, who allocated particular sections of fighters to individual ships to control. To coordinate the four groups there was a Task Force fighter director, who had to maintain the balance between the fighters sent out to deal with immediate threats and those retained in reserve, and during air attacks effectively directed the launching and recovery of fighters. Each Task Group usually maintained two eight-plane combat air patrols, and when one of these patrols was committed to a target another eight fighters were launched to replace it, so that there was always a reserve if any raiders broke through the initial interceptions.

For dive-bombing, SB2C Helldivers had replaced nearly all the old Dauntlesses, while all the torpedo-aircraft were TBF or TBM Avengers. The greatest American weakness was in reconnaissance, in which they were still outclassed by the Japanese. The scouting squadrons had been merged into the dive-bombing squadrons, and in the forthcoming battle virtually all reconnaissance from the carriers was carried out by the F6F Hellcats and TBF Avengers which were the only aircraft fitted with radar.[10]

During the battle, tactical command was in the hands of Mitscher, but Spruance had to approve or acquiesce in the major decisions, in accordance with his directive from Nimitz that his

A Curtiss SB2C Helldiver banks over its carrier before landing.
(*National Archives, 80-G-469319*)

task was to 'capture, occupy and defend Saipan, Tinian and Guam'. Spruance told Mitscher that he was leaving the selection of dispositions and movements 'best calculated to meet the enemy under [the] most advantageous conditions' to the latter's discretion, but he would 'issue general directives when necessary'.

The first of these directives was issued early on 18 June, when Spruance vetoed Mitscher's announced intention of steaming south-westwards at high speed to where the first submarine report had suggested the main body of the Japanese fleet lay, locate the enemy ships precisely with afternoon searches, then engage them in a surface action that night. Instead, Spruance told Mitscher and Lee that Task Force 58 must cover forces engaged in the Saipan operation 'by advancing to the westward during daylight and retiring to eastward at night so as to reduce the possibility of enemy passing us during darkness'.

Ozawa had clear knowledge, obtained from American news releases, of who his key opponents were.[11] On the other hand US intelligence could provide no information on the command of the Mobile Fleet. Spruance tried to read the mind of this unknown Japanese admiral, and decided that his objective would be the destruction of the ships supporting the Saipan landing. He figured that attacks would probably begin with long-range carrier strikes, followed by a surface attack on the landing area. The tactical aim of the Japanese would, Spruance thought, be to lure Task Force 58 away from Saipan so that the battleship force could turn his flank and attack the Saipan shipping behind his back.

Spruance was reinforced in his expectation of how the Japanese would act by the study of a captured Japanese document containing the current battle doctrine, which recommended just such a manoeuvre. In all his decisions during the battle, Spruance was to be influenced by this appreciation, although, as we have seen, Ozawa's target was not shipping but the American carrier fleet, which was not strictly in accordance with his orders from Toyoda to 'annihilate the invasion fleet'. It is also likely that Spruance overestimated the importance of the transports off Saipan. By the time a Japanese naval force could have reached them, the American troops were well established ashore.

At dusk on 18 June Spruance and Mitscher still had no recent news of Ozawa's fleet. During the day Mitscher's aircraft had made two thorough searches westwards to a depth of 325 miles, the afternoon one falling short of Ozawa's van by a mere 60 miles. Spruance was satisfied that Ozawa was still well to the west, and ordered Mitscher to head back towards Saipan during the night, so as to eliminate the possibility of Ozawa slipping past them in the dark.

At last came news, for Ozawa used his radio at 8.28 p.m. to tell Guam and the other airfields of his intentions for the following day, and the transmission was immediately detected by American radio direction-finding stations. At 10 p.m. Spruance knew that a Japanese ship had been about 300 miles west of him 90 minutes earlier, but since that time he had been retiring and by dawn would be beyond effective striking distance.

Mitscher, eager to close with the enemy, urged a reversal of course to the west and a dawn air attack, but Spruance was more cautious. Perhaps Ozawa had divided his fleet: the radio intelligence meant no more than that one ship had been in the reported position.[12] His doubts were reinforced shortly before midnight when he was told that the US submarine *Stingray*, patrolling about 175 miles to the south-east of the position given by the direction finders, had sent a message which had been jammed and could not be read. Spruance jumped to the conclusion that this submarine might have been trying to report part of Ozawa's fleet; if this were so, it meant that the Japanese were much closer than previously believed, and were already working round his southern flank. (Actually the report from the submarine was only a routine one, and the Japanese had not been jamming.) At 1.15 a.m. the Japanese fleet was sighted on radar by a patrol aircraft from Saipan, but owing to an equipment failure no message got through to Spruance until eight hours later, when the aircraft had returned to base.

Soon after midnight Spruance decided that the fleet would continue on its easterly course. He was still worried that his scout planes had seen nothing of the Japanese, although the presence of snooping Japanese aircraft during the night made it obvious that his enemy counterpart was in no such doubt regarding the location of the American carriers. Meanwhile, Mitscher did not neglect his scouting role. Soon after 2 a.m. fifteen radar-equipped Avengers set off to search to the westward to a distance of 325 miles, but this search again fell short of Ozawa's nearest ships, this time by 50 miles. It was not until nearly 9 a.m. on 19 June that the contact report from the Saipan-based flying-boat—the first reconnaissance news of Ozawa's ships for more than three days—reached Spruance.

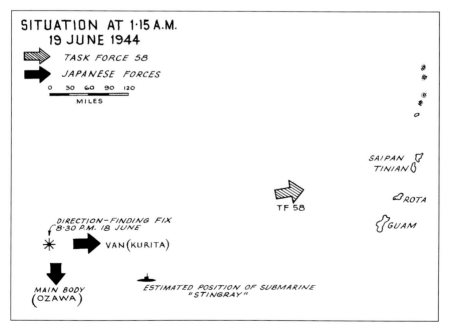

SITUATION AT 1·15 A.M.
19 JUNE 1944

TASK FORCE 58

JAPANESE FORCES

0   30   60   90   120
MILES

SAIPAN
TINIAN

ROTA

GUAM

TF 58

DIRECTION-FINDING FIX
8·30 P.M. 18 JUNE
VAN (KURITA)

MAIN BODY
(OZAWA)

ESTIMATED POSITION OF SUBMARINE
"STINGRAY"

The situation at 1.15 a.m., 19 June 1944

This day was to begin as a clear trial of strength between the Japanese strikes and the American defence. Of Mitscher's five battle groups, the one nearest Ozawa was Vice-Admiral Lee's. The seven battleships in this group were in a circular formation round the flagship *Indiana,* where they were intended to take the first shock of air attack and were also in a good position to manoeuvre

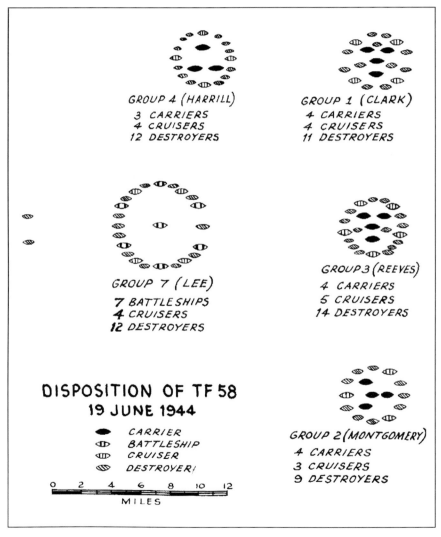

GROUP 4 (HARRILL)
3 CARRIERS
4 CRUISERS
12 DESTROYERS

GROUP 1 (CLARK)
4 CARRIERS
4 CRUISERS
11 DESTROYERS

GROUP 7 (LEE)
7 BATTLESHIPS
4 CRUISERS
12 DESTROYERS

GROUP 3 (REEVES)
4 CARRIERS
5 CRUISERS
14 DESTROYERS

**DISPOSITION OF TF 58
19 JUNE 1944**

CARRIER
BATTLESHIP
CRUISER
DESTROYER

0 2 4 6 8 10 12
MILES

GROUP 2 (MONTGOMERY)
4 CARRIERS
3 CRUISERS
9 DESTROYERS

The disposition of TF58, 19 June 1944

independently if a surface action became imminent. Two picket destroyers were stationed ten miles further west, to give warning of any low-flying aircraft which might attempt to sneak in under the radar cover. To the east of the battleships were Mitscher's other four groups disposed like a figure 7, with the carriers in each group surrounded by a close circular screen of cruisers and destroyers.

Alarms and diversions were frequent in the first hours after sunrise. At 5.50 a.m. the opening shots were fired, when a Zeke fighter-bomber scouting from Guam attacked one of the US picket destroyers and was promptly shot down by the other. Between 6.30 and 10 a.m. there was almost continuous fighting over Guam. Ozawa's plan relied on heavy support from Guam, but instead of the 500 aircraft he expected there was barely one-tenth that number there. This was the measure of the success of the Fifth Fleet's earlier operations. Vice-Admiral Kakuta, on Tinian Island, made desperate efforts to use the surviving aircraft against the Americans, and to bring up reinforcements from Truk and Yap, but he achieved little. Hellcat fighters from the carriers shot down more than 30 Japanese aircraft over Guam, until at 10 a.m. they were hastily recalled to deal with a more serious threat which was developing.

Ozawa had flown off two searches before sunrise. The first, of sixteen float planes from the cruisers and battleships in Kurita's van force, had made contact with Lee's battleship group and the northern carrier group, but it lost more than half its strength in the process. But Ozawa had enough information, and at 8.30 a.m. he ordered Obayashi to launch the first heavy raid—45 Zeke fighter-bombers and eight torpedo-carrying Jills, escorted by sixteen Zeke fighters. It was the detection of this raid by the American radar at 10 a.m. which caused the hasty recall of the US fighters over Guam.

The battle which ensued followed a simple pattern. The Japanese flew at 20 000 feet, and at this height were detected by American radar 150 miles away. The American carriers had ample time to turn east into the wind, strike below or order away the bombers and scouts, and get more fighters into the air. By 10.20 a.m. this first raid was within 70 miles of Mitscher's flagship, *Lexington*, but there they paused for fifteen minutes, forming up. The delay was fatal, for it helped last minute preparations in the American ships. When the Japanese closed in, they were fiercely attacked by the defending fighters and nearly half fell without ever sighting the American groups. Some struggled on and unsuccessfully attacked the picket destroyers, while three or four reached the battleship group, where one managed to hit *South Dakota*, without causing serious damage. This was to be the only Japanese bombing success of the whole battle.

By 10.50 a.m. the surviving Japanese aircraft, by now numbering less than 30, were in full retreat, but their place was taken by a second large raid more than 100 strong. This strike had been launched from Ozawa's carrier group a little over two hours earlier, but had many vicissitudes on the way. Eight pilots had to turn back because of engine trouble, one had crash-dived his aircraft in an unsuccessful attempt to save his carrier from a torpedo fired by a US submarine, and ten more aircraft had been destroyed or damaged as the formation flew over Kurita's group. (Airmen on both sides knew what it was to suffer from over-enthusiastic naval gunners.)

This second strike was detected by American radar at a range of 115 miles at 11.07 a.m., and was met more than 60 miles out by the Hellcats. One of the Judys was carrying sixteen packets of

Hellcat F6F fighters of TF58 ready to intercept a Japanese strike. (*National Archives, 80-G-255017*)

'window', its job being to drop its load north-east of Mitscher to draw off some of the American fighters; this task was successfully accomplished, although the amount of 'window' used in the attack was far too small to have any significant tactical influence.

The Jills and Judys were no match for the Hellcats, while the escorting Zekes were hard pressed to save their own skins. Seventy Japanese aircraft were shot down within a few minutes, but the survivors flew gamely on. About twenty unsuccessfully attacked the exposed picket destroyers and the battleships, and a few even found the nearest carrier group, to the north of the battleships. One torpedo-bomber crashed into the waterline of *Indiana* but the torpedo did not explode, and two carriers were slightly damaged by bomb splinters. That was all, and by noon the second raid was over. There were only 31 survivors from the 128 aircraft that Ozawa had launched three hours earlier.

Ozawa's offensive was still not spent, for two further large groups were on their way. The handling of the first of these, the third strike, quickly became a muddle. Forty-seven aircraft were despatched at 10 a.m. towards the 7.30 a.m. position of the Americans as reported by the first Japanese search. But while the strike was taking off new reports of American ships began to be received from the second search, according to which there appeared to be two American carrier groups about 200 miles apart, each consisting of three carriers with other ships in company. Unfortunately for Ozawa, both positions were seriously in error, owing to compass errors in the scouting aircraft; one report placed the American carriers too far north by 60 miles, the other by no less than 260 miles.

The aircraft of the third strike had just set course when a radio instruction was sent directing them towards the more southerly of the newly-reported American groups. About half the aircraft in the third strike received the order to change their target, while the remainder flew steadily on towards the original position. The latter pilots at least did find some American ships, Lee's battleships. Their orders, however, were to attack carriers, and it was not until they had fruitlessly searched the position they had been given that they turned back towards the battleships. By chance their course took them over the north-westerly carrier group, but the American fighter-defence was ready for them. They were met fifty miles out by 40 Hellcats and dispersed, though a few managed to break through and drop some ill-aimed and ineffective bombs at the carriers.

The other half of the strike, those which had obeyed the order to divert to the inaccurate position 60 miles too far north, naturally found nothing, and after searching for some time returned disconsolately to their carriers. The only redeeming feature of this third strike, from the Japanese point of view, was that 40 aircraft returned of the 47 which set out.

The fourth and final strike had been launched in the half-hour after 11 a.m., and consisted of 82 aircraft, 30 of them being Zeke fighters. They set out towards the phantom targets 260 miles to the north of Spruance's real position. Not surprisingly they found nothing, but they searched for so long that they had insufficient fuel to return to their carriers and had to head for Rota and Guam.

The group heading for Rota, about 33 strong, was fortunate enough to sight the southernmost American carrier group, and immediately bore in to attack. The American fighter defence shot down a number of the Japanese aircraft but it was not as effective as usual, and nine bombers managed to sneak in unopposed and drop bombs at two of the carriers. So intense was the anti-aircraft fire that only one bomber survived, and the carriers were unscathed. The remnants of the Japanese group—nine fighters and one bomber—headed for Rota and landed safely.

The group making for Guam was even more roughly handled. At 2.49 p.m., as they were nearing their objective, they were detected by the radar in the American ships. Twelve Hellcats were sent after them, and the leader soon reported 'forty enemy planes circling Orote field at angels 3, some with wheels down'. Fifteen more Hellcats quickly joined him, and the fighters wrought great execution. Thirty Japanese aircraft were swiftly shot down and the nineteen which somehow managed to land were all wrecked beyond repair.

This was the end of the last serious Japanese effort. Although Mitscher kept up the attacks on Guam and Rota airfields all afternoon, there was little incident, and it was obvious that the Japanese offensive was spent, at least for the present. Ozawa was still unaware of the extent of the disaster. True, few of his aircraft had returned, but he hoped that many had landed safely on Guam or Rota. He could not overlook, though, two heavy blows which had been struck by US submarines. Soon after 9 a.m. his flagship *Taiho* had been hit by a torpedo fired by the submarine *Albacore*. (This was the torpedo on which one of the pilots in the second strike had unsuccessfully crash-dived his aircraft.) Ozawa was not perturbed, for surely his flagship could not be seriously endangered by a single torpedo hit? It seemed that he was justified, for the carrier did not list and could still make better than 26 knots, but a serious disaster was impending.

The explosion of the torpedo had ruptured aviation-fuel tanks, and wretchedly incompetent damage control allowed highly-inflammable petrol vapour to spread. At 3.30 p.m. the inevitable spark occurred, vast explosions rocked the ship and fierce fires broke out everywhere. It was immediately obvious that the carrier was doomed, and Ozawa was rescued by a destroyer, ultimately re-hoisting his flag in the cruiser *Haguro*. *Taiho*, burning so furiously that the rescuing ships could not approach her, sank soon after 5 p.m., carrying with her thirteen aircraft and more than 1600 men. *Taiho* was the second Japanese carrier to sink on this disastrous day, for although she was not struck until 12.20 p.m., *Shokaku* was damaged so severely by three torpedo hits inflicted by the US submarine *Cavalla* that she sank within three hours.

Ozawa, in his new flagship, was without adequate communications, and was almost blind and dumb. He knew that he had lost two carriers, but believed that his bombers had sunk at least four American carriers and damaged others. He had no idea of the extent of his losses of aircraft, and had no intention of breaking off the action. He decided that he would refuel his ships on 20 June and resume battle the following day, so at 6.20 p.m. he ordered his ships to head north-west towards the fuelling rendezvous.

Spruance and Mitscher had their worries too. While the air battles had raged the carriers had steamed into the easterly wind, landing, rearming and refuelling and launching fighters as fast as the flight-deck crews could contrive. Spruance was anxious to chase the Japanese, but when he gave the order to head westward in pursuit he was only twenty miles from Guam, and more than 400 miles from Ozawa's main body. Even then there was a further delay of five hours while fighters took off and landed, for it was essential to keep a tight defence in the air lest Ozawa strike another blow, and thus it was not until 8 p.m. that Task Force 58 headed west, at 23 knots. One of the carrier groups had to be left behind to fuel, and it was given the task of keeping the Japanese airfields' on Guam and Rota quiet, a job which was most efficiently carried out.

Mitscher had disposed his remaining three carrier groups on a north-south axis, twelve miles apart, with the battleships 25 miles ahead. When would contact be made? Nobody knew, for Ozawa's ships had not been sighted since 12.15 p.m., when *Cavalla* reported torpedoing *Shokaku*. Nothing was known of Ozawa's movements since then, of the sinking of *Taiho* and *Shokaku*, or of the alteration of course to the north-westwards. Mitscher believed his aircrews and flight-deck crews to be exhausted, and did not order the all-out efforts to locate the Japanese fleet which were necessary if a decisive victory was to be won. Mitscher flew only a routine afternoon search which fell well short of the Japanese, and no night searches at all despite the fact that he had radar-fitted Hellcats and Avengers with fresh crews which could have searched to a depth of 400 miles. He decided to rely on the Saipan-based flying boats, which found nothing. Not for the first time in battle, tenderness for one's own men resulted in the loss of a decisive advantage.

Dawn on 20 June saw Spruance and Mitscher still heading west, in considerable doubt about the general position, and hoping against hope that the dawn search would find the Japanese fleet. Their hopes were destined to be frustrated.

All the survivors of Ozawa's Mobile Fleet were heading for the refuelling rendezvous, in great confusion because Ozawa could not control his ships from his temporary flagship. The tankers were ready to deliver fuel by 9 a.m. on 20 June, but there was no proper control and it was not until 12.30 p.m. that Ozawa could give the order to start fuelling. This order was cancelled almost immediately, when a false report was received that the Americans were approaching. Only after Ozawa transferred his flag to the carrier *Zuikaku* at 1 p.m. was he able to re-assert control. Then he also finally learnt the bitter truth about the previous day, when he had lost 330 aircraft—the most disastrous losses in a single day in the history of air combat—leaving barely 100 aircraft in the seven surviving carriers.[13] Ozawa was tough, however, and stuck to his decision to strike the next day with everything he had, hoping that Guam and Rota aircraft would be able to help.

Ozawa's immediate problem, though, was to parry the inevitable American counter-attack. He was well aware how vulnerable his fleet was while fuelling, particularly as the heavily-armed van had been ordered to fall back on the main body. Fifteen aircraft had been sent out on morning searches to the eastward, which found no ships but one of the Japanese scouts saw two American carrier aircraft. This led Kurita to recommend that the Mobile Fleet forthwith return to Japan, but this Ozawa refused to do until at 4.15 p.m. the cruiser *Atago* intercepted an American message saying that the Japanese had been sighted. This time Ozawa was convinced, for he knew his fleet was in no condition to withstand a heavy American attack. Reluctantly he ordered fuelling to be abandoned, and set course to the north-west towards Okinawa at 24 knots. The stern chase had started.

Mitscher had found his quarry at last, when one of the aircraft engaged in the routine afternoon search reported having seen something—but what or where it was nobody knew, for the message was mostly indecipherable. Mitscher had to act quickly, for it was

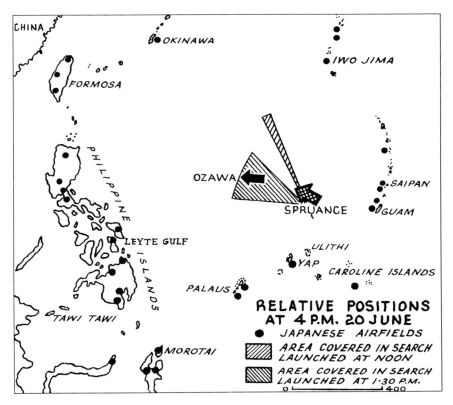

Relative positions at 4.00 p.m., 20 June 1944

3.40 p.m. and the sun would set at 7 p.m. At 3.53 p.m. he told Spruance that he was going to strike with everything he had, even though the aircraft would inevitably return after dark. Soon further reports began to come in from the scouting aircraft, and the position of the Japanese, when plotted, proved to be 275 miles from Task Force 58, dangerously near the maximum radius of the American bombers. But Mitscher had made his decision, and Spruance supported him.

At 4.20 p.m.—less than three hours before sunset—the whole task force turned majestically into the wind and within ten minutes 216 aircraft had taken the air—85 fighters, 77 dive-bombers, and 54 Avengers (most of which carried bombs rather than torpedoes). A second strike of similar size was made ready as soon as the flight decks were cleared by the departure of the first strike. Because of the loss of ground while steaming eastwards when launching aircraft, however, this second strike would be at even longer range than the first one. Mitscher decided that it was not justified.

The sun was just setting as the first American aircraft sighted the Japanese fleet. There was no time to organise attacks, for the Americans were too near the limit of their endurance—they simply attacked as they arrived, aiming at the most valuable targets they could see. Fortunately for them, Ozawa had not been able to regroup his fleet for effective defence.

Kurita's powerful van force, with three carriers and most of the battleships and cruisers, was the furthest away of any of the four Japanese groups, although it had originally been designed to take the shock of an American attack. Eight miles north of Kurita were the three fast carriers of the 2nd Carrier Division, supported by the battleship *Nagato*, a cruiser and eight destroyers. Eighteen miles further to the north-east was Ozawa's new flagship, the fast carrier *Zuikaku*, screened by three cruisers and seven destroyers. All were retiring to the north-west at their best speed of 24 knots, leaving the oilers and their meagre destroyer screen lumbering far behind. Ozawa had his ships grouped in very compact formations, not more than $2\frac{1}{2}$ miles in diameter, in the hope that the intensity of their gunfire would compensate for the lack of fighter defence.

Ozawa was still prepared to be aggressive, and at about 4 p.m. Kurita's carriers had launched a strike of sixteen aircraft. But the position they had been given for the Americans was false, so they found nothing and they were just landing when the first American aircraft arrived. Ozawa's fleet was nearly defenceless. He had only 50 fighters left, and although these took to the air they could do little to stop the Americans. Many American pilots did not sight a single Japanese aircraft during the attack.

Nearly all the American attacks were made on the two northern carrier groups, and in half-an-hour they were over. As darkness fell over the scene, it could be seen that the carrier *Hiyo* was sinking, and four others had sustained varying degrees of damage. In *Zuikaku* the order to abandon ship was actually given, and was only cancelled when it was seen that the fires were being brought under control; *Chiyoda* had her flight deck wrecked by a bomb hit; flying operations in *Junyo* had to be suspended. The battleship *Nagato* had been damaged also, along with two oilers which were scuttled that night.

That the Americans did not achieve more was partly due to the fact that they were operating at the very limit of their range and had to attack without delay, and partly because over half of the Avengers were not carrying torpedoes. *Hiyo* had been the victim of two torpedoes, and others might well have followed her if more torpedoes had been fired. But the slaughter of the Devastators at Midway was still well-remembered, and torpedo attacks were unpopular with many—despite the fact that the problems with the Mark 13 torpedo had been overcome and it was now an excellent weapon.[14]

After completing their attacks the American aircraft withdrew unmolested, for the Japanese fighter force was far too weak to attempt pursuit. The Americans still had the problems of finding their carriers and landing in the dark. Only twenty aircraft had been lost in the attacks on Ozawa's fleet, but four times as many were to be lost that night in crashes on the flight decks or landings in the sea. Mitscher did all he could. He ordered the carriers to switch on their lights (which was normal for night landings), and other ships to burn searchlights and fire star shell, but despite this the landings were chaotic—or perhaps because of it, for one of the pilots thought that 'blame for the panic must go to the excessive amount of lights on the ships'.[15] The night was pitch-black, and the pilots, untrained in night landings and almost out of fuel, tried to land at any cost. Some disregarded wave-offs; many landed on the wrong carrier; one tried to land on a destroyer. Perhaps the miracle is that nearly 120 landed safely, but the losses were heavy. Fortunately many of the crews were saved, only sixteen pilots and 33 aircrewmen being lost.

Meanwhile Ozawa was having similar difficulties, and when the last aircraft had landed or crashed he had only 35 fit survivors. There could be no thought now but retreat. He had actually ordered a forlorn surface attack at 7 p.m., and Kurita had headed eastwards with most of the heavy ships. Kurita had no chance of success, for Mitscher was 230 miles away and would have had no difficulty in dealing with the clumsy Japanese thrust. Finally at 8.46 p.m. Toyoda, watching the disastrous progress of the battle from his headquarters, ordered a general retreat. Fortunately for Ozawa all his surviving warships could make at least twenty knots and, after recalling Kurita, he had no difficulty in making his way to Okinawa.

Ozawa had done all he could. Japanese carrier air power had been committed to battle in a favourable situation, and had been destroyed. Ozawa should undoubtedly have retreated after his reverse on 19 June, but he did not know the extent of the disaster and was reluctant to admit defeat. Besides, what was the point of saving the carriers if the aircraft and crews they bore were lost and could never be replaced? It was a disconsolate Mobile Fleet which anchored off Okinawa on 22 June. The battle had sealed the fate of the Japanese troops on Saipan, although they fought on gallantly but hopelessly for another three weeks.

The American pursuit of Ozawa was not a headlong affair. It could not be, for most of the ships were dangerously short of fuel. It was not until after 11 p.m., when the last of the returning strike force had landed or crashed, that Task Force 58 turned westwards in pursuit, and then only at a comfortable sixteen knots. Spruance had given up all hope of catching Ozawa's main fleet, a decision which was confirmed when the night search revealed that the Japanese were 360 miles ahead (well out of range) and were hourly increasing the gap. Spruance spent all the next day searching for crippled Japanese ships, and picking up survivors of crashed American aircraft. When night fell, and no damaged Japanese ships had been found, Spruance turned back for Saipan. The battle of the Philippine Sea was over.

The immediate American reaction was not jubilation but frustration. Mitscher growled about the enemy having been allowed to escape, and even Nimitz wrote that there 'may be some disappointment that . . . there was not also a decisive "fleet action"'.[16] Much of the undercurrent of criticism was directed at Spruance, for being too cautious and for not understanding air power. Yet the chief blame for the failures, such as they were, must fall on Mitscher.

The most serious American shortcoming was in scouting, and in particular the failure to order a thorough search during the night of 19 June and an earlier second search on 20 June, for by the time Ozawa was found it was too late to complete the strikes in daylight. For both of these failings Mitscher bears the prime responsibility. Even when Ozawa was finally found, Mitscher struck with only half his strength, though it is true that it is doubtful whether a second strike could have reached Ozawa in daylight; and the Avengers in the first strike were not all armed with torpedoes as they should have been.

The battle clearly illuminated the limitations of daylight bombing attacks on well-defended targets. If the target force had efficient radar-directed fighter defence, the prospects of daylight bombing were grim, unless the bombing force was well-armed and had high-performance fighter escorts. The Japanese had neither. In view of the overwhelming superiority of the American fighter defence, it is curious that the Japanese did not make more use of 'window', for the little that was used did succeed in causing some of the American fighters to be temporarily lured out of the action. Perhaps even worse for the Japanese was the obvious sharp drop in the efficiency of their aircrews, caused by the lack of sustained sea training. The Americans clearly had far superior radar, and much better anti-aircraft gunnery and fighter aircraft, and the Japanese, courageous though they were, were simply outclassed.

The recriminations which followed this battle must not be allowed to conceal the fact that the Americans had won a great victory. Japanese carrier air power had been finally destroyed. The Japanese lost 476 aircraft and 445 irreplaceable aviators; the Americans lost 130 aircraft and 43 aviators. The Japanese lost three carriers sunk and two others seriously damaged without inflicting any significant damage on the American ships. Spruance, a most modest and unassuming man, would have agreed that perhaps he had failed to make the most of his opportunities, but he believed his mission was to support and cover the landing on Saipan, and he kept this aim in the forefront of his mind throughout the battle. Leyte Gulf, four months later, would show the perils which can arise when the command is held by a less clear-sighted and more impetuous man.

17

Leyte Gulf:

20–25 October 1944

The capture of the Marianas was inevitable after Spruance's victory in the Philippine Sea, and the Palau Islands fell to Nimitz in mid-September. Simultaneously MacArthur seized Morotai, off the northern tip of the Halmaheras. After prolonged argument it was at last agreed that the Philippines should be the next main objective, and the invasion of Mindanao was set for mid-November, to be followed a month later by an attack on Leyte. This timing was in accordance with MacArthur's belief that each successive amphibious leap should be made under the cover of shore-based fighters.

Admiral Halsey had recently relieved Spruance in the Pacific Fleet command. Nimitz's idea was to use Halsey and Spruance in alternate operations, one planning the next operation while the other was executing the present one. The ships were the same under either, but while Spruance was in command they were known as the Fifth Fleet, and with Halsey the Third Fleet, Mitscher's seventeen fast carriers being the core in each case. In addition to the carriers, Halsey had under his command six modern battleships, thirteen cruisers and 58 destroyers—this fleet being divided into four task groups of roughly equal size.

In the first two weeks of September Halsey's aircraft had attacked targets in Palau and the Philippines. The lack of opposition caused him to jump to the conclusion that the Japanese air strength was spent, and he accordingly suggested an immediate invasion of Leyte, dispensing with the intermediate landing on Mindanao. This bold proposal was based on a faulty premise, for Japanese air strength was merely being husbanded. Halsey's idea was nevertheless accepted, and on 15 September the Joint Chiefs of Staff set 20 October as the date for the landing in Leyte.

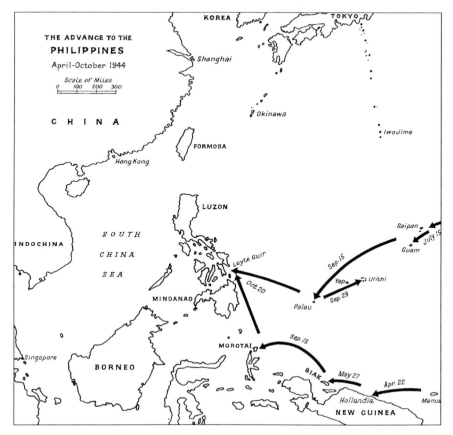

The advance to the Philippines

The command system for the invasion of the Philippines was extraordinarily cumbersome. There was MacArthur, who commanded all the ground forces. The air forces operated under no less than four authorities. Finally two fleets were involved, the Seventh (Kinkaid) under MacArthur and the Third (Halsey) under Nimitz. In this clumsy organisation lay the seeds of a near-disaster.

After his crushing defeat in the Philippine Sea, Ozawa had led his surviving carriers to the Inland Sea of Japan to refit. The outlook was gloomy indeed when he hoisted his flag in the new carrier *Amagi* in August.[1] He had four other carriers under his command—*Zuikaku*, *Zuiho*, *Chitose* and *Chiyoda*—and two hybrid carriers, *Ise* and *Hyuga*.[2] He began desperately training aircrews to replace his losses, but efficient new squadrons could not possibly be ready before November 1944, and this was going to be too

271

late. In mid-October Toyoda ordered Ozawa to send most of his aircraft—more than 170—to bolster the land-based air forces in Formosa and southern Japan. This order marked a recognition by Toyoda that Ozawa's carriers were no longer an effective striking force, for carriers without trained aircrews are useless weapons of war.

Kurita had all the available battleships at Lingga Roads, near Singapore, where he had been sent by Toyoda so as to be near their oil supplies, for Japanese shipping was by now so depleted

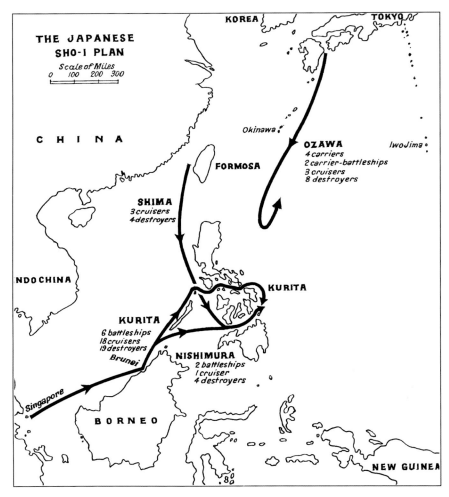

THE JAPANESE SHO-1 PLAN

Scale of Miles
0   100   200   300

KOREA

TOKYO

C H I N A

Okinawa

FORMOSA

IwoJima

OZAWA
4 carriers
2 carrier-battleships
3 cruisers
8 destroyers

SHIMA
3 cruisers
4 destroyers

NDO CHINA

KURITA

KURITA
6 battleships
18 cruisers
19 destroyers

Brunei

NISHIMURA
2 battleships
1 cruiser
4 destroyers

Singapore

B O R N E O

NEW GUINEA

The Japanese SHO-1 plan

that a large fleet could not be supplied at a more distant base. His force was a formidable one, comprising *Yamato, Musashi* and six older battleships, thirteen cruisers and nineteen destroyers. Intensive efforts were made to reduce the vulnerability of these ships to air attack by increasing their already-heavy armaments of 25mm guns.[3]

Toyoda's SHO–1 plan[4] to counter an American invasion of the Philippines was based on the use of Ozawa's carriers as a decoy to lure the US fast carriers northwards, while Kurita's fleet debouched through the San Bernadino and Surigao Straits and converged on the US assault shipping in Leyte Gulf. For the penetration of Surigao Strait two old battleships, a cruiser and four destroyers were detached from Kurita and placed under the command of Vice-Admiral Nishimura. An additional group of ships—three cruisers and four destroyers—under Vice-Admiral Shima was to sail from the Inland Sea and cooperate with Nishimura in forcing Surigao Strait. If the intricate SHO–1 plan was to work, it would clearly need admirable timing.

The Japanese Navy and Army cooperated better in their control of the available aircraft than they ever had before, and in the two areas all maritime-strike aircraft operated under a single commander. Vice-Admiral Fukudome commanded in Kyushu, the Ryukus and Formosa, and Vice-Admiral Teraoka in the Philippines.

Toyoda had planned to hold back his shore-based aircraft until the Americans were about to land, when all available aircraft would be flung against the assault shipping, but on 10 October he was on a tour of inspection in Formosa when news came of a strike on Okinawa by Halsey's carriers. Deciding that this was the preliminary to the 'general decisive battle', he reversed his original intention and ordered his full air strength against Halsey. By 17 October, when Toyoda belatedly reverted to his original policy of holding back, it was clear he had suffered a severe defeat. The Japanese had lost more than 180 aircraft in attacks on the US ships, plus another 150 in the air and on the ground in Formosa. Halsey had lost a mere 89 aircraft, and the only impact upon his ships was two damaged cruisers. The American success marked a new stage in the development of carrier warfare—for the first time a carrier fleet had engaged and decisively defeated a shore-based air force of superior strength. The striking power of Toyoda's shore-based air force had been effectively blunted.

At 10 a.m. on 20 October the Americans stormed over the beaches of Leyte. There was no attempt to achieve tactical surprise. The Americans had such overwhelming firepower to support the landing that they could afford to dispense with this element, although there was an attempt to persuade the Japanese, by jamming some of their radars and by the use of 'window', that a landing was being made on the neighbouring island of Mindanao. The ploy was unsuccessful, probably because Japanese radar techniques were not sufficiently advanced to fall for the deception.

The Seventh Fleet commander, Vice-Admiral Kinkaid, had more than 700 ships under his command. For gunfire support he had six old battleships, nine cruisers and dozens of destroyers, while off the coast eighteen escort carriers in three task groups under Rear-Admiral Thomas Sprague had about 200 Avengers and 260 fighters, and were providing fighter and anti-submarine cover, giving close support to the troops ashore, and attacking the Japanese airfields. By the evening of 22 October Kinkaid could reckon the landing was going well, for the army was securely ashore and although Takloban airfield had not yet been captured its fall was obviously imminent. Very few ships had been sunk or damaged, for the Japanese had as yet made no serious attempts to interfere. The dangerous part of the assault was over, and far to the north the seventeen carriers of Halsey's fleet were giving cover and support, with instructions to 'destroy enemy naval and air forces in or threatening the Philippines area'. This they could surely do.

The first clear hint of impending danger came during the early hours of 23 October, when two American submarines sighted eleven heavy Japanese ships and six destroyers, of Kurita's force, heading north-east along the narrow passage off the west coast of the island of Palawan.[5] By the afternoon Nishimura had been located heading for Surigao Strait, and Shima steaming southwards off the west coast of Luzon. The only group not so far located was the one the Japanese most wanted to be found—Ozawa's decoy force.

The two American submarines not only reported Kurita's whereabouts, but had struck him heavy blows, sinking two of his heavy cruisers (one of them his flagship) and severely damaging a third. While Kinkaid prepared to defend Surigao Strait, Halsey moved towards Kurita. At noon on 23 October three of his carrier groups—Bogan's Task Group 38.2, Sherman's Task Group 38.3 and Davison's Task Group 38.4—were 350 miles east of Luzon, while McCain's Task Group 38.1 was on its way to Ulithi (350 miles east of Palau) for rest and replenishment. Halsey did not recall McCain, but ordered his other three task groups to close the coast and be ready to strike Kurita at dawn the following day. By then Bogan was close to San Bernadino Strait, with Sherman and Davison respectively 150 miles to the north-west and south-east of him. At first light dozens of Hellcats and Helldivers took off from the American carriers to search the seas to the westwards. Kurita was to have no chance of evasion.

Nevertheless the Japanese struck first. The Second Air Fleet had arrived in the Philippines from Formosa, and Fukudome was convinced that the best way to protect Kurita was to strike at the American carriers. Kurita was given a meagre fighter escort (rarely more than four fighters at a time) while everything else was flung against Halsey's carriers. Fukudome's policy was clearly wrong, for his role at this time under the SHO–1 plan was to see that Kurita got safely through. Lacking adequate reconnaissance,[6] Fukudome had only a sketchy idea of the location of the American carrier groups, and he lacked the strike power to do them serious harm; and at a critical time Kurita was left almost unsupported.

This is not to say that Fukudome's attacks achieved nothing, but fortunately for the Americans his target was the northernmost American carrier group, Sherman's Task Group 38.3 off central Luzon, and Bogan's Task Group 38.2, the one best placed to deal with Kurita, was left unmolested. The Japanese attacked Sherman's task group between 8.30 a.m. and 10 a.m. in three waves each of 50–60 aircraft. Sherman was well-prepared for them. Given plenty of warning by radar, dozens of Hellcats met the attackers well away from the carriers, broke up the formations and wrought great damage.

One lone Judy managed to evade the American fighters by using cloud cover skilfully, and unexpectedly dived down on the carrier *Princeton*. The 550-pound bomb penetrated three decks, and exploded deep in the ship's vitals. *Princeton* was doomed. The light carriers were converted from cruiser hulls, and were without the hangar-deck armour of the larger carriers. The aviation fuel in the hangar was soon blazing fiercely, followed by vast explosions as torpedoes in the hangar exploded. Despite every endeavour the ship could not be saved. Soon after 5 p.m., more than nine hours after she was hit, the carrier was sunk by two torpedoes fired by the cruiser *Reno*. Thus went the only fast carrier of any navy to be sunk as a result of shore-based bombing attack during the entire war.

Meanwhile the Americans were striking vigorously at Kurita, who one of Bogan's scouts had found east of Mindoro at 8.10 a.m. In the next seven hours more than 250 aircraft attacked the Japanese fleet, the Americans having no difficulty in brushing aside the feeble fighter defence. Fourteen fighters had been sent to Kurita's assistance, but most of them had been driven off by gunfire from the ships they were supposed to protect.

The Americans found the Japanese gunfire, although intense,

to be highly inaccurate, and they lost only eighteen aircraft in all the attacks. The attackers concentrated on the battleship *Musashi*, almost ignoring her consorts, and by 1.30 p.m. she had been hit by torpedoes and bombs and was trailing twenty miles astern of the rest of the formation. During the afternoon the crippled battleship was hit by more torpedoes and bombs,[7] and she became completely unmanageable. By 7.30 p.m. the list had increased to thirty degrees, and her captain at last gave up the fight and ordered her abandoned. Five minutes later she rolled over and sank, the first Japanese battleship to be sunk by air attack alone.

Musashi's sacrifice was not in vain, for nearly all the American attacks had been concentrated on her and the other four battleships were almost unscathed. *Yamato* and *Nagato* had each been hit twice by bombs, *Haruna* had had five near-misses, and the cruiser *Myoko* had been forced to turn back after being hit by a torpedo. That was all. Kurita still had a formidable force of four battleships, eight cruisers and ten destroyers, but he passed the afternoon in a state of painful indecision. He could not decide whether to fall back

The battleship *Yamato* hit by a bomb on 24 October. (*National Archives, 80-G-325952*)

and support the lagging *Musashi* or push on without her. At 3 p.m. he retired to the westward, informing Toyoda an hour later that he considered it 'advisable to retire temporarily from the zone of enemy air attacks', but at 5.14 p.m. he changed his mind and turned back towards the San Bernadino Strait. His decision was soon strengthened by a cryptic message from Toyoda in the Inland Sea: 'All forces will dash to the attack, trusting in divine guidance'.[8]

Kurita was now several hours behind schedule, and informed Toyoda that he would pass through San Bernadino Strait at 1 a.m. and reach Leyte Gulf ten hours later. From 7.30 p.m. onwards Kurita was tracked by night-flying American aircraft, and as he debouched into the Philippine Sea he was ready for an immediate bitter battle with Halsey's battleships. Instead, nothing happened. There was no sign of any American ships. The shadowing aircraft

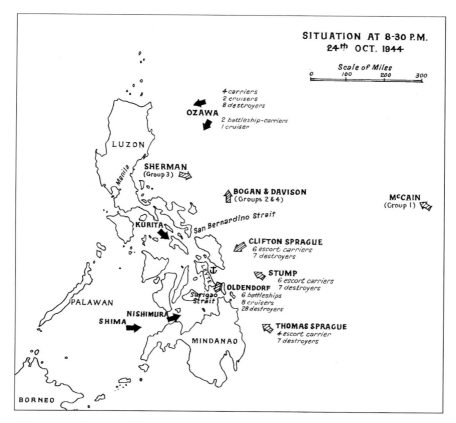

The situation at 8.30 p.m., 24 October 1944

had disappeared. Scarcely believing his good fortune, Kurita headed for Leyte Gulf.

Ozawa had been increasingly concerned. By noon on 24 October he was only 200 miles from Halsey's northerly carrier group, yet the Americans still had not sighted him. Kurita was due to pass through the San Bernadino Strait in six hours, and Halsey must at all costs be lured northwards before then. Ozawa had only 116 aircraft—less than half their normal complement—in his four carriers, *Zuikaku*, *Zuiho*, *Chitose* and *Chiyoda*; the two converted battleships *Ise* and *Hyuga* had no aircraft at all. Ozawa had launched 76 aircraft against Sherman at 11.45 a.m., the strike representing virtually all his air strength, for he retained only about twenty fighters for the defence of his force. The Japanese strike-pilots were very inexperienced, and were instructed to land at airfields in the Philippines if they were in any doubt about their ability to return to their carriers. Half of them were shot down by the American fighters, most of the remainder headed for Luzon and very few aircraft returned to Ozawa's carriers.

Worse still, the strike had achieved nothing and had provoked no retaliation, the Americans assuming that the Japanese aircraft came from airfields in Luzon. In desperation Ozawa detached Rear-Admiral Matsuda at 2.30 p.m. with the two carrier-battleships and a small screen to head southwards and attack the American ships with gunfire. Even so it was not until 3.40 p.m. that Matsuda was sighted by an American aircraft, and another hour before Ozawa himself was sighted. At last the deception could begin.

At 8 p.m. Ozawa received Kurita's message that he was retiring westwards, which obviously threw out the complicated timetable on which the SHO–1 plan was based, but an hour later he received the order from Toyoda to attack as originally planned. Ozawa accordingly recalled Matsuda and at midnight headed south with all his ships. His sole aim was to lure Halsey north. He expected to lose his entire force.

Halsey was confident that he had crippled Kurita's fleet, and that all the battleships and most of the cruisers could no longer be a serious menace to Kinkaid.[9] Now he had a chance to destroy the Japanese carriers, which he erroneously believed to be still the backbone of their fleet. When the orders for the Philippine operation were being prepared, Nimitz had included in the plan the words 'in case opportunity for destruction of the major portion of the enemy fleet offer or can be created, such destruction becomes the primary task'.[10] This was an attempt to avoid a repetition of what was regarded as Spruance's failure at the battle of the Philippine Sea, but for Nimitz to give such latitude to an impulsive leader like Halsey was courting disaster.

Soon after 8 p.m. on 24 June Halsey made his decision. He would concentrate all his strength against the Japanese carriers, ignoring Kurita, and he accordingly ordered Bogan's and Davison's groups to join Sherman off central Luzon and attack Ozawa at dawn. McCain, on his way back from Ulithi, was also ordered to join in. Not a ship was to be left off the San Bernadino Strait, and even the aircraft which had been shadowing Kurita had to be recalled shortly before midnight because their carrier, *Independence*, was on her way north with the rest of Task Force 38.

Halsey had indeed contemplated using his battleships against Kurita, and had issued a preparatory battle plan (which was intercepted by both Kinkaid and Nimitz) in which he stated that the six battleships and other heavy units 'will be formed as Task Force 34' under Vice-Admiral Lee; this order was subsequently modified by a message to his own fleet that Task Force 34 would be formed 'when directed', but he sent this second message on very-high-frequency radio and it was not received by either Kinkaid or Nimitz. Now that Ozawa's carriers had been sighted, Halsey wanted the battleships to accompany his carriers to deal with any crippled Japanese ships and as a shield against any possible surface threat. Moreover, if he left the battleships off San Bernadino, he felt he would have to leave behind at least one carrier group to give them air cover, and this would weaken his blow against Ozawa. Halsey apparently did not consider asking Kinkaid to use some of his escort carriers to give fighter cover to the battleships off San Bernadino, support which could have been provided although at the expense of the support for the land forces, and in any case Lee later said that he would have been quite happy to operate his battleship task force there without fighter support.

Not all of his admirals agreed with Halsey's decision. Bogan asked if Halsey knew that Kurita had turned eastwards again and that the lights in San Bernadino Strait were burning, while Lee told Halsey that he believed that Ozawa's carriers were acting as decoys and that Kurita's force was coming out. Neither received more than a bare acknowledgment. Commodore Arleigh Burke, Mitscher's chief of staff, tried to induce Mitscher to recommend to Halsey that the battleships should be left behind, but Mitscher refused. Halsey had been encroaching on Mitscher's tactical responsibility for the handling of Task Force 38, and relations between the two admirals were somewhat strained. 'If he wants my advice he'll ask for it', said Mitscher, and went to sleep. So Task Force

38 continued to head northwards to join battle with Ozawa's carriers.

Meanwhile Kinkaid, confident that his northern flank was being protected by Halsey, had been dealing with the threat to his southern flank. He had received ample warning of the approach of the two Japanese groups, for aircraft from Davison's Task Group 38.4 had sighted Nishimura in the Sulu Sea at 9 a.m. on 24 October, and Shima had been located three hours later by one of Kenney's bombers in almost the same position. The two Japanese admirals made no attempt to cooperate with each other, Nishimura pushing ahead so as to pass through Surigao Strait in darkness, while Shima followed 50 miles astern and attacked independently.

Soon after noon on 24 October Kinkaid warned all his ships to prepare for a night engagement. His escort carriers were fully occupied in supporting the landing and could not be spared for an attack on Nishimura and Shima, so the Japanese would have to be turned back by an old-style surface action. At 2.43 p.m. Kinkaid ordered Rear-Admiral Jesse Oldendorf to take command of the six old battleships and all the cruisers, destroyers and motor torpedo-boats that could be spared, and with this force to bar the northern end of Surigao Strait.

Oldendorf was overwhelmingly superior to his opponents in strength and efficiency, particularly in the availability of radar to control his surface gunfire. His only worry was the shortage of shells, particularly armour-piercing shells. Nishimura had no real chance as he plodded steadily into the trap Oldendorf had prepared for him. The first contact was made at 10.36 p.m. by one of the far-flung motor torpedo-boat squadrons, 100 miles from the battle line, and within six hours the battle was over. Harassed by motor torpedo-boats, damaged and disorganised by destroyers, and finally overwhelmed by the gunfire of battleships and cruisers, Nishimura's force was almost annihilated. Both his battleships, *Fuso* and *Yamashira*, were sunk, as were two of his four destroyers. The only survivors were two destroyers—one completely disabled—and the heavily-damaged cruiser *Mogami*, which was limping out of the action.

At this point Shima entered the fray with his three cruisers and four destroyers. He was 40 miles behind Nishimura, and imagined that he was coming to his aid. At 3.25 a.m. one of his cruisers was damaged by a torpedo fired by a motor torpedo-boat, and 45 minutes later he passed the burning wreck of *Fuso*, by then in two halves. Shima decided that it was the wreckage of both Nishimura's battleships, and in that case he was too late and should retire, which he did. During his withdrawal, one of his cruisers collided with the damaged *Mogami*. At 4.33 a.m. Oldendorf released a few cruisers and destroyers to pursue Shima and destroy any cripples, at the same time asking Kinkaid to arrange for air attacks on the surviving Japanese ships. The threat from the southern flank was clearly removed.

Kinkaid had some reason to feel satisfied, but he was still slightly uneasy about the threat from Kurita. The previous evening he had sent a radar-fitted Catalina up the coast towards San Bernadino, but this aircraft was looking for small craft close inshore, and had seen nothing of Kurita. Kinkaid had been told by Halsey that the Central Force (Kurita's) was badly damaged, and that three carrier groups were now going north after Ozawa; however, he assumed that Task Force 34 was still guarding San Bernadino. But was it? Some of his staff were doubtful. At 1.55 a.m. Kinkaid ordered Sprague to fly three dawn-searches, one of them covering the northern sector to a depth of 135 miles. At 4.12 a.m., when telling Halsey of Oldendorf's success, Kinkaid asked directly whether Task Force 34 was guarding San Bernadino.

The answer did not come from Halsey. At 7.04 a.m. Kinkaid received an emergency signal from Rear-Admiral Clifton Sprague, in the northern group of escort carriers, that he was under gunfire attack by four battleships, eight heavy cruisers and many destroyers, at a range of 30 000 yards. The destruction of the escort carriers seemed inevitable, for Oldendorf's ships were still deep in Surigao Strait, more than 60 miles or three-hours steaming away, and in any event they were certain to be short of ammunition and torpedoes. Halsey was the only one who might be able to give immediate assistance, and from 7 a.m. Kinkaid addressed to him a series of appeals.

Soon after 8 a.m. Kinkaid received the discouraging news, in answer to his first signal, that Lee's battleships were with Halsey. An hour later came word that Halsey was still engaging the Japanese carriers, but that McCain with five carriers and four heavy cruisers had been ordered to assist him. McCain had been fuelling on his way back from Ulithi and was actually further from Leyte Gulf than Halsey himself, so it would be several hours before help could be looked for from that source. By that time the escort carriers must surely have been annihilated.

Thomas Sprague's three carrier task units were operating in the approaches to Leyte Gulf, about 40 miles off the coast. The northern unit, Clifton Sprague's, was off Samar Island; the centre unit (Rear-Admiral Felix Stump), was about twenty miles to the south and directly off Leyte Gulf; and the southern unit, commanded by Thomas Sprague himself, was off northern Mindanao,

The escort carrier *Gambier Bay* straddled by Japanese shells during the battle off Samar, 25 October. A Japanese cruiser is barely visible on the horizon at the right. (*National Archives, 80-G-287505*)

more than 100 miles further south. Clifton Sprague and Stump each had six escort carriers and Thomas Sprague four, and each unit had a screen of seven destroyers or destroyer escorts, chiefly for protection against submarines. Each escort carrier had an average of twelve Avengers and seventeen Hellcats or Wildcats with which to perform routine tasks such as providing fighter cover over the beaches, and anti-submarine patrols over the whole area.

On 25 October Clifton Sprague and Stump had been instructed to provide air support for the army, while Thomas Sprague was to strike at the Japanese ships retreating from Surigao Strait. *Ommaney Bay*, in Stump's task unit, had been selected to fly the three dawn-searches ordered by Kinkaid, but the order was not received until after 5 a.m., and reorganising the aircraft on the tiny flight deck was a lengthy task. It was not until 6.55 a.m. that the ten-aircraft search took to the air, and by then it was too late.

By this time many other aircraft were in the air. At 5.30 a.m. Clifton Sprague sent twelve fighters to cover the ships in Leyte Gulf, and fifteen minutes later Thomas Sprague had launched a strike at the Japanese ships retreating from Surigao Strait. Soon after 6 a.m. all the routine fighter and anti-submarine patrols were in the air, and it was one of the latter that gave the first alarm at 6.47 a.m., reporting the sighting of a major Japanese force only twenty miles from Clifton Sprague's task unit. Simultaneously anti-aircraft fire was sighted to the north-west from Clifton Sprague's ships, and one of the escort carriers obtained a surface radar contact. Any doubt about the identity of the ships was soon resolved when the unmistakable superstructure of Japanese battleships loomed over the horizon, and at 6.59 a.m. shell splashes began to fall near Clifton Sprague's carriers.

Clifton Sprague had already acted. At 6.57 a.m. he had altered course to the eastwards, as far away from Kurita as he could while still retaining the ability to fly-off his aircraft. He increased speed to the maximum his carriers could make—a mere $17\frac{1}{2}$ knots—and ordered every ship to make smoke. Within five minutes Thomas Sprague had ordered all the escort carriers in the three task units to attack the Japanese ships with every available aircraft, though many were not available because they had already been dispatched on different missions.

Kurita was as surprised as Clifton Sprague at the sudden contact. He was in the process of forming his ships into a circular anti-aircraft formation on a new course when the American carriers were sighted, and without waiting for the manoeuvre to be completed he ordered 'general attack'. Singly or in small groups, without coordination, his ships dashed into battle. Kurita did not even know who his targets were. He thought they might be 30-knot carriers of Task Force 38, while some of his staff saw battleships, and others saw several cruisers. In so far as Kurita had a plan, it was to get to windward of the carriers to prevent them from launching their aircraft into the north-easterly wind.

Soon after 7 a.m. the Americans had some temporary relief when they were suddenly covered by a rain squall, which made the Japanese gunfire ineffective, but when they emerged fifteen minutes later Kurita's cruisers had closed to within 25 000 yards. Clifton Sprague ordered his three destroyers, and later his four destroyer escorts, to counter-attack. This they did with great gallantry, scoring several hits with torpedoes and gunfire, and although three of them were sunk they gained a respite for the carriers who headed south under cover of a smokescreen.

The destroyers were not Kurita's only worry, for aircraft from

Clifton Sprague's carriers were attacking his ships continually, forcing frequent changes of course. At first they attacked only in twos or threes, many making repeated runs even though they were without any weapons to drop. By 7.30 a.m. practically every serviceable aircraft from Clifton Sprague's carriers was in the air, but it was not until 8.30 a.m. that the first coordinated attack was made, by six torpedo-bombers and twenty fighters. By this time aircraft from Stump's task unit were on the way. Stump's carriers had been ordered to be ready to arm their Avengers with torpedoes in case they were required in the Surigao Strait, and within ninety minutes of the first alarm 36 fighters and 43 torpedo-bombers were despatched in three waves. These orderly attacks had much to do with turning the tide of battle, one Japanese officer reporting that 'the bombers and torpedo planes were very aggressive and co-ordination was impressive'.[11]

The third task unit, that of Thomas Sprague, could do little to help, for many of its aircraft were already committed to the pursuit in Surigao Strait (in which they finished off the crippled cruiser *Mogami*). It also had problems of its own, having found itself under attack from Zeke fighters of the 201st Air Group which were intent on crashing into the US carriers. The pilots of these aircraft were from a special squad of Kamikaze volunteers organised by Vice-Admiral Ohnishi, a veteran pilot who had been one of Yamamoto's principal assistants in directing the expansion of Japan's naval air arm.[12]

Thomas Sprague's task unit of four escort carriers had just launched a strike to go to Clifton Sprague's help when Zekes dived onto the carriers *Santee* and *Suwanee*, causing fires and putting them out of action. Both were converted tankers of the *Sangamon* class, however, and such ships were difficult to sink. *Santee* rapidly got her fire under control, but she was then hit by a torpedo fired by the submarine *I-56*. Even so she was still capable of sixteen knots, despite a slight list. *Suwanee* also quickly got her fire under control, and within two hours flying operations were resumed.

By 9.11 a.m. one of Clifton Sprague's six escort carriers had been sunk and only two were undamaged. The five surviving carriers were heading south-westwards at their best speed, with their destroyers still trying to fend off the Japanese attacks. The Japanese had not escaped unscathed, for two of Kurita's heavy cruisers had been sunk and a third was sinking, but Kurita still had four practically-undamaged battleships, five cruisers and two squadrons of destroyers.

To Clifton Sprague's amazement Kurita suddenly broke off the engagement and turned north. Kurita's original intention was merely to reorganise his ships, which had become widely scattered in the hectic chases, but he was also sorely perplexed. He had been told that Nishimura's force had been almost annihilated and he knew that Shima had turned back. He had heard of Kinkaid's appeals for help, and imagined that the fast battleships would be near and that a strike from Halsey's carriers was imminent. He had intercepted a message from Kinkaid directing any aircraft not able to land on an aircraft carrier to put down on the newly-captured Takloban airfield, and built this up in his imagination to a powerful air force which would attack him if he entered Leyte Gulf. For over three hours the Japanese steamed around aimlessly with Kurita in a state of indecision, every hour his estimate of the American strength increasing and his own prospects decreasing.[13] At 12.36 p.m. he made his decision, and his entire force turned north and headed back towards the San Bernardino Strait.

Clifton Sprague's carriers could still hardly believe their miraculous escape from Kurita when, at 10.30 a.m., they were attacked

The escort carrier *St Lo* after a Kamikaze hit. (*National Archives, 80-G-270516*)

by five of Ohnishi's suicide Zekes. Two were shot down and one, badly-damaged, narrowly missed *White Plains*, but *St Lo* and *Kitkin Bay* were heavily hit. *St Lo* caught fire, torpedoes and bombs in the hangar blew up, and she was soon blazing from end to end before she sank at 11.25 a.m. Before she went down yet another carrier, *Kalinin Bay*, had been damaged in an attack by about ten Zekes, of which apparently about four were intent on suicide. Clifton Sprague's flagship, *Fanshaw Bay*, was now the only un-damaged carrier in his unit. Ohnishi's pilots had sunk an escort carrier and damaged four others, and had achieved as much, at far less cost, as had Kurita's formidable force of surface ships. But even the desperate gallantry of the Japanese pilots could not alter the course of the battle, for Ohnishi's attack had been too late, and on far too small a scale.

Meanwhile, when Halsey received Kinkaid's increasingly des-perate appeals for help he was heavily engaged with Ozawa, who had done his task perfectly. Even two years later Halsey believed (or purported to believe) that he had been 'rushing to intercept a force which gravely threatened not only Kinkaid and myself, but the whole Pacific strategy'.[14] The three carrier groups (Bogan's, Sherman's and Davison's) were together by midnight, when Mitscher assumed tactical command; McCain was still hundreds of miles to the east, but moving up as fast as he could. At 1 a.m. Mitscher sent off five radar-equipped aircraft from *Independence* to search the north-western sector to a depth of 350 miles, and soon after 2 a.m. the reports began to come in, first on Matsuda's two battleship-carriers, then on Ozawa's main body.

The opposing forces were now 210 miles apart, but reporting errors gave Mitscher and Halsey the impression that they were actually within 90 miles of each other, and Halsey at once ordered Lee's Task Force 34 to push ahead of the carriers. For nearly five hours there was no more news of the Japanese, but Mitscher did not hesitate. As soon as it was light, at about 5.40 a.m., he began launching his first strike, together with scouting aircraft to search around Ozawa's last reported position. When Ozawa was located at 7.10 a.m. the strike aircraft were waiting less than 100 miles away.

Ozawa had no chance, for after the losses during his strike the previous day he had only 29 aircraft (24 of them fighters) in his four carriers, and these were brushed aside by the massive American strikes. Ozawa's flagship, *Zuikaku*, was hit by one torpedo in the first attack, the light carrier *Chitose*, hit by several bombs, was left sinking and a destroyer was sunk. Worse still, Ozawa by now had only six serviceable fighters left, and a second strike was on

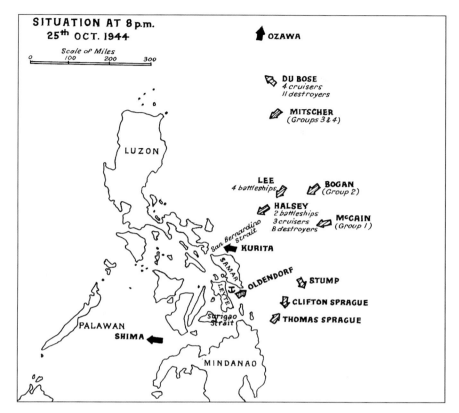

SITUATION AT 8 p.m.
25th OCT. 1944

Scale of Miles
0   100   200   300

OZAWA

DU BOSE
4 cruisers
11 destroyers

MITSCHER
(Groups 3 & 4)

LUZON

LEE
4 battleships

BOGAN
(Group 2)

HALSEY
2 battleships
3 cruisers
8 destroyers

McCAIN
(Group 1)

San Bernardino Strait

KURITA

SAMAR

OLDENDORF

STUMP

CLIFTON SPRAGUE

Surigao Strait

THOMAS SPRAGUE

PALAWAN

SHIMA

MINDANAO

The situation at 8.00 p.m., 25 October 1944

its way, arriving shortly before 10 a.m. The carrier *Chiyoda* was mortally damaged in this second attack, and the Japanese seemed doomed, for more heavy air-attacks were surely inevitable and Lee's battleships were waiting to deal with any stragglers.

Respite was to come from an unexpected quarter. At 8.22 a.m. Halsey received Kinkaid's first message about the arrival of Kurita off Samar, but he ignored it, apart from ordering McCain to support Kinkaid. Halsey steeled himself to disregard Kinkaid's increasingly desperate appeals, including a message sent in the clear: 'Where is Lee? Send Lee', but by 10 a.m. Nimitz had entered the fray, asking pointedly 'where is (repeat) where is Task Force 34? The world wonders'.[15] Nevertheless Halsey held out for another hour, until at 10.55 a.m. he ordered Bogan's group and Lee's battleships (including his own flagship, *New Jersey*) to turn south and go to Kinkaid's assistance. He had left it too late. Even by pushing ahead with two battleships—at the risk of being out-numbered in the first instance by Kurita—Halsey could not reach San Bernadino before 1 a.m. the following day, and Kurita had passed through the strait three hours earlier.

Mitscher still believed that his two carrier groups could destroy Ozawa. Shortly before noon he launched his third strike, 200 strong and the largest of the day. This strike finished off *Zuikaku*—the last surviving carrier from the Pearl Harbor attack—and severely crippled the only undamaged carrier, *Zuiho*. Mitscher then sent ahead a force of four cruisers and eleven destroyers under Admiral Du Bose to sink the derelict *Chiyoda* and any other cripples he might find. Three more strikes in the afternoon achieved compar-atively little, although the damaged *Zuiho* was sunk. Much effort was concentrated on the two carrier-battleships, but neither of these tough ships received more than superficial damage. Ozawa was aggressive to the end, and when he heard of the advance of Du Bose he turned south with *Ise*, *Hyuga*, one cruiser and a destroyer, forcing Du Bose to make a prudent withdrawal.

Turning north again at 11.30 p.m., Ozawa resumed his retreat. An American submarine sank another of his cruisers, and it was a sorely depleted little force of two carrier-battleships, one cruiser and five destroyers which finally reached Japan. Ozawa had lost all four of his carriers, but he had done what he set out to do.

Leyte Gulf was an overwhelming American victory. In the four days of fighting the Japanese had lost four carriers, three battle-ships, nine cruisers and thirteen destroyers; the Americans had lost only a light carrier, two escort carriers and three destroyers. The Imperial Japanese Navy was finished. Ozawa said later that 'after this battle . . . there was no further use assigned to surface vessels, with the exception of some special ships'.[16] Well might Nimitz write that 'the Imperial Japanese Navy no longer existed as a fighting force, and the United States Navy commanded the Pacific'. Japan, cut off from its strategically-critical supplies, faced inevitable defeat, and after Leyte its eventual surrender was certain, invasion or no invasion, atom bombs or no atom bombs.

The battle showed the immense superiority the Americans had built up, in numbers, in quality of equipment and efficiency of its use. For the first time a carrier force had taken on and defeated a numerically-superior land-based air force. The fighter and anti-aircraft gunfire defence of the Americans was of a very high standard, and made daylight bombing attacks on them a forlorn

A carrier battleship in action on 25 October. Neither *Ise* nor *Hyuga* carried any aircraft during the battle, but both survived. (*US Naval Historical Center, NH63440*)

undertaking. Unable to mount effective night attacks, the Japanese had to look elsewhere.

Yet the tactical direction of both sides was surprisingly defective. Of the Japanese admirals, only Ozawa performed well. He performed his decoy role with exemplary efficiency, and maintained his aggression to the end. The Commander-in-Chief, Admiral Toyoda, totally misjudged the ability of his shore-based aircraft to take on Halsey's carriers, and blunted their striking power before the crucial stage of the battle was reached. Kurita, by his indecision and pusillanimity, lost a wonderful opportunity to inflict serious damage on the American invasion fleet and its supporting ships. True, he would almost certainly have eventually been sunk by Task Force 38 (though he might have been able to escape through Surigao Strait, Kinkaid's old battleships being probably too low in ammunition to stop him) but there was no point in aiming to save his battleships for a future battle, for it was highly improbable that such a chance to destroy American ships would recur. (In fact none of Kurita's surviving battleships achieved anything useful during the remainder of the war, and all except *Nagato* were sunk before the end of it, and *Nagato* was heavily damaged.) Finally, the total lack of coordination between the two admirals taking their forces through the Surigao Strait was extraordinary.

Things were no better on the American side. Nimitz was most unwise to confuse the aim of the naval part of the operation, which surely was the assault and the subsequent protection of the landing force, and not the destruction of the Japanese fleet. If that fleet threatened the landing its destruction became part of the aim, but it should not have been made separate, particularly when its execution was in the hands of the impulsive Halsey. It is fascinating to consider what would have happened had Spruance rather than Halsey been in command of the Third Fleet. Spruance, a clear-sighted strategist and cautious tactician, would surely have concentrated on Kurita, and not allowed himself to be drawn off on a chase after Ozawa until Kurita had been completely destroyed, when he could have turned on Ozawa and overwhelmed him.

Halsey made five critical mistakes in his conduct of his part of the battle. The first was when he failed to order adequate air searches to the northward, the direction from which Ozawa's carriers could be expected to approach, despite his preoccupation with those carriers. (It is however a moot point whether Halsey's conduct of the battle would have been better or worse if he had detected Ozawa earlier.) Halsey's second mistake was when he failed to concentrate his forces by recalling McCain's task group of five carriers from its visit to Ulithi when Kurita was first detected. His third mistake was when he accepted the pilots' reports of the damage inflicted on Kurita in the Sibuyan Sea, reports which his experience should have led him to discount, and which he later implicitly recognised when he admitted the 'difficulty of crippling by air strikes, alone, a task force of heavy ships at sea and free to manoeuvre.'[17] The fourth mistake was when he set off after Ozawa, leaving San Bernadino completely unguarded and his aircraft no longer shadowing Kurita, without making his intentions clear and misleading both Kinkaid, his colleague, and Nimitz, his superior. The fifth was when, after learning from Kinkaid that Kurita was attacking the Seventh Fleet, he failed either to detach his battleships in time to block Kurita's retreat through San Bernadino, or to keep them with his carriers so as to win an annihilating victory over Ozawa, the fast battleships thus not being permitted to contribute anything to the victory. Five serious mistakes is a lot.

Leyte was not only one of the decisive battles of the Pacific War, it also marked a turning point in naval tactics. It was a great long-range amphibious operation. It was the last conflict that will ever be fought between lines of battleships, and the last surface action between battleships and aircraft carriers. It was the last battle between fleets of aircraft carriers, and the first occasion on which aircraft carriers had overwhelmed shore-based air power. It also marked the introduction of mass attacks by guided weapons, although the guidance system required a level of valour unexcelled in the history of war. For one battle, that is enough.

18

Tirpitz:

11 November 1944

No ship had more influence on the conduct of the war than the 42 600-ton German battleship *Tirpitz*. For more than two years she had been a brooding menace over the vital Allied sea-communications across the Atlantic and to North Russia. As Churchill said, she 'rivetted our attention' and forced Britain to maintain much larger forces to defend the Russian convoys and to prevent a break-out into the Atlantic. Yet in all that time *Tirpitz* did not sink a single ship, and her powerful guns were never fired against an Allied surface vessel.

Tirpitz's first year after commissioning in January 1941 was ill-starred. She suffered many minor breakdowns and was forced to remain in the Baltic, training her crew and trying to remedy the defects, while her sister ship *Bismarck* made her fatal foray into the Atlantic without her.

In December 1941 Hitler suddenly decided that a British invasion of Norway was imminent. Such an operation must be stopped, he believed, because 'the fate of the war will be decided in Norway'. Admiral Raeder was ordered to redeploy the German fleet, for 'every ship which is not stationed in Norway is in the wrong place'.[1] *Tirpitz* accordingly sailed for Trondheim in January 1942, and a month later *Scharnhorst* and *Gneisenau*, which had been blockaded in Brest for some months, broke through the English Channel and returned to the North Sea. However, both these ships had struck mines during their escape, and could not be sent to Norway until repairs were made.

At Trondheim *Tirpitz* was well placed either to break-out into the Atlantic or to pounce on convoys to Russia. She made her first attempt to intercept a convoy in March 1942 but was reported

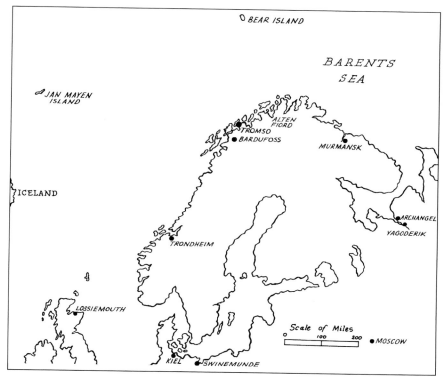

Norway and *Tirpitz*'s hiding-places

by a British submarine and Admiral Tovey—who was covering the convoy with the battleship *King George V* and the aircraft carrier *Victorious*—headed to intercept. Unluckily for Tovey the Luftwaffe failed to hold contact with the convoy, and *Tirpitz* abandoned the attack and headed for home before she could be cut off. An attack was attempted by twelve Albacores from *Victorious*, but it was poorly handled. The torpedoes were dropped at too great a range and *Tirpitz* had no difficulty in avoiding them before escaping to Foettenfiord, near Trondheim, having shot down two of the attacking aircraft.

There was little peace to be had at Foettenfiord. Churchill had already written to the Chiefs of Staff about *Tirpitz*:

> The destruction or even the crippling of this ship is the greatest event at sea at the present time. No other target is comparable to it . . . A plan should be made to attack with carrier-borne torpedo aircraft and with heavy bombers by daylight or at dawn.[2]

293

Tirpitz lies at her berth in Foettenfiord, January 1942. (*Imperial War Museum, HU50946*)

The problems of attacking the battleship were formidable, for her position was one of immense natural strength. The mountains rose steeply around her berth, and she nestled close to the cliffs on one side and spread extensive nets on the other. It was certain that a torpedo-bombing attack would be abortive so the only hope was a bombing attack, but even here nature gave shelter to the German battleship. Thick mists abounded in the area, and on the few clear days *Tirpitz* was able to cover herself quickly with a smokescreen whenever danger threatened.

Bomber Command was nonetheless prepared to attempt attacks. In the first raid, on 31 March, only one bomber found the target, and its attack was baffled by the smokescreen. On 28 April 32 heavy bombers attacked, and the following day 30 more. Most managed to find *Tirpitz*, but again they were frustrated by the smokescreen. This attack did have one original feature. While Lancasters bombed from a high level, a group of Halifax bombers flew in low and dropped small mines on the mountainside, in the hope that they would roll down and detonate under the ship. These attacks had no chance of seriously damaging the battleship. The 4000-pound blast-bombs dropped by the Lancasters could not hope to penetrate the thick armour which protected her vitals, while the

100 pounds of explosive in the mines meant they were too light to cause much harm. They were also too light to roll down the mountainside, and none reached the ship although several were caught in obstructions on the cliff above it.[3] Twelve bombers were lost in the three attacks, bombers which could ill be spared. For more than two years thereafter Bomber Command took no part in the campaign against *Tirpitz*.

In July 1942 *Tirpitz*, without firing a shot, played a vital role in a major victory. She was in Altenfiord in the north of Norway as convoy PQ17 passed on the way to Russia. The First Sea Lord, Sir Dudley Pound, was mistakenly convinced that *Tirpitz* was about to attack and ordered the convoy to scatter. The almost defenceless merchant ships were massacred by submarines and the Luftwaffe, and only eleven of the 34 who set out finally limped into Murmansk.

The career of *Tirpitz* nearly ended in January 1943, as the result of a blow from a quite different direction. An attempted attack on another Russian convoy by *Lützow*, *Hipper* and six destroyers had been ignominiously beaten off by the convoy escort. Hitler was furious, and ordered that all heavy ships should be scrapped and their guns mounted on land for coast defence. Göring enthusiastically supported this decision, claiming that the heavy ships were tying down squadrons of his aircraft which could be better used elsewhere, and in any case the Luftwaffe could do anything heavy ships could. Unable to alter Hitler's decision, Admiral Raeder resigned and was succeeded by Dönitz, previously the Admiral of Submarines.

At first Dönitz welcomed Hitler's decision to scrap the heavy ships. He soon realised their strategic value, though, and by tactful treatment gradually managed to talk Hitler into reversing his order. When he proposed to move the repaired *Scharnhorst* to Norwegian waters to join *Tirpitz* and *Lützow*, Hitler was sceptical of the value of the move but finally consented.

The British were in no doubt about the value of the move, and the new concentration was watched with concern. The Allies were forced to suspend the convoys to Russia in the spring and summer of 1943, and again the German ships had achieved much while risking little. Except for a brief raid on Spitzbergen in September, they remained at Altenfiord. With the coming of the autumn darkness the convoys would start again. The German battleships would be ready.

The Royal Navy was not prepared to wait passively for the Germans to attack their convoys. On 22 September *Tirpitz*, lying behind her defences in Altenfiord, was disabled by British midget submarines. Three of the six craft which set out managed to penetrate the intricate net-defences around the battleship, and two laid their explosive charges before being destroyed. The explosions immobilised *Tirpitz* for six months. *Lützow* had already gone to the Baltic, leaving *Scharnhorst* as the only operational battleship in Norwegian waters. Attempting a lone foray against a convoy, *Scharnhorst* was destroyed by the Home Fleet on Christmas Day 1943. The sands of fortune were running out for the German heavy ships.

The vigilant British naval intelligence never relaxed its concentration on *Tirpitz*. In mid-March 1944 it was known that the battleship had been repaired and was running trials in Altenfiord. During February she had been attacked by a group of Russian bombers, each carrying a 2000-pound bomb. Fifteen set out on a moonlight attack, but only four found the battleship, and they did her no harm. The RAF Bomber Command was preoccupied with other targets, for the invasion of France was imminent. Another attack by midget submarines was unlikely to be successful. If *Tirpitz* was to be immobilised, it would have to be done by carrier aircraft.

By this time, the vast output of American shipyards was making itself felt, and the Home Fleet at last possessed a powerful force of carriers. *Victorious*, the old *Furious* and four escort carriers—*Emperor*, *Fencer*, *Searcher* and *Pursuer*—were available to deal with *Tirpitz*. Between them the carriers had 164 aircraft, of no less than six different types. Forty-two of the new Barracuda dive-bombers were to perform the strike function, supported by Hellcats and Wildcats, with Corsairs flying top cover against Luftwaffe fighters. Intensive practices had been held in Loch Eriball, where attempts had been made to simulate the conditions in Altenfiord.

For the actual attack, the carriers followed some distance behind a convoy to Russia. The transports were certain to rivet German attention, and the carriers were thus able to approach undetected. Soon after 3 a.m. on 3 April 1944 the first strike of 21 Barracuda bombers and 45 fighters took off. Flying low over the water to avoid German radar, they reached the Norwegian coast without being detected and then climbed to clear the mountains before diving into the snow-covered valley where *Tirpitz* lay. Although the British strike was detected by a shore radar-station as it crossed the coast, the warning took twenty minutes to reach *Tirpitz* and arrived almost simultaneously with the Barracudas.

Surprise was complete. *Tirpitz* was preparing to leave her berth for trials, most of her guns were not manned, there was no time to lay a smokescreen and she lay naked and almost defenceless in the fiord. The fighters swept the decks of *Tirpitz* with their machine-guns, while close behind came the dive-bombers. Seven bombs hit and there was one damaging near-miss; within a minute the attack was over. *Tirpitz*'s War Diary recorded that 'as it was doubtful if the trials could be carried out, it was decided to return to the net enclosure'. But *Tirpitz* had still not reached her berth when the second wave (of nineteen Barracudas) arrived, and although she was by now fully alert the smokescreen did not cover her completely and the Barracudas scored five more hits.

The Luftwaffe fighters never appeared, despite increasingly desperate appeals. The battleship's anti-aircraft gunfire was poor, caused by the surprise of the first strike and the difficulty of seeing the attacking aircraft through the smoke which was developing during the second strike. One Barracuda was lost in each strike (as well as one which crashed shortly after take-off). The fighters were unscathed. Although 300 of her crew were killed, the material effects on *Tirpitz* were slight. Within a month the battleship was again ready for action. Dönitz took a robust view of *Tirpitz*'s prospects, reporting to Hitler on 11 April that:

> This ship is to be repaired and to remain stationed in northern Norway. This course will be followed even if further damage is sustained . . . After all, the presence of the *Tirpitz* ties up enemy forces.[4]

Despite their comparative lack of success the Home Fleet carriers tried again—on 17 July, twice on 22 August, and then on 24 and 29 August. Four of the five attacks were complete failures, but one—on 24 August—was a remarkable feat of bombing, scoring two hits with 1600-pound bombs and ten more with 500-pounders, but little damage was done.[5]

So the Fleet Air Arm had failed. They had attacked with courage and skill, but their bombs were too small and their dive-bombing technique unsuitable for the destruction of such a target, even if they could find it. Yet something had to be done to dispose of *Tirpitz*. The focus of naval operations was shifting to the Pacific, where the Royal Navy was about to join with the Americans for the final onslaught on Japan, but the Admiralty would not denude the Home Fleet of its battleships and aircraft carriers while *Tirpitz* was capable of putting to sea.

Some means of disabling her must be found. Bomber Command was the last hope. Sir Arthur Harris, the Commander-in-Chief of Bomber Command was, like Göring, a poor strategist. He strongly resisted any diversion of his bombing effort from the sustained attack on German industry, and was prepared to cooperate with

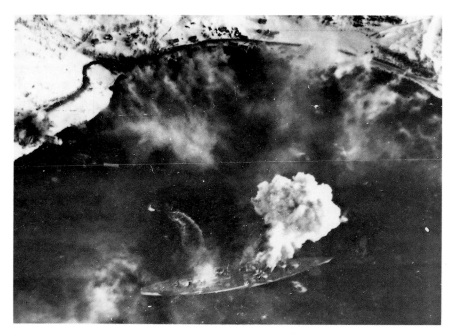

Bombs hit during the carrier attack on *Tirpitz* in Altenfiord. (*Imperial War Museum, A22633*)

the other services to the very limited extent of providing one squadron of bombers for use on special operations. This was the famous 617 Squadron, which had breached the Möhne and Eder dams in the Ruhr. The unit was serving under Air Vice-Marshal Cochrane, and it was to him that Harris gave the task of sinking *Tirpitz*.

The problem with which Cochrane was confronted was three-fold: how to get his bombers to Altenfiord (and back); how to prevent *Tirpitz* from hiding in a smokescreen; and what bombs to use in order to sink her. At this time the only battleships which had been sunk by bombs during the Second World War were the old *Arizona* at Pearl Harbor and the Italian *Roma*, sunk by a German 'Fritz X' radio-controlled armour-piercing bomb on 9 September 1943 while on her way to Malta to surrender.

The first German experiments with a radio-controlled bomb had been made in 1938, and when it entered service in August 1943 the Fritz X weighed 3000 pounds, including a 600-pound warhead. It was fitted with dive-brakes to limit its velocity, and a flare in its tail to make it more visible to the aimer. The parent aircraft had to drop the bomb from at least 13 000 feet to give the bomb-aimer time to bring the bomb under control. Once the bomb-aimer had the bomb in his sights his task was relatively simple, provided the pilot maintained his direction of flight. The bomb-aimer had to manipulate his controls, which moved spoilers on each of the bomb's four tail-fins, so as to keep the bomb in line with the target. If he managed to do this, a hit was certain. During trials it was found that 50 per cent of the bombs landed in a five-metre square.

The HS 293 was a small aircraft with a nine-and-a-half-foot wingspan, powered by a rocket motor which lifted it on to the sightline between the bomb-aimer and the target. Thereafter it glided towards its target at a speed of 330 knots, the aimer controlling it by radio signals. It could be released at ranges of up to ten miles from the target, and its accuracy was of the same order as Fritz X.

These two guided weapons were used successfully, particularly in the Mediterranean, but they had two vulnerable points—the radio control, which could be jammed, and the fact that the parent aircraft had to remain in the vicinity until the bomb hit. The Germans had foreseen the possibility of jamming and had developed a wire-guidance system, by which the control orders were passed along a fine wire connecting the bomb to the parent aircraft, thus making the controls immune to jamming. Yet although the wire-guidance system worked well, it was never used in action, for the Germans were not aware that the Allied ships were vigorously jamming the control signals. When inexplicable failures occurred, the Luftwaffe suspected faulty wiring in the parent aircraft, or blamed the unfortunate bomb-aimer.

The Fritz X had some impressive successes, apart from the sinking of the *Roma*. In the same action the battleship *Italia* was also hit by a Fritz X, but survived. The British battleship *Warspite* was later hit by two of them and narrowly missed by two more, and was left dead in the water, managing to reach Malta after a lengthy and perilous tow. A cruiser was sunk and two others severely damaged. Other ships were sunk, and in February 1944 ships at Anzio were in such peril that the Allied command ordered that the port was to be used only in an emergency. The HS 293, too, had its successes, chiefly against merchant ships and destroyers. Despite jamming and intense gunfire by the ships (aimed at the glider-bombs, for the launching aircraft were usually well outside range) 60 per cent of the bombs scored hits or near-misses on their targets. This accuracy was unapproached by any comparable weapon.

Yet the campaign by the guided-weapons was a failure. Although both types of bomb could be released beyond the range of effective gunfire, the parent aircraft were very vulnerable to fighters, particularly as accuracy could be achieved only in daylight attacks. By August 1943 the Luftwaffe was in decline, and Allied fighters made short work of the Dornier Do.217 and Heinkel He.177 carriers of the guided-weapons. On average only one aircraft of every ten which set out was able to release its weapon, and soon only moonlight attacks were possible. Finally by early 1944 the air superiority of the Allies became so great that the bombers could not operate at all. In all, only about 100 guided-weapons were successfully released.

The RAF had nothing as sophisticated as the German guided-weapons, but fortunately certain bombs had been developed during the war which held out some hope of being effective against *Tirpitz*. The best hope lay in the peculiar bombs being designed by Dr Barnes Wallis, one of those eccentric geniuses that England so often produces. Against strong official obstruction and lack of interest he had persevered with his proposals for unusual bombs, and had eventually convinced the government of the merit of his plan for an attack on the Ruhr dams with specially-designed bombs. The success of this attack had led those in authority to consider seriously his other proposal—for an 'earthquake' bomb, which would penetrate far into the ground and bring structures crashing down by its shockwave. Approval was eventually given for the manufacture of a six-ton version of this bomb, called the 'Tallboy', and in its final version it was no less than 21 feet long.

The Tallboy bombs were ready by the time Normandy was invaded in June 1944, but only in small quantities. They were used by 617 Squadron sparingly, but with spectacular success against suitable targets. They caused immense waves which swamped small craft in Le Havre and Boulogne, they inflicted severe damage on the V1 bomb sites, and penetrated more than sixteen feet of concrete when used against the submarine pens in Brest. Cochrane had no doubt that these were the bombs to sink *Tirpitz*.

The selection of a base for the Lancaster bombers was more difficult. Altenfiord was beyond the range of a Lancaster bomber based in the British Isles and carrying a Tallboy. Cochrane decided that the only solution was to shift the aircraft to Russia, which might have the subsidiary advantage of confusing the German smokemakers by attacking from an unexpected direction. Thus it was that on 10 September 1994 two squadrons of Lancasters—617 Squadron and 9 Squadron—took off from Lossiemouth in Scotland and headed for Yagoderik, twenty miles from Archangel. The flight was nearly a disaster, for the Lancasters were more than a ton overweight with fuel and their special bombs, and the weather over Russia was foul. The squadrons became dispersed during the long flight, and six of the heavy bombers were lost before the attacks had even started.

For the next three days the impatient crews had to stay on the ground, waiting for the weather to improve. On 15 September the sky cleared, and while the Lancasters were made ready a Mosquito flew over Altenfiord to see if the weather was clear there too. It was, and minutes later 28 Lancasters took off and headed west. The plan was to approach at maximum height from the south-east, descending to 12 000 feet for the bombing run. It was hoped that the unexpected direction of attack would confuse the German radar operators, perhaps making them believe that the British bombers were friendly aircraft, or at least puzzling them for a few critical minutes. This stratagem may have succeeded, for the Germans were certainly late in laying their smokescreen, and the leading bombers could see the battleship lying in the fiord before the smoke pots began to belch smoke.

It now became a race against time to aim the bombs accurately before the battleship disappeared under the smoke. The Lancasters attacked in compact groups of six or seven, but the bombers were just too late—the battleship disappearing beneath the smoke just as the first bomb-aimer dropped his bomb. The aircraft following could see nothing but swirling smoke, and although most dropped their bombs blindly into the murk, seven held back, not considering it worthwhile.

It was a dejected group which returned to their Russian airfield, for they had been so near success. The 26-year-old commander of 617 Squadron, Wing Commander Tait, contemplated mounting a second attack with the remaining Tallboys, but the heavy rain-curtain descended again and the idea was abandoned. The two squadrons returned disconsolately to England. They had, however, struck a harder blow than they knew. One Tallboy— probably from Tait's aircraft—had passed through the ship and exploded under the bow, wrecking the forepart of the ship and flooding the first 120 feet.

A rough estimate showed that repairs, if they could be made without interruption in a dockyard, would take nine months, and with German industrial cities under day and night air bombard-ment this was a hopeless prospect. The German naval staff decided that the best thing to do was to turn *Tirpitz* into a floating battery for the defence of northern Norway. A berth was selected near Tromso, and the battleship was moved there

301

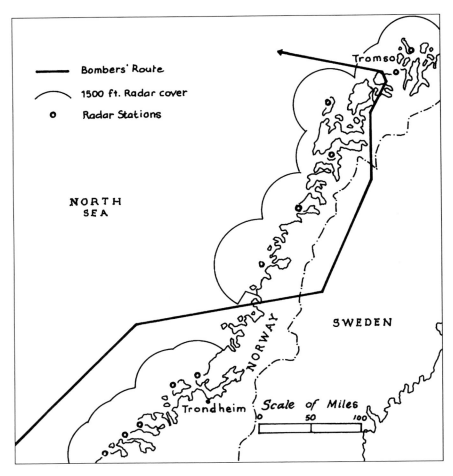

The attack on *Tirpitz*

on 15 October. A double net barrage to protect her from torpedoes was speedily erected, and the anti-aircraft guns and the smoke-making apparatus were transferred from Altenfiord as rapidly as possible. The plan had been to moor *Tirpitz* in shallow water, so that she could neither sink nor capsize, but the berth chosen had a big hollow under the centre of the ship. Dredgers were called up to fill in the hole, but meanwhile the ship was vulnerable.

Little of this was known in England. All that was known was a report from a Norwegian agent that *Tirpitz* had arrived in Tromso, and that her bow was badly damaged. Tromso was 200 miles closer than Altenfiord for bombers based in Scotland, and the Lancasters could just reach Tromso, but only if they had more powerful engines and were stripped of weight by removing the pilot's armour and the upper gun-turrets. This was done in three days of feverish activity, leaving the weather as the critical factor. The skies were clear enough for visual bombing only on two or three days a month at this time of year, and after 26 November the sun does not rise at all in Tromso. If *Tirpitz* could not be sunk before then, accurate attacks would be impossible in the long Arctic night.

The weather forecasts for 28 October were favourable, and 617 and 9 Squadrons again moved to Lossiemouth. At midnight a Mosquito on a weather-reconnaissance flight over Tromso reported that the wind was veering east, and if this wind held the skies would be clear over the target. Within an hour 32 overloaded Lancasters took off and headed for Tromso, but by the time they arrived the wind had changed and great masses of cloud were blowing in from the Arctic Ocean. The Lancasters could not attack from beneath the cloud, for their Tallboys had to be dropped from at least 10 000 feet to have a chance of penetrating *Tirpitz*'s heavy armour, so they bombed as best they could through the clouds. The only damage done was by a near-miss, which damaged the port propeller-shaft and flooded the after end of the ship.

As far as Cochrane could tell *Tirpitz* had not been damaged by this attack. His Lancasters would have to try again. But now a new complication arose, for intelligence reports indicated that the Germans had moved between twenty and thirty fighters to Bardufoss airfield, 30 miles from Tromso. The Lancasters, bombing in daylight, and without even the normal guns and armour, would be easy targets for these fighters. Yet *Tirpitz* was still a major preoccupation of the Admiralty, and still containing many valuable ships in the Home Fleet—ships which were urgently needed in the Pacific. Cochrane decided that the attack would have to be made.

Surprise was obviously essential, both to help the bombers evade the German fighters and also to prevent *Tirpitz* from disappearing under a smokescreen. RAF radar-reconnaissance aircraft plotted the location and coverage of the German radar stations placed along the Norwegian coast, and found that there was a gap in the low cover over the central part of Norway, and also that the Norwegian mountain range blocked low coverage to the eastwards. It was decided that the bombers would keep below 1500 feet and make for the gap in the radar cover in this sector; having penetrated the radar chain, they would continue east until they had the cover of the mountain range before turning northwards, even though this required them to fly over neutral Sweden, and finally they were to approach *Tirpitz* from the landward side, where they would be least expected.

On 11 November the weather forecasts were hopeful, and the two squadrons again moved to Lossiemouth. At 3 a.m. the following day they took off, hoping that the weather would be clear enough over Tromso for the aircraft to bomb visually from 12 000 feet, hoping that their radar-evasion plan would work, hoping that the German fighters would be ineffective, and hoping that *Tirpitz* would not be smoke-covered. All went well. When the British bombers arrived unchallenged over the fiord *Tirpitz* was lying clear amid her torpedo nets. It was all over within ten minutes. Struck by at least two Tallboys and near-missed by a third, the great battleship rolled over to port and lay on the bottom with her keel exposed. More than 1000 men were trapped when the ship capsized. A few (less than 100) eventually escaped through holes cut in the ship's bottom. The remainder died a futile death in a ship which was no longer a seagoing fighting unit.

The sinking of *Tirpitz* meant the end of the German battlefleet. *Bismarck* and *Scharnhorst* had already been sunk by the British. *Gneisenau*, damaged by a mine during her escape up the Channel from Brest, had been further damaged by the RAF in March 1942 when almost the entire forepart of the ship was wrecked. At first it was proposed to rebuild the ship, rearming her at the same time with 15-inch guns, but work was abandoned at the end of 1942.

The long struggle in Europe was almost over. The disappearance of the German battlefleet made the defence of Russian convoys much easier, for the ships previously required for a covering force could now be used to reinforce the close escort. Despite a recurrence of German submarine and Luftwaffe attacks on the northern convoy routes in the winter of 1944, the convoy escorts, strengthened by the addition of several escort carriers, had no difficulty in beating them off. Between August 1944 and the end of the war only two ships out of 250 were lost on the northern route.

The sinking of *Tirpitz* was not the last blow struck by Bomber Command at the German Fleet. In April 1945 both the surviving pocket battleships, *Lützow* and *Scheer*, were sunk. *Lützow* was attacked by 617 Squadron at Swinemunde in the Baltic and sent to the bottom of the shallow harbour, and *Scheer* was capsized alongside a wharf at Kiel after a heavy night raid.

The campaign against *Tirpitz* illustrated many lessons, mostly old lessons which had to be re-learnt. There was a major technical problem—how to score hits on a battleship when bombs had to be dropped from more than 10 000 feet in order to have sufficient terminal velocity to penetrate the deck armour. Such accuracy was possible when the ship was in harbour (if it was visible) but only with a weapon such as a Fritz X was it possible at sea. This brought up a new problem—with the techniques of the time such bombing had to be done in daylight and therefore required air superiority. *Tirpitz* was in a very strong position in harbour in northern Norway, fully defended against torpedo attack, invisible to bombers when under a smokescreen, and (in the final stages) with fighter support which should have been effective against the Lancasters operating in daylight far beyond the range of fighter escort. Only when two of *Tirpitz*'s defences failed simultaneously— the fighters did not intercept the Lancasters, and the smokescreen was not ready in Tromso—was she sunk.

It is curious, and an example of the lack of inter-service co-operation, that the Home Fleet was not asked whether it could provide fighter escorts for the Lancasters in their final attack. Cochrane could not have known that the German fighters would not intercept. It is true that the use of carriers might have ultimately been rejected because of the possibility of their detection and the loss of vital surprise, but at least the use of carrier fighters should have been considered.

There were two minor lessons which should be noted. Firstly, if you are using a weapon which requires surprise to be effective (rolling mines down a hillside) always make sure that it is used in sufficient strength to be effective if surprise is achieved, because you probably will not get a second chance. Secondly, if your tactical plan is to hide (*Tirpitz* under a smokescreen) do not give away your hide-out by opening fire (*Tirpitz* with her 15-inch guns).

While the Germans were far in advance of other powers in the development of radio-controlled anti-shipping weapons, the weakness of a navy without integral air power was shown once again, and was well illustrated by Raeder's desperate and very belated attempt to complete *Graf Zeppelin*.

Finally, the campaign against *Tirpitz* illustrated once again the value of 'a fleet in being', although in the later stages of *Tirpitz*'s life it was a ship rather than a fleet that was 'in being'. The effect on British naval dispositions caused by the presence of the German battleships was dramatic, although if such a force is to be effective in this role it must, as Raeder realised, be willing and able to make occasional sorties. The Germans did this effectively, and *Tirpitz* was able to continue the decoy role in Tromso even when she was too badly damaged to go to sea operationally.

When the war ended the only German ships bigger than destroyers still in commission were the cruisers *Prinz Eugen* and *Nürnberg*, which had been protecting the Baltic flank of the German army during the long retreat from Russia. In 1918 the powerful and almost undamaged High Seas Fleet had steamed across the North Sea to Scapa Flow and into the custody of the Grand Fleet. In 1945 there was almost no German surface fleet to surrender.

19

Okinawa:

1 April–21 June 1945

Vice-Admiral Ohnishi was not the only Japanese officer who had considered the possibility of mass suicide attacks. Early in 1944 Sub-Lieutenant Ohta, a pilot engaged in flying transport aircraft to Rabaul, had produced a design for a piloted rocket-powered bomb. He realised that the US carriers were the key to their victories, and argued that since conventional attacks on them were clearly ineffective, volunteer airmen should crash his piloted-bombs into the American ships. His idea received ready acceptance from his superiors.

Thus it was that in August 1944 the Japanese Naval Air Research Centre received urgent orders to develop Ohta's piloted bomb, which was given the code name of Oka ('cherry blossom'); these bombs were later to be known by the Americans as Bakas (which is Japanese for 'fool'). The design produced by the Centre was for a small wooden powered-glider with a 2645-pound warhead—powerful enough to cripple the largest ship—and was driven by three rockets, giving it a range of about fifteen miles. The Okas had, of course, to be carried to their launching position by larger aircraft, and the Betty bomber was usually chosen. The Oka pilot would remain in the parent aircraft until the target area was reached, when he climbed through the bomb bay into the cockpit of his glider-bomb. When ready he would release the Oka from the parent aircraft, and from that point there was no chance of return, no hope of survival.[1]

In September 1944 Captain Okamura was ordered to form a corps of suicide pilots to fly these glider-bombs. The reason Okamura was chosen was that for several months he had been campaigning for such a corps of volunteers, telling Vice-Admiral

BOMBERS VERSUS BATTLESHIPS

Fukudome that with such a group and 300 aircraft he could turn the tide of war. Now he had his chance. His corps became known as the Jinrai Butai—the Divine Thunderclaps. The first volunteers were all experienced pilots, and were trained on an unpowered glider version of the bomb, the MXY7. While the pilots were still training and awaiting the operational version of the glider-bomb, news was received of the first Kamikaze attacks in the Philippines, which caused bitter disappointment among the Jinrai Butai that they had not been first.

In November the program received a setback, when 50 Okas were lost aboard the 68 000-ton carrier *Shinano*. This carrier, converted from the hull of the third *Yamato* class battleship, was sunk by six torpedoes fired by a US submarine. She was on her maiden voyage, with an untrained crew and cluttered with dockyard workmen, and the desperate but ill-directed efforts of her crew could not save her.

By March 1945 the Jinrai Butai was at last ready. Mitscher's fast carriers were battering the Japanese homeland, sinking ships, attacking airfields and bombing factories, and these carriers were clearly a suitable target for the Jinrai Butai. On 21 March sixteen Betty bombers, each carrying an Oka, took off for an attack but the defences of the US carriers were too formidable. Despite an escort of 30 Zekes all the bombers were shot down, as well as fifteen of the fighters.

Meanwhile the Kamikaze attacks continued. Ohnishi had intended a short campaign by a small number of volunteers, but as the disastrous events of the Leyte Gulf battle unfolded he came to the conclusion that the only hope of stemming the American advance lay in the mass use of Kamikazes. When Fukodome's Second Air Fleet arrived in the Philippines from Formosa on 23 October, they were invited to join in the suicide missions. Fukudome refused, still confident that he could achieve results by conventional means. Over the next two days he sent 250 aircraft against the American ships, but despite the lucky sinking of the carrier *Princeton* they achieved nothing commensurate with their losses, and meanwhile Ohnishi's Kamikazes were having considerable success.

On 26 October Fukudome capitulated and agreed to organise suicide attacks by volunteers, and soon army pilots—not to be outdone—joined in. A special seven-day course was given to Kamikaze volunteers, many of whom were barely trained to fly. Kamikazes were at first instructed to release their bomb-safety switches as soon as they were over the sea, but this meant that a pilot had to jettison his bomb if he failed to find a target, and this was considered to be wasteful. The instructions were therefore altered so that the switches were not to be released until just before the final dive. Inevitably some pilots forgot their switches in the heat of the attack and facing imminent death, with the result that their bombs did not explode and only slight damage was done to their targets.

The suicide aircraft nevertheless achieved a great deal during the three months of the campaign in the Philippines, despite the loss of 480 naval aircraft and 50 army aircraft, with of course their pilots. They sank 60 ships and scored hits on nine fast carriers and thirteen escort carriers, but even this does not tell the full tale for some ships were hit as many as six times. More than one in four of the Kamikaze pilots reached their targets despite the best efforts of the defending fighters and the ships' gunfire.

Yet all the efforts of the Kamikazes could not halt the inexorable advance of American amphibious power. Mindoro in the central Philippines was invaded in December, and Luzon (the main island) in January 1945. Iwo Jima, midway between Saipan and Japan, was seized in the following month, to be used as a fighter base and an emergency landing-ground for B–29 Superfortress bombers. All was now ready for the next step, the capture of Okinawa. With this island in American hands the vital Japanese communications to the south would be finally severed, and as Okinawa is only 360 miles from the southern Japanese island of Kyushu it could be made into an excellent bomber base from which to attack Japan's industrial centres.

The importance of Okinawa made it certain that Japan would defend it desperately, and its proximity to Kyushu meant that the invasion force would inevitably be subjected to intense attacks from the numerous airfields in southern Japan.

Admiral Spruance, who had directed the attack on Iwo Jima, was again in command, with Mitscher leading Task Force 58, now consisting of sixteen fast carriers with more than 1200 aircraft. The carrier complements had recently been altered to provide an increased proportion of fighters, for these were the aircraft chiefly required for defence against Kamikazes, attacks on Japanese airfields and support of troops ashore. The standard number of dive-bombers in each large carrier was reduced from 24 to fifteen, torpedo-bombers from eighteen to fifteen, and the number of fighters raised from 54 to 73.

There were also substantial changes in fighter-direction procedures to meet the mass Kamikaze threat, which posed entirely new problems, for instead of approaching in formations which could be intercepted by formations of defending fighters, the Kamikazes came in at all altitudes and from all directions. The combat air patrols over each Task Group were increased to 20–24 fighters, and there was also two pairs of fighters with each Task Group (nicknamed 'Jack Patrols') who were visually directed by fighter-direction officers against Kamikazes who had penetrated the normal fighter defence.

Pairs of 'Tomcat' destroyers were stationed as pickets 40–50 miles from the carriers, in the most likely direction of attack, both to provide early warning and to watch for Kamikaze 'tag-alongs' with returning American strikes, which were usually routed over the 'Tomcat' destroyers. These pickets were given standing fighter patrols of four aircraft, and were later moved out as far as 80–100 miles from the carriers, to compensate for the lack of long-range low-level cover of the ship-fitted radars.[2] A better solution to this problem was being quickly developed by the fitting of downward-looking 10cm radar sets in TBM Avengers, with the resultant picture being transmitted to the parent ship's PPIs; flying at 5000 feet they could detect bombers flying at 500 feet at ranges of 60 miles, and ships at 200 miles, but despite the rapid development these aircraft were not available in time for the Okinawa campaign.

Another weakness in the American defence was the lack of radar coverage of aircraft which were directly overhead. If a Kamikaze survived until directly above his target, that ship's radars could not see him, so the distance between the carrier task groups was adjusted so that one task group's radars covered another's blind spots, the restrictions on independent manoeuvring being accepted. Some urgent work was going on to produce a new aerial for the 10cm SG surface-warning radar set, so that the set would scan vertically upwards, but the war ended before the sets saw service. The Kamikazes gradually found and exploited the weak points in the American defences, and tended to attack about dusk, though the large American carriers each had four to six radar-equipped night-fighters, and they were supported by shore-based fighters controlled from ground stations in the Ryukus.

The increasing use of radar by the Japanese caused the Americans to employ countermeasures much more extensively. By early 1945 it was standard practice for striking carrier-aircraft to carry intercept sets to determine the extent of Japanese radar coverage and to use 'window' when attacking heavily-defended targets; and jammers were available if required. For example, each squadron of carrier-based Avengers had sufficient equipments to give five aircraft two jammers each. In the event of a fleet engagement (which did not eventuate), it was policy that aircraft should keep the surface forces continuously covered with 'window'.

Finally, jammers were widely fitted in surface ships, including small craft and landing craft. Japanese radar technology, which was at about the level the Germans had been in 1941, was overwhelmed.

One of the few limitations of the American 5-inch gunfire had been the inability of the radars mounted in the directors (the Mark 4 and its successor, the Mark 12) to track aircraft which were below ten degrees elevation; they could range on them, but interference with the sea surface made it impossible to track them in elevation, making blind fire ineffective. The answer was a separate 30cm set (the Mark 22) with a narrow beam which could scan in elevation any target more than one degree above the horizon. With this set used in conjunction with the Mark 4 or Mark 12, all mounted on a stable platform, US ships could provide highly effective 5-inch fire against the dusk Kamikaze attacks, though the arrangements for the initial acquisition of blind targets remained crude.

There was also pressure to increase the weight of close-range gunfire. The 20mm Oerlikons fell into disfavour as having too light a shell to stop a Kamikaze, and wherever possible they were replaced by 40mm Bofors.[3] The twin and quadruple Bofors guns remained very effective weapons, particularly as a new radar-fitted tachometric director (the Mark 52) began to be fitted in the second half of 1944, and before the war ended 500 had been installed. The radar ranging increased the accuracy of the tachometric system, and it had a blind-fire capability as well. To launch a successful air attack on the US ships was clearly going to be a formidable task.

Spruance organised his fleet into six principal task forces. Task Forces 53 and 55 were the northern and southern amphibious assault forces. Task Force 52 (Rear-Admiral Blandy) was the Amphibious Support Force, and had 240 ships ranging from escort carriers (of which there were fourteen) to net-layers and gunboats. Task Force 54 (Rear-Admiral Deyo) comprised ten old battleships and 45 other ships, and was instructed to prevent Japanese surface interference with the landings, and also to provide bombardment ships to Task Force 52. Mitscher's Task Force 58 usually operated to the east of Okinawa, to cover the landing against air and surface interference, and to strike against the airfields in Japan and Formosa.

In this operation Mitscher had the support of the fast carriers of the Royal Navy for the first time. Task Force 57, under the command of Vice-Admiral Sir Bernard Rawlings, consisted of two modern battleships, the fleet carriers *Indomitable*, *Victorious*, *Illustrious* and *Indefatigable*, a cruiser squadron and a destroyer screen.

311

The British carriers had been largely re-equipped with American aircraft—Hellcats, Corsairs and Avengers—though *Indefatigable* did operate predominantly British aircraft, with a complement of 40 Seafires and nine Fireflies (a new twin-seat fighter, replacing the Fulmar) as well as twenty Avengers. Through the use of a permanent deck park they had increased the number of aircraft each carrier could operate—up to 69 in the case of *Indefatigable*—but their numbers were still well below those carried in American ships of comparable size. On the other hand, their armoured flight decks, which had so restricted them in the past, were about to come into their own.

The Seafires, though beautiful aircraft, were not sturdy enough for carrier operations.[4] Worse still, the Seafires had very short endurance, and could not remain on patrol for much more than an hour, meaning that the carriers had to be constantly turning into the wind to recover and replace them. Increasing their endurance by fitting them with long-range tanks was not popular, because the tanks were not easily jettisoned before combat and they made deck landings even more difficult. The problem was eventually solved by 'scrounging' from the Americans (that is, obtaining without going through the usual supply procedures) some long-range tanks designed for Kittyhawk aircraft. Fitted with these, the Seafires became much more useful, being employed in the fighter-bomber role in the final attacks on Japan. The deck-landing problems were never solved, more than three times as many Seafires being lost in landing accidents as in combat. Nevertheless the Commander-in-Chief, Sir Bruce Fraser, could report that 'in July the Seafires were flying twice as many sorties and about three times as many hours per aircraft per day as in March and April'.[5]

The Americans had insisted that the British Pacific Fleet should be logistically self-supporting, and this posed enormous problems for the Admiralty.[6] The problem of supporting a fleet in the Pacific had actually been looked at by an Admiralty committee between 1936 and 1938, but the committee had been instructed to assume that the Singapore base would be available, and oilers (and methods of replenishing at sea) most regrettably were excluded from its brief.

Although the Admiralty accepted the committee's recommendations, little was done to provide the necessary ships, and in 1944, when planning for the support of the new Pacific Fleet began, there was a long way to go. Replenishment at sea was still primitive in the Royal Navy. At this time all the British battleships and aircraft carriers were refuelled by the cumbersome 'astern' method, and in fact it was not until June 1945 that *King George V* became the first British battleship refuelled by the much more efficient abeam method. Rear-Admiral Vian, commanding the carriers in the British Pacific Fleet, described the British method of fuelling big ships at sea as 'an awkward, unseamanlike business' and complained that 'for some reason we had failed to benefit from American experience'.[7] His Commander-in-Chief, Admiral Fraser, agreed with his criticisms, saying that 'the fuelling of the Fleet proceeded with constant interruptions and delays caused by hoses parting etc. Aircraft carriers experienced great difficulty in obtaining Avgas for this reason.'[8]

There were other problems, too. The endurance of the British destroyers was little more than half that of their American equivalents, and obviously made more frequent replenishments necessary. These refuellings were usually done at slow speed because of the poor performance of most of the tankers, and the destroyers were difficult to steer at such speeds. Few of the tankers had sufficiently powerful pumps to deliver fuel at an adequate rate, so fuelling usually took an inordinate time.

In the broader area of logistic support, the main base was at Sydney (4000 miles from Okinawa) and the initial advanced base was at Manus, north of New Guinea, but 2000 miles from the scene of action. The advanced base was later moved to Leyte Gulf, but that was still 1000 miles from Okinawa. In order to establish a fleet train, the Admiralty had to prise ships out of the Ministry of War Transport, no easy task with the war in Europe and the battle of the Atlantic still continuing.

Despite all the difficulties, by early 1945 a motley collection of ships was assembled, a force which (with escorts) was by the end of the war in the Pacific to total 125 ships, of 712 000 tons, and manned by 26 200 men. There were warships, civilian-manned Royal Fleet Auxiliaries and chartered merchantmen, ships from Britain, Australia, New Zealand, Panama, Denmark, Holland, Norway and Belgium. Their role was to support the operations of the British Pacific Fleet, and this ultimately meant the striking power of that fleet, the 200 aircraft in the carrier force. They had to provide not only fuel (including aviation fuel), but replacement aircraft, ammunition, food and other stores, as well as repair and servicing facilities.

The fleet train did have serious deficiencies—the fighting ships were much handicapped, according to Fraser, 'by its few, small, slow tankers'. (He might have added that they had very slow pumping rates as well.) But for the first time for nearly a century a British fleet could be maintained at sea for prolonged periods; during the Okinawa campaign Task Force 57 operated off the enemy's coast for 32 days.[9] Although the American task groups, with their much greater experience of replenishing at sea and better equipment could operate for twice the time, it was still a remarkable effort by an improvised fleet train.

The anti-aircraft gun defence of the British ships had also improved. The 40mm Bofors guns were widely fitted (including numerous local conversions of twin 20mm mountings into single 40mm ones), and VT fuses were available for the medium-calibre anti-aircraft guns, although the crudity of the predictors controlling these guns was unaltered. The changes in the close-range armament of the carrier *Victorious* give a good example of the progressive steps taken by the Royal Navy. On commissioning in 1941 *Victorious* had six 8-barrelled pom-poms, each with its own director, but without a tachometric sight or remote power control of the mountings. Soon after commissioning five of the six directors were fitted with a Type 282 radar set for ranging, but the defects of the current director system were so obvious that in March 1943 the six directors were removed; by March 1944 the pom-poms had been modified so that they followed a director automatically and four directors with tachometric sights were reinstalled.

With regard to 20mm Oerlikons, the increase was dramatic. The first fitting of these guns occurred during 1942, when three were fitted around the island structure. In January 1943 when the ship was being refitted in America twenty additional single 20mm Oerlikons were fitted, and in March six more were fitted in place of the pom-pom directors, and ten more were placed on a sponson outboard of the island structure. In March 1944 fourteen twin-Oerlikon mountings replaced the same number of single mountings, and in early 1945, when it became obvious that Oerlikons did not have the stopping power to deal with Kamikazes, six 40mm Bofors guns were fitted in place of twin-Oerlikons. *Victorious* already had a number of American-built 40mm Bofors guns, which had been acquired in Pearl Harbor in March 1943, when two quadruple and two twin mountings had been fitted, each automatically following its own tachometric director.

Fighter direction was well-developed, with each carrier having two long-range air-warning sets (a Type 79 and a Type 281), each using only a single aerial. The battleships and cruisers were fitted with either Type 281 or Type 79 approximately in the ratio 2:1. PPIs were readily available for the Type 281s (the Type 79 had too wide a horizontal beam-width to be displayed on a PPI) and there were also Skiatrons, a plotting version of the PPI, useful for intercepts. Specialist fighter-direction officers were now available, but the greatest weakness was the lack of an efficient radar set for detecting low-flying aircraft and for height-finding. The 10cm Type 277 had proved a disappointment in this role, with reliable detection of low-flying aircraft at only 25–30 miles and no useful height-finding capability. One of the carriers, *Indomitable*, was fitted with an American SM–1 set, which could detect aircraft above the radar horizon out to 50 miles and had good height-finding capability, but could not do both jobs at the same time; the other ships could not help.

Rawlings' Task Force 57 was given the task of neutralising the Japanese airfields in the Sakishimas, but there was insufficient strength for it to be possible for him to divide the task force into two carrier task groups so that the attacks could be continuous, one group striking while the other was replenishing. And replenishment had to be frequent, because the earlier armoured-hangar carriers—*Illustrious*, *Formidable* and *Victorious*—contained only enough aviation fuel for two or three strike days. When Rawlings had to withdraw his task force for rest and replenishment, the neutralising role was taken on, in addition to their other duties, by Blandy's hard-worked escort carriers.

Such was the organisation of Spruance's powerful fleet, which comprised 525 fighting ships, including 34 aircraft carriers and twenty battleships.

SUICIDE ATTACKS

On 1 April 1945 the Tenth US Army landed over the beaches on the south-west shore of Okinawa. Nine days before the landing the carriers of Task Force 58 began attacking the island, and a day later the surface ships had joined in with practically every type of gun. The early landings were weakly opposed and the northern half of the island was quickly overrun, but any jubilation was premature. The Japanese were firmly entrenched in the southern bastion, and a bitter and prolonged campaign of extermination was necessary before the island could be captured. It was not until 21 June, after 82 days of fighting, that organised Japanese resistance ended.

So for more than two long months the Fifth Fleet had to remain near Okinawa, to give protection, aid and succour to the embattled troops ashore, while itself under constant attack by Kamikaze pilots, Oka glider-bombs and conventional bombers. The Japanese High Command hoped that the mass suicide attacks would isolate the American assault troops on Okinawa, and enable their Thirty-Second Army to drive them back into the sea. For the first time the suicide pilots of the navy and army worked together, in a series of attacks called Kikusui operations. Ten of these were carried out between 6 April and 22 June, and in between there were sporadic attacks by individuals or small groups.

Practically any aircraft which could fly was pressed into the attack, but for the first time there began to be a shortage of Kamikaze volunteers. According to Commander Nakajima:

> Many of the new arrivals seemed at first not only to lack enthusiasm, but, indeed, to be disturbed by their situation. With some this condition lasted only a few hours, with others for several days. It was a period of melancholy that passed with time and eventually gave way to a spiritual awakening. Then, like an attainment of wisdom, care vanished and tranquillity of spirit appeared as life came to terms with death, mortality with immortality.[10]

Apparently not all the pilots became reconciled to their lot, another Japanese officer commenting that:

> difficulties became especially apparent when men in aviation training were peremptorily ordered to the front and to death. When it came

A comrade tightens the 'Hachimaki' for a Kamikaze pilot. The Hachimaki was a Samurai symbol of courage and pre-battle composure that was worn by all Kamikaze pilots. (*US Naval Historical Center, NH73096*)

time for their take-off, the pilots' attitudes ranged from the despair of sheep headed for slaughter to open expressions of contempt for their superior officers. There were frequent and obvious cases of pilots returning from sorties claiming they could not locate any enemy ships, and one pilot even strafed his commanding officer's quarters as he took off.[11]

For the first few days after the landing, the Kamikaze attacks were much less violent than the Americans had expected, although five ships were damaged, including the battleship *West Virginia*. The first massive attacks came on 6 and 7 April when about 355 Kamikazes and the same number of conventional aircraft were launched against the shipping off Okinawa. There was a furious air battle in which more than 300 Japanese aircraft were destroyed, most of them by Mitscher's carriers. Suicide crashes sank two destroyers, two ammunition ships and two other ships; 22 other ships, many of them destroyers, were damaged. The Japanese used 'window' to try to deceive the American fighter directors, but they were not very successful.[12]

On the same day a new menace appeared, a sortie by the battleship *Yamato*, for it was not only Japanese aircraft which were intended to make suicide attacks. The Commander-in-Chief, Admiral Toyoda, intended to use his surviving surface ships to distract the attention of the US carriers so that the Kikusui aircraft would have easier targets, but if they could do some damage to the American ships off Okinawa, so much the better. Because of the shortage of oil Toyoda could muster only a small force, so he decided to use the 64 000 ton *Yamato*, accompanied by a cruiser and eight destroyers, the sortie being timed to take place at the same time as the first Kikusui attack on 6–7 April. There was no hope of survival for *Yamato*, and little chance of success.

On the afternoon of 6 April the force sailed from the Inland Sea of Japan, under the command of Vice-Admiral Ito. At 8.10 p.m. the ships were detected by a US submarine as they emerged from the Inland Sea at 22 knots. The submarine was soon joined by a second and contact was held until nearly midnight, by which time they had identified Ito's force as two large ships and at least six destroyers. Mitscher's three carrier groups (the fourth was 500 miles to the south on its way back from Ulithi) were in their usual operating position east of Okinawa. Spruance was reluctant to send them northwards prematurely, for the Japanese might merely be transferring their ships to Sasebo, and he did not want to deprive the hardpressed Okinawa forces of much of their air support until the situation was clearer.

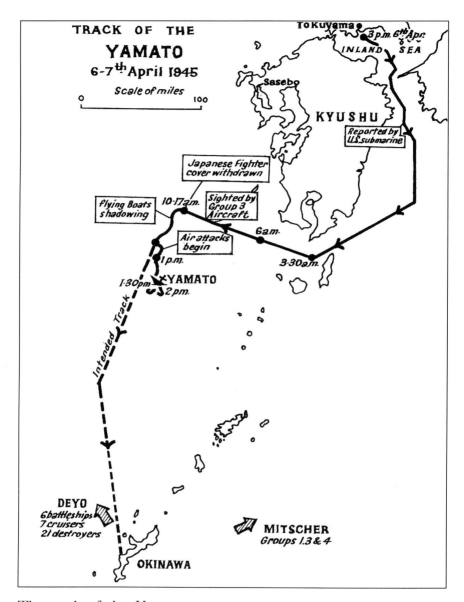

The track of the *Yamato*

As at Saipan, Spruance intended that the enemy should come to him. He realised that the Japanese ships could reach the Okinawa beaches by midnight on 7 April, and had to take precautions in case Mitscher's air attacks failed to stop them during the daylight hours of 7 April—a failure which was not inconceivable in the prevailing squally weather. He therefore ordered Rear-Admiral Deyo to hold Task Force 54 ready to deal with the Japanese ships if they approached Okinawa, and at 3.30 p.m. Deyo accordingly took his six battleships, accompanied by numerous cruisers and destroyers, to a position north-west of Okinawa.

By that time Task Force 58's dawn searches had found *Yamato*, heading westwards off the southern end of Kyushu, and Spruance ordered Mitscher to attack that afternoon. Rear-Admiral Sherman, commanding Task Group 58.3, had launched sixteen fighters at 9 a.m. to track Ito's ships, and an hour later his group and task Group 58.1 (Rear-Admiral Clark) began launching a strike of 250 fighters, fighter-bombers, torpedo-bombers and dive-bombers, and this was followed 45 minutes later by 130 aircraft from Rear-Admiral Radford's Task Group 58.4. Mariner flying boats from Okinawa also joined in the search.

Yamato had no real chance, although the low cloud at 3000 feet gave her some faint hope of avoiding detection. There was a gap of nearly two hours between the time that the dawn searchers had to return to their carriers and the arrival of the first Mariner at 10.30 a.m. During this interval Ito altered course abruptly to the southwards, but he could not evade the searchers. Sherman's fighter team arrived at 11.15 a.m., and the massive first strike was already on its way. Ito had no fighter defence, for he had no carriers and his shore-based fighter cover had to be withdrawn at 10 a.m. when he passed beyond its range. Without fighters no ship could withstand attacks of the weight Mitscher now flung against Ito.

Ito had his ships formed in a circle around *Yamato* with a radius of 1200 yards. *Yamato*'s radar detected the first wave of attackers at a range of 60 miles, and when they had closed to twenty miles he ceased zig-zagging and increased speed to 24 knots. Two minutes later, at 12.34 p.m., he opened fire, and soon his ships were firing with practically every gun they had, from 18-inch to 25 mm. Considering its great strength, the first strike achieved comparatively little. *Yamato* was hit by a torpedo and two bombs, but was not seriously damaged. The cruiser *Yahagi* had been hit and stopped, and two of the eight destroyers sank and two more were seriously damaged. The conditions were admittedly difficult, for the Helldiver dive-bombers had been trained to dive from 10 000 feet and found the 3000-foot cloud ceiling very frustrating. The strength of the American attack added to the confusion, for the Target Coordinator simply lost control, at least partly because Ito was vigorously jamming the US voice communications. It looked as if Deyo's battleships might be needed after all. As it turned out they were not, for the smaller second strike was much more effective.

At 1.33 p.m. Radford's 130-strong attack arrived over Ito's force, which by now was battered and scattered, with only two or three destroyers remaining with *Yamato*. She was hit five times in rapid succession by torpedoes, her speed fell to twenty knots, and she was listing so heavily that it was almost impossible to fire her guns. Soon after 2 p.m. six torpedo-bombers from *Yorktown* delivered the *coup de grâce*. Hit by four more torpedoes the great battleship struggled on for a few more minutes and then rolled over and sank in 150 fathoms, carrying with her Vice-Admiral Ito, her captain and 2496 officers and enlisted men. Four Japanese destroyers, one of them seriously damaged, managed to struggle into Sasebo. The Americans lost a mere four dive-bombers, three torpedo-bombers and three fighters.

This was the last sortie by the Japanese battle fleet. Mitscher returned to his task of protecting and supporting the army on Okinawa. Spruance recalled Deyo's battleships, and they reluctantly turned to the more mundane tasks of bombarding the Japanese ashore and defending themselves against suicide attacks.

The air threat was not so easily disposed of. The pattern of the air battle was soon established, with sporadic attacks—some by Kamikazes, others by conventional bombing—being carried out every day, while every few days there were Kikusui mass-suicide attacks, usually by more than 100 aircraft. The Japanese used radar-equipped aircraft as pathfinders for the Kamikazes and other aircraft tried to help them by dropping 'window' to confuse the American radars. The Kamikazes themselves tried to use the sun and clouds to conceal their approach and sometimes managed to infiltrate behind a returning American strike. Not even constant vigilance could prevent occasional successes by the Kamikazes.

The US Army Air Force was very slow to establish fighter aircraft and radar-warning stations on Okinawa. The first captured airfield was useable on 6 April, and 100 Marine Corsairs were flown in on that day, but it was several weeks before they were ready for large-scale operations. Only on 13 May did the first Army Thunderbolt fighters begin to arrive, to be followed by other groups as repairs to the captured airfields were completed, but it was not until 10 June—more than two months after the landing—that Mitscher's carriers could be spared. They badly needed to rest and replenish so that they would be ready for the next operation, the assault on Japan.

Meanwhile the Japanese air attacks had taken a heavy toll. The Kamikaze attacks were by far the most damaging, for the conventional attacks were ineffective and the Okas were a failure. After the fiasco of the attack on 21 March their next use, on 12 April, was a modest success. The destroyer *Abele* had shot down two Kamikazes and been crashed into by a third when it was hit by an Oka. The destroyer broke in two and sank immediately. But after this success the Okas had a dismal record, and they failed for exactly the same reason as had the German HS293s: their range was too short. This forced their parent aircraft to come within range of the formidable American fighter defences, which made short work of them. During the whole Okinawa campaign only 74 Oka-carrying aircraft were sent out, and *Abele* was the only ship sunk, although four others were damaged.

The Kamikazes were a different proposition. The most difficult Kamikaze to counter was the low-level attacker, who flew under the long-range radar coverage and was detected too late for

A Kamikaze diving on the US cruiser *Columbia*. (*US Naval Historical Center, NH79449*)

interception by fighters patrolling above the carrier group. Although the gunfire of the US ships was impressive in volume and accuracy, it could not be relied on to destroy all such attackers, particularly as a Kamikaze, heavily hit and blazing furiously, still frequently crashed into its selected victim. The picket destroyers were stationed on a circle round Okinawa, about 70 miles from the island, and similar picket lines were maintained round the carriers. Originally these pickets had been intended merely to give warning of approaching Japanese aircraft, but as the operation progressed they took on more and more fighter direction, which necessitated a change in their radar outfit. The speed with which these modifications were made was remarkable.

The Japanese concentrated much of their effort on these pickets, and although between eight and sixteen fighters were usually maintained by day over the picket line they could not prevent some of the fiercest air attacks of the entire war being launched against the isolated pickets.

The Japanese campaign against the outlying pickets was very ill-conceived. If they could have destroyed the pickets covering a particular sector, and launched an attack against the carriers before the gap was plugged, the campaign might have had some merit. But they never attempted such a plan—the attacks seemed almost random, against a carrier if one could be found, but failing that any convenient warship would do. The pickets were all too often the convenient targets, and suffered accordingly. Of the nineteen ships originally provided as pickets, one was sunk by a mine and four by Kamikazes, who also damaged eleven of the remaining fourteen. Of the fourteen replacement ships one was sunk, five were seriously damaged and two slightly damaged, all by Kamikazes.

Yet the Japanese made a serious mistake in concentrating on the pickets, for with the war in Europe nearly over, the Americans had no difficulty in providing replacements for any destroyers sunk or damaged. The only Japanese chance, albeit a forlorn one, was to damage sufficient of the US fast carriers to delay the advance on Japan. The US carriers were proving very vulnerable to the Kamikazes, the sporadic and surprise nature of the attacks often catching them with large groups of fully-fuelled and armed aircraft on the flight deck. Their lack of an armoured flight deck meant that many of the Kamikazes, despite their comparatively low terminal-velocity, penetrated the flight deck and exploded in the hangar, causing hideous damage.

The British carriers, with three-inch armour on their flight decks, were almost immune to this type of damage, and their

The flight deck of a British carrier after a Kamikaze attack. The Kamikaze did not penetrate the flight-deck armour. (*Imperial War Museum, A29312*)

design at last paid dividends. It had not been successful in preventing them from being put out of action by conventional bombing, and severely limited the number of aircraft which could be carried and the speed with which they could be operated, but now there was a pay-off. During the Okinawa campaign eight of the fast carriers—four British and four American—were hit by Kamikazes.[13] All four of the American carriers had to be withdrawn for repairs—one of them having suffered 650 casualties, including 400 dead or missing—but the four British carriers were only slightly damaged, though there were heavy losses of aircraft on the flight deck or in the hangar, such losses being one of the most serious operational results of the Kamikaze attacks.

The success rate of the Kamikazes against their prime target, the fast aircraft carriers, is interesting in another respect. The Americans were operating four times as many fast carriers as the British, and the weight of Kamikaze attack against them was many times greater again: ten Kikusui (massed suicide attacks) being flung against them whereas there were no such attacks on the British carriers. Yet the same number of carriers of each navy was damaged, which is a fair indication of the relative effectiveness of the fighter and gunfire defences of the two carrier task forces.

THE LOSSES

The Japanese aircraft losses in the campaign were staggering. Their air attacks cost them 6810 aircraft—1900 in suicide attacks, 2255 in combat and 2655 in operational accidents, and more than 1000 were destroyed on the ground.[14] The Allied losses in aircraft were 825, of which 565 were lost by the US carriers and 160 by the British. The exchange rate was better than eight to one, but nevertheless the logistic problems of maintaining the carrier aircraft and crews were enormous. During the Okinawa campaign, of a total aircraft complement in the British carriers of 218, no less than 203 replacements were required—32 aircraft destroyed by Kamikazes, 30 in a hangar fire, 33 in combat, 61 (mostly Seafires) in deck-landing accidents, and 47 from other causes.

The Fifth Fleet suffered some other severe losses, with 36 ships sunk and a further 371 damaged. Twenty-seven of the ships were sunk by Kamikaze or Oka attacks, and such suicide attacks accounted for nearly half of the damaged ships. One suicide pilot in ten struck his target, but the Fifth Fleet gradually gained the upper hand as experience was gained and the quality of the Kamikaze pilots fell off. The Japanese pilots were too inexperienced to make much use of attacks on moonlit nights, when the fighter and gun defences were seriously hampered, or to attack in the early dawn when the carriers were flying off masses of aircraft and Kamikazes might infiltrate without being identified. The few attacks made at dawn or by moonlight were generally successful, but as the veteran pilots were killed the partially-trained newcomers had to limit themselves to simple daylight attacks.

The Fifth Fleet was not content with a purely defensive role, and with the assistance of the B–29 Superfortresses of XXI Bomber Command it launched attacks on the Japanese airfields, particularly those in Kyushu. Spruance was aware that the numerous airfields there were not rewarding targets for his aircraft, but felt that the attacks had to be made so as to reduce the number of Kamikazes. Mitscher disagreed, preferring to deal with the Japanese over Okinawa rather than tackling them in their heavily-defended bases. In retrospect it is clear that Mitscher was right, for there is no evidence that the attacks on the Kyushu airfields had any significant effect on the Kamikazes. The Japanese could ferry in new aircraft at will, but the limiting factors on their use were pilots and aviation fuel, and the attacks on the Kyushu airfields caused very little attrition to either.

Yet this must not be allowed to conceal what the Fifth Fleet achieved. For nearly three months they lay off Okinawa, within easy range of the numerous airfields in southern Japan. They landed the army and kept it supplied, they provided it with air and gunfire support, they fended off the forlorn attack by the Japanese surface fleet, and they destroyed eight Japanese aircraft for every one they lost themselves. In attaining all this, not a single major warship was lost. When Spruance was relieved by Halsey on 27 May and Mitscher by McCain the following day, much of the Japanese shore-based air power lay in ruins before them, and they had written a new chapter in the history of carrier warfare.

For the Royal Navy, too, the campaign represented a dramatic advance. By the end of the campaign Admiral Spruance was able to report that the British Pacific Fleet had gained sufficient experience to be able to undertake operations with the US Fast Carrier force, which was certainly not the case at the beginning of the campaign.

The fall of Okinawa was a clear sign that Japan had lost the war. The shipping position was disastrous; in 1943 17 per cent of supplies sent overseas for the army had been sunk, the figure rising to 30 per cent in 1944, and after March 1945 all overseas shipments were stopped. In the following month, after the US landing on Okinawa, attempts to fight convoys carrying crucial supplies (principally oil) to Japan through the South China sea were finally abandoned. Japan was thus cut off from the vital supply areas which in 1941 she had risked everything to secure. The B–29 Superfortresses, assisted by the aircraft from the fast carriers, were tearing the industrial heart out of Japan, and the Kamikazes, the last desperate hope, had proved unable to stay the advance of American sea power.

Japan's plight was hopeless, but it was not until two nuclear bombs were dropped early in August that she received the final impetus to surrender. On 15 August the Emperor ordered all Japanese forces to lay down their arms and surrender, and the world, or at least the major part of it, was at peace.

20

Post-war developments:

1945 onwards

At the end of the Second World War in 1945 the victory of aircraft carriers over battleships seemed complete. No further battleships were laid down, although the 42 500-ton British battleship *Vanguard* was completed; she was never to see any operational service but was relegated to a training status after only three years in commission, and was scrapped in 1960. On the other hand aircraft carriers spread widely, and by the 1950s were present in ten navies.

Naval requirements were dominated by the Cold War and the existence of nuclear weapons. Technology moved fast. The first deck landing by a jet aircraft was made in November 1945 by an American XFR–1 Fireball, an experimental aircraft with both a piston engine and a jet engine; it managed to make a deck landing after its piston engine failed. A month later a Vampire jet-fighter landed without difficulty on HMS *Ocean*. Operational jet fighters began to be carried by US carriers in 1948 and in the Royal Navy in 1951, and a few years later such fighters were standard in virtually all carriers. Some strike aircraft were also jet powered, the twin-engined Savage bomber of the US Navy being the first carrier aircraft able to deliver an atomic bomb.

A radical change in carrier design was necessary to cope with the new jet aircraft, which were increasingly heavy and had higher landing-speeds. The old system of crash barriers protecting a deck park at the forward end of the flight deck became unworkable. The answer was simple, even obvious—after it had been thought of. Aim the landing deck off a little to port, so that if an aircraft missed all the arrester wires it could simply go around again. This also meant the area at the forward end of the flight deck could continue to be used as a parking area, for it would not now be in the path of aircraft attempting to land. The concept came from the Royal Navy, and the first trials were carried out by HMS *Triumph* in 1952. The idea was speedily adopted by the US Navy, with the flight deck skewed 10.5 degrees and extended over the port side, and the arrester wires suitably re-aligned.

Another problem arose with catapulting, again because of the increasing weight of carrier aircraft. (The US Navy was planning to operate aircraft of up to 40 000-pounds weight, an enormous increase on the 16 671 pounds of the heaviest version of the Second World War TBM Avenger.) There were going to be severe problems in producing hydraulic or compressed-air catapults capable of launching such aircraft, for the old-style catapults were reaching their design limits. The Royal Navy developed a new style of catapult, which used steam from the carrier's main boilers, and was capable of launching any conceivable naval aircraft. The steam catapult was first fitted in a British carrier in 1951, and was adopted by the US Navy in the following year.

The third new device was the mirror landing sight, which replaced the batsman (the 'Deck Landing Control Officer') in guiding the aircraft in to land. As landing speeds rose the old system became unworkable, and a new system was needed by which

The angled deck on HMS *Bulwark*. (*FAA Museum, CARS B/96*)

An early mirror landing sight aboard HMS *Albion*. (*FAA Museum, CARS A/395*)

the pilot could monitor his own approach. The mirror landing sight was stabilised, and could be adjusted to give different approach paths for different aircraft. What the pilot had to do was to keep a reflected 'source light' in line with a row of horizontal datum lights each side of the mirror, and he remained responsible for correctly aligning his aircraft on the centre line of the angled deck and for monitoring his landing speed. A 'wave-off' for any reason could be given by the illumination of red lights either side of the mirror. This new device was introduced into service in 1954, and proved an immediate success.

It is interesting that the three key post-war developments in the operation of aircraft from carriers all originated in Britain. Clearly, the Royal Navy's air arm had recovered from the two disastrous decades of the 1920s and 1930s.

It took the Korean War to restart the programs of building aircraft carriers. The US Navy did take delivery of two 45 000 ton *Midway* class carriers in 1945 (but too late to see any active service in that war) and a third in 1947, but then there was a pause, although a program was begun in June 1948 to modernise the wartime *Essex* carriers so they would be capable of operating

40 000-pound aircraft. In 1949—before the Korean War—the keel of a giant new aircraft carrier, *United States*, was laid, only to be cancelled after a week. Two years later, after the experiences of the Korean War, the program began again, with four of a new 59 650-ton *Forrestal* class being approved, followed by four more of the slightly larger *Kitty Hawk* class.

There was a dramatic development in 1961 when the first nuclear-powered carrier, *Enterprise*, entered service. She was 75 700 tons standard (89 600 tons deep load), with a crew of nearly 6000; this immense carrier—at this time the biggest warship ever built— was 1040 feet long and fitted with four steam catapults. Six more nuclear-powered carriers of the larger *Nimitz* class were built, each displacing 93 400 tons at combat load, and with improved nuclear reactors enabling it to steam for thirteen years between refuellings (although naturally it needs regular replenishment with aviation fuel, replacement aircraft, spare parts and food). By the end of the century the US Navy could expect to have eleven carriers in commission, eight of them *Nimitz* class (as well as *Enterprise*), the new carriers gradually replacing the conventionally-powered carriers of the *Forrestal* and *Kitty Hawk* classes; the Second World War carriers had of course long since disappeared.

The US Navy had used its surplus Second World War carriers—initially principally the escort carriers—for a multiplicity of purposes. They were used for aircraft transport and as ferries, as command ships, as communications relay ships, and most notably to operate the newly-developed anti-submarine helicopters, which had 'dunking' sonar—a set which could be lowered into the sea while the helicopter hovered. Numerous helicopter carriers were also built to support amphibious assaults, including one class of 39 300 tons.

The aircraft-carrier situation was much less happy in the Royal Navy. The massive wartime construction program was inevitably cut back with the coming of peace, and no new carriers were laid down for nearly 30 years. The three 45 000 ton carriers never left the drawing board, and of the four planned vessels of the 36 800 ton *Audacious* class only two—*Eagle* and *Ark Royal*—were completed. The order for eight of the 20 300 ton *Hermes* class was cut back to four, and although sixteen of the 13 350 ton *Colossus* and 14 000 ton *Majestic* classes were completed, two of them were converted to aircraft maintenance ships and no less than eight were eventually sold to other navies (one of them actually fighting against the Royal Navy).

The main strength of the Royal Navy in 1945 had been the six armoured-deck carriers, but there were real problems with continuing to employ these ships because of their large crews and the restrictions imposed on aircraft size and servicing by the enclosed armoured-box hangars, and they were hardly used operationally after the war. *Victorious* was modernised, being rebuilt from the hangar deck upward, but she did not return to operational service until 1958 and was scrapped in 1969 after a disastrous fire on board. *Indomitable* and *Illustrious* were partially modernised by rebuilding their flight decks to increase the usable space for deck-parking, but they did not remain operational for long.

By the mid-1970s Britain was withdrawing from her worldwide military commitments and concentrating on her role as a member of NATO in any future war against the Soviet Union. All the fixed-wing aircraft carriers were paid off, *Ark Royal* in 1978 being the last to go. *Bulwark* and *Hermes* were retained as helicopter carriers, with no capacity to operate fixed-wing aircraft. There was still thought to be a need for large ships to carry the anti-submarine helicopters which were too big to operate from frigates and destroyers, and also to act as command ships; two cruisers were converted for this role, but they were unsuccessful. With some diplomatic finesse (not to say trickery) the navy managed to gain approval for the construction of three 'through-deck' cruisers, of 20 600 tons full load; they were in fact helicopter carriers, and the first of them, *Invincible*, was delivered in 1980. The 'through-deck' cruisers had a flight deck running the full 685-foot length of the ship, and a carrier-type island, but they could not operate normal fixed-wing aircraft.

In 1960 there was the first flight of the prototype of an aircraft designed to take-off and land vertically, and also able to alter the angle of engine thrust and fly forwards in normal flight. From this 'VTOL' aircraft evolved the Hawker Siddeley Harrier, which entered RAF service in 1969, and a US version, the McDonnell Douglas AV–8A Harrier, which was first delivered to the US Marine Corps in 1971. Trials of these aircraft were carried out by nine navies, and a squadron was embarked for eight months on board the US carrier *Franklin D Roosevelt*.

In 1975 approval was given to convert the RAF Harrier into the Sea Harrier, and the first Royal Naval squadron commissioned in 1980. The efficiency of the Sea Harriers was dramatically improved by a change in flight-deck design, nicknamed the 'ski jump'. This was an upward-curving structure at the forward end of the flight deck, which enabled a Sea Harrier to carry a greater payload by changing the take-off attitude of the aircraft and giving it an upward impetus. The payload was increased by up to 2000 pounds and take-offs were possible when the carrier was not heading into the wind.

Both the new *Invincible* and *Hermes* were fitted with ski jumps in time to operate Sea Harriers in the Falklands; a seven-degree ski jump in *Invincible*, twelve degrees in *Hermes*, the steeper ski jump improving the operational capability of the Sea Harriers. In fact the two ships were lucky to survive for the Falklands campaign because the 1981 'Statement on Defence' proposed to make radical cuts to the Royal Navy, including the sale of *Invincible* to Australia and *Hermes* to India, and the phasing-out of the amphibious force. If the Argentine government had waited another year the British would have been unable to do anything effective about the Falklands.

Two sister ships of *Invincible*—*Illustrious* and *Ark Royal*—were completed after the end of the Falklands war, and by 1988 the three ships of this class were the only carriers left in the Royal Navy, the sale of *Invincible* to Australia having been cancelled. The Sea Harrier was becoming obsolete, and the Royal Navy was very interested in a new supersonic V/STOL strike/fighter aircraft being designed in America, primarily for the US Marines. Studies were commenced in 1995 for a replacement carrier to be in service by 2010.

In its rebirth after the end of the Second World War, the French Navy acquired a number of aircraft carriers from Britain

A Sea Harrier takes off from the ski-jump on HMS *Hermes*. (*FAA Museum, FALKLANDS/161*)

and America. From the Royal Navy came the escort carrier *Biter* (renamed *Dixmude*) and the light fleet carrier *Colossus* (renamed *Arromanches*), while from the US Navy came two fast light carriers of the *Independence* class (renamed *Lafayette* and *Bois Belleau*). In the 1960s two new French-designed carriers of 32 000 tons—*Foch* and *Clemenceau*—were commissioned, and they were the only French carriers to survive into the 1990s. However, a nuclear-powered carrier, *Charles de Gaulle*, to carry 35–40 aircraft as well as helicopters, is due to commission just before the end of the century.

A shipborne element of the Soviet Navy's air arm began in the late 1960s, with the appearance of two 16 300-ton anti-submarine 'cruisers', each carrying eighteen helicopters. A much more important development was the commissioning in the late 1970s and 1980s of four 33 300-ton *Kiev* class aircraft carriers with 30–35 aircraft. There was no attempt to operate conventional fixed-wing aircraft, but by this time the Soviet Navy had developed its own vertical/short take-off and landing aircraft, the Yak–36 'Forger', and a typical complement of these carriers was eighteen helicopters and twelve Forgers. The Forger was withdrawn from service in 1992, leaving the *Kievs* as helicopter carriers, unless they undergo substantial reconstruction, which is very unlikely in view of their age and their poor state of maintenance following the disintegration of the USSR. In 1990 the new 57 000 ton carrier *Admiral Kuznetsov* operated Su–27 and MiG–29 fighters—the first Soviet carrier to operate conventional fixed-wing aircraft—but like the *Kiev*-class her future is uncertain, as is that of a sister-ship launched in 1988. Even more uncertain is the future of a proposed 70 000 ton nuclear-powered carrier.

Seven other navies acquired aircraft carriers in the early post-war years: Argentina, Australia, Brazil, Canada, India, Netherlands and Spain. All but one were British light fleet carriers of the *Majestic* or *Colossus* classes; the exception was Spain, which acquired an American *Independence* class carrier in 1967. As aircraft weights increased, it became increasingly difficult to find suitable aircraft to operate from such relatively small carriers; besides, the rapid development of helicopters made it possible to carry them in destroyers and frigates, and from such ships they could carry out many of the roles—anti-submarine work, and limited reconnaissance and anti-shipping strike—for which a carrier had until then been essential.

By 1970 the Dutch and Canadian navies had both abandoned fixed-wing flying from aircraft carriers, and the Australian Navy followed in the early 1980s.[1] The Indians and the Spanish adopted the Sea Harrier solution. The Indians operated Sea Harriers from their old carrier *Vikrant*, and continued to do so in *Hermes* (renamed *Viraat*) which was purchased from the British in 1988. The Spanish built a new carrier, *Principe de Asturias*, to operate American-built ground-attack Harriers. *Principe de Asturias* has a full-load displacement of 17 188 tons, a speed of 26 knots, and normally operates between six and twelve AV–8B Harriers as well as a dozen helicopters.

The Italians built a similar ship, the 10 100 ton *Giuseppe Garibaldi*, which commissioned in 1987 and can carry either sixteen Sea Harriers or eighteen helicopters, or a mixture of the two. The Brazilians acquired a *Colossus* class carrier from the UK in 1961, but have used it chiefly as a helicopter carrier, although it operates some anti-submarine fixed-wing Tracker aircraft. The Argentinians also acquired a similar carrier from the UK (in 1958) and ten years later replaced it with *Karel Doorman*, which the Dutch had acquired from the British in 1948 and substantially modernised. The Argentinians renamed the carrier *25 de Mayo*, and continued to operate conventional fixed-wing aircraft as well as helicopters from it; the performance of this carrier in the Falklands War will be considered later.

The sophistication of methods of launching air attacks on ships was also developing at a comparable rate, and as a result enormous efforts were being directed to improving air defence at sea. The reason for this was that all of the major navies saw their principal role as being participants in a major war between NATO and the Warsaw Pact, and in such a war extremely advanced forms of attack were to be expected.

The pace of change in weaponry since 1945 has been staggering. At the end of the Second World War the only operational anti-shipping guided-weapon was the American Bat glider-bomb. The Soviet Union began experimenting with anti-ship missiles in the 1950s, aiming to develop weapons to be carried both by aircraft and in surface ships. These began to be fitted by the end of the decade, and in 1962 were fitted in submarines. By 1967 the Soviet Union had a missile (codenamed by NATO as 'Kitchen') which could be launched by an aircraft, had a range of 150 miles, a speed of Mach 3.5 and a 2200-pound warhead. It carried its own radar set, and homed automatically.

Many other missiles were produced over the following years, some of which had infra-red homing and others homed on radar or jamming transmissions. The longer-range weapons normally used inertial guidance until they were within the detection range of their homing systems. Various flight patterns were also possible:

sea-skimming, or 'bunting' to achieve a steep final dive, or just flying directly at the target. Comparable weapons were produced by other countries, particularly the US but also the UK, France, Italy, Israel, Norway and Sweden. The threat to ships was very much greater than anything that had been faced in the Second World War.

How to deal with this new threat? Obviously the best way is to destroy the bearer of the missile—aircraft, ship or submarine—before the missile can be launched. Then anti-ship missiles launched from over the horizon by ships or submarines would usually require mid-course guidance, and the aircraft or helicopter providing this guidance might be vulnerable. If all else failed, it might be possible for the defending ships to shoot down the missile, but this would be particularly difficult with sea-skimming missiles, coming in low above the waves, and difficult to detect until the last moment.

The first requirement was more efficient aircraft-detection radar, particularly in height-finding. The initial approach was to devise an aerial array which would emit a large number of pencil beams set at different elevations. Such a system—commonly called 3D radar—would provide instant height-finding, but it required a heavy aerial. Later a more sophisticated approach was devised, using electronic scanning, with a multiplicity of beams directed in both azimuth and elevation. The weight of this aerial, too, was considerable, as was the cost of the system, so although major warships could expect 3D radar, smaller vessels had to accept less efficient systems.

The second requirement was airborne early warning, which had been very successfully pioneered by the Americans at the end of the Second World War. The frequencies used by warning radars meant that the radar beam followed the line of sight, and detections could not be made round the curvature of the earth. An aircraft coming in at sea level could not be detected by a ship at more than fifteen miles or so, far too late for a controlled interception, but a look-down radar set in an aircraft could give far greater warning. The first airborne early warning aircraft, the Grumman Avenger, was succeeded by several other aircraft, both carrier and land-based, and including the Fairey Gannet in British carriers.

Of its generation the best one for air defence at sea was the twin turbo-prop Grumman E–2 Hawkeye, which entered service in 1968. It had a 24-foot radar dome on top of the fuselage, and could detect low-flying aircraft at ranges of up to 200 miles, and could also detect sea-skimming missiles. The Hawkeye transmitted its radar picture to the ships below, but as it carried three or four systems-operators in addition to its flying crew it could also act as a fighter direction centre and could control strikes. This latter capability is particularly useful in dealing with surface units that have to come in close in order to fire missiles. Ships at sea may also of course have the assistance of shore-based radars in certain circumstances, as well as land-based AEW aircraft.

The third requirement is effective fighters. Jet fighters began to be embarked in carriers in the late 1940s, and from the 1960s onwards the USN in particular had highly-effective fighters, at least as good as their shore-based opponents. The F–4 Phantom II became operational with the US Navy in December 1960. It was a twin-engined jet fighter with a speed of over Mach 2, as well as a weapons load of 15 000 pounds. It was a superb aircraft, and was adopted by many countries, as well as the US Air Force. Its successor, the F–14 Tomcat, was even better. Air-to-air missiles were used by all the fighters, and in fact the Phantom did not have any guns at all, a lack which was sometimes felt by pilots involved in close dog-fights. Another development of the times was the use of tanker aircraft to refuel other aircraft in the air, to increase the range of strikes or the time-on-task of fighters. Sometimes aircraft carrying extra fuel were sent out with strikes to refuel their colleagues on the way.

But no matter how efficient the fighter defence, it was most unlikely that all the attacking aircraft would be shot down, particularly before they had launched their anti-ship missiles. The obvious answer was homing rockets or jet-powered missiles. By the mid-1950s the major navies were all fitting or developing air defence missiles of considerable range. The most popular form of guidance was 'semi-active', with the missile responding to radar reflections from the target, which would be 'illuminated' by a radar in the launching ship. Some of the early ones were 'beam-riders'—the launching ship continuously aimed at the target with a pencil beam radar, and the missile held its flight along the pencil beam—but only a single target could be engaged at any time by each radar, and there were also accuracy problems.

By the 1980s the most widely-fitted anti-aircraft missile was the American Standard; it was also probably the best. The SM–2 Standard missile is a two-stage rocket with semi-active homing and a range of 80 miles and, when fitted in conjunction with advanced radars and command systems (such as the American AEGIS), its control system can deal successfully with multiple targets. The Standard system is also effective against anti-ship missiles, except for the 'sea-skimming' variety, which is a threat that has to be dealt with separately.

Although at one stage it looked as if guns might disappear

from warships (as they did from F–4 Phantom fighters), there has been a resurgence of interest in them. This is partly because of their usefulness for shore bombardment, partly because of their anti-ship role, but largely because they provided a reassuring last line of defence against old-fashioned bombing attacks by aircraft and might even achieve something against missiles.

As a result guns in the 76–130mm range continue to be widely fitted. The problems they face are the same as their Second World War predecessors, but the solutions are much more elegant and the performance much higher. Rates of fire have improved (a French 100mm gun has a rate of fire of 90 rounds per minute); automatic following of the guns is universal; computers are much more compact and effective; blind-fire radars are common; and proximity fuses have been improved even further. The systems are better than the best available in the Second World War, and would have been very effective if available in that war. They are still effective against direct-bombing attacks, but are of limited value against missiles, particularly the sea-skimmers.

The picture is the same with the smaller, close-range weapons—those between 76mm and 20mm. Higher rates of fire, and better radar and computers, have greatly improved their capability against Second World War-style attacks, but their effectiveness against missiles is limited. To try to deal directly with the missile threat no less than six navies have been developing short-range ('point defence') missile systems, all of them rockets with ranges of up to ten miles employing various guidance systems. An alternative approach is to have a mounting of 20mm, 25mm or 30mm guns, capable of up to 4200 rounds per minute, with automatic radar detection and aiming, and a very fast reaction time; these mountings are particularly designed to deal with last-minute detections of sea-skimming missiles.

But if fighter, missile and gun defence against missile attacks could never be expected to be totally effective, could not missiles be decoyed or deceived? This brings up the whole complex question of electronic warfare, in particular detection of radar transmissions and the jamming or suppression of radar sets, and the use of decoys, which may be 'window', or flares to seduce missiles which use infra-red either as their primary or supplementary homing-device. The purpose of the decoys may either be to cause confusion about the size of the surface force, or to produce false targets at the acquisition phase, or to lure a missile away from its target ship onto a false objective.

The techniques of electronic warfare can be used by attackers as well as defenders. Reconnaissance aircraft are usually fitted with receivers to detect radar transmissions (for these can be detected well beyond the range at which the radar set would have an echo), and attacking aircraft often hear warning signals if they are illuminated by radar. Specially-equipped electronic-warfare aircraft have also been developed, particularly by the Americans.

The performances of all these radars, missiles and guns, and the techniques of electronic warfare are extremely complicated subjects. It is worth noting, though, that equipments do not always achieve in action the results their propagandists claim for them, and no matter how complex a computerised control-system may be there is still scope for human error. Moreover the latest equipments are never universally fitted, and ships are often forced to operate with equipments which would have been appropriate against much less sophisticated threats.

In more than half a century since the end of the Second World War the global war for which the principal navies were preparing has not occurred, but there have been many smaller conflicts. In nearly all of these minor conflicts sea power has performed its traditional roles: protection of one's own sea lines of communication and disruption of the enemy's, amphibious assaults, and bombardment of the enemy's coastline. The existence of aircraft carriers has given much greater significance to the last role, for carrier aircraft are not limited to coastal targets. Aircraft carriers have been used as mobile bases to deliver tactical air power in nearly every war since 1945, as well as in many 'brush fires'.

One peculiarity of these post-1945 conflicts, as far as the navies are concerned, is that all of them, with the exception of the Falklands War, were extremely one-sided. The maritime dominance of the Western powers was not seriously challenged. The Americans used some of their Second World War battleships for bombardments, but they were never threatened. The opposition never had effective submarines, though they were beginning to become more widespread, but in small numbers: India in 1968, Pakistan in 1970, Argentina in 1974 and Libya in 1976. The opponents of the Western powers also never had effective surface fleets, though mines were sometimes used very effectively, particularly in the Gulf of Iran, and anti-ship missiles began to come into their own.

In the Second World War submarines had been major destroyers of aircraft carriers. More than 200 aircraft carriers saw service in the American, British and Japanese navies during the six years of the war, and 40 of them were lost. Of those which were lost from all causes during that war, seventeen were sunk by submarines.[2] No aircraft carrier has been sunk or damaged by enemy action in any of the post-war conflicts, though the *threat* of nuclear-powered submarines was enough to take the Argentine carrier out of the Falklands War.

The first significant post-1945 operational use of aircraft carriers occurred in 1947, when the French escort carrier *Dixmude* operated Douglas SBD dive-bombers off the Vietnamese coast, being replaced by the *Colossus*-class carrier *Arromanches* in 1948, and the two *Independence* class carriers joining in later. In the Korean War (from 1950 to 1953) American, British and Australian carriers operated off both coasts, and provided a crucial level of support to the army. In the attack on Suez in 1956 the British provided three carriers—*Eagle*, *Albion* and *Bulwark*—and the French provided two—*Arromanches* and *Lafayette*; in addition the British had two helicopter carriers, which conducted the first helicopter-borne assault landing in history, bringing ashore the 524 men and 23 tons of stores of 45 Commando in 90 minutes. The aircraft from the five fixed-wing carriers dominated the Egyptian Air Force, and provided much of the tactical support for the amphibious landing.

The US Navy provided immense carrier effort in the Vietnam War. In the early days, between 1960 and 1964, it was limited to photographic reconnaissance, but from 1964 onwards until the armistice in 1973 the carrier force off the coast, sometimes numbering as many as six carriers, carried out sustained attacks on shore targets as the ships ranged up and down the coast. In the fourteen-day war between India and Pakistan in December 1971 the Indian carrier *Vikrant* dominated the Bay of Bengal (the Pakistanis did not have a carrier), attacked shore targets in East Pakistan and laid mines in the harbour approaches.

In the Falklands War in 1982 the British used two carriers, initially carrying a mere twenty Sea Harrier fighters between them, against shore-based aircraft which outnumbered them seven to one. The Argentines also had an aircraft carrier, which raised the possibility of the first carrier-versus-carrier battle since Leyte Gulf, though this did not eventuate. After one sortie, the Argentine carrier *25 de Mayo* retreated to harbour for fear of British nuclear-powered submarines, and there she stayed for the remainder of the war, though her aircraft were used from shore bases.

The Falklands campaign was a small war, but a sharp one. There were no battleships involved on either side. By maintaining its fleet so far from its base, in a tempestuous southern autumn, the Royal Navy demonstrated how far it had come in replenishment techniques since 1945. The Sea Harriers, armed with superior air-to-air missiles, dominated the Argentine fighters below 15 000 feet, but they were not sufficiently numerous, and had inadequate endurance, to defend both the fleet and the landing area.

The British ships proved to be very vulnerable to low-level attacks by Exocet cruise-missiles, although the decoy arrangements worked reasonably well when they were used. They had no airborne early warning, and achieved no interceptions of the aircraft carrying the Exocets, nor were any missiles fired at them. The ships' missiles and guns also proved ineffective against the cruise missiles themselves.[3] Fortunately the Argentine Navy had only five such air-launched missiles, the French having cut off supplies when the war started.

Argentine Air Force and Navy aircraft attacked the ships in the landing area with great gallantry, flying in from a low level to avoid the British missiles, whose control radars were confused by land echoes in the assault anchorage. The Argentine aircraft scored numerous hits, but most of the bombs failed to detonate because they had not had time to be armed. The lessons of the Bismarck Sea battle nearly 40 years earlier had obviously not been grasped.

In 1981 and 1985 there were serious brushes in the Mediterranean

HMS *Sheffield* after being hit by an Exocet. (*Imperial War Museum, FKD64*)

between Libyan aircraft and US carriers. In 1981 two carriers, *Forrestal* and *Nimitz*, shot down (after some provocation) two Libyan aircraft in the Gulf of Sirte, and four years later there was a much more serious confrontation, culminating in massive strikes on Tripoli and Benghazi by US aircraft based in England as well as carrier aircraft.

American carriers also provided crucial air power during the turmoils in the Gulf of Iran during the late 1980s and early 1990s. Finally American, British and French carriers offered air support to the UN forces trying to keep the peace in Bosnia, though the offer was seldom taken up because the process of asking for it was so cumbersome. Although none of the carriers involved was damaged in any of these wars, this is not to say that they were not threatened or unsuccessfully attacked.

The Gulf War against Iraq in 1991 was perhaps the most remarkable of all for providing the occasion for a dramatic reappearance of the battleship, in the form of two members of the *Iowa* class, *Wisconsin* and *Missouri*, which had been laid up at the end of the 1960s but were recommissioned during the 1980s to form the cores of surface battle groups.[4] The ships were modified

A Tomahawk land-attack cruise-missile is fired towards an Iraqi target from USS *Missouri*. (*Department of Defence Still Media Records Center*)

by removing four of the original ten twin 5-inch turrets, and replacing them with 32 Tomahawk cruise-missiles in eight armoured launchers, and sixteen Harpoon anti-ship missiles in four quadruple launchers. The radar and other electronic equipment were also updated, and four six-barrelled Phalanx automatic anti-missile mountings were fitted.

The attraction of the battleships was that, with their heavy armour, they would be almost invulnerable to contemporary anti-ship missiles. The problem was their age—nearly 50 years. Nevertheless, with their missiles and their 16-inch guns for bombardment, they were a formidable threat to the Iraqis. Too much should not, however, be read into their reappearance. They were used because they were available. To build new, heavily-armoured ships would be very expensive, and if they ever became a serious force it would not be difficult to develop air-to-surface and surface-to-surface missiles which would strike their targets beneath the waterline. As someone said, it is easier to sink a battleship by letting water into the bottom than air into the top.

While the two battleships played important roles in the Gulf conflict, it was the final fling for these naval dinosaurs. Both were paid off on their return from the campaign, though *Missouri*—the ship on which the Japanese surrender was signed in 1945—was allowed a brief reprieve so that she could take part in the fiftieth anniversary commemoration of Pearl Harbor. On 31 March 1992 she, too, was finally paid off.

There will be no new battleships, and the only one remaining in service will be HMS *Victory*, Nelson's flagship at Trafalgar—in dry dock, but still in commission.

Notes

CHAPTER 1

1 *Aeroplane*, 25 January 1911.
2 *Aeroplane*, 18 January 1912.
3 The circular letter of 1 July 1914 did in fact mention that the Royal Naval Air Service formed the naval wing of the Royal Flying Corps, and the formal act of separation from the Royal Flying Corps did not take place for another year.
4 *Flight*, 18 February 1911.
5 *Flight*, 30 September 1911.
6 These were the strengths when the Royal Naval Air Service was incorporated into the Royal Air Force on 1 April 1918. Only 397 officers and 821 sailors were regulars.
7 The first Zeppelin for the German Navy was ordered in 1912, and three of these airships had been delivered before the war began. Two of these had already been lost however—the first crashed in a storm, the second exploded in mid-air.
8 Perhaps not the first brush, because during the German battlecruiser bombardment of Yarmouth on 3 November 1914 a Short aircraft attacked them with a 14-inch torpedo, but no-one noticed.
9 Report of flight by Flight Commander C.H.K. Edmonds (Roskill 1969, p. 222).
10 Letter from Admiral Sir David Beatty, Commander-in-Chief Grand Fleet, to the Admiralty, 11 September 1917 (Roskill 1969, pp. 541–43).
11 Admiralty letter of 25 September 1917 to Admiral Sir David Beatty, Commander-in-Chief Grand Fleet (Roskill 1969, pp. 549–54).
12 Beatty had requested 200 in a letter of 31 August 1917.
13 During the four years of war there were 51 airship and 52 aeroplane raids on England; of these London was the target for twelve raids by

342

airships and nineteen by aeroplanes. The total number of people killed by the raids was 1413.

14 There had been an earlier trial of deck-landing arrangements in September 1916. The arrester-gear was very similar to that used by Eugene Ely.

15 That at least was the feeling of the British ships, but the Zeppelins were much less effective in reconnaissance than they thought.

CHAPTER 2

1 Reynolds 1968, p. 14.

2 Hurley 1975, p. 101.

3 This board was headed by the Chief of Naval Operations, Admiral Eberle, and was therefore known as the 'Eberle Board'.

4 Quoted in Ranft 1977, p. 122.

5 Life in the *Langley* was not always easy. The flight deck had been built over the bridge, so that those on the bridge could not see to navigate. The executive officer's quarters were in an old pigeon-loft, which had become available when a plan to use homing pigeons to carry messages was abandoned (Reynolds 1991, p. 198).

6 Pride 1986, p. 28.

7 There was a great deal of controversy about the displacement of the *Lexington* and *Saratoga*. The maximum displacement of an aircraft carrier was set at 27 000 tons by the Washington Treaty of 1922, but the Americans managed to get a special dispensation allowing for two 33 000-ton ships, to permit them to convert two partly-constructed battlecruisers, though there was to be no increase in their total aircraft carrier allowance of 135 000 tons. In fact the two carriers, when their conversion was complete, were nearly 3000 tons over the limit, but the Americans managed to calm their consciences by arguing that at the time of the Washington Conference the two ships were actually battlecruisers, and it was permissible to increase the displacement of a battlecruiser by up to 3000 tons to improve its protection. Nevertheless official US publications usually referred to the *Lexington* and *Saratoga* as displacing 33 000 tons, when in fact they were nearly 36 000 tons.

8 *Lexington* and *Saratoga* were originally intended to operate 72 aircraft, but by 1929 *Lexington* was putting to sea with 120 fighters and bombers, although less than 90 of them could be accommodated in the single hangar, vast though it was.

9 The landing signal officer evolved from the actions of Commander Whiting, of the USS *Langley*. He saw a pilot repeatedly approaching too high and being forced to go around again, so he grabbed the caps from two nearby sailors and held them out to show the pilot he was too high, and then gradually lowered them to coach the pilot in.

10 *Ranger* had some unusual features, such as additional arrester wires on the forward end of the flight deck so that, if the flight deck was damaged, she could land her aircraft while going astern. This capability was never used operationally, but was installed in all US carriers until 1943. *Ranger* also had two athwartship catapults on the hangar deck, but as one pilot

said, 'I made one catapult shot from the hangar deck and that was enough'. The hangar-deck catapults were intended to be used only in an emergency when the flight deck was out of action, but were not fitted in later carriers.

11   The requirement was that the captain of an aircraft carrier should be qualified either as a pilot or observer. As an example, the future Admiral Halsey qualified as a pilot at the age of 51, so that he could take command of the carrier *Saratoga*. The presence of senior officers such as Halsey in a flying course caused some social problems. It was the custom that the pilot who took the greatest number of flying hours before being allowed to go solo should be thrown in the pool by his classmates, and Halsey did take the most in his class. Nearly all the rest of his course were ensigns, and they hesitated, briefly, before imposing the penalty on such a senior officer.

12   Till 1979, p. 39.

13   The RN started 'Senior Officers Flying Courses' in 1945; the course consisted of pilot training in Tiger Moths, which were biplane trainer aircraft. Unfortunately very few senior officers applied for the courses, the vacancies being filled by young lieutenants. The scheme was soon scrapped.

14   An American carrier-aircraft had only 'a small steel hook under its belly to which one end of a wire strop was attached while the other end went around a shuttle fitted almost flush in the forward end of the carrier's deck. This innovation brought simplicity in carrier design, a weight and drag saving on the aircraft, and the further advantage that the aircraft got airborne at an angle of attack giving it maximum lift without the pilot having to rotate it immediately after launch' (Brown 1987, pp. 47–48).

15   *Illustrious* was the first British fleet carrier to be capable of doing tail-down launches. The modifications to the catapult were made while the ship was being refitted in America in 1941 after being damaged in the Mediterranean, but British aircraft (and US aircraft built to British specifications) still had to be launched by trolley. It is curious that the Royal Navy was so slow to adopt efficient catapulting from its carriers, for as far back as 1922 a naval staff decision was made to 'go slow' on local catapult design and to watch foreign catapult development.

16   *Eagle* (21 850 tons) was converted from the Chilean battleship *Almirante Cochrane*, which was requisitioned during the war while under construction. *Hermes* (10 850 tons) was often claimed to be the first ship to be designed as an aircraft carrier, though it was, in fact, built on the hull of a *Hawkins*-class cruiser.

17   The hangar was divided into three bays by fire curtains, which caused difficulties in moving aircraft. The lifts were not armoured, but were separated from the hangar by armoured doors. However these doors could not be closed or opened quickly, and they therefore had to be left open when the carrier was handling aircraft, rendering the hangars vulnerable to hits outside the protected hangar area. In the two post-war armoured carriers of the *Ark Royal* class the problem was overcome by fitting power-operated armoured doors, which were open only when an aircraft was actually being moved between the hangar and the lift.

18 In *Illustrious*, for instance, the flight deck was 745 feet long (compared to 825 feet in the contemporary US carrier *Yorktown*), but of this only 620 feet was usable. When *Illustrious* was repaired in America in 1941, the long round-down aft was partially flattened out, adding 50 feet to the available flight deck length.

19 FAA Committee Report, 12 April 1935, ADM 116/3008, Admiralty, London.

20 Till 1979, p. 149.

21 Designed to have a displacement of 23 450 tons (about the same size as the *Yorktown* and *Illustrious* classes), *Graf Zeppelin* was intended to carry 30 Messerschmitt Bf109T–1s. These were a variant of the standard Luftwaffe fighter, with manually-folded wings, a slightly larger wing area and the fuselage strengthened to withstand catapulting and arresting. The strike aircraft were Ju.87s, which were converted from the standard Luftwaffe dive-bomber by being fitted with arrester hooks. They retained their fixed undercarriage but it could be jettisoned in the event of a forced landing on the sea. The Ju.87s did not have wing-folding, and only twelve were intended to be carried.

22 Commissioned in December 1922, *Hosho* was the first purpose-built carrier. The British ship *Hermes*, to whom this distinction is usually given, was commissioned in February 1924.

23 During the Second World War the Allies used code names to describe Japanese aircraft, and although they did not come into general use until late 1942 they have been used throughout this work. The only aircraft about which this might cause confusion is the Zeke, called the Zero by the Japanese and many others. Aircraft put into production for the Japanese Navy received a type number which was the last two digits of the Japanese year, which is 660 years ahead of the Christian year. Thus the Zeke was given the type number zero because it went into production in the Japanese year 2600 (1940 AD). Similarly the dive-bomber Val was Type 99, and the torpedo-bomber Kate was a Type 97.

24 Marder 1981, pp. 305–6.

25 Minute to the First Lord of the Admiralty, 15 September 1940 (Churchill 1949, p. 592).

26 Only the first four *Atlanta* class had sixteen 5-inch guns. The later seven (including three commissioned after the end of the war) had the number of 5-inch guns reduced to twelve so as to permit the fitting of new radar sets and large numbers of 40mm Bofors guns and 20mm Oerlikons. The *Juneau*, completed in 1946, had 28 40mm and numerous 20mm guns.

27 There were delays with the production of 5.25-inch turrets, and the final five ships had four instead of five turrets. Two of the earlier ships were fitted with 4.5-inch turrets instead of the 5.25-inch. Five of the sixteen *Dido* class ships were sunk during the war (all but one by air attack), as were five of the eight earlier conversions.

28 The last two classes of pre-war British destroyers—the L and M classes; eight destroyers in each—did have 4.5-inch turrets capable of higher elevation, but subsequent classes went back to the low-elevation mountings.

29 One of them, Admiral Henderson—the Rear-Admiral, Aircraft Carriers—
said in 1932 that 'the primary defence of the fleet against air attack [by
gunfire] is not justified by data or experience. No realistic firing against
aircraft has taken place since the last war and, in my opinion, the value
of our own High Angle Control System Mk 1 is rated too high. In
common with others we are apt to over-rate the capabilities of our
weapons in peacetime.' (Quoted in Ranft 1977, p. 116) Some years later
Henderson's views were supported by the findings of an Admiralty
committee—actually the Sub-Committee on Bombing and A-A Gunfire
Experiments—which in January 1939 estimated that for each aircraft shot
down by ships' gunfire one hit would be scored on a cruiser, or two on
a carrier, and stated that destroyers were virtually defenceless against air
attack (Roskill 1976b, p. 420).

30 At the time Chatfield and the Chief of the Air Staff, Air Chief Marshal
Sir Edward Ellington, were advisers to the sub-committee of the Committee of Imperial Defence, which investigated the vulnerability of capital
ships to air attack. The sub-committee came to no clear conclusions,
concentrating mainly on the direction of further trials, but some interesting views were expressed. Aircraft carriers were assessed as being 'far
more vulnerable to air attack than battleships'. Torpedo attacks against
heavily armoured ships, the sub-committee reported, 'is not regarded by
the Staffs to be as good a method of attack as [level or dive bombing]'.
The Admiralty view was also reported to be 'that there is no reason why
the ship cannot be designed to meet air attack just as in the past she
had been designed to meet other dangers'. This sanguine view was to
be exploded in the first naval campaign of the coming war.

31 In fact, when the Bofors guns first went to sea in the Royal Navy in
1941—a few were installed in *Prince of Wales* and some cruisers—they
were fitted on army mountings.

32 In late 1941 *Saratoga* reported that her CXAM was 'very unreliable. The
darn thing would catch aircraft one day and not catch surface craft, and
then they'd do some tinkering with it and it would catch surface craft
this side of the horizon but would not catch any airplanes. And you
couldn't know whether it was working or not' (Stern 1993, p. 127).

33 In March 1942 attempts were made to salvage sets from the sunken
Prince of Wales, but although *Repulse* was located in the area and some
ammunition and anti-aircraft guns brought up by divers, *Prince of Wales*
was not found at the time, despite being only eight miles to the east of
Repulse, at a depth of 150 feet.

34 The resonant cavity magnetron was designed in 1940 by a team at
Birmingham University under the supervision of an Australian, Professor
Oliphant.

CHAPTER 3

1 Vice-Admiral Sir Guy Royle (ADM 116/3722: Admiralty, London).
2 Martienssen 1948, p. 52.
3 The German naval organisation B Dienst had cracked the British naval

ciphers before the war, and obtained much information until the ciphers were changed in late 1940. The Germans also penetrated the British and Allied Merchant Ship code, and they used the information from this with devastating effect in the Battle of the Atlantic until the code was changed in mid-1943.

4   This was the destroyer *Gurkha*, whose captain was frustrated by the ineffectiveness of his guns against the German aircraft, and turned to a course away from the wind and sea in the hope of improving the performance of his gunfire. In the process he became widely separated from the rest of the British ships, and was overwhelmed by the German aircraft (Vian 1960, p. 37).

5   Quoted in Roskill 1976a, p. 179.

6   Troubridge 1940, p. 2.

7   Forbes 1940.

8   At least the lifts on *Glorious* were large enough to carry the Hurricanes; on board *Ark Royal* there were plans to chop the ends off their wings so they could be taken down on the lifts into the hangar.

9   Roskill 1977, p. 107. The captain of the *Glorious*, D'Oyly-Hughes, was apparently a very difficult, almost impossible, man to deal with. He was not an aviator, and had fallen out with his Commander (Air), who had been left behind in Scapa Flow facing a probable court martial.

10 Not perhaps to everyone. The rear-admiral who commanded the Home Fleet destroyers was flying his flag in a cruiser and had witnessed the first air attacks. He decided that whether a ship was or was not struck by bombs was purely a matter of the competence of individual captains in taking avoiding action (Vian 1960, p.38).

11 Quoted in Cunningham 1951 p. 227. There were some other lessons which should have been learnt too, notably the urgent need for higher-performance fighters, better anti-aircraft gunfire and the ability to replenish warships at sea.

12 Till 1979, p. 85.

13 It was already standard practice for ships to make a flag hoist when an aircraft was sighted, but this was to alert the gunfire defence of the fleet, not to provide direction for fighters, if any happened to be present. For a time there was an attempt to pass information to fighters by flags but this was hopeless; although the fighters might be alerted by a flurry of flag-hoisting that something was going on (but not what or where).

CHAPTER 4

1   The Commander-in-Chief at the time of the Munich crisis was Admiral Sir Dudley Pound. He eventually approved Lyster's plan, but added the caveat 'unless, as I hope will be the case, shore-based aircraft are available'.

2   As an example of economy of force, Taranto might be rivalled by the attack by three Italian 'human-torpedoes' (torpedoes with a 600-pound warhead, each ridden and guided by a crew of two) on the battleships

Queen Elizabeth and *Valiant* in Alexandria on 19 December 1941; both battleships were seriously damaged and put out of action for months.

Taranto was also not the first torpedo attack on warships in harbour during the Mediterranean war, for more than a month earlier a single Italian bomber had dropped two torpedoes in Alexandria Harbour, near the cruiser *Gloucester*. At first it was thought that influence mines had been dropped, but it was later decided that they were torpedoes, which had become stuck in the mud. Alexandria had no barrage balloons, so all ships were instructed to fly kites while in harbour, and the submarine tender *Medway* was given the task of attaching explosive charges to its kites, and setting them off occasionally, to give the impression to watchers onshore that all the kites carried explosives. The torpedo attack was apparently a solo effort, and there were no further such attacks (Cunningham 1951, p. 270).

CHAPTER 5

1 Churchill 1950, vol. 3, p. 250.
2 Cunningham 1951, p. 375.
3 Cunningham 1951, p. 379.
4 Cunningham 1951, p. 384.
5 Cunningham 1951, p. 373.
6 The F4F Wildcats Mark 1 to Mark 4 were called Martlets by the Royal Navy. The later Mark 5 and Mark 6 versions were called Wildcats.
7 In September 1941 the Air Ministry was asked to transfer 400 up-to-date Spitfires to the navy, and with some reluctance 250 were ultimately provided. The first version, called the Seafire IB, was a Spitfire V fitted with an arrester hook. The early Seafires (like the Hurricanes) did not have folding wings, which was a problem in the first three armoured-decked carriers, *Illustrious*, *Formidable* and *Victorious*, whose lifts were too small to strike them down into the hangars. The first folding-wing Seafire flew in November 1942. The Seafire's performance was lower than that of the land-based Spitfires because navalisation incurred both weight and drag penalties, particularly in the early models which had external spools for catapult launching from a trolley. The Seafire L Mk III, which was produced in larger numbers than any other Seafire variant, began to reach squadron service early in 1944. It had a maximum speed of 305 knots at 6000 feet, and a maximum range (with a 409 litre drop-tank) of 450 miles (its lack of endurance was a continuing problem). The armament was four 0.303-inch machine guns and two 20mm cannons. The fragile undercarriage caused continuing deck-landing problems. Later versions, with strengthened undercarriage and the more powerful Griffon engine, did not see service during the war.
8 The hoses used for refuelling at sea at this time were the standard wound-copper hoses used for refuelling in harbour. These hoses were very inelastic, and if the refuelling ship accidentally got too far away they would burst with a spectacular gush of fuel oil. They were replaced in the following year with rubber hoses.

9   Although *Formidable* did cease to operate aircraft, during her passage back to Alexandria she did manage to fly off her serviceable aircraft to an airfield in Egypt.

10 Grantham 1943.

11 The official historian, Captain S.W. Roskill, actually claimed that it was 'a revolutionary change in carrier design which was to pay a very good dividend in war' (Roskill 1976b, p. 224). In fact the Royal Navy suffered greatly from the small number of aircraft which could be operated by its armoured carriers. Consider, for example, the operations in the Indian Ocean in April 1942, when the Royal Navy had the same number of carriers as the Americans were to have at Midway, but could not contemplate taking on the Japanese carriers in daylight. The *Illustrious* class carriers did perform well in 1945 under Kamikaze attack, for the suicide aircraft had low terminal-velocity and could not penetrate the deck armour, but the threat from Kamikazes was certainly not a factor in the design of the British carriers.

12 The Luftwaffe losses in Crete were as follows:

	In action		Operational	
	Destroyed	**Damaged**	**Destroyed**	**Damaged**
LR recce	4	–	–	1
SE fighters	16	3	11	3
TE fighters	19	10	6	3
Bombers	19	4	7	14
Dive-bombers	9	2	9	2
Transport	80	45	39	61
Coastal	–	–	1	–
Totals	147	64	73	84

(CAB 106/711, 15 July 1947)

13 The same set was being fitted in British destroyers, where it was known as Type 286. The first version had a fixed aerial as it had when fitted in aircraft, but later versions had a rotating aerial which gave a better indication of bearing. A Type 286 could pick up a battleship at about ten miles, but was very little use against aircraft.

CHAPTER 6

1   ASV Mark 2, with a detection range on a battleship of about 20 miles.

2   There had been a plan to erect a dummy second funnel in the *Bismarck*, but it was not proceeded with. With a second funnel, the *Bismarck* might easily have been confused, in poor visibility, with *Renown* or *King George V*, and the confusion might well have disorganised the second Swordfish strike (Von Müllenheim-Rechburg 1981, p. 162).

3   Quoted in Barnett 1991, p. 315. It was an extract from a letter from Tovey to the official naval historian, Captain S.W. Roskill.

4   Churchill 1950, p. 663.

CHAPTER 7

1   Some cabinet members were even more bellicose. Interior Secretary Ickes wrote to Roosevelt, on the day after the German invasion of the USSR, that 'to embargo oil to Japan would be as popular a move as you could make . . . and might . . . make it, not only possible but easy, to get into this war in an effective way. And if we should thus indirectly be brought in, we would avoid the criticism that we had gone in as an ally of communistic Russia' (Toland 1970, p. 85).

2   Fuchida and Okumiya 1955, p. 24.

3   Ugaki 1991, p. 249.

4   7 December, west-longitude date. Japan and Pearl Harbor were of course separated by the date line.

5   From here onwards, west-longitude dates are used.

6   *The Pearl Harbor Operation*, p. 15: ATIS Research Report No. 132, 1 December 1945.

7   It has been claimed that the Japanese JN–25B fleet code was 'partly readable' by December 1941, by the code-breakers in Washington and the Philippines. (The code-breakers in Honolulu, on orders from Washington, were concentrating on a task which proved to be fruitless, the cracking of the Japanese flag-officers code.) It is not known what useful information was obtained from the JN–25B code, but none of it was passed to Kimmel (Layton 1985, pp. 230–3).

8   Edwin Layton, Kimmel's intelligence officer, claims that the 'Purple' decryption machine which had been intended for Pearl Harbor was diverted to the British, on orders from President Roosevelt (Layton 1975, p. 81).

9   Investigation of the Pearl Harbor Attack. Report of the Joint Committee (79th Congress, 2nd session, Doc. No. Z44, 1946) part 24, p. 1363; part 8, p. 3838.

10   After the Pearl Harbor attack, air searches were carried out over an arc of nearly 270 degrees, only the sector to the eastwards being omitted. The sectors to the east and south were covered to a depth of 200 miles, to the north-westwards to 375 miles, and to the north 300 miles (Morison 1948, p. 136, based on a chart presented to Joint Congressional Committee, Item 18). By the time the new search plan was implemented Nagumo was out of range, but he might have been detected if the search plan had been in place before 7 December, although probably not until after he had launched his strikes. The American aircraft were not fitted with radar and were not really effective at reconnaissance by night. At dusk on the night before the launch Nagumo was 490 miles from Pearl Harbor, and the first launch was made at dawn at a range of 275 miles.

11   Morison 1948, p. 139.

12   Rear-Admiral Bellinger had been co-author of an assessment dated 31 March 1941 in which it was pointed out that in the past Japan had never preceded hostile actions by a declaration of war, and that a dawn attack on Pearl Harbor by carrier aircraft was the most likely and dangerous form of attack. In fact carrier attacks on Pearl Harbor had

been carried out successfully several times in US fleet exercises in the years before Pearl Harbor. The problem for the defenders was that a carrier force could be more than 500 miles from Pearl Harbor at dusk, make a rapid transit during the night and be within strike range at dawn. To cover the approaches to a distance of 500 miles without radar assistance would have required 250 reconnaissance aircraft; Bellinger had only 69, and nearly half of these were obsolescent.

13 Twelve B–17s, on their way to the Philippines, arrived during the Japanese attack. In order to carry the necessary fuel for the flight from the mainland they were without ammunition, and the armour plate in the rear had been shifted forward to improve the aircrafts' balance. They could do nothing but attempt to evade the Japanese fighters (and American anti-aircraft gunfire), and one of them was destroyed and three badly damaged.

14 There was some confusion in the attack, for Fuchida noticed that the fighters, which had been in the clouds, were not following instructions after he fired his first signal pistol, so he fired a second time. Some of the dive-bombers mistook this for the signal for an opposed attack, and attacked the battleships instead of the airfield (Fuchida in O'Connor (ed) 1969, p. 22).

15 No fighters were able to take to the air until 35 minutes after the initial attack, when four P–40s and two P–36s took off from Wheeler Field. Only 25 fighter sorties were flown against the Japanese attacks.

16 The only total losses among the battleships were the *Arizona* and the *Oklahoma*. The *West Virginia*, *California* and *Nevada* were sunk or beached, but all three were repaired in time to take part in the later campaigns of the war. The *Tennessee* got under way on 20 December, and was then given a thorough overhaul and modernisation. The *Maryland* rejoined the fleet in February 1942, the *Pennsylvania* soon afterwards.

17 Toland 1970, p. 211.

18 Evidence of Kimmel's assistant war plans officer, Pearl Harbor Attack, part 26, p. 207.

CHAPTER 8

1 Churchill 1950, p. 772.

2 CAB 79/2, Public Records Office, Kew.

3 'It was decided to send as the first instalment of our Far Eastern Fleet both the *Prince of Wales* and the *Repulse*, with four destroyers, and as an essential element the modern armoured aircraft-carrier *Indomitable*. Unhappily, the *Indomitable* was temporarily disabled by an accident. It was decided in spite of this to let the two fast capital ships go forward, in the hope of steadying the Japanese political situation, and also to be in relation to the United States Pacific Fleet.' (Churchill 1950, p. 524; see also Marder 1981, p. 229, and Roskill 1960, p. 176.)

4 Phillips' appointment was initially as Deputy Chief of the Naval Staff, but the post was later renamed Vice Chief of the Naval Staff.

5   Admiral Sir Guy Grantham, letter to Arthur J. Marder, quoted in Marder 1981, p. 370.
6   Willis vol. 1, p. 31.
7   In the event, several hours after the attack on Pearl Harbor MacArthur's air force was virtually wiped out on the ground by Japanese aircraft, half his bombers and three-quarters of his fighters being destroyed in a 30 minute raid. This was far more culpable than anything that happened at Hawaii. There were eight investigations into the Pearl Harbor disaster, both Kimmel and Short were sacked, yet there was never an inquiry into MacArthur's bungling and he went on to Supreme Command.
8   Marder 1981, p. 402.
9   Ibid., p. 406.
10 This area is now Vietnam, and Saigon has been renamed Ho Chi Minh City.
11 Pearl Harbor was attacked at 2 a.m. (Singapore time) the following morning.
12 In addition to Churchill and the three Chiefs of Staff, those present were A.V. Alexander (the First Lord of the Admiralty), Admirals Moore and Harwood, and General Ismay from the Office of the Minister of Defence (CAB 79/55).
13 Churchill 1950, p. 547.
14 Some time earlier Phillips had detached the destroyer *Tenedos* to return independently to Singapore to refuel. The captain of *Repulse* had been asked if his ship could refuel the destroyer, but when Phillips was told that speed would have to be reduced to eight knots for this to be possible, he decided to detach the destroyer instead. *Tenedos* had been given a message to transmit by radio when well clear of the main body, but the message said nothing of Phillips' changed plan.
15 A Walrus amphibian aircraft from *Prince of Wales* had landed on Sembawang airfield on Singapore island at 11.30 a.m., but it does not seem that any message from her got through to Palliser. The Walrus had been catapulted soon after sunrise to search the Kuantan area (preserving radio silence), and then to fly on to Singapore if nothing was found.
16 A later report from *I-58*, that the British had altered course to 240 degrees—that is, towards Kuantan—was not received, and the Japanese command remained ignorant of this important piece of information.
17 According to the radar officer of *Prince of Wales*, that ship's air-warning radar had been shut down overnight because of a policy of radar silence, and was not switched on until the Japanese attacks developed (Howse 1993, p. 124).
18 Flight Lieutenant H.C. Plenty, quoted in Shores 1992, p. 120.
19 Roskill 1976, p. 558.
20 It must not be assumed that the Japanese had no problems. They did have serious defects in their logistic organisation, which became increasingly damaging as the war progressed. 'Supply plans for the invasion of Malaya demonstrated the limited capabilities of the Navy's service forces at the war's very outset, even before combat losses began their debilitating

erosion of the fleet train units; only major combatant vessels could
approach stores ships for replenishment, fresh water quantities were
limited, and the support fleet had to rely on minesweepers to transport
these minimal supplies' (Sadkovich 1990, p. 64).

21 Okumiya and Horikoshi 1958, p. 90.
22 See, for example the views of Admiral Sir Andrew Cunningham,
    Vice-Admiral Sir James Somerville and Admiral Sir Frederick Dreyer,
    quoted in Marder 1981, pp. 365–6.
23 Ismay 1960, p. 240.
24 Middlebrook and Mahoney, p. 181, quoting Lieutenant-Commander
    Harland, the Torpedo Officer of the *Prince of Wales*. Harland was not
    sure of the exact wording of Phillips' reply.
25 The only reasonable interpretation of the message sent by Palliser to
    Phillips about the unavailability of fighter support over Singora was that
    it was because the airfield at Kota Bharu had been captured or neutralised
    by the Japanese. It would have been absurd to have deduced from this
    message that fighter cover could not be provided over Kuantan.
26 Some have argued in favour of Phillips' handling of his force. An extreme
    (but not very convincing) example is given in Stephen 1991.

CHAPTER 9

1 It is interesting that Ciliax was apparently not aware of the possibility
   of being detected by British radar-fitted aircraft.
2 Roskill 1956, p. 151. The cruiser *Prinz Eugen*, having evaded pursuit
   after the sinking of the *Bismarck*, had joined the battleships in Brest.
3 This was not actually the first detection, for the German ships were
   detected at 10.14 a.m. by the Beachy Head RAF radar station, at a
   range of 40 miles, but the telephone line to Dover was dead and the
   report was delayed for more than half-an-hour.
4 It is interesting that the German jamming served to alert the British.
   Churchill attributes the failure to detect the German ships to this
   jamming, and states that 'our sea-watching radar was in fact useless'
   (Churchill 1951 p. 99). Watson-Watt makes it quite clear that the
   performance of the sea-watching radar was completely unaffected by the
   jamming, and that the German ships were detected as soon as they came
   within range (Watson-Watt 1957, p. 335 et seq.).
5 Beamish's actions were supported by the Board of Inquiry set up after
   the German escape, but Fighter Command soon changed its instructions
   on radio silence to permit the immediate reporting of sightings of
   warships of destroyer size or above, or convoys of more than twenty
   ships.
6 The remaining four squadrons of fighters, having missed Esmonde at
   the rendezvous, made for the reported position of the German ships.
   Two squadrons were engaged with German fighters during Esmonde's
   approach. The other two squadrons failed to make contact at all.
7 It was sent by morse code. The four Beauforts had recently been fitted

with voice-radio sets in place of their W/T (morse) sets, and consequently did not receive it.

8   Richards 1953 p. 372.
9   *The Times*, 14 February 1942.
10 Raeder 1960, p. 360.
11 Robertson 1958, p. 191.

CHAPTER 10

1   Churchill 1951, p.156.
2   *Formidable*: 12 Martlets, 21 Albacores and 1 Swordfish.
3   *Indomitable*: 12 Fulmars, 9 Sea Hurricanes and 24 Albacores.
    Hermes: 12 Swordfish.
4   In fact PPIs were not entirely suited to the Type 281 radar, because for a PPI to work well the radar aerial had to be in continuous power-rotation. The leads to the aerial of the Type 281 at this time were such that the aerial could not rotate more than 360 degrees, so with a PPI in use the aerial had to rotate 360 degrees one way, and then 360 degrees the other, resulting in an inferior picture on the PPI.
5   The first height-finding radar (Type 277), was not available for ship-fitting until 1944. The Type 277, originally intended as a surface-warning set, had a wavelength of 10cm and had a focussed beam like a searchlight. By simultaneously measuring the elevation and range of a target it could accurately assess its height, but it was not a success in this role, for its reliable detection range of 25–30 miles was insufficient for fighter direction. Besides, its rotation had to be stopped while it was measuring the height of a target, and such loss of warning coverage was rarely acceptable to the Command.
6   Roskill 1977, p. 203.
7   The code-breakers could rarely give complete information, either because some messages were not intercepted, or complete decryption was not possible, and in any case there was frequently a delay of some days before a decrypted text was available. (In May 1942 only about 60 per cent of Japanese naval high-frequency transmissions were being inter-cepted, and of these less than half were being analysed.) The information made available to Somerville on 28 March was that 'Operation CX [thought to be a carrier strike in the Bay of Bengal] to be carried out. Attack on shipping in vicinity of DC [wherever that was]'. On 31 March he was told that 'First Air Attack force scheduled 1 April against ships as primary objectives. Time and area unknown but believed Bengal Bay'. On 1 April he was told that 'Unknown callsign using highest priority requests weather Indian Ocean Coastal regions. Believe all this adds up to launching air offensive Bay of Bengal region today 1 April' (Winton 1993, p. 25). Of course code-breaking was not the only form of radio intelligence. Much information was gained by traffic analysis—watching the volume of traffic, the callsigns and procedures used; occasionally information was gained by the peculiarities of particular transmitters or operators; and direction finding of radio and radar transmissions was

important. All were used, and could often be used to confirm each other, but code-breaking was easily the most dramatic. Information gained from code-breaking, traffic analysis and captured enemy documents was given the codename 'Ultra'.

8 These ships had been designed for service in the North Sea. In the tropics they ran out of fresh water after about four days of operations. Although water for the crews could be (and was) rationed, there remained the problem of feed-water for the boilers.

9 Fuchida and Okumiya 1955, pp. 41–2, and Shores 1993, p. 396.

10 Roskill 1956, p. 28. It was a pity that Somerville was not given the discretion earlier, when Churchill first raised the issue.

11 Grenfell 1951, p. 172.

12 Account by Captain Crockett, Royal Marines, the gunnery officer of *Hermes* (Richards and Saunders 1954, p. 55).

13 Although the Japanese had at one time contemplated asking the French for bases in Madagascar they had long since dropped this project. By the end of March they had definitely abandoned the idea of a sustained Indian Ocean offensive in favour of operations to isolate Australia and capture Midway.

14 Willis vol. II, p. 8.

15 Letter from Sir James Somerville to the Admiralty, 17 April 1942.

16 Quoted in Tomlinson 1976, p. 103.

CHAPTER 11

1 Fuchida and Okumiya 1955, p. 60.

2 The B–25s of course could not land back on the *Hornet* so they were instructed to land on friendly airfields in China, 1200 miles from Tokyo. Only four aircraft managed to crash-land in China, one landed at Vladivostok where the crew was interned by the Russians, but most of the crews of the other aircraft survived by baling out; none were shot down over Japan.

3 The SC was an attempt to produce a new radar without the bulk of the CXAM aerial, but the detection range fell dramatically to no more than 30 miles on a bomber at 10 000 feet. Such poor performance was very unpopular with seagoing personnel, so in January 1942 a new version, the SC-1, appeared, with twice the power and approximately twice the detection range, and all SCs were soon converted. Later versions had enlarged aerials and more power.

4 The PPI (plan position indicator) is essentially a radar-made map, the radar concerned being at the centre. Echoes are shown as bright spots, and have afterglow so that they remain visible until the aerial makes another sweep. The operator can see the range and bearing of all echoes, and their relative positions, but there is no indication of altitude. PPIs were developed, apparently independently, in Britain and America at much the same time. In the case of the US Navy, the PPI was developed in 1939–40, the first model going to sea in April 1941. For a PPI to be efficient, the width of the beam of the radar set must be reasonably

narrow and the aerial must rotate continuously. Both of these requirements caused problems for the Royal Navy with its air-warning sets.

5 A factor in Fletcher's decision might have been the difficulty of
manoeuvring the two Australian cruisers in an American formation.
Although the Australian ships were using American signal codes, they
were not fitted with the American voice-radios (called TBS) used for
tactical manoeuvring, so any manoeuvring signals would have to be
separately transmitted to them by flag hoist or by light.

6 Nor was the cruiser force damaged (except in its feelings) by a
subsequent high-level attack by three US Army Air Force B–17s, an
attack which was considerably less accurate than the Japanese high-level
bombing.

7 It is interesting to compare the consequences of bomb hits on the flight
decks of carriers with and without deck-armour. The small hole in the
flight deck of the *Yorktown* was easily repaired, and her ability to operate
aircraft was not interrupted, whereas bomb hits on the British armoured-
deck carriers had forced the cessation of flying activities in each case.
Armoured flight decks were not without supporters in the US Navy, and
the *Midway* class, ordered in 1942, had a 3-inch armoured flight-deck
and armoured lifts, as well as 2-inch armour on the hangar deck. The
primary purpose was, however, to make the flight deck the integral
strength member. In previous US carriers the hangar deck had been the
strength member, with the flight deck as a superstructure, but as the
ships became longer and longer this ceased to be practicable. The *Midway*
class did not have the anti-gunfire side-armour of the British carriers,
so could have large open hangars and deck-edge lifts. These carriers
were of 45 000 tons with a flight deck 986 feet long and could carry
137 contemporary aircraft.

CHAPTER 12

1 After the loss of *Lexington* Nimitz had only three carriers, for *Saratoga*
had been torpedoed on 11 January by the submarine *I–6* near Pearl
Harbor and was undergoing repairs in America. She was substantially
modified while in the shipyard, her four twin 8-inch turrets and twelve
obsolete single 5-inch mountings being removed and replaced with sixteen
modern 5-inch guns in four twin and eight single turrets, with up-to-date
fire control and gunnery radar. She also received four additional twin
1.1-inch mountings and the 0.50-inch machine guns were replaced by
20mm Oerlikons, and her radar outfit was strengthened by a surface-
warning radar and a second air-search radar.

2 The assessments of the personalities of Spruance and Halsey are taken
largely from Potter 1969.

3 Although the code-breakers on Hawaii and Washington had penetrated
the Japanese ciphers, there was still room for confusion about the
designators used in the messages to describe geographical places. The
designator 'AF' frequently appeared as the target for the operation;
Nimitz's code-breaking staff thought it meant Midway, but the code-

breakers in Washington felt it might be Hawaii or even the West Coast of America. Nimitz's staff managed to resolve the issue by sending a message by cable to Midway telling the garrison commander to make an emergency radio report, in plain English, that his water-distillation plant had broken down. Within a day the Japanese were being told by radio that 'AF' was running short of water and that the invasion force should take extra supplies. The story that the code-breakers provided Nimitz with a detailed order of battle for the Japanese is apparently completely false (Layton 1975, p. 125). The part played by traffic analysis in deducing Japanese dispositions should not be underestimated.

4 Morison 1948, p. 84.
5 Throughout the account of this battle, west longitude dates and zone plus 12 time are used.
6 Commander Fuchida, who normally led such strikes, had appendicitis.
7 Morison 1948, p. 103.
8 Fuchida and Okumiya 1955, p. 143.
9 The two battleships in the Aleutians Protection Force—the *Ise* and *Hyuga*—had Type 2 Mark 2 10cm radars fitted two days before they sortied for the operation, but they took no part in the Midway action. These radars proved unsatisfactory in the air-warning role, and were modified to a 1.5m wavelength, but this version did not become available until August 1943.

   The Japanese used a complicated system of designating their radars. The 'type' was based on the year the set entered service, in terms of the Japanese Imperial calendar, by which 1940 was the year 2600 (usually rendered as 'zero'). Within a year, mark numbers indicated different sets. Different models of a set were indicated by a 'Mod' number, and finally changes within a Mod were identified by a 'Kai' number. Thus a set might be a Type 2 Mk.2 Mod 1–Kai 3. To add to the confusion, sets were often referred to by their mark/model numbers only—'21' for the Type 2 Mk.2 Mod 1, for instance (Friedman 1981a).
10 Fuchida and Okumiya 1955, p. 178.
11 Yamamoto, a former captain of *Akagi*, was very reluctant to give the scuttling order, but finally decided to do so, out of a fear that the Americans could capture the wreck and she 'would become a museum piece in the Potomac River'.
12 Office of Naval Intelligence 1947, p. 11.
13 Eleven new *Essex* class carriers of 27 200 tons displacement were on order before Pearl Harbor, and this number was increased after the US entered the war; seventeen of these ships were completed before Japan surrendered, but the first was not ready for operations until August 1943. *Essex* class ships were easily the most effective carriers to see service on either side, with ten of their number damaged (eight of them by Kamikaze attacks) but none sunk. They were designed to have a complement of 83 aircraft (27 fighters, 38 scout-bombers, 18 torpedo-bombers), plus 25 per cent spares, but in practice often operated more than 100 using a permanent deck park.

   In addition there was a new class of nine light carriers—the

Independence class—being built on the hulls of *Cleveland* class cruisers. Ordered in March 1942, these were fast enough to operate with the fleet but were only 10 600 tons and normally operated 24 fighters and nine torpedo-bombers. Then there were the escort carriers, which were first ordered in March 1941 and were beginning to pour from building yards. Before the end of the war, 77 of these ships were commissioned into the US Navy, and a further 38 supplied to the Royal Navy. Typically, the escort carriers had a speed of nineteen knots and could operate about 30 aircraft by using a permanent deck park.

14 The third of the giant *Yamato* class battleships, the 64 800 ton *Shinano*, was to be completed as a heavily-armoured aircraft carrier. The construction of the 29 300 ton *Taiho* was sped up, and five more of this class were ordered. *Taiho* was designed to operate 84 aircraft, but on commissioning she carried only 60, because the Judy dive-bombers with which she was equipped did not have folding wings. Fifteen more of the 17 300 ton *Hiryu* class were also ordered. Two large, fast merchant ships and a cruiser were ordered to be converted into carriers. An 11 200 ton seaplane carrier, *Chiyoda*, was already being converted into a 29 knot carrier capable of operating 30 aircraft, and would become available late in 1943; a similar ship, *Chitose*, would soon follow her. Two battleships, *Ise* and *Hyuga*, and the cruiser *Mogami* were to be converted into hybrid carriers, with a flight deck fitted in place of the after turrets.

15 An almost undamaged Zeke had been recovered in the Aleutians, and experiments with this aircraft and the experience of the pilots who had flown Wildcats against the Zekes resulted in a more powerful engine being fitted in the second Hellcat prototype.

16 The B–17s claimed hits on two battleships or cruisers and two transports in the Midway Occupation Force on 3 June, three hits on two carriers in Nagumo's Carrier Striking Force early on 4 June and two hits on a 'smoking carrier' later the same day.

CHAPTER 13

1 All but one of the Spitfires reached Malta. That one developed a defect and landed on *Indomitable*. Despite the Spitfire having no arrester-hook and the pilot having no deck-landing experience, the aircraft was only slightly damaged.

2 Syfret 1942, (Report of the Rear-Admiral, Home Fleet Aircraft Carriers, part II, para. 6).

3 The Italians had been supplied with some Ju.87 dive-bombers by the Germans, and some of the 'Stuka' attacks were carried out by the Italians, though at the time the British ships assumed that all such attacks were by the Luftwaffe.

4 Syfret 1942 (Report from Commanding Officer, H.M.S. *Victorious*, Appendix 1, p. 3). It had intended that the Reggianes should each carry a 630kg armour-piercing bomb (a converted shell), but the plan was changed because of last minute faults.

5   Because the convoy was behind schedule, the Spitfires initially operated at a range of 170 miles from Malta, instead of 120 miles as had originally been planned.

6   The RAF in Malta had prepared a force of fifteen Beauforts and fifteen escorting Beaufighters to attack the Italian ships in daylight on 15 August, if the Italian ships attempted to intercept the convoy. The force available for a night strike was no more than two Albacores and one hastily-repaired Wellington. During the night three Wellingtons shadowed the Italian force, dropping flares, carrying out bombing attacks, and transmitting spurious calls for Liberators to join them, although in fact no Liberators were available.

7   The Germans and Italians lost a total of 36 aircraft in the whole three days of intense fighting. The German Air Force carried out eighteen raids on the convoy, the Italian Air Force eleven.

8   Syfret 1942, p. 3. The Hurricane was the fighter with the highest prestige, but even in its RAF version it was regarded as obsolescent. The carrier-based version, the Sea Hurricane 1B, which was fitted with catapult spools and arrester-hook, was 25 knots slower.

9   Four Liberators were temporarily flown in from Egypt to attack an Italian airfield in Sardinia, but only two found the airfield and they did not achieve anything; all four then returned to Egypt. Nine Beaufighters from Malta carried out bombing attacks on Sardinian airfields, destroying six aircraft on the ground and damaging a further nineteen with bullets and splinters. The RAF also provided reconnaissance and anti-submarine patrols, with Hudsons and Sunderland flying boats, but there were protests from the British carriers that the IFF (the radar-identification system) of the RAF aircraft was not properly calibrated and this caused much wasteful carrier-fighter effort to intercept and identify them.

10 Two oil tankers had been used in the June convoys to Malta from Alexandria and Gibraltar. Admiral Syfret wrote, in his report to the Admiralty on Operation Pedestal, about 'the extreme efficiency shown by [the oilers] *Dingledale* and *Brown Ranger*. In previous similar operations it has not been necessary to provide for so large an oiling program since ships going to Malta have been able to fuel there. In this case Malta had no oil to spare. The problem of oiling 3 cruisers and 26 destroyers at sea, under enemy observation and in U-boat infested waters was an anxious one, failure of which could have seriously upset the whole plan'. (Syfret 1942, p. 3) There were nevertheless still problems with the fuelling technique. The oiler *Abbeydale* broke seven hoses (the old-style metal ones) during the day, and *Indomitable* found it impossible to fuel from her during the night.

11 *Indefatigable* had been laid down in November 1939 and *Implacable* in February 1940. They were enlarged versions of the *Illustrious* class, with a full length lower hangar, and four propellers instead of the three in the earlier ships. As in *Indomitable* the height of the hangars had to be reduced to fourteen feet to compensate for the added weight. Both ships suffered many delays because Churchill, as First Lord of the Admiralty, had ordered in September 1939 that the Admiralty was 'not to worry

about vessels that cannot come into service until 1942'. The restrictions were gradually relaxed, but the ships did not commission until May and August 1944 respectively.

12 Syfret 1942 (Report by the Rear-Admiral, Home Fleet Aircraft Carriers, part II, para. 19).

13 The Type 281B (the single-mast version) was capable of continuous rotation, which greatly improved the picture on its PPIs. The Type 281 was better than the Type 79 for low and medium cover, but it gave cover only to an altitude of about 28 000 feet compared to 40 000 feet for the Type 79. The Type 79 had too wide a beam to be used with a PPI.

CHAPTER 14

1 In April 1942 the Pacific had been divided into two commands: the South-West Pacific Area under General MacArthur, and the Pacific Area under Admiral Nimitz. The South Pacific Commander was a subordinate of Nimitz.

2 Ghormley was indignant about the way Fletcher had handled the carrier group, claiming that it had remained too long in an area where Japanese submarines were suspected. The charge was furiously disputed, but Fletcher was never given another carrier command.

3 The US Navy had doubts about the surviveability of the *Wasp*, which had been built to the *Ranger* design in order to keep within Treaty limits. She was a carrier of only 13 800 tons, capable of high speed and intended to operate 72 aircraft, but in order to achieve these characteristics was very lightly constructed. In the early months of the war she had been employed in the Atlantic, and did a number of aircraft-ferrying trips in the Mediterranean. She had been called to the Pacific when the carrier shortage there became acute.

4 Morison 1951, p. 189.

5 The complements of aircraft were:
Enterprise: 34 F4F Wildcat, 36 SBD Dauntless, and 13 TBF Avenger;
Hornet: 36 F4F Wildcat, 36 SBD Dauntless and 16 TBF Avenger;
Junyo: 24 Zekes, 21 Vals and 10 Kates;
Shokaku: 18 Zekes, 20 Vals and 23 Kates;
Zuiho: 18 Zekes and 6 Kates;
Zuikaku: 27 Zekes, 27 Vals and 18 Kates.

6 The radar set was the Type 2 Mk 2, operating with a low-output magnetron on a 10cm wavelength. Accuracy was about one mile, resolution one mile and twenty degrees. It was fitted with a rotating aerial in the carriers, but in other ships it sometimes had fixed horn-aerials on either side of the bridge structure.

7 Halsey had taken the experienced fighter-direction officer in the *Enterprise* with him as a member of his staff.

8 The forces involved were:

Class	Japanese	Americans
Aircraft Carriers	4	2
Battleships	4	2
Cruisers	10	9
Destroyers	29	20

9 IFF (Identification Friend or Foe) was a transponder fitted in aircraft. It was activated by reception of a radar transmission, and modified the echo received by the radar set. The IFF sets fitted at this time were far from perfect, but properly used they should have reduced the confusion between the Japanese aircraft and the returning American strikes.

10 *Zuiho* was hit by two 500-pound bombs, *Shokaku* by five or six 1000-pound bombs, and *Enterprise* by two 1000-pound bombs.

CHAPTER 15

1 A key element in this poor performance was the air force's high-level bombing technique, which depended on the use of large numbers of aircraft in a compact formation. A contemporary estimate was that a formation of at least eighteen to twenty bombers would be required to give a reasonable chance of scoring a hit on a manoeuvring ship, even if the bombs were dropped from as low as 10 000 feet. Eighteen to twenty bombers! At this time the Americans considered themselves lucky if they could muster as many as half-a-dozen for a single mission.

2 Inevitably there were occasional penalties, such as when the destroyer *Mutsuki* was rescuing survivors from a transport which had been set on fire by Marine Dauntless dive-bombers. When a formation of eight B–17s approached, the captain of the destroyer ignored them and paid for his temerity when three direct hits sank his ship, though as he was rescued he admitted that 'even the B–17s could make a hit once in a while' (Morison 1959, p. 105). He could consider himself unlucky, for his was the first Japanese warship to be sunk by level-bombing since the war began.

3 Horner 1982, p. 208.

4 The US aircraft available to participate in the convoy attack (not including reconnaissance aircraft) were 35 P–38 and 43 P–40 fighters; 28 B–25 medium bombers; fifteen A–20 light bombers; and 28 B–17 and nine B–24 heavy bombers. From the RAAF there were seventeen P–40 fighters, thirteen Beaufighters, six Boston light bombers and thirteen Beaufort torpedo-bombers. The total strength available was 207 aircraft.

5 Although pre-war studies had shown that hundreds of escorts were necessary to protect Japan's vital trade routes against submarine attack, only four escorts were built in the decade before Pearl Harbor, and only two more in the first eighteen months of the war. At the time of the Bismarck Sea battle there were only three anti-submarine escorts in the whole East Indies area, and it is not surprising that US submarines, once they had overcome the early problems with their torpedoes, created mayhem.

6 The scatter of bombs dropped from a low level is much greater along than across the direction of flight.

7 To balance the many charges of war crimes laid against the Japanese, this should be compared with the exemplary behaviour of the Japanese pilots to the survivors of the *Prince of Wales* and *Repulse*, the *Dorsetshire* and *Cornwall*, and the *Hermes*.

8 General MacArthur's press release of 4 March claimed that the Allied Air Forces had destroyed 22 Japanese ships (fourteen transports and eight destroyers) and killed 15 000 troops. The gross exaggerations in the claims caused some bitter disputes, and General MacArthur went so far as to suggest that disciplinary action might be taken against anyone disputing the claims made in the communique.

9 Okumiya and Horikoshi 1956, p. 238.

10 The 75 mm gun was not the largest to be fitted in an aircraft. In early 1943 the Italians fitted a 102 mm gun in a Piaggio twin-engined bomber, but Italy surrendered before the preliminary trials were completed.

CHAPTER 16

1 The merchant ships, renamed *Shinyo* and *Kaiyo*, carried only 24 aircraft each and could not make more than 22 knots. While the converted seaplane carriers, *Chitose* and *Choyoda*, had the speed (29 knots) to operate with the fleet they were of only 11 190 tons, although they could carry 30 aircraft each.

2 The Sam fighter was both faster and more manoeuvrable than the American Hellcat, but its development was delayed by difficulties with the engine and chaotic production arrangements; the prototype did not fly until May 1944 and it was clear that many months must elapse before the type came into service.

3 Only two of these sets—the Type 2 Mark 2, and the Type 3 Mark 1—were useful against aircraft, with the latter being slightly more effective. Introduced into service in February 1944, the Type 3 set had a wavelength of 2 metres and could detect high-flying aircraft out to about 50 miles; it also had a rough height-finding capability from the range of initial detection. The problem of the performance of the radars was compounded by the fact that they were unreliable, being highly susceptible to the effects of vibration and gunfire.

4 The SK was first installed in January 1943, and 250 were fitted before production was completed in April 1944. The SK could detect a medium bomber flying at 10 000 feet at a range of 100 miles.

5 The SM began to be fitted in September 1943. It was heavy, with the aerial weighing 4400 pounds. A lightweight successor, the SP, began to be fitted in battleships, cruisers and even destroyers towards the end of 1944. Its overall performance exceeded that of the SM, though it was not as accurate in height-finding.

6 Morison 1959, p. 129.

7 As one experienced flying-instructor put it: 'Men who could never have even dreamed of getting near a fighter plane before the war were now

362

thrown into battle . . . We were told to rush the men through, to forget the fine points, just to teach them how to fly and shoot . . . It was a hopeless task. Our facilities were too meagre, the demand too great, the students too many' (Sakai 1957, p. 269).

8 Price 1977, p. 142. The Japanese were in fact the first nation to use 'window'. They had developed 'Giman-shi' (deceiving paper), made from the metal screening cut off electric cables, backed with paper tape. It was cut to a length of 75cm—half the wavelength of the American gunnery radar sets—and from May 1943 was used with some success in the later stages of the Solomons campaign.

In Europe both the RAF and the Luftwaffe were aware of the potential of such a technique, but were reluctant to use it for offensive missions for fear that the other side would find out what was going on and develop their own 'window' for use against them, wrecking their fighter-defence system. It was not until July 1943 that Bomber Command started to use 'window' in its raids on Germany, with spectacular success. In the Pacific, Japanese radar was at this time not sufficiently developed for it to be worthwhile for the Americans to attempt to confuse it.

9 *Zuiho* was a converted submarine support ship and, like *Chitose* and *Chiyoda*, displaced about 11 000 tons and had a speed of about 28 knots. It also could carry 24–30 aircraft.

10 Task Force 58 had 24 F6F and three F4U night-fighters, and 37 TBF Avengers equipped with radar. The night fighters carried the A1A radar equipment which covered a 120-degree arc ahead of the aircraft, but as they were single-seaters there was a problem operating the radar. The Avengers had the ASB radar which was supposed to detect a ship at about 32 miles.

11 Quoted in Dickson 1975, p. 171. The use of such assessments was even more dramatically shown in the Japanese plan for the battle of Leyte Gulf, when Halsey was the principal American commander.

12 It will be remembered that Admiral Phillips in *Prince of Wales* had detached the destroyer *Tenedos* to return to Singapore while he headed northwards. *Tenedos* was given a message to transmit when she was well clear of Phillips' other ships. If detected by the Japanese (it was not), the radio transmission could have misled them.

13 See Morison 1953 pp. 319–20 for a detailed calculation. To this figure must be added about 50 Guam-based aircraft lost on the same day.

14 The early performance of the Mark 13 torpedo had been very poor, but the fitting of a plywood cylinder to the head of the torpedo stabilised it while it was airborne, and a shroud structure over the tail blades cured the problems with the underwater running. Torpedoes were authorised to be dropped at heights of up to 800 feet and at speeds of up to 300 knots. These improved Mark 13 torpedoes were widely available by mid-1944.

15 Ramage 1982, p. 6.

16 CINCPAC Summary of Action, June 1944.

CHAPTER 17

1   *Amagi* was a 17 460 ton carrier of a modified *Hiryu* design. After Midway fifteen of this class were ordered, but only six were ever laid down and only three of these were completed.

2   *Ise* and *Hyuga* were converted battleships, modified by the removal of their after 14-inch turrets and the erection of a small flight deck, which was really only a catapult deck and a parking area for aircraft. Both ships first put to sea in their new role in December 1943, but because of the shortage of trained aircrew they never actually carried any aircraft.

3   The armament of the 64 170 ton *Yamato* is a good example. On commissioning in 1941 her anti-aircraft defences comprised twelve 5-inch guns in six twin turrets and twenty-four 25mm weapons. In June 1944 two triple 6.1-inch turrets were removed and replaced with six more twin 5-inch turrets, and the number of 25mm guns increased to 152.

4   This was one of four SHO-GO plans for 'general decisive battle'. SHO–1 was for the Philippines; SHO–2 for Formosa-Ryukus; SHO–3 for Honshu-Kyushu; SHO–4 for Hokkaido-Kuriles.

5   Morison 1958, p. 57. Kurita had actually been sighted two days earlier off northern Borneo by one of the electronic-warfare Catalina flying boats, but the report was not passed on by its seaplane tender because the Japanese force had not been sighted by other aircraft searching in the general area!

6   All he could provide was two radar-equipped flying boats, which could operate only by night because of the threat of American carrier fighters. They searched to the eastwards to a depth of 450 miles.

7   As an example of the tendency of aircrews to exaggerate the number of hits—'creative vision', it was sometimes called—the American aircrews claimed nineteen torpedo hits on the *Musashi* whereas the actual number was eleven.

8   Morison 1958, pp. 187 and 189.

9   Halsey's *Action Report*, p. 4.

10 Operation Plan 8–44 of 27 September 1944, section 3x, quoted in Morison 1958, p. 58.

11 Quoted Morison 1958, p. 280.

12 Ohnishi was not the first to propose suicide attacks. In July 1943 Rear-Admiral Kuroshima had asked for the approval of volunteer suicide attacks by aircraft, but at this time the navy and army high commands refused to adopt such a drastic solution. In March 1944 Prime Minister Tojo ordered the army to make preparations for special suicide missions, and the first officially-planned suicide attack by an aircraft occurred in May 1944. In July the army ordered a study to be made of specially-designed suicide aircraft.

13 Prange 1990, p. 135.

14 Halsey and Bryan 1947, p. 219.

15 Actually the last three words were not part of Nimitz's message but padding put in to confuse possible Japanese code-breakers; but they were left in the copy shown to Halsey, and caused him considerable upset.

16 Field 1947, pp. 230–1.
17 Quoted in Morison 1958, p. 187.

CHAPTER 18

1 Brassey's 1948, p. 256.
2 Churchill 1951, p. 98.
3 A later attack with heavier mines might have been successful, but the Germans, now forewarned, took the obvious precautions to prevent the success of such an attack.
4 Dönitz to Hitler. See Woodward 1953 p. 185.
5 One of the 1600-pound bombs struck the heavily-armoured roof of a turret and exploded harmlessly, while the other somehow penetrated though the main armoured-deck and came to rest near the main electrical switchboard and gunnery control rooms—without exploding.

CHAPTER 19

1 The US was developing a similar weapon, although it was to be guided by radar rather than a human pilot. The Americans had entered the field in the search for an anti-submarine weapon. The preference for the guidance system was for radar rather than television, because of the problems of television in poor visibility. Three radar options were looked at—homing on enemy radar, guidance from a radar-fitted aircraft, or self-contained radar. All were pursued, although the American authorities favoured the last. The only such weapon to see service in the Second World War was the Bat, a glider with a 10-foot wingspan, a load of 1000 pounds of explosives, and self-contained radar. Once the Bat's radar had locked on to the target, the glider homed automatically and the parent aircraft was free to take any necessary evasive action. In early 1945 a squadron of Privateers was equipped with the Bats, the aircraft carrying one under each wing. By the time they were ready for service Japanese shipping had almost disappeared, but they sank one Japanese destroyer and several small merchant ships. Japanese fighter power had by this time been virtually eliminated, so the Bats did not have to face the problem of their parent aircraft being shot down before release. This would have been an even bigger problem for the Bats than it was for the Japanese Okas, for the Bat had no rocket power and had to be released even closer to the target than did the Oka.
2 Picket destroyers were first used in 1943. The picket destroyers had improved VHF radios to communicate with fighters and a specialist fighter-direction officer, and by 1945 most destroyer divisions had one fighter-direction picket among its members. These pickets had limitations, because they had no height-finding radar and their aircraft-warning radar was not the best available. In December 1944 twelve destroyers (later increased to 24) were ordered to be more extensively converted for picket duty, by removing the two sets of torpedo tubes and fitting a tripod mast with an SP height-finding radar. (With the virtual elimination of

the Japanese surface fleet, surface-ship torpedoes were no longer a high priority.) The conversions took 6–9 weeks. The British Task Force also used picket destroyers, though its destroyers were not nearly as suitable in fighter-direction and anti-aircraft gunfire capabilities.

To show the value of the picket destroyers, the following figures (Vian 1960, p. 201) from the attacks on the fleet during July and August 1945 are illuminating:
Carrier-directed interceptions (US carriers 12, British 5)   17
Undirected visual sightings by combat air patrols 5
Picket-directed interceptions 26

3 Looking for an even heavier weapon, the Americans converted the 3-inch anti-aircraft gun (a hand-loaded gun fitted in small naval vessels and merchantmen) into an automatic weapon, capable of a rate of fire of 50 rounds a minute. Two of these guns were fitted on a quadruple Bofors mounting, and a single gun on a twin Bofors mounting, but the war ended before they were ready for ship-fitting.

4 The Seafires did have a history of deck-landing problems. For instance 106 Seafire LIICs were employed in support of the invasion of Italy at Salerno in 1943. During the three-and-a-half days of operations by the escort carriers, two German aircraft were shot down by the Seafires without loss, but 42 Seafires were either damaged beyond repair or destroyed in deck-landing accidents.

5 Fraser 1945, p. 4.

6 The logistic support arrangements for Spruance's fleet were awesome. The monthly consumption of oil was 750 000 tons, which had to be met by commercial tankers bringing oil from the American West Coast to the advanced base at Ulithi. From there a shuttle service of 40 fleet-tankers brought the oil to the operating area off the Ryukus. Four converted escort carriers brought replacement aircraft from Guam and Ulithi to the carriers in the operating areas, while seventeen more escort carriers shuttled aircraft between the West Coast and the forward bases. Provisioning at sea had long been provided, but replenishment of ammunition at sea had first been seriously attempted during the Iwo Jima campaign, and by the Okinawa campaign had become standard. The result of all this support was that the fighting ships could remain in the operational area for unprecedented periods.

7 Vian 1960, p. 175.

8 Fraser 1945, p. 4.

9 Naval Staff History 1950, p. 107.

10 Inoguchi and Nakajima 1959, p. 148.

11 Yokoi 1954, p. 511. Rear-Admiral Yokoi was Chief of Staff to the Fifth Air Fleet during the Okinawa campaign.

12 One American carrier reported that 'the enemy used window extensively throughout this operation. In the case of night raids, window was detected immediately and at no time did it conceal the bogey's movements . . . A good deal of window was dropped during the day raids . . . [but] once a raid was located and a track established, it was not difficult to

maintain the track and spot the window drops' (USS. *Independence* CVL 22, Action Report, 14 March–11 May).

13 *Enterprise* and *Bunker Hill* (US) and *Formidable* (British) were each hit on two occasions.

14 There was an immense disparity between the two fast carrier task forces in the number of Japanese aircraft destroyed during the campaign. Task Force 58 (the fifteen US fast carriers) was credited with 1908 and Task Force 57 (the four British carriers) with 75. The difference was largely caused by the much heavier Japanese attacks flung against the US carriers (Naval Staff History 1959, pp. 202–3).

CHAPTER 20

1 The Australian Navy arranged to purchase the 'through-deck cruiser' *Invincible* when the third of that class was commissioned in the Royal Navy, and paid off its carrier HMAS *Melbourne* in preparation. The Falklands War broke out before the ship was delivered, and following its success in that war an agreement was reached that the sale of HMS *Invincible* should be cancelled. The Australian Navy was offered the older carrier *Hermes* as a substitute, but in March 1983 the newly-elected Labor government decided not to accept the offer. The *Melbourne* was never re-commissioned.

2 **Aircraft carriers sunk during the Second World War**

	Britain	USA	Japan
Total number of carriers	79	110	25
Number destroyed by:			
submarine	5	3	9
surface gunfire	1	1	–
carrier attack	1	2	12
Kamikaze	–	3	–
shore-based bombing attack	–	1	–
shore-based torpedo attack	–	1	–
accidental explosion	1	–	–

Note: 'aircraft carrier' is taken to include all ships capable of launching and landing-on fixed-wing aircraft, i.e. including ships such as escort carriers and MAC ships. Ships with catapults but without deck-landing facilities—CAM ships, seaplane carriers, battleships and cruisers, and the two Japanese carrier-battleships—are excluded. Some damaged and abandoned carriers were sunk by surface ships; these are shown under the heading of the method of attack which caused them to be abandoned.

3 In the final attack, the fate of the Exocet is unclear. It certainly did not hit anything. It was probably decoyed, but may have been destroyed by a Sea Dart missile fired by HMS *Exeter*. The story that it was hit by a 4.5 inch shell is very unlikely.

4 There were originally four battleships of the *Iowa* class, of 57 353 tons full load and with a main armament of nine 16-inch guns. The *Iowa* and *New Jersey* were placed in 'mothballs' in October 1990 and February 1991.

Bibliography

GENERAL

Agawa, Hiroyuki 1979, *The Reluctant Admiral*, Kodansha International, Tokyo

Air Ministry 1948, *The Rise and Fall of the German Air Force (1933 to 1945)*, Air Ministry Pamphlet, London

Andrew, C. 1985, *Secret Service*, Heinemann, London

Apps, Michael 1971, *Send her Victorious*, William Kimber, London

Association for Publication of a History of Naval Gunnery 1975, *Kaigun Hojutsu Shi*, Tokyo

Auphen, Paul and Mordal, Paul 1957, *The French Navy in the Second World War*, (translated by Sabolot, A.C.T.), Naval Institute Press, Annapolis, Maryland

Barker, Edward L. 1950, 'German Naval Aviation', *United States Naval Institute Proceedings*, vol. 76, no. 7, July 1950

——1954, 'War Without Aircraft Carriers', *United States Naval Institute Proceedings*, vol. 80, no. 3, March 1954

Barnett, Correlli 1991, *Engage The Enemy More Closely*, W.W. Norton, London

Bassett, Ronald 1988, *HMS Sheffield*, Arms and Armour Press, London

Beaver, Paul 1982, *The British Aircraft Carrier*, Patrick Stevens, Wellingborough

Belote, James H. and Belote, William M. 1975, *Titans of the Seas*, Harper & Rowe, New York

Birkenhead, Frederick 1961, *The Prof. in Two Worlds*, Collins, London

Bogan, G.F. 1986, *Reminiscences of Vice-Admiral G.F. Bogan*, US Naval Institute, Annapolis

Bragadin, Marc' Antonio 1957, *The Italian Navy in World War 2*, Naval Institute Press, Annapolis

Brassey's 1948, *Naval Annual*, William Clones, London

Brown, David 1974, *Carrier Operations of World War II* (two volumes), Ian Allan, London
——1977, *Aircraft Carriers*, Alco Publishing, New York
Brown, Eric 1961, *Wings on my Sleeve*, Anchor Press, Tiptree
——1987, *Wings for the Navy*, Airlife, Shrewsbury
——1988, *Duels in the Sky: World War 2 Naval Aircraft in Combat*, Naval Institute Press, Annapolis
Buell, Thomas B. 1974, *The Quiet Warrior: A Biography of Admiral Raymond A. Spruance*, Little, Brown and Company, Boston
Burns, Russell (ed.) 1988, *Radar Development to 1945*, Peter Peregrinus, London
Chesneau, Roger 1984, *Aircraft Carriers*, Naval Institute Press, Annapolis
Churchill, Winston S. 1923, *The World Crisis 1911–1914*, Thornton Butterworth, London.
——1948, *The Second World War: Vol. 1: The Gathering Storm*, Cassell, London
——1949, *The Second World War: Vol. 2: Their Finest Hour*, Cassell, London
——1950, *The Second World War: Vol. 3: The Grand Alliance*, Cassell, London
——1951, *The Second World War: Vol. 4: The Hinge of Fate*, Cassell, London
——1952, *The Second World War: Vol. 5: Closing the Ring*, Cassell, London
——1954, *The Second World War: Vol. 6: Triumph and Tragedy*, Cassell, London
Clark, Ronald 1965, *Tizard*, Methuen, London
Colitta, Paolo E. 1987, *Patrick N.L. Bellinger and U.S. Naval Aviation*, University Press of America, Lanham
Costello, John 1981, *The Pacific War*, Collins, London
Cunningham, Andrew 1951, *A Sailor's Odyssey*, Hutchinson, London
D'Albas, Andrieu 1957, *Death of a Navy*, Robert Hale, London
Davies, Richard Bell 1967, *Sailor in the Air*, Peter Davies, London
Douglas-Hamilton, James 1981, *The Air Battle for Malta*, Mainstream Publishing, Edinburgh
Drea, Edward J. 1992, *MacArthur's Ultra*, University Press of Kansas
Dull, Paul S. 1978, *A Battle History of the Imperial Japanese Navy 1941–1945*, Naval Institute Press, Annapolis
Friedman, Norman 1981a, *Naval Radar*, Conway Maritime Press, London
——1981b, *Carrier Air Power*, Conway Maritime Press, Greenwich, England
——1983, *U.S. Aircraft Carriers: An Illustrated Design History*, Naval Institute Press, Annapolis
——1985, *U.S. Cruisers*, Arms and Armour, London
——1986, *U.S. Battleships*, Arms and Armour, London
——1988, *British Carrier Aviation: The Evolution of the Ships and their Aircraft*, Naval Institute Press, Annapolis
Fuchida, Mitsuo and Okumiya, Masatake 1955, *Midway: The Battle that Doomed Japan*, Naval Institute Press, Annapolis
Genda, Minoru 1969, *Tactical Planning in the Imperial Japanese Navy*, Naval War College Review, October 1969
Gray, Edwyn 1990, *Operation Pacific*, Leo Cooper, London
Grove, Eric J. 1987, *Vanguard to Trident*, Naval Institute Press, Annapolis

Halsey, William F. and Bryan, J. 1947, *Admiral Halsey's Story*, McGraw-Hill

Hata, Ikuhito and Izawa, Yasuho 1989, *Japanese Naval Aces and Fighter Units in World War 2*, (translated by Gorham, Don Cyril), Naval Institute Press, Annapolis

Hezlet, Arthur 1975, *The Electron and Sea Power*, Peter Davies, London

Hinsley, F.H. and Stripp, A. 1993, *Code Breakers. The Inside Story of Bletchley Park*, Oxford University Press

Hodges, Peter and Friedman, Norman 1979, *Destroyer Weapons of World War 2*, Conway Maritime Press, London

Howarth, Stephen 1983, *The Fighting Ships of the Rising Sun*, Athaneum, New York

Howse, Derek 1993, *Radar at Sea*, Macmillan, Basingstoke

Hurren, B.J. 1949, *Perchance. A Short History of British Naval Aviation*, Nicholson and Watson, London

Hurst, Mike 1993, *Airborne Early Warning*, Osprey Publishing, London

Inoguchi, Rikihei and Nakajima, Tadashi 1959, *The Divine Wind*, Hutchinson of London

Ito, Masanori 1962, *The End of the Imperial Japanese Navy*, W.W. Norton, New York

Jacobsen, Hans-Adolf and Rohnar, Jürgen 1965, *Decisive Battles of World War 2: The German View*, André Deutsch, London

Jameson, William 1957, *Ark Royal 1939–1941*, Rupert Hart-Davis, London

Jentschura, Hansgeorg, Jung, Dieter and Mickel, P. 1977, *Warships of the Imperial Japanese Navy, 1869–1945*, (translated by Preston, Anthony and Brown, J.D.), Naval Institute Press, Annapolis

Johnson, Brian 1981, *Fly Navy. The History of Naval Aviation*, William Morrow, New York

Jones, R.V. 1978, *Most Secret War*, Hamish Hamilton, London

Kingsley, F.A. (ed.) 1995, *The Development of Radar Equipments for the Royal Navy, 1938–45*, Macmillan, London

——1995, *The Applications of Radar and other Electronic Systems in the Royal Navy in World War 2*, Macmillan, London

Lawson, Robert L. (ed.) 1985, *History of U.S. Naval Air Power*, Temple Press, Middlesex

Layton, Edwin T. 1975, *Reminiscences of Rear-Admiral Edwin T. Layton*, US Naval Institute, Annapolis

——1985, *And I Was There*, (with Pineau, Roger and Costello, John) William Morrow, New York

Lenton, H.T. 1975, *German Warships of the Second World War*, Macdonald and Jane's, London

Lewin, Ronald 1978, *Ultra Goes to War*, Hutchinson, London

Lundstrom, John B. 1984, *The First Team*, Naval Institute Press, Annapolis

Macintyre, Donald 1962, *Wings of Neptune*, Peter Davies, London

——1966, *The Battle for the Pacific*, Angus & Robertson, Sydney

Marder, Arthur J. 1981, *Old Friends, New Enemies: Vol.1: Strategic Illusion*, Clarendon Press, Oxford

Marder, Arthur J., Jacobsen, Mark and Horsfield, John 1990, *Old Friends,*

New Enemies: Vol. 2: The Pacific War 1942–1945, Clarendon Press, Oxford

Martienssen, Anthony 1948, *Hitler and his Admirals*, Secker and Warburg, London

Melhorn, Charles M. 1974, *Two-Block Fox. The Rise of the Aircraft Carrier, 1911—1929*, Naval Institute Press, Annapolis

Monserrat, John 1985, *Angel on the Yardarm*, Naval War College Press, Newport

Morison, Samuel Eliot 1948, *History of United States Naval Operations in World War II: Vol. IV: Coral Sea, Midway and Submarine Actions*, Little, Brown & Co., Boston

Musciano, Walter A. 1994, *Warbirds of the Sea*, Schiffer Military/Aviation History, Altglen, Pennsylvania

Naito, Hatsuho 1989, *Thunder Gods: The Kamikaze Pilots Tell Their Story*, Kodansha International, Tokyo

Naval Staff History 1954a, *The Development of British Naval Aviation, 1939–1945*, Admiralty, London

——1954b, *Defensive Phase*, vol. II, Admiralty, London

——1957, *War With Japan*, vol. IV, Admiralty, London

O'Connor, Raymond (ed.) 1969, *The Japanese Navy in World War II*, US Naval Institute, Annapolis

Office of the Chief of Naval Operations 1947, *US Naval Aviation in the Pacific*, United States Navy

Okumiya, M. and Horikoshi, J. 1956, *Zero*, E.P. Dutton, New York

——1958, *The Zero Fighter*, (with Caidin, Martin), Cassell, London

Polmar, Norman 1969, *Aircraft Carriers*, Macdonald, London

Poolman, Kenneth 1972, *Escort Carrier 1941—1945*, Ian Allen, London

Popham, Hugh 1969, *Into Wind*, Hamish Hamilton, London

Potter, E.B. and Nimitz, Chester W. (eds) 1960, *The Great Sea War*, Prentice Hall

Potter, John Deane 1965, *Admiral of the Pacific*, Heinemann, London

Prados, John 1995, *Combined Fleet Decoded*, Random House, New York

Prange, Gordon W. with Goldstein, Donald M. and Dillon, Katherine V. 1990, *God's Samurai: Lead Pilot at Pearl Harbor*, Brassey's (US), New York

Price, Alfred 1977, *Instruments of Darkness: The History of Electronic Warfare*, Macdonald and Jane's, London

——1984, *History of U.S. Electronic Warfare: Vol. 1*, The Association of Old Crows, Massachusetts

Raeder, Erich 1960, *My Life*, Naval Institute Press, Annapolis

Raven, Alan and Roberts, John 1976, *British Battleships of World War Two*, Arms and Armour Press, London

Reynolds, Clark G. 1968, *The Fast Carriers: The Forging of an Air Navy*, McGraw-Hill, New York

——1991, *Admiral John. H. Towers: The Struggle for Naval Air Supremacy*, Naval Institute Press, Annapolis

Richards, Denis 1953, *Royal Air Force 1939–1945, Vol. 1 The Fight at Odds*, HMSO, London

Richards, Denis and Saunders, Hilary St. G 1954, *Royal Air Force 1939–1945: Vol. 2: The Fight Avails*, HMSO, London

Robinson, Walton L. 1948, *Akagi, Famous Japanese Carrier*, United States Naval Institute Proceedings, May 1948

Rochefort, Joseph J, 1983, *Reminiscences of Captain Joseph J. Rochefort*, US Naval Institute, Annapolis

Roskill, Stephen 1976a, *The War at Sea 1939–1945: Vol. 1: The Defensive*, HMSO, London

——1956, *Vol. 2: The Period of Balance*

——1960, *Vol. 3 Part 1: The Offensive 1st June 1943— 31st May 1944*

——1961, *Vol. 3 Part 2: The Offensive 1st June 1944— 14th August 1945*

——1969 (ed.), *Documents relating to the Naval Air Service: Vol.1: 1908–1918*, Navy Records Society

——1977, *Churchill and the Admirals*, Collins, London

Rowland, Buford and Boyd, William B. 1953, *U.S. Navy Bureau of Ordnance in World War II*, Bureau of Ordnance, Department of the Navy, Washington

Russell, James S. 1986, 'The Essex Class', *United States Naval Institute Proceedings*, Supplement 1986

Sadkovich, James J. (ed.) 1990, *Reevaluating Major Naval Combatants of World War II*, Contributions in Military Studies, Number 92, Greenwood Press, New York

——1994, *The Italian Navy in World War 2*, Greenwood Press, Westport, Connecticut

Sakai, Saburo 1957, *Samurai*, E.P. Dutton, New York

Seuter, Murray 1928, *Airmen or Noahs?*, Pitman, London

Sigwart, E.E. 1969, *Royal Fleet Auxiliary*, Adlard Coles, London

Smith, Peter C. 1988, *Dive Bombers in Action*, Blandford Press, London

Stern, Robert 1993, *The Lexington-class Carriers*, Arms and Armour Press, London

Sturtivant, Ray 1984, *The Squadrons of the Fleet Air Arm*, Air Britain (Historians) Ltd

——1990, *British Naval Aviation*, Arms and Armour Press, London

Tedder, Lord 1966, *With Prejudice*, Cassell, London

Thach, John S. 1977, *Reminiscences of Admiral John Smith Thach*, US Naval Institute, Annapolis

Thetford, Owen 1991, *British Naval Aircraft since 1912*, Naval Institute Press, Annapolis

Till, Geoffrey, 1979, *Air Power and the Royal Navy*, Jane's, London

Tillman, Barrett 1976, *The Dauntless Dive Bomber of World War II*, Naval Institute Press, Annapolis

Toland, John 1970, *The Rising Sun: The Decline and Fall of the Japanese Empire, 1936–1945*, Random House, New York

Turnbull, Archibald D. and Lord, Clifford L. 1949, *History of United States Naval Aviation*, Arno Press, New York

Ugaki, Matome 1991, *Fading Victory*, University of Pittsburgh

Van Deurs, George 1966, *Wings for the Fleet*, US Naval Institute, Annapolis

Van der Vat, Dan 1991, *The Pacific Campaign*, Simon and Schuster, New York

Vian, Philip 1960, *Action This Day*, Frederick Muller, London

Von der Porten, Edward 1969, *The German Navy in World War II*, Arthur Barker, London

Warner, Denis 1983, *Kamikaze—the Sacred Warriors, 1944–45*, Oxford University Press, Melbourne

Watson-Watt, Robert Alexander 1957, *Three Steps to Victory*, Odhams Press, London

Watts, Anthony J. 1966, *Japanese Warships of World War II*, Ian Allan, London

Willis, Algernon U. (unpublished), *Memoirs*, vols. I and II, Churchill College, Cambridge

Winton, John 1978, *War in the Pacific*, Sidgwick & Jackson, London

——1986, *Carrier Glorious*, Leo Cooper, London

Woods, Gerard A. 1985, *Wings at Sea*, Conway Maritime Press, London

Y'Blood, William 1987, *The Little Giants: U.S Escort Carriers against Japan*, Naval Institute Press, Annapolis

Yokoi, Toshiyuki 1960, *Thoughts on Japanese Naval Defeat*, United States Naval Institute Proceedings, October 1960

Yoshida, Mitsuru 1985, *Requiem for Battleship Yamato*, Kodansha International

The following additional books and articles were consulted in the preparation of particular chapters.

CHAPTER 1

Cooper, Malcolm 1986, *The Birth of Independent Air Power*, Allen & Unwin, London

Corbett, Julian S. 1921, *Naval Operations: Vol. II*, Longmans, Green and Co, London

'Gradatim' 1964, 'The Fleet Air Arm—Another Fiftieth Anniversary', *Naval Review*, vol. 52, no. 4, October 1964

Layman, R.D. and Drashpil, Boris V. 1971, 'Early Russian Shipboard Aviation', *United States Naval Institute Proceedings*, vol. 97, no. 1, January 1971

Moore, John Hammond 1981, 'The Short, Eventful Life of Eugene B. Ely', *United States Naval Institute Proceedings*, vol. 107, no. 1, January 1981

Newbolt, Henry 1931, *A Naval History of the War 1914–1918: Vol. 5*, Longmans, Green and Co, London

Nowarra, Heinz J. 1966, *Marine Aircraft of the 1914–1918 War*, Harleyford Publications, Letchworth, England

Owsley, Frank L. and Newton, Wesley Phillip 1986, 'Eyes in the Skies', *United States Naval Institute Proceedings Supplement*

Powers, Barry D 1976, *Strategy without Slide-rule*, Croom Helm Ltd, London

Ray, Thomas 1971, 'Naval Aviation. The Beginning', *United States Naval Institute Proceedings*, vol. 97, no. 1, January 1971

Robinson, Douglas H. 1966, *The Zeppelin in Combat*, G.T. Foulis, London

Roskill, S.W. 1960, 'The Destruction of Zeppelin L.53', *United States Naval Institute Proceedings*, vol. 86, no. 8 (August 1960)

Samson, Charles Rumney 1930, *Fights and Flights*, Ernest Benn, London

CHAPTER 2

'C.C.C.H.' 1980, 'The Adoption of the Oerlikon', *Naval Review*, vol. 68, no. 3, July 1980

Committee of Imperial Defence 1936, *The Vulnerability of Capital Ships to Air Attack*, Report by a Sub-Committee

Foley, Francis 1986, 'We Had Fun', *United States Naval Institute Proceedings Supplement*

Friedman, Norman 1965, 'Anti-Aircraft Cruisers: The Life of a Class', *United States Naval Institute Proceedings*, vol. 91, no. 1, January 1965

Goldrick, J.V.P. 1983, 'For Want of a Nail . . . Royal Naval Anti-Aircraft Gunnery 1919–1939', *Journal of the Royal United Services Institute of Australia*, vol. 6, no. 1, April 1983

Hurley, Alfred F. 1975, *Billy Mitchell. Crusader for Air Power*, Indiana University Press, Bloomington

Macintyre, Donald 1967, 'Shipborne Radar', *United States Naval Institute Proceedings*, vol. 93, no. 9, September 1967

Moore, W. Geoffrey 1963, *Early Bird*, Putnam, London

Morison, Elting E. 1942, *Admiral Sims and the Modern American Navy*, Russell and Russell, New York

Pelz, Stephen E. 1974, *Race to Pearl Harbor*, Harvard University Press, Cambridge

Pride, Alfred M. 1986, 'Pilots, Man Your Planes', *United States Naval Institute Proceedings Supplement*

——1984, *The Reminiscences of Admiral Alfred M. Pride U.S. Navy (retired)*, US Naval Institute, Annapolis

Ranft, Brian (ed.) 1977, *Technical Change and British Naval Policy 1860–1939*, Hodder & Stoughton, London

Richardson, James O. 1973, *On the Treadmill to Pearl Harbor*, Department of the Navy, Washington

Roskill, Stephen 1968, *Naval Policy Between the Wars: Vol. 1: The Period of Anglo-American Antagonism 1919–1929*, Collins, London

——1976b, *Naval Policy between the Wars: Vol. 2: The Period of Reluctant Rearmament, 1930–1939*, Collins, London

——1978, 'Anti-Aircraft Gunnery between the Wars', *Naval Review*, vol. 66, no. 2, April 1978

——1980, 'The Adoption of the Oerlikon Gun—1939–40', *Naval Review*, vol. 68, no. 2, April 1980

Ross, George 1981, 'How the Oerlikon Gun came to Britain', *Naval Review*, vol. 69, no. 1, January 1981

Russell, James S. 1986, 'The Ranger: Atavistic Anomaly', *United States Naval Institute Proceedings Supplement*

Snow, C.P. 1961, *Science and Government*, Oxford University Press, London

Trimble, William 1994, *Admiral William A. Moffett*, Smithsonian Institute Press, Washington

Wildenberg, Thomas 1993, 'Chester Nimitz and the Development of Fueling at Sea', *Naval War College Review*, Autumn 1993

CHAPTER 3

Assmann, Kurt 1952, 'The Invasion of Norway', (translated by Krause, Roland E.) *United States Naval Institute Proceedings*, vol. 78, no. 4, April 1952

Forbes, C. 1940, *Dispatch of 15 July 1940*, ADM 199/393

French, Godfrey 1962, 'Some Operations of H.M.S. Furious and Her Aircraft, 1939–1940', *Naval Review*, vol. 50, no. 1, January 1962

Naval Staff History 1950, *Naval Operations of the Campaign in Norway*, (Battle Summary no. 17), Historical Section, Admiralty

Roskill, Stephen 1981, 'The Adoption of the Oerlikon Gun—An Addendum', *Naval Review*, vol. 69, no. 1, January 1981

Troubridge, T.H. 1940, *Report of Proceedings, HMS Furious*, 30 April 1940, ADM 199/479

CHAPTER 4

Janvrin, Richard 1991, 'The Fleet Air Arm Attack on Taranto', *Naval Review*, vol. 79, no. 1, January 1991

Naval Historical Branch 1970, *Operation 'MB8' including the Naval Air Attack on Taranto*, Admiralty, September 1970

CHAPTER 5

Boyd, D.W. *H.M.S. Illustrious—Action Report*, 26 January 1941, Admiralty, London

Grantham, G. 1943, *Initial Report for Repair of Damage H.M.S. Indomitable 20 July 1945*, (ADM 199/555) Admiralty, London

Naval Staff History 1960, *Naval Operations in the Battle of Crete*, ADM 234/320 (Battle Summary no. 4), Admiralty, London

CHAPTER 6

Garzke, William H. Jr. and Dulin, Robert O. Jr 1991, 'Who Sank the Bismarck?', *United States Naval Institute Proceedings*, vol. 117, no. 6, June 1991

Grenfell, Russell 1948, *The Bismarck Episode*, Faber & Faber, London

Naval Staff History 1950, *The Chase and Sinking of the 'Bismarck'*, (Battle Summary no. 4) Admiralty, London

Von Müllenheim-Rechburg 1981, *Battleship Bismarck*, (translated by Sweetman, Jack), Bodley Head, London

Wellings, Joseph H. 1983, *On His Majesty's Service*, ed. Hattendorf, John B., Naval War College Press, Rhode Island

CHAPTER 7

Beach, Edward L. 1991, 'Who's to Blame?', *United States Naval Institute Proceedings*, vol. 117, no. 12, December 1991

Beard, Charles 1948, *President Roosevelt and the Coming of the War 1941*, Yale University Press, New Haven, Connecticut

Cook, Charles O. Jr 1978, 'The Strange Case of Rainbow–5', *United States Naval Institute Proceedings*, vol. 104, no. 8, August 1978, and vol. 104, no. 9, September 1978

Costello, John E. 1983, 'Remember Pearl Harbor', *United States Naval Institute Proceedings*, vol. 109, no. 9, September 1983

Craven, Wesley Frank and Cate, James Lea (eds) 1948, *The Army Air Force in World War II: Volume One: Plans and Early Operations*, University of Chicago Press, Chicago

Goldstein, Donald M. and Dillon, Katherine V. 1993, *The Pearl Harbor Papers. Inside the Japanese Plans*, Brassey's (US), Washington

Kimmel, Husband E. 1954, *Admiral Kimmel's Story*, Henry Regnery, Chicago

Meigs, Montgomery C. 1985, '. . . This Must Mean the Philippines!', *United States Naval Institute Proceedings*, vol. 111, no. 8, August 1985

Miller, Edward S. 1991, *War Plan Orange*, Naval Institute Press, Annapolis

Morison, Samuel Eliot 1948, *History of United States Naval Operations in World War II: Vol. III: The Rising Sun in the Pacific*, Little, Brown & Co, Boston

Prange, Gordon W. with Goldstein, Donald W. and Dillon, Katherine V. 1991, *Pearl Harbor: The Verdict of History*, Penguin Books, London

——1988, *December 7, 1941*, McGraw-Hill, New York

Richardson, David C. 1991, 'You Decide', *United States Naval Institute Proceedings*, vol. 117, no. 3, December 1991

Rushbridger, James and Nave, Eric 1991, *Betrayal at Pearl Harbor*, Summit Books, New York

Sweetman, Jack 1991, 'To Cut a Sleeping Throat', *United States Naval Institute Proceedings*, vol. 117, no. 3, December 1991

Wohlsetter, Roberta 1962, *Pearl Harbor: Warning and Decision*, Stanford University Press, Stanford, California

CHAPTER 8

Cabinet Office 1976, *The Principal Telegrams relating to Operations in the Far East (4 December 1941 to 25 December 1941)*, HMSO, London

Grenfell, Russell 1951, *Main Fleet to Singapore*, Faber & Faber, London

Hart, Thomas C. 1942, *Narrative of Events, Asiatic Fleet Leading up to War and From 8 December 1941 to 15 February 1942*, World War II Action Reports, US Operational Archives

Hough, Richard 1963, *The Hunting of Force Z*, Collins, London

Ismay, Hastings Lionel 1960, *The Memoirs of General Lord Ismay*, Heinemann, London

Japanese Defence Agency's Research Section, *The Book of Military History, the Malayan Area*

Layton, Geoffrey 1941, 'Loss of H.M.Ships Prince of Wales and Repulse, 17 December 1941', the supplement to *The London Gazette*, 20 February 1948
Middlebrook, Martin and Mahoney, Patrick 1977, *Battleship*, Allen Lane, London
Pound, Dudley 1942, *Loss of HMS Prince of Wales and Repulse*, ADM 199/1149, Admiralty, London
Shores, Christopher 1992, *Bloody Shambles Vol. 1*, Grubb St, London
Stephen, Martin 1991, *The Fighting Admirals*, Leo Cooper, London

CHAPTER 9

Bucknill 1942, *Report of Board of Inquiry*, Tabled 1946 (Command 6775), HMSO, London
Busch, Fritz-Otto 1956, *The Drama of the Scharnhorst*, Robert Hale, London
Galland, Adolf 1955, *The First and the Last*, Methuen, London
Garrett, Richard 1978, *Scharnhorst and Gneisenau*, David & Charles, Newton Abbot
Robertson, Terence 1958, *Channel Dash*, Evans Brothers, London
Vulliez, Albert and Mordal, Jacques 1958, *Battleship Scharnhorst*, (translated by Malcolm, George), Hutchinson, London

CHAPTER 10

Macintyre, Donald 1961, *Fighting Admiral*, Evans Brothers, London
Shores, Christopher and Cull, Brian with Izawa, Yasuho 1993, *Bloody Shambles Vol. 2*, Grubb St, London
Tomlinson, M. 1976, *The Most Dangerous Moment*, William Kimber, London
Winton, John 1993, *Ultra in the Pacific*, Leo Cooper, London

CHAPTER 11

Brennan, James W. 1968, 'The Proximity Fuze. Whose Brainchild?', *United States Naval Institute Proceedings*, vol. 94, no. 9, September 1968
Doolittle, James H. with Grimes, Carroll V. 1991, *I Could Never Be So Lucky Again*, Bantam Books, New York
——1987, *Reminiscences of General James H. Doolittle*, US Naval Institute, Annapolis
US Naval War College 1947, *The Battle of the Coral Sea, May 1 to May 11 Inclusive, 1942, Strategical and Tactical Analysis*, Newport, Rhode Island

CHAPTER 12

Cross, Richard F. III 1976, 'Essex: More than a Ship, More than a Class', *United States Naval Institute Proceedings*, vol. 101, no. 9, September 1976
Office of Naval Intelligence 1947, *The Japanese Story of the Battle of Midway*, United States Navy, Washington DC
Potter, E.B.1969, 'The Command Personality', *United States Naval Institute Proceedings*, vol. 95, no. 2, February 1969

Prange, Gordon W. 1982, *Miracle at Midway*, Penguin, Harmondsworth
US Naval War College 1948, *The Battle of Midway Including the Aleutian Phase, June 3 to June 14, Strategical and Tactical Analysis*, Newport, Rhode Island

CHAPTER 13

Naval Staff History 1957, *Malta Convoys: Battle Summary no. 32*, (revised) ADM 234/353, Admiralty, London
Pawle, Gerald 1956, *The Secret War 1939–45*, George G. Harrap, London
Poolman, Kenneth 1970, *The Catafighters*, William Kimber, London
——1978, *Scourge of the Atlantic*, Macdonald and Jane's, London
Shores, Christopher and Cull, Brian, with Malizia, Nicola 1991, *Malta: The Spitfire Year*, Grubb St, London
Smith, Peter 1970, *Operation Pedestal*, William Kimber, London
Syfret, E.N. 1942, *Report on Operation 'Pedestal'*, Admiralty, London
Wise, James E. Jr 1974, 'Catapult Off—Parachute Back', *United States Naval Institute Proceedings*, vol. 100, no. 4, September 1974

CHAPTER 14

Morison, Samuel Eliot 1951, *History of United States Naval Operations in World War II: Vol. V: The Struggle for Guadalcanal*, Little, Brown & Co., Boston

CHAPTER 15

Craven, Wesley Frank and Cate, James Lea (eds) 1950, *The Army, Air Forces in World War II: Vol. 4: Guadalcanal, to Saipan*, University of Chicago Press, Chicago
Gillison, Douglas 1962, *Royal Australian Air Force 1939–1942*, Australian War Memorial, Canberra
Horner, David 1982, *High Command*, Australian War Memorial, Canberra
Morison, Samuel Eliot 1959, *History of United States Naval Operations in World War II: Vol. VI: Breaking the Bismarcks Barrier*, Little, Brown & Co., Boston

CHAPTER 16

Buell, T.B. 1974, 'Battle of the Philippine Sea', *United States Naval Institute Proceedings*, vol. 100, no. 7, July 1974
Dickson, W.D. 1975, *The Battle of the Philippine Sea June 1944*, Ian Allan, London
Morison, Samuel Eliot 1953, *History of United States Naval Operations: Vol. VIII: New Guinea and the Marianas*, Little, Brown & Co., Boston
Ramage, James D. 1982, *A Review of the Philippine Sea Battle June 20, 1944*, US Naval War College, Newport, Rhode Island

CHAPTER 17

Ahlstrom, John D. 1984, 'Leyte Gulf Remembered', *United States Naval Institute Proceedings*, vol. 110, no. 8, August 1984
Cutler, Thomas J. 1994, *The Battle of Leyte Gulf*, Harper Collins, New York
Field, James A. Jr. 1947, *The Japanese at Leyte Gulf. The SHO Operation*, Princeton University Press, Princeton, New Jersey
Jones, Ken and Kelley, Hubert Jr. 1962, *Admiral Arleigh (31-knot) Burke*, Chilton Books, Philadelphia
Morison, Samuel Eliot 1958, *History of United States Naval Operations in World War II: Volume XII: Leyte, June 1944—January 1945*, Oxford University Press, London
US Naval War College 1957, *The Battle for Leyte Gulf, October 1944*, (three volumes), Newport, Rhode Island

CHAPTER 18

Bogart, Charles H. 1976, 'German Remotely Piloted Bombs', *United States Naval Institute Proceedings*, vol. 102, no. 11, November 1976
Brown, David 1977, *Tirpitz, the Floating Fortress*, Arms and Armour Press, London
Woodward, David 1953, *The Tirpitz*, William Kimler, London

CHAPTER 19

Fisher, Douglas 1953, 'The Fleet Train in the Pacific War', *Quarterly Transactions of the Institute of Naval Architects*, vol. 95, no. 2 (April 1953)
Fraser, Bruce 1945, *The British Pacific Fleet in Operations against Japan*, (ADM 199/199) Admiralty, London
Hirst, Mike 1983, *Airborne Early Warning*, Osprey, London
Morison, Samuel Eliot 1960, *History of United States Naval Operations in World War II: Vol. XIV: Victory in the Pacific*, Oxford University Press
Naval Staff History 1960, *Naval Operations in the Assault and Capture of Okinawa, March–June 1945 Operation Iceberg*, (Battle Summary no. 47) ADM 234/368, Admiralty, London
——1959, *War with Japan: Vol. VI: The Advance to Japan*, Admiralty, London
Reynolds, Clark G. 1986, 'Taps for the Torpecker', *United States Naval Institute Proceedings*, vol. 112, no. 12, December 1986
Ruck-Keene, P. 1945, *Action Damage Report—4th May 1945*, (HMS *Formidable*) ADM 199/2071, Admiralty, London
Spruance, Raymond 1945, *Commander Fifth Fleet. Report of Operations 14 March through 28 May*
Wardroom Officers, HMS *Formidable* 1947, *A Formidable Commission*, Seeley Service, London
Winton, John 1969, *The Forgotten Fleet*, Michael Joseph, London
Yokoi, Toshiyuki 1954, 'Kamikazes and the Okinawa Campaign', *United States Naval Institute Proceedings*, vol. 80, no. 5, May 1954

CHAPTER 20

Almond, Denise L. (ed.) 1991, *Desert Score: US Gulf War Weapons*, Naval Institute Press, Annapolis

Baker, A.D. 1984, 'Aircraft Carriers in the Falklands', *United States Naval Institute Proceedings*, vol. 110, no. 2, February 1984

Braisco, Jesus Romero and Huertas, Salvador Mafé 1985, *Falklands Witness of Battles*, Federico Domenech, Valencia, Spain

Brown, David 1987, *The Royal Navy and the Falklands War*, Leo Cooper, London

Burden, Rodney A., Draper, Michael I., Rough, Douglas A., Smith, Colin R. and Wilton, David L. 1987, *Falklands: The Air War*, Gould Publishing, London

Cigar, Norman 1992, *Soviet Aircraft Carriers*, Naval War College Review, Spring 1992

Colombo, Jorge Luis 1984, '"Super Etendard" Naval Aircraft Operations during the Malvinas War', *Naval War College Review*, May–June 1984

Ethell, Jeffrey and Price, Alfred 1987, *Air War South Atlantic*, Macmillan, New York

Friedman, Norman 1989, *The Naval Institute Guide to Naval Weapons Systems*, Naval Institute Press, Annapolis

——1991, *Desert Victory: The War for Kuwait*, Naval Institute Press, Annapolis

Hastings, Max and Jenkins, Simon 1983, *The Battle for the Falklands*, Pan Books, London

Hill, J.R. 1988, *Air Defence at Sea*, Ian Allan, London

Huertas, Salvador Mafé 1983, *South Atlantic Air War*, Air International, May 1983

Ministry of Defence 1987, *Implementing the Lessons of the Falklands Campaign*, HMSO, London

Oxenbould, C.J. 1991, 'Maritime Operations in the Gulf War', *Journal of the Australian Naval Institute*, vol. 17, 1991

Philippi, Alberto Jorge 1983, 'The Odyssey of a Skyhawk Pilot', *United States Naval Institute Proceedings, Naval Review 1983*

Polmar, Norman 1992, 'Going Downtown the Safe Way', *United States Naval Institute Proceedings*, vol. 118, no. 8, August 1992

Price, Alfred 1984, *Harrier at War*, Ian Allan, London

Scheina, Robert L. 1983, 'The Malvinas Campaign', *United States Naval Institute Proceedings, Naval Review 1983*

Secretary of State for Defence 1982, *The Falklands Campaign: The Lessons*, (Command 8758) HMSO, London

Stumpf, R.E. 1986, 'Air War with Libya', *United States Naval Institute Proceedings*, vol. 112, no. 8, August 1986

Swanborough, Gordon 1983, 'Harriers for the Task Force', *United States Naval Institute Proceedings*, vol. 109, no. 11, November 1983

Ward, N.D. 1992, *Sea Harriers over the Falklands*, Leo Cooper, London

Winton, John 1987, *Air Power at Sea*, Sidgwick & Jackson, London

Woodward, Sandy and Robinson, Patrick 1992, *One Hundred Days*, Harper Collins, London

Index

385